Rethinking Regulation of International Finance

International Banking and Finance Law Series

VOLUME 33

Series Editors

Professor Joseph Norton, Professor Ross Buckley and Professor Douglas Arner.

Subjects

Topical issues in international banking and financial services law, such as regulatory responses to the global financial crisis or regulation of alternative investment funds.

Objective & Readership

To provide authoritative analysis of trends and complex subjects for academics, regulators and practitioners involved in international banking and financial services law.

The titles published in this series are listed at the end of this volume.

Rethinking Regulation of International Finance

Law, Policy and Institutions

Uzma Ashraf Barton

Published by:
Kluwer Law International B.V.
PO Box 316
2400 AH Alphen aan den Rijn
The Netherlands
Website: lrus.wolterskluwer.com

Sold and distributed in North, Central and South America by:
Wolters Kluwer Legal & Regulatory U.S.
7201 McKinney Circle
Frederick, MD 21704
United States of America
Email: customer.service@wolterskluwer.com

Sold and distributed in all other countries by:
Air Business Subscriptions
Rockwood House
Haywards Heath
West Sussex
RH16 3DH
United Kingdom
Email: international-customerservice@wolterskluwer.com

Printed on acid-free paper.

ISBN 978-90-411-8838-0

e-Book: ISBN 978-90-411-8918-9
web-PDF: ISBN 978-90-411-8949-3

© 2018 Kluwer Law International BV, The Netherlands

All rights reserved. No part of this publication may be reproduced, stored in a retrieval system, or transmitted in any form or by any means, electronic, mechanical, photocopying, recording, or otherwise, without written permission from the publisher.

Permission to use this content must be obtained from the copyright owner. More information can be found at: lrus.wolterskluwer.com/policies/permissions-reprints-and-licensing

Printed in the United Kingdom.

To my late father, Muhammad Ashraf whose vision empowered me to choose the paths I endeared most

Table of Contents

Preface and Acknowledgments ... xiii

CHAPTER 1
Introduction ... 1
§1.01 Setting the Agenda ... 1
§1.02 Why Reforms Indispensable? ... 3
§1.03 What's Next? ... 5
§1.04 Some Definitions ... 6
§1.05 Some Questions ... 9
§1.06 Why Answers Matter? ... 10
§1.07 Let's Find Answers ... 11

CHAPTER 2
Cyclic Financial Crises and the Development of IFL ... 15
§2.01 IFL and the Controlled Regimes ... 17
    [A] The Classical Gold Standard ... 18
    [1] Politicization of the Monetary System (1919-1928) ... 19
    [2] The Great Depression (1929-1939) ... 21
    [3] Death of the Old and the Birth of the New ... 22
    [B] The Bretton Woods and Domestic Finance ... 23
    [1] The Formation: Keynes and White's Plan ... 24
    [2] Problems and Consequences (1945-1971) ... 26
§2.02 The Era of International Finance (1970-1993) ... 32
    [A] Systemic Risk Episodes (1983-2000) ... 35
    [1] The 1980s Debt Crisis: Mexico and Brazil ... 36
    [2] Russia 1996-1999 ... 37
    [3] IFL Through the 1990s ... 38
    [4] The Asian Crisis 1997-1998 ... 39
    [5] Argentinian Crises 2000-2007 ... 41
    [B] New Millennium and the Global Finance ... 42

Table of Contents

§2.03   The GFC 43
        [A]   The Context, Course and the Destruction 43
              [1]   Phase I: Nascent Shocks, Fledgling Responses 44
              [2]   Phase II: The Onslaught of the Crisis 46
        [B]   A Probe into the Origins 47
              [1]   Why the GFC? 47
              [2]   The Controversial Gramm-Leach-Bliley Act (GLBA) 1999 49
        [C]   IFL in Action 51
§2.04   Conclusion 55

Chapter 3
IFL and the Development of Its Regulatory Architecture 57
§3.01   Financial Market Development 58
        [A]   The Institutional Heritage 58
              [1]   The Post-War Controlled Financial Markets 58
              [2]   The Post-Bretton Woods and the Emergence of Risk 58
              [3]   Graduated Financial Markets 60
        [B]   Theories of Institutional Development 61
              [1]   Where Stands the Law? 61
              [2]   Institutions Matter 63
        [C]   FML and Institutional Correlations 66
              [1]   The WC (the Consensus) 68
              [2]   The NIFA 70
§3.02   The Pillars of IFRA 70
        [A]   The BIS 71
              [1]   The Second World War: Of Justifying Continued Existence 72
              [2]   The Post-War Period: Of Building Strengths 72
              [3]   The Bretton Woods Era: Of Faltering Convertibility and Strengthening Cooperation 73
              [4]   The BIS, Banking Supervision and Financial Stability 74
              [5]   The Changing Role of the BIS 74
        [B]   Securities Regulation 75
              [1]   International Organization of Securities Commissions (IOSCO) 77
        [C]   International Association of Insurance Supervisors 79
              [1]   Organizational Structure of IAIS and Nature of Insurance Markets 80
              [2]   The IAIS Standards 80
        [D]   Reinsurance 82
        [E]   The Joint Forum and Mutual Assistance 83
        [F]   International Accounting Standards (IAS) 84
        [G]   Credit Rating Agencies (CRA) 86
        [H]   The FSF 87
        [I]   The FSB 88

		[1]	The Transformation	89
		[2]	Membership	89
		[3]	Internal Structure	92
		[4]	Functions	93
		[5]	Decision-Making	96
		[6]	Enforcement	98
		[7]	The Role of the FSB in Post-crisis Financial Reforms	99
	[J]	The G's Group and the G20		101
		[1]	The Group of Twenty (G20)	102
§3.03	Evaluating the Existing Financial Architecture			105
§3.04	Conclusion			108

CHAPTER 4
Regulatory Regimes and IFL — 109

§4.01	Regulation and Risk Management			111
	[A]	Some Distinctions		111
		[1]	Regulation and Supervision	111
		[2]	Key Regulatory Structures	111
		[3]	Twin-Peak Structure	113
		[4]	Regulatory Risk Management	114
		[5]	The Regulatory Objective	116
§4.02	The Basel: Inception and Development			118
	[A]	Historical Evidence I: Basel I and II		118
		[1]	An Assessment	120
	[B]	Historical Evidence II: Newly Emergent Operational Risk		121
		[1]	Defining Operational Risk	123
		[2]	Historical Recognition	124
		[3]	The Three Pillars and a Critical Assessment	126
		[4]	Operation Risk Approaches	128
		[5]	An Assessment	131
	[C]	Spineless Regulation: Past Failures, Future Bets		132
§4.03	Post-2008 Reform Initiatives			133
	[A]	A Look at the Inner Thresholds		133
		[1]	Impact Studies	134
		[2]	The European Situation	134
	[B]	Basel III: Adoption and Implementation Timeline		136
	[C]	Basel III: A Critical Assessment		148
§4.04	From Self-regulation to Reregulation: Myth or Reality			149
§4.05	Conclusion			152

CHAPTER 5
Enforcement in IFL: The Precarious Case of the EU — 155

§5.01	Old Fissures, New Lessons	155
§5.02	Financial Market Integration	158

Table of Contents

	[A]	Inception of the European Experiment	159
	[B]	The Development of the Treaty-Based Mechanism	161
		[1] Stage I: The Economic Integration	162
		[2] Stage II: Infancy and the Minimum Harmonization	164
		[3] Stage III: Maturity and the Maximum Harmonization	166
§5.03	The Single Market and the Existential Crises		168
	[A]	External Shocks	168
	[B]	Internal Vulnerabilities	169
		[1] The Icelandic Banking Crisis	170
		[2] The Fortis Bank's Case	172
		[3] The SDC	172
§5.04	The Single Market and Imperative Reform		174
	[A]	Preliminary Responses	174
		[1] Stage I: EFSF and the New Developments	175
		[2] Stage II: The ESRB	177
		[3] Stage III: The Worsening Crisis	178
	[B]	Postliminary Responses	181
		[1] Crisis Management Framework: The EBA	181
		[2] The Long-Awaited Panacea: The SSM	182
		[3] Redefining Roles: The ECB	184
		[4] The DGS	186
§5.05	Continuing Challenges		188
§5.06	Epilogue: Can There Be a Global Treaty?		190
§5.07	Conclusion		193

CHAPTER 6
IFL: Contemporary Issues, Rethinking Alternatives — 195

§6.01	What's Wrong with the World of Finance?		197
§6.02	Financial Stability: What Is This Undefined Term?		198
§6.03	Contemporary Critical Issues in IEL		203
	[A]	IFL and the Conflict of Laws	203
	[B]	Consolidating the Discipline: Is it a Good Idea?	206
		[1] Consolidation and Arbitrage	207
		[2] The US Case	208
		[3] Consolidation Through Increased Regulation?	209
§6.04	Select Structural Inconsistencies in IFL: Rethinking Alternatives		211
	[A]	The Soft-Law of International Finance	211
		[1] Understanding the Soft Law	211
		[2] The Dialectics of Hard Law	213
		[3] What Soft Law Offers?	216
§6.05	Processes and Legitimacy Critique in IFL		218
	[A]	What Is Legitimacy: Defining the Gaps	218
§6.06	Financial Institutions and the Soft Reform Agenda		220

	[A]	The IMF	221
		[1] Facts, Beyond Facts, and to Challenges	221
		[2] The Reform Process at the Fund	223
	[B]	The World Bank and the Emergent Challenges	225
§6.07	Thinking Alternatives		228
	[A]	Scenario I: Whether a Global Regulator	228
	[B]	Scenario II: If Less Is More	231
§6.08	Conclusion		234

CHAPTER 7
Conclusions, Challenges and Recommendations — 235

§7.01	Overview		235
§7.02	Challenges and Limitations		238
	[A]	Where Do We Stand Today?	238
		[1] The Anti-regulatory Debate and Misaligned Incentives	239
		[2] The Reform Fatigue	239
		[3] Markets Have Failed Us	240
	[B]	Is Financial Stability Still an International Public Good	241
§7.03	Conclusions and Recommendation		242
	[A]	Approach I: Strengthening Responsiveness Within	242
	[B]	Approach II: Looking Ahead, Beyond Within	245
		[1] Financial Market Risk Prevention and Management Mechanism	245
		[2] Further Research	249

Index — 251

Preface and Acknowledgments

The inspiration for this work "Rethinking Regulation of International Finance" dates back to 2007 when the "Run on the Rock" raised many questions regarding regulation of risks in the financial system. It was the first run on retail deposits of a United Kingdom's (U.K.) bank since Victorian times; however, for me on my first visit of an international financial center, it was a passive admission of the fact that the U.K. can be as much susceptible to reckless financial practices as one of its erstwhile colony, Pakistan. The run-on incident brought flashbacks of the Punjab Cooperatives Societies scandal and of the Savings and Loans crisis.

Not too long ago in another, rather developing country, Pakistan, over 700,000 people, mostly poor, lost all their savings in the Punjab Cooperative Societies bankruptcy in 1992. The Cooperatives collapsed due to irresponsible granting of loans in violation of banking codes and ethical standards. Almost at the same time, in another advanced economy, the Savings and Loan Association (S&L) collapsed. The S&L in 1989 was the greatest bank collapse since the Great Depression of 1929 in the United States (U.S.). Amongst other issues, the S&L used federally insured deposits to make risky loans, somewhat like the Punjab Cooperatives Societies, which irresponsibly issued politically motivated loans. In both cases, regulators lost race to the market participants and failed in keeping pace with market nuances.

Right after the S&L went bust, investigators in the U.S. and in the U.K. found major anomalies in the conduct of a Luxembourg-based world's seventh largest private bank, the BCCI. Despite years of investigations, the USD 5 billion hole in the BCCI's balance sheet remained unresolved; however, the bank's malpractices in extending loans (lack of due diligence) were brought to the fore. The auditors, Pricewaterhouse-Coopers, only belatedly admitted that the BCCI was one of the most complex deceptions in banking history. Only retrospectively, regulators were able to spot that the BCCI was set up deliberately to avoid centralized regulatory view. Regulators again lost the race to BCCI.

Arguably, Northern Rock's run was primarily due to liquidity shortages, regulatory slipups were common along all of the crises. The promising and sanguine stock market optics were being reflected through advertisements full of economic euphoria

Preface and Acknowledgments

until the last day before the 1929 crash. Irving Fisher's statement – only days before the Black Days of late October – "[S]tock prices have reached what looks like a permanently high plateau" would become one of his most frequently quoted, albeit, the wrongest market reading of all times. Not so surprising that the regulators in the U.S. lost their gaze on the crisis Frisbee just like they lost in 2007 (and many times in between). Despite the Bank of England confirming emergency support to the Rock announced on September 13, the bank's customers in thousands rushed to the Rock's branches to empty their accounts on September 14 – triggering the classic run on a bank. By September 17 when Chancellor Darling pledged government guarantee on all deposits, it was already *"too late."* In less than a year, the Lehman Brothers (and what followed its aftermath) met similar response by the U.S. regulator (too late). The underlying reasons of the Lehman collapse (followed by the Global Financial Crisis) were not too different from the issues that brought on the Cooperative Societies or the BCCI bankruptcy. The worst losers from these crises were the end users: the consumers of the financial services and the masses in each country.

Not that the Northern Rock, S&L crisis or the Cooperatives Scandal were the most jagged crises in the history of the world but witnessing the Run on the Rock triggered many questions in my mind about fragility of our financial system and its constituent elements: fiat currency, emptiness of the existing debt-based banking system, irresponsible lending and borrowing, government guarantees and moral hazard, regulators as competitors, and the dominance of animal spirits in the financial markets. While listening to Prof. George Walker's talk on the Northern Rock crisis in 2007 at Queen Mary University in London, I wondered how a financial scandal of the magnitude of the BCCI can continue to simmer for so long. The BCCI continued its shady business despite that the Bank of America had spilled the beans more than a decade ago. The regulatory watch, its 1.2 million bank depositors (mostly from the third world), and auditors collectively failed. I wondered about the relevancy of Basel regime: whether lack of enforcement of standards by member countries was the cause or the regulatory regime itself was inadequate. I wondered about the countries at the periphery of the international financial system, their interests, complexity of the regulatory regimes, the implications of implementing complex (and burdensome) international regimes, and the devastating effects of international crises (external to them). These were the questions in my head when I commenced my doctoral research on "rethinking international finance" at the University of Hong Kong in 2010.

The questions, which the Northern Rock triggered in London, Hong Kong, supported me in my journey to find answers. Compliance or lack thereof came out to be a fundamental issue in my understanding of the functioning of our financial system. Hong Kong is a resilient financial center. In many respects, Hong Kong's financial system characterizes the many complexities of financial world albeit at a miniscule scale, it fully reflects regulatory limitations. My work on the Hong Kong Research Grants Council's Theme-based Research Scheme, titled "Enhancing Hong Kong's Future as a Leading International Financial Centre" (2012-2017) – a striking project led by Prof. Douglas Arner – complemented research for my doctoral dissertation and refined my experiences on which I base this book (and I am greatly thankful). Observing closely the development of Hong Kong's financial markets and its compliance with policy and laws, reflected on the gaps in financial market infrastructure around the world: the gaps in good governance, gaps in adequate and effective regulation, gaps in compliance, gaps in due diligence by market actors (including consumers, market watch agencies, credit ratings, and institutions), and gaps in expert knowledge. David Kennedy points out the complexities of global governance and observes in his book, "Struggle for Power" that conflicts, unexamined assumptions, and assertions of power and entitlement lay at the center of expert rule. My experiences in Hong Kong partly focused on the "unexamined assumption" of seeking for an alternative financial system, which is stable. In my quest for "Rethinking Regulation of International Finance," I examined the innate foundation of our existing financial system, which my research found in want of serious reform. Inspired with contemporary scholarship in particular from Douglas Arner, Emilios Avgouleas, Chris Brummer, Ross Buckley, Chin Leng Lim, Paul Lejot, David Zaring, and others, I initiated the quest for finding answers to many of the unanswered questions regarding the intrinsic instability of our debt-based financial system. In the process, the work of many notable scholars and my peers including, Paul Lejot, Christian Tietje, Jasper Finke, David Southern (QC), Rosa Lastra, and Philip Wood (QC) enlightened my journey.

The research for this book thus has been informed by my experiences working (part-time/full-time) on many related assignments during the past seven years: as Senior Researcher for the project, "Hong Kong as an International Financial Center;" for Asian Development Bank's project on Asian Financial Reform (along with Prof. Emilios Avgouleas); as part of the Taskforce on "Renminbi Ascending: How China's Currency Impacts Global Markets, Foreign Policy, and Transatlantic Financial regulation" led by Chris Brummer; at the World Bank with the Global Governance Practice and Finance & Markets Practice. Although Hong Kong's financial market as such has not been discussed independently in this book, nonetheless, Hong Kong's distinct yet ingenious financial markets (with its many constituent elements) bear direct influence on my understanding of the functioning of an international financial center. I owe my utmost thanks for this seven-year journey – from the doctoral research to the publication of this book – to my supervisor Prof. Douglas Arner. Doug is an extremely methodical supervisor, in particular when it comes to understanding the most confusing thoughts. I reckon my not too infrequent encounters with him along with a long list of questions. Doug has been brilliant not only as my supervisor but he was most helpful in the critical instances as I needed his help. This book would not have been completed without his support.

I am grateful to the Asian Institute of International Financial Law (AIIFL), Department of Law, University of Hong Kong, Hong Kong for hosting my research and providing me University Fellowships as well as assisting me throughout the research. I would like to acknowledge AIIFL's support for the travel/conference grants that enabled me in presenting parts of this research at international conferences in London and Frankfurt. Likewise, I am thankful to the Federal Board of Revenue, Government of Pakistan (my employer in 2010) for their grant of study leave to complete my doctorate. I feel fortunate having the auspicious opportunity to work for the government's implementing arm. Working as a bureaucrat (despite all the drawbacks) made me learn that drafting a legislation and subsequent regulation is cumbersome

Preface and Acknowledgments

especially at an international level, yet it is only the beginning of an uphill task. The work on ground in implementing reforms and enforcing laws is in so many arduous ways challenging. I can appreciate the practical reasons why reforms do not work one hundred percent and I understand how bureaucracies (both national and international) suffer from inertia and can thwart the success of the reform process. This title, "rethinking regulation of international reform" is based on these insights that take into account such impeding elements from national and international institutions that hamper progress of law and policy.

If the Run on the Rock was the moment that raised my curiosity to undertake this research, reading the report from my dissertation defense committee defined my decision to undertake this book project. I reckon my first meeting with Douglas Arner in 2010 which he dropped the idea about book; it sounded like a wishful dream to me at that time. I owe my gratitude, in particular to Prof. Ross Buckley, whose specific notes on publishing a book volume prompted the "original idea" to commence work and guided me during my writing.

Some of the issues discussed through the various chapters in this book have been presented at the various conferences and workshops in Asia, Europe, and the U.S. during 2010-2017. I am thankful to the comments and feedback provided by many of my peers, participants of the conferences, and anonymous reviewers of the published papers. Specifically, I would like to mention, the Institute of Global Law and Policy (IGLP), Harvard Law School's intensive workshops (2012-2017). Participation in those intense workshops helped refine my ideas in many ways. The detailed comments from Christine Desan in 2012 (Chapter 2 of this book) were helpful in broadening my angle of looking at the international financial law, amongst others. More recently, in 2017, at another IGLP's workshop, Leo Specht (Specht & Partner) and Jason Jackson (MIT) provided detailed comments on the initial proposal for this book. I am also thankful to Shanthi Elizabeth Senthe (Windsor Law) for coordinating the writing workshop panel and its participants in providing me useful feedback on the initial work for this book.

I am grateful to the Department of Law, University of Hong Kong's staff, in particular, Coria, Flora, and the Law Library staff, who were always available to help me even when I was away from Hong Kong. I extend my thanks to Georgetown Law School, USA (and Prof. Chris Brummer) for accepting me as Visiting Fellow (June-December 2014) and providing me the opportunity to stay in Washington DC (where I was destined to meet the man who is my husband now). I am thankful to Law & Economics Centre, George Mason University, USA for accepting me to their Henry G. Manne Program in Law & Economics workshop. I am indebted to Dean, Henry Butler (George Mason) and Todd J. Zywicki (George Mason) in having me as a fellow at the School and offering me access to the scholarly resources during the process of writing this book.

I want to acknowledge the indirect support from my colleagues and friends from the World Bank, in particular, Nagavalli Annamalai, Khuram Farooq, Raul Félix Junquera-Varela, Munawer Sultan Khwaja and Amitabha Mukherjee. I have special regards for my dear friend Dr. Simone Raudino who – may not have an idea – has been a motivation throughout. I thank my many colleagues and friends, especially in Hong Kong who always made themselves available during my frequent visits. I cannot thank my friends and family enough for their thoughtful views and many discussions that we have had during several of my trips to Hong Kong. I am thankful to Dalal Ag, Prof. Cyra Akila Choudhury, Sharron Fast, Muhammad Kamran, Dr. Hoda Mahmoudi, Muhammad Nadeem, and Samina Seth.

I express my utmost thanks to the team at Wolters Kluwer for assisting me throughout this project and bringing it to its present shape. I am thankful to Lisa Zoltowska and Ms. Pradhiba for their laborious task of coordinating the project. I am indeed highly indebted to R. Srinivasan, Rohini Murugesan, R. Suganthi, and Krithika Shekar, my editorial team, for the insights, comments, and carrying out the proof.

Last, but by no means least, I have immense love for Patrick, my life partner, who in an unsuspecting way deepened my quest for alternative perspectives on financial system. I reckon our discussions on gold standard and on prospects for a return to gold standard – not for the lack of a better topic but for our mutual affinity to realize a solid, responsible, and freer financial system – dominated our honeymoon years.

Uzma Ashraf Barton
AIIFL, University of Hong Kong
Hong Kong

CHAPTER 1
Introduction

§1.01   SETTING THE AGENDA

International Financial Law (IFL) advanced under the classical liberalism during the early twentieth century however increasing capital controls towards the later part of the century shaped further development of the IFL institutions, which continue to exist today.[1] In the beginning governments while adhering to the gold standard were able to maintain fixed exchange rates and thereby controlled capital flows to an extent.[2] With a mechanical effort, the system was set to the free flow of capital subject to a control mechanism under the Bretton Woods institutions. The post-Second-World-War period was of relative stability in the financial system until the 1970s. Finance (and financial intermediation), at this stage, emerged as a distinct activity – not related to production or consumption – and posed different kinds of regulatory challenges compared to the conventional regulations previously required for the orderly functioning of financial markets.

An absence of major financial distress for over quarter of a century under the Bretton Woods Institutions characterized this period as more of stability, which did not last long. By the early 1970s with the breakdown of capital controls, pro-market forces brought a deluge of structured innovative financial products under the spirit of the

---

1. Classical Liberalism is a political philosophy built upon Enlightenment sources, marked by commitment to limited government, rule of law, individual liberties and free markets, developed during the eighteenth and nineteenth centuries in the US and the UK as an intellectual response to industrial revolution. *See also*, Crane & Kritzer's classic empirical legal study of the European and Americal financial systems and institutions, taking into account not only the normative interpretations of law but social, political, economic and ethical. *See*, Cane, P., & Kritzer, H. M. (Eds.). (2010). *The Oxford Handbook of Empirical Legal Research*. Oxford University Press.
2. The faith that the gold standard and general domestic prosperity are mutually reinforcing imparted credibility to the financial system despite divergent critical opinions. *See*, Eichengreen, B. (1992). Golden Fetters: *The Gold Standard and the Great Depression*. Oxford University Press. *See also*, Kindleberger, C. P. & Aliber, R. Z. (2005). *Manias, Panics, and Crashes: A History of Financial Crises* (5ed), John Wiley & Sons. Ch. 2 covers this topic in detail.

Washington Consensus (WC). It did not take long for the financial world to find itself in a series of serious crises and resulting defaults. Each of these disruptions followed renewed commitments of reform and laudable promises to act.[3] Yet these piecemeal initiatives taken only weakened the discipline and added to the existing fragmentation of law, regulation as well as risk management mechanisms. The post-2009 period was not an exception to this pattern.[4] Not surprisingly, after a lapse of almost a decade, financial markets remain vulnerable and IFL remains a weaker bulwark of risk preventing regulatory standards.

Continued existence of higher risks in financial markets builds a case for substantive and procedural reform of IFL regulatory content and enforcement mechanism respectively. Rethinking about the discipline of IFL requires a better understanding of *how the law works and how it does not.*[5] The pre-2008 institutional structures and legal frameworks meant for ensuring financial stability lacked comprehensive crisis-management and crisis-prevention mechanisms. Although, some regulatory standards (like the Basel I and II) and some institutions (like the FSF) were in place during this time, however, IFL and its regulatory ambit remained inherently weak – and continues to remain so – devoid of a mechanism to ensure compliance, lack of procedural accountability in the operation of IFL networks (though the Basel Committees and the Financial Stability Board (FSB) are becoming more representative) and an arbitration platform (to be invoked in cases of defiance).[6] In a way, murky nature of regulatory compliance serves less protection especially to the poor countries – for instance, the uncontrolled capital flows of the 1990s were especially damaging to those vulnerable states.[7] The crisis in 2008 has confirmed the truly interconnected nature of global financial markets and institutions. The spread of the Global Financial Crisis (GFC) around the globe in almost no time, the aftershocks and the massive losses incurred have also made us believe that in fact *[T]his time is [really] different.*[8]

---

3. Reform as a response to a crisis episode is distinct from taking up steps necessary to the development of the discipline itself. Lim and Mercurio argue that the post-2008 reform has neither led to a *grand redesign* of the financial architecture nor enhanced the capacity of the financial system to accommodate issues and events that result in the progression of the discipline. See, Lim.C. L. & Mercurio, B. (ed). (2015). *International Economic Law after the Global Crisis: A Tale of Fragmented Disciplines.* Cambridge University Press.
4. Bellis brings out the interrelationship of domestic legal systems and international law regulatory regimes to reflect on the issues of accountability, legitimacy, employing different models of private norms as used in public regulation within domestic legal orders. See, Bellis, M. D. (2010). *Public Law and Private Regulators in the Global Legal Space* Jean Monnet Working Paper No. 17/10.
5. See, for a discussion and analysis of legal restraints to the functioning of IFL and its role in maintaining FMS, Brummer, C. J. (2010b). How International Financial Law Works (and How it Doesn't). *Georgetown Law Journal, Forthcoming.* Retrieved from http://ssrn.com/paper = 1542 829.
6. See, for details on the interrelationship of soft IFL and compliance, Brummer, C. (2012). He uses the term, 'compliance pull' to characterize the latent force of sanction working behind the 'soft' international law that transforms it into 'hard' IFL.
7. See, Buckley, R. P. (2008). *International Financial System: Policy and Regulation.* Kluwer Law International. p. 155. See also, Buckley, R. P. & Arner, D. W. (2011). *From Crisis to Crisis: The Global Financial System and Regulatory Failure.* Kluwer Law International.
8. This term owes its popularity to Reinhart and Rogoff who employed it to mark the moment just before a crisis hits. As we have seen, market tends to keep believing *'this time is different'* and

§1.02 WHY REFORMS INDISPENSABLE?

This time the risks are different too, and require a different strategy to outmaneuver the overly devastating risk potentials from interconnected financial products and institutions. Crises usually break out when market actors do not deliberate the system-wide consequences of their policies.[9] For example, de-regulatory practices being adopted by the market participants did not consolidate risk management policies (nor raised appropriate capital, liquidity or leverage requirements), thus exposing themselves to higher financial costs in crisis situations. It did not surprise many who spotted black swans[10] after the 2008 crisis.

In today's world, the cost of financial crises has become humongous. A study conducted by a group of International Monetary Fund (IMF) economists, in a sample of countries representing just over 50% of the world's Gross Domestic Product (GDP), the total amount of government recapitalization, asset purchases and guarantees during the period 2007-2011 amounted to nearly USD 5 trillion. This is equivalent to 16% of the GDP of these economies, or translates into nearly USD 5,000 per person. And, this was only a very conservative guess on the (immediate) cost of the crisis. There are estimates that banking crises that occurred between 1970 to 2000 resulted in output losses of more than 20% on an average if we look at all the countries, and more than 30% of GDP in advanced economies.[11] These results are in line with the Bank for International Settlements (BIS) finding that the median discounted cumulative loss of output over the course of a crisis in the same period was about 19% of pre-crisis GDP.[12] The last quarter of the twentieth century was shaped mostly under the dominant neoclassical spirit where the markets were to define the sphere, extent and nature of

---

   thus they cannot fail and that there are no looming crisis. Here, this term emphasizes that actually *this time in 2008 is different* from many angles (Ch. 6 talks about the changed political realities of today's world): financial, legal and more importantly political and technological. The prolonged aftereffects of the GFC have pushed us into an era marked by nationalism, trade-barriers, financial cut downs and inward-looking insecure nations. This makes it absolutely necessary to address the ideological flaws in our regulatory, economic and political reforms. *See*, Reinhart, C. M. & Rogoff, K. S. (2009). *This Time Is Different: Eight Centuries of Financial Folly*. Princeton University Press.
9. *See*, Dale, R. (1992). Also, Taylor, L., & Eatwell, J. (2000). *Global Finance at Risk: The Case for International Regulation*. The New Press.
10. *See*, Taleb, N. (2007). *The Black Swan-The Impact of the High Improbable*. Random House.
11. Calculation of costs is based on Laeven and Valencia's data from the banking crisis database and calculations of the BIS and the Riksbank. Output losses are computed as the cumulative sum of the differences between actual and trend real GDP over the crisis period in relation to pre-crisis GDP. *See*, Laeven, L., & Valencia, F. (2012). Systemic Banking Crises Database: An Update. *IMF Economic Review*, 61(2), 225-270 available at http://www.imf.org/external/pubs/ft/wp/2012/wp12163.pdf.
12. *See*, the BCBS. (2010). An assessment of the long-term economic impact of the new regulatory framework. In the report loss of output has referred to represent the median cumulative discounted output loss reported by a number of academic studies assessed in the study measured over the period from the peak to the end of the crisis. The output loss does not include permanent losses in GDP, i.e., where the GDP trend does not recover to the pre-crisis level. Ingves, M. S. (November 2014). *Implementing the regulatory reform agenda – the pitfall of myopia*. Speech by the Chairman, BCBS, the FRB Chicago. Retrieved from http://www.financialstabilityboard.org/wp-content/uploads/Stefan-Ingves-Implementing-the-regulatory-reform-agenda-the-pitfall-of-myopia.pdf.

regulatory parameters. It was mostly WC and then the New International Financial Architecture (NIFA)[13] steering liberalization of monetary and exchange policies, which brought many benefits to the markets (both developed and developing), expanded financial activities through greater interconnectedness and enhanced welfare by providing a variety of choices to the users of financial products. It however, brought considerable risks to the system as well. There is already an increasing mismatch between the globally integrated finance and its fragmented mostly national regulatory structures. This fragmentation is unfortunately on the rise with the recent nationalist-cum-populist political approaches defining trade, economic and financial contours. This disproportion has led to damaging crises as Kaminski and Reinhart have documented ample empirical evidence.[14] There are many pitfalls of fragmented regulatory policies implemented arbitrarily by various jurisdictions without regard to the systemic consequences, which may include negative externalities, deepening fragmentation and segmentation of the global financial system.

As we will *see* in Chapter 2, recent systemic crises have brought rich countries almost to the brink of bankruptcy.[15] Employing a historical approach, Buckley and Arner[16] have shown *how misconceived economic policy responses have paved way for the next crash* and have, amongst others, strongly advocated for *game-changing reform* like establishing a global sovereign bankruptcy regime. The *Animal Spirits*[17] reiterated the need for an active role of government (national or international institutions as the case may be) in economic policy-direction to keep the animal spirits in check. Taleb interprets the *repeating follies* behavior from an unconventional angle. Accordingly, these crises events, when looked at retrospectively, do not seem that improbable. Black Swan[18] portrays exquisitely the post-2008 state of affairs, which bore remarkable euphoric similarities, and contrast to the pre-1929 crash. Black swans are not infrequent in the world of finance.

---

13. Chapter 3 has discussed the philosophy in detail.
14. *See,* Kaminsky, G. L., & Reinhart, C. M. (June 1999). The Twin Crises: The Causes of Banking and Balance-of-Payments Problems. *American Economic Review, 89*(3), pp. 473-500.
15. *See,* on repeated mistakes, Buckley, R. P., & Arner, D. W. (2011). *From Crisis to Crisis: The Global Financial System and Regulatory Failure.* Kluwer Law International http://ssrn.com/paper = 1 980010. *See also,* Petersmann, E.-U. (2014). Global Justice and International Economic Law: Three Takes. By Frank J. Garcia. *Journal of International Economic Law, 17*(1), 183-189. And, Petersmann, E.-U. (2014). Need for a New Philosophy of International Economic Law and Adjudication. *Journal of International Economic Law, 17*(3), 639-669.
16. *See,* Buckley & Arner, *supra* n. 15.
17. A term that described the changing patterns of mind after the great depression of 1929. It was used by Keynes in his book in 1936, *see,* Keynes, J. M. (1936). *The General Theory of Employment, Interest and Money.* Collected Writings, vol. VII, Macmillan for the Royal Economic Society.
18. A Black Swan is a highly improbable event with three principal characteristics: It is unpredictable; carries a massive impact; and, after the fact, we concoct an explanation that makes it appear less random, and more predictable than it was. The astonishing success of Google was a black swan; so was 9/11.

§1.03 WHAT'S NEXT?

So, if black swans are frequent visitors to the financial horizon, what are our choices? Usually, crises offer the best political opportunity to undertake otherwise difficult reform in particular questions involving matters of sovereignty and national interest. We lost many such opportunities not to mention the Asian financial crises of the late 1990s. There was a major reform debate in the 1990s[19] without significant gains. Post-2008 era, the scholarship once again brainstormed and policy makers went on to G20 forums repeatedly committing to the best solutions available to weather the financial catastrophe in the western world and its spillovers to the emerging economies. Once again, *this time was different* as the industrialized as well as emerging economies all had high stakes in fixing the system. Not surprisingly, in the early years of the GFC, the G20 and the various Basel Committees were able to achieve much both in advancing their regulatory contents and more importantly, in addressing some of the structural, procedural and legal deficiencies.[20]

Authority springs from legitimacy and accountability. Although, IFL and its institutions are gradually adopting reform yet these efforts are far from being sufficient. In an ideal world, states surrender part of their sovereignty only to enjoy collective sovereignty through a legal contract[21] by the states thereby holding themselves accountable collectively and individually to the rules, regulations or laws they craft collectively. However, in the real world, the basic elements of legitimacy and collective accountability are not always followed and thereby such rules and regulations remain

---

19. *See,* Ch. 3 for major reform initiatives, including the WC, NIFA, and G20s role; Griffith-Jones, S. Proposals for Regulatory Reform: IPD Policy Brief: Columbia University. Available at: http://www.un.org/ga/president/63/commission/ipd_proposals_regulatory.pdf accessed 21 July 2017.
20. *See,* Ch. 4 analyses Basel III and its reaching out to all countries; Ch. 6 on lack of legitimacy in Basel processes, and the long-standing governance/quota reform at the IMF and steps taken to rectify.
21. Thomas Hobbes (1588-1679)'s social contract brought civil liberties for individuals when they surrendered part of their sovereignty to the state. For a supra-national body, as in the formation of other international bodies and institutions under the customary law, states need to surrender a part of sovereignty for the collective benefit of all. This is in fact not as unusual as it sounds. Even today for example, capital adequacy requirements for a bank in Iowa are being determined by a committee of experts sitting in Basel, which is not accountable to US Congress. Eatwell and Taylor responded to the review by Hutton of their book, Taylor, L., & Eatwell, J. (2000). Hutton has contested their argument that 'America has no intention of ceding any regulatory authority at the moment'. That was in 2000 where the world especially the developed countries had not weathered any major crisis since 1929. This is year 2012 where the crisis in the financial markets have changed the world-view of the most developed countries and this fact in itself presents a strong case for surrendering state sovereignties in a bid for entering into a 'legal contract' for the collective welfare. Hutton, W. (1999). *The Stackholding Society Writings on Politics and Economics*. Polity Press, Cambridge. *See also,* Xiaochuan, Z. (March 23, 2009). Reform the International Monetary System. An Essay by Dr. Xiaochuan, Governor of the People's Bank of China, available at http://www.bis.org/review/r090402c.pdf where he suggested creating a global reserve currency. This was not the only call many scholars including American have been dwelling on the idea.

far from empowering the financial system. This study questions the fundamentals[22] of the existing architecture and explores possibilities for putting in place a stable and resilient financial system empowered to legislate reform and authorized to seek compliance from its members.

The need is to take bold decisions that conform with procedural justice and distributive equity to the ongoing development of relevant laws and standards. A resilient enforcement mechanism with judicious regulatory substance can make the financial system safer for all the actors including the taxpayers. Certainly, the measures are tough and some entities may see a short-term decline in profits or higher costs of compliance to a more prudent legal framework. However, for the stability of financial markets and long-term market stability, states need to *provide teeth* in the soft jaws of supervisors and regulators to strengthen enforcement of laws, rules and regulations vested in these agencies. Since we are going talk about enforcement of IFL in the subsequent chapters, let's first have a look at what this term implies in order to better understand it.

§1.04　SOME DEFINITIONS

This book centers on the concept of enforcement in the discipline of IFL that continues to be an unresolved issue. The arguments *for and against* instituting enforcement provision in IFL continue to be substantial both in the academic as well as policy debate. The Oxford dictionary defines the term *enforcement* simply as an *act of compelling observance of or compliance with a law, rule or obligation.*[23] In legal and IFL scholarship the term has profound meaning. In addition to seeking observance it essentially entails provision for disciplinary measures ensuring effects of the expected requirements.

The distinguishing characteristic of soft law is that it remains unenforceable by legal means (such as law suits)[24] as it is not legally binding.[25] According to some, it is not law at all.[26] Traditionalists view soft law as *neither soft nor hard and any soft lawbased obligations not a law at all*. The term enforcement in legal discourse refers to a specific transformation leading to the hardening of the soft law of international finance. The term hard law as used in this research implies *[l]egally binding obligations that are precise (or having potential to be made precise through further regulation, adjudication) delegating authority to interpret and implement the law.*[27] The concept of enforcement in legal terms is a detailed legalization process and has been analyzed in

---

22. A fundamental is what an average opinion believes to be fundamental, where an average opinion is the overall opinion held by market participants and so shapes well-respected conventions.
23. A simple dictionary definition, *see*, https://en.oxforddictionaries.com/definition/enforcement.
24. The commitments and undertakings, e.g., for the Universal Declaration of Human Rights, and the Helsinki Final Act impact behavior of a signatory state being quasi-legal in character.
25. Giovanoli, M. (2000). *The IMF Law: Issues for the New Millennium*. OUP. 2000. p. 35.
26. *See*, Guzman, A. T. & Meyer, T. (2010). International Soft Law. *The Journal of Legal Analysis*, 2(1). Available at http://ssrn.com/paper = 1353444.
27. *See*, Abbott, K. W., et al. (2000). The Concept of Legalization. *International Organization*, 54(3), 401-419.

sufficient detail to present a three-dimensional theory of the legalization process.[28] Gu and Liu expanded on the concept of legalization in IFL (used by Abbott et al.) to include the term *delegation*, thus, *[e]nforcement calls for disciplinary measures ensuring compliance, while delegation refers to a third party authorized to administer the execution of law.*[29] Accordingly, the three-dimensional theory of the legalization of IFL comprises of (a) *an obligation:* that is, a requirement having binding effects, for example to comply with the Financial Sector Assessment Program (FSAP) of the IMF, (b) *stringency:* spelling out the specifics to be achieved or targets to meet, for example Basel regulation quantitatively defines various ratios and targets to achieve) and, (c) *delegation:* third-party authorization to administer the requirements, for example, as it operates in the World Trade Organization (WTO)).[30]

Abbott and Snidal[31] apply the three-dimensional theory of legalization on various modes of international law along a continuum, which on the one end provides for soft law structures (an absence of obligations and no stringent numbers and marked by anarchy like in the G7), and on the other end, it provides for hard-law based structures (precise, legally binding and treaty-based with an authority to administer). They also bring forward a *soft-legalization* model with various combinations of reduced precision, less stringent obligation and weaker delegation (usually a preferred option by many IFL actors as it offers an advantage to deal with uncertainty and facilitates compromise. Giovanoli espouses not a very different view from the *soft-legalization* model of Abbot and Snidal as expounded above. Accordingly, a unique balance could be achieved by combining soft law and hard law in an optimal manner to get to a strengthened soft-law based mechanism for IFL. Therefore, the standards on which an international consensus has been established in an informal way could be made the object of an international treaty under which countries could sign up to specific standards, thereby commit themselves to implement and enforce these within their national jurisdictions.[32] Pauwelyn et al., call it informal international lawmaking (IN-LAW), which can include private actor participation but excludes cooperation involving only private actors. They construct a three-dimensional theory of soft law marked by informality at each step of the process. The soft law or the *IN-LAW* thus comprises of (a) *output informality*– in the sense of not necessarily leading to a treaty or other traditional sources of law but rather a standard, declaration or even a policy exchange); (b) *process informality*– through a loosely organized network or a forum rather than a traditional treaty-based international organization); and (c) *actor informality*– not the traditional state or diplomatic delegates but other public authorities like domestic regulators, independent or semi-independent agencies).[33] There are however

---

28. Ibid.
29. Gu, B. & Liu, T. (2014). Enforcing International Financial Regulatory Reforms. *Journal of International Economic Law 17*(1).
30. Ibid. p. 3.
31. Abbott et al. *supra* n. 27.
32. Giovanoli, *supra* n. 25, p. 53.
33. Pauwelyn, J., Wessel, R., & Wouters, J. An Introduction to Informal International Lawmaking, in, Pauwelyn, J., Wessel, R. A. & Wouters, J. (Eds.). (2012). *Informal International Law-Making*. Oxford University Press. pp. 15-20. *See also*, Pauwelyn, J. (2012). *Dealing with the Increasing Complexity of Investment-Related Treaties: A Framework and Some Policy Guidelines*. Available

many questions on the process including for example, how states would prefer, what kind of formal or informal processes states may approve or disapprove. There are also issues to consider with keeping formal and informal boundaries especially when the same actor fancies both formal and informal lawmaking for two sets of subjects in contrast to another opposing actor/s.

International finance[34] is dotted with sporadic and incoherent choices for an enforcement mechanism due to the lack of a judicial or quasi-judicial apparatus in its design. This research explores the theme of enforcement of regulatory reforms within the domain of IFL as a number of important reforms are being processed (and have been adopted) in the post-GFC era as crises provide an excellent opportunity to strengthen legal global as well as domestic framework and legislation.[35] Nonetheless, enforcement of laws is central to ensure the credibility of institutional processes in the traditional realm of law. A comprehensive legal framework comprising all three elements of legalization (obligation, delegation and enforcement) of IFL can be one option to provide for a stable financial system, we are going to find out in this volume. If public enforcement of regulation is the most contested issue (as being largely criticized by pro-market forces), *a private regulation and enforcement system*[36] could be another option. The idea is not to legislate to put in place traditional state diplomats or regulators micromanaging every act of market. Considering the IN-LAW framework as developed by Pauwelyn et al., the regulators and the regulated could actually become essential *partners* in maintaining a stable financial system.[37] Miller and Cafaggi, while distinguishing between private and public regulation and enforcement said that *private regulation and enforcement can manifest independence of action and judgment, as compared with public regulation.*[38] They add a new perspective to the analysis of how regulation could and should respond to the GFC by focusing on the private as opposed to the public aspect of regulation.

---

at https://www.iisd.org/itn/2012/10/30/dealing-with-the-increasing-complexity-of-investment-related-treaties-a-framework-and-some-policy-guidelines/.

34. To define the term international finance, *see*, part I of the chapter in Scott, H. S. (December 15, 2005). An Overview of International Finance: Law and Regulation, *available at http://papers.ssrn.com/sol3/papers.cfm?abstract_id = 800627*. See also, Scott, H. S., & Wellons, P. A. (2010). *International Finance: Transactions, Policy, and Regulation* (17 ed.) Foundation Press.

35. *See*, for example, financial regulation has more often than not been a by-product of, or a reaction to crises episodes. *See* for instance, Goodhart, C. A. E. & Lastra, R. M. (2010). Border Problems. *Journal of International Economic Law, 13*(3), 705-718.

36. For an economic analysis, *see*, Polinsky, A. M. & Shavell, S. (2006). Public Enforcement of Law, *SIEPR Discussion Paper No. 05-16*. Retrieved from http://web.stanford.edu/group/siepr/cgi-bin/siepr/?q = system/files/shared/pubs/papers/pdf/05-16.pdf *See also*, Pauwelyn et al. *supra* n. 33 for a discussion of the private and public enforcement.

37. Sykes develops a theory regarding rules for international trade and investment agreements. *See*, Sykes, A. O. (2005). Public v. Private Enforcement of International Economic Law: Standing and Remedy. *Journal of Legal Studies, 34*(2), 631-666. *See also*, Becker, G. S. & Stigler, G. J. (1974). Law Enforcement, Malfeasance, and Compensation of Enforcers. *The Journal of Legal Studies, 3*(1), 1-18.

38. Miller, G. P. & Cafaggi, F. (2013). *The Governance and Regulation of International Finance*. Edward Elgar Publishing.

Chapter 1: Introduction §1.05

It is important to differentiate between enforcement and implementation.[39] Enforcement is a legal concept meaning that competent authorities take measures to *apply legally binding rules*, implementation however, is a factual concept. It implies *achieving of certain results* either through appropriate domestic legislation or by any other means.

Another distinction is pertinent to make between the concept of law, legal effects and enforceability. Law and non-law standards and norms both have legal effects, whereas only *the law is binding* and has *enforceability*. For soft law, it mostly is *at will adoption* or through *incentives*[40] one can compel compliance to financial standards. However, peer pressure and regulatory competition can work in opposite directions resulting into either adoption by all of the members or in a scenario marked by fragmented interests (part of the informal lawmaking process) and preferences, which can create arbitrage opportunities.[41]

§1.05 SOME QUESTIONS

Absence of an effective international regulatory framework continues to be a challenging area in want of serious theoretical and policy research. Stanley Fischer raised a set of questions:

> [h]ow do you encourage countries to adopt a standard? If a standard is adopted, how do you monitor implementation? If we look at the international economy, the international regulatory framework is in its infancy. And if we ask why international financial crises have erupted on such a scale and frequency…the answer may have a lot to do with the absence of an adequate international regulatory and legal framework.[42]

Let's look at these questions narrowly. These questions relate to a fundamental issue of seeking compliance in IFL. No matter how many international forums we devise or how many well-researched regulatory regimes we bring up, it would not make our financial world safer if such new standards (or even the old ones) do not incentivize compliance. Chapter 2 reflects on the tumultuous, crisis-ridden and mostly reactive developmental processes of IFL and regulation and thus the issue of *compliance* hardly gets a line on the immediate agenda. From the discussion in the next six chapters, we are going to seek answers. This book evaluates the developmental processes (or the lack thereof) of the discipline of IFL[43] and its regulatory architecture.

---

39. Giovanoli, *supra* n. 25, p. 46.
40. The incentives could be either official or market: former would include *'name and shame'* practice, the use of the IMF conditionality etc., while the latter would include credit-risk rating, differentiated interest rates, inter-bank exposure and others. Market incentives are typically voluntary and require a high degree of transparency.
41. Giovanoli, *supra* n. 25.
42. Fischer, S. (1999). *Capital Account Liberalization and the Role of the IMF*. Available at https://piie.com/fischer/pdf/Fischer141.pdf last accessed 7 July 2017.
43. *See,* Ch. 2.

More critically, it looks at the weaknesses (structural[44] as well as substantive[45]) in its conduct (or misconduct), from various angles (including from a treaty-bound hard-law perspective).[46] The working thesis it poses is whether a hard-law-based IFL (based on enforcement of regulation) is essential for maintaining global financial stability. It looks at alternative perspectives to treaty-based framework by incorporating much talked-about reforms to the existing soft-law-based framework of IFL and to evaluate financial stability options.[47] As successive episodes of financial crises raise the question of *whether there is a need for an enforcement mechanism in the post-crisis reconstruction of an international financial regulatory architecture* (IFRA) to support global financial stability? If the answer to the above question is *no*, then we look at what alternative risk management system or reform to the existing system are required to achieve international market stability? We also explore conceptual, institutional and practical *challenges* in framing and implementing such reform to IFRA in order to prescribe risk management strategies. In doing so, we explore all options including any lessons from similar historical initiatives with a view to learn. Of course this book takes into account the many contemporary instances from trade and monetary systems pertinent in particular for the development of the discipline of IFL.

§1.06   WHY ANSWERS MATTER?

We're now at an important juncture. Broadly speaking we experienced 30 years of Keynesian economic ideas in the post-war period before we moved to a much more free market, Hayekian approach, which the GFC has reflected to be flawed in a number of ways. As always, post-GFC research has been in search for a new set of ideas, which dramatically change the world in order to implement the ideal recommendations to resolve the jinx of financial crisis forever. The *big* objective of this research is to add to the development of IFL as a discipline.[48] Importantly, it seeks for a financial law structure embodying tools for early-warning system, predictability and yet for unseen, unknown unknowns, having crisis-management mechanism fully in place. A strengthened IFRA is a corollary of a stronger IFL regime.

Although, the subject of this book has been the focus of much of the post-crisis scholarship the reform debate has not been conclusive. It is still striving for a *consensus*

---

44. *See*, Ch. 3.
45. *See*, Ch. 4.
46. *See*, Ch. 5.
47. *See*, Ch. 6.
48. Primary objective of IFL is to create international financial stability. This stability has to be created in an environment of national jurisdictions where each is in pursuit of narrow national interests and is constantly threatened by consequences from increasing globalization, technological development and financial innovation. *See*, reference work by, Wood, P.R., (2008). *Law and Practice of International Finance*, Sweet and Maxwell. And, Bamford, C.G., (2011). *Principles of International Financial Law*, Oxford University Press. *See also*, International Financial Law. Peace Palace Library. Retrieved from http://www.peacepalacelibrary.nl/research-guides/economic-and-financial-law/international-financial-law/ date accessed August 20, 2015.

even on the fundamentals.[49] The argument on *enforcement v. voluntary adoption of standards, regulation v. de-regulatory regimes, and hard-law v. soft-law* based reform remains indecisive even today. Mario Giovanoli remarked in 2000 that the major challenge for the specialists of monetary law is no doubt the strengthening of the IFRA with a view to promoting international monetary stability.[50]

Therefore, answers to the above issues are analyzed in the chapters below using institutional analogy,[51] qualitative analysis and by combining comparative[52] and historical approaches. The subject matter of this research entailed a continuous update of the vast literature cited on a range of issues (development of IFL, of regulatory architecture, of treaty-based mechanisms, of regulatory regimes etc.).[53] This book is being published at a critical time when not only financial and monetary reforms are being adopted but also our politico-economic and social landscape is in a big transition. It is the latter that impacts the former in many consequential ways. Karl Polanyi argued that the emergence of market-based societies in modern Europe was not inevitable but historically contingent as economies are embedded in society and culture.[54]

§1.07 LET'S FIND ANSWERS

Going forward, Chapter 2 looks at the development of IFL during the twentieth century and how recurring financial crises shaped its present day formulation. Chapter 3 looks at the development of international financial institutions (IFIs), their role in maintaining international FMS and the current regulatory architecture as it has evolved especially trough the WC, NIFA and GFC. In Chapter 4 we look at the Basel process (Basel I, II and III): its development and the various risk management strategies to evaluate Basel's effectiveness during crises. Chapter 5 looks at the possibilities of

---

49. See, *supra* n. 22.
50. *Supra* n. 29.
51. The EU, a treaty-based IL structure has been analyzed in Ch. 5 to review possibilities for replicating a similar structure at the global level, since the EU especially in the aftermath of the SDC presents an excellent laboratory for stress testing various hypotheses. Also, Ch. 3 takes into account the critical pillars of the existing regulatory architecture to provide analytical insights. For example, the IMF, another treaty-based institution presents another setting of formal hard-law-based mechanism binding on its members and bestowed with surveillance and monitoring powers in addition to force of sanction. The international trade law is considered a successful model in international-trade-sector hard-law-based regulations. It comes with an effective arbitration and dispute settlement mechanism that anchors stability and effectiveness to the system to an extent.
52. Comparative law is defined as the study of the relationship between systems or between rules of more than one system ... in the context of a historical relationship. This definition underlines that to qualify as a true comparative law enterprise it also requires comparison of two or more legal systems, or two or more legal traditions, or of selected aspects, institutions or branches of two or more legal systems. See, Watson, A. (1974). *Legal Transplants: An Approach to Comparative Law*. Scottish Academic Press. See also, for a more modern perspective on the subject, Cruz, P. D. (2007). *Comparative Law in a Changing World*. (3ed.) Routledge-Cavendish.
53. See, for an overall overview of international financial law annotated bibliography, Arner, D. & Ashraf, U. (2012). International Financial Law, In T. Carty (Ed.), *Oxford Bibliographies in International Law*. Oxford University Press.
54. Polanyi, K. *The Great Transformation: The Political and Economic Origins of Our Time*. Beacon Press. Available at http://inctpped.ie.ufrj.br/spiderweb/pdf_4/Great_Transformation.pdf.

having a treaty-based structure for IFL by examining closely the EU's integration framework. Chapter 6 summarizes the various regulatory issues raised in Chapters 2-5 and weighs in on the post-GFC reform initiatives for their adequacy in establishing a stable, resilient and robust IFL. It looks at the role of the law in defining institutional dynamics and financial stability. This leads us to the final chapter, which reiterates the need for fundamental reform of the existing international financial system and provides alternative ways of achieving the goals.

In Chapter 2, I begin by looking at the chronological development of IFL during the twentieth and twenty-first century. It starts under the controlled regimes (the Gold Standard, still considered a stable time in terms of international FMS), the Bretton Woods System (based on the precept of domestic finance), and follows through the era of comparative liberalization and de-regulation (frequent financial disruptions and global imbalances). The next section examines the various crises episodes and how these shaped the development of IFL regime. Alternatively, how IFL and its regulatory bodies responded to various crises and those crises in turn shaped the architecture. This section looks at this drastic transformation of *finance from a domestic concept to an international phenomenon* under the de-regulatory philosophy of market fundamentalism. This period is dotted with innumerable instances of financial, banking and at times, systemic crises across the globe. On an average, the world had a major financial crisis every three years since 1971. Section §1.03 evaluates the GFC, current state of IFL and the post-GFC reforms leading us to the next chapter, which looks at the development of the IFRA.

Chapter 3 addresses two distinct streams: the first stream focuses on ideological and political ethos underpinning the development of financial markets and how this has contoured the formation of regulatory institutions. Stream II focuses on the substantive regulatory apparatus – the bodies and institutional networks established mostly in response to various crises. In exploring these structural manifestations of IFL, section §1.02 looks at the institutional heritage financial markets carried from the post-War and post-Bretton Woods time to analyze the interplay of the role of law and institutional underpinnings in the development of international financial markets. In the next part, we study the interplay of liberalization and de-regulation under the ethos of the WC and NIFA. Section §1.03 looks at the structure, role and functions of IFRA and brings out the gaps undermining the credibility of these institutions. It identifies factors delaying implementation of reforms after a lapse of almost 10 years since the GFC. Section §1.04 questions if the regulatory architecture as it exists today is resilient enough to prevent future financial disruptions? The answer summarizes what regulatory reforms have achieved so far and whether the existing IFRA presents the ideals those post-GFC commitments envisioned achieving? The next three chapters evaluate whether *an enforcement mechanism* in the realm of IFL is indispensable in the post-crisis reconstruction of a credible regulatory architecture.

Chapter 4 is focused exclusively on risk prevention and management regulation. The basic question (in line with the objectives of this research) is to look at *whether the newly evolving soft law based regulatory framework, the Basel III would be resilient against future crises?* Two issues are specifically explored: first, the regulatory substance (i.e., resilience) of the new standards against future risks and; second, the requisite legal backstops to oblige compliance to the new regulatory standards. We compare and contrast the pre- and post-2008 Basel regimes (Basel I, II and III) and evaluate for its effectiveness as a risk prevention tool. This focused *substance and processes* analysis reviews *global v. national* regulatory standards and practices. The pre-2008 period focusses on capital adequacy regulation and the emergence of various risks especially the operational risk. Their key objective was to a create buffer against future losses and to provide for a mechanism discounting the costs of a financial crises. We find the pre-2008 capital buffers inadequate and scanty, while the Basel III framework is yet to be judged against future financial flare-ups. The post-2008 phase focuses on Basel III critique in terms of strength of its contents (compared to Basel II), its adoption timeline and the glitches, if any, in its ultimate implementation.

Chapter 5 explores a treaty-based hard-law structure in order to evaluate if a binding framework of integration can work in globalized financial markets. The EU in the context of the GFC, the Sovereign Debt Crisis (SDC) of 2012, the Eurozone fear of disintegration that followed the Greek bailout, the *Brexit* and even the most recent fall outs from the refugee crisis and rising political populism provide a perfect laboratory to analyze the various options regarding devising a treaty-based global market framework. The failure of the crisis prevention/management mechanism in the EU as crisis unfolded in dealing with the GFC and the SDC provides an insight on the functioning of hard-law-based supra-national financial governance. Section §1.02 sketches an analytical overview of economic and institutional developments leading to the establishment of a treaty-based EU single market for financial services. It discusses threats to the integration framework posed by the GFC and intensified by the SDC and how these disruptions gradually challenged the most advanced integrated regional market. The discussion here extends to the evolution of institutional infrastructure safeguarding financial stability and effective supervision of financial institutions in the EU from its early stages. It reviews the post-crisis European effort at reinventing the integration mechanism (through the formation of the European Financial Stability Facility (ESFS)), the European Systemic Risk Board (ESRB), the European Banking Authority (EBA), the Integrated Fund and Deposit Guarantee Scheme (DGS) on the one hand, and how this new set of institutions would strengthen EU's economic and political integration on the other. We end with the discussion on future challenges to the treaty-based mechanisms and on possibilities of replicating a single market framework in a global setting.

In Chapter 6 we look at the inconsistencies in the development of a responsible regulatory framework and reflect on the objectivity, adequacy and credibility of each of the major pending reforms. The analysis has a focused coverage of issues that directly stem from the nature of IFL and have arisen from the *pre-and-post-crisis reregulation* including: financial market liberalization (FML), weaker crisis-management and crisis-prevention systems, legitimacy deficit, pending governance and faulty representational structures of the regulatory infrastructure. These factors have rendered the existing institutions weak delivery, legal mandate and credibility. Thus short-to-medium-term solutions are being provided here while living within the existing soft law based IFL, which operates on a consensus-oriented regulatory compliance model.

The chapter starts by looking at theoretical underpinnings of the relationship between institutions and development of financial markets. It employs a three-pronged strategy to study the role of these institutions in development, their relationship with law, and how this nexus between the two has developed over time. While defining the *undefined term, financial stability, we expand* the debate to instability and its inherent challenges. This argument combines theoretical conceptualization from the post-2008 IFL and identifies significant paradoxes therein. The next section draws on the current reforms taking place at the global level in response to the crisis to highlight *inconsistencies* in the reform processes. Gaps, in compliance to and in the enforcement of financial standards engender the debate whether to strengthen the IFIs' governance or the field of IFL itself needs to be revisited. The argument for inherent flexibility to support global applicability results mostly in partial compliance of these soft standards. Frequently, a number of jurisdictions embracing these standards have lesser or at times insignificant contribution in the drafting processes signaling *democratic deficit* in the formation of IFL and its regulatory regimes. Analysis of these institutions reveals legitimacy gaps and democratic deficit in the standard-formulation processes, representation imbalances in their membership, and skewed decision-making models forms the third sub-theme of this chapter. The conceptual foundations of these legitimacy and ingenuity-related questions form the fourth sub-theme. If FMS is the optimal end, then IFL as it exists today faces multiple inconsistencies on a number of fronts. These multi-faceted reforms as suggested in this chapter would support the existing structures through improved functioning of IFL.

Chapter 7 however concludes the discussion by providing unconventional alternatives for further development of IFL as a discipline as well as for subsequent development of the IFRA to realize stable, predictable and robust international financial markets. Based on the previous analysis, it provides conclusive recommendations to build an IFRA embodying early-warning systems and yet for unseen, unknown unknowns, crisis-prevention mechanism fully primed to address such situations. It recommends for a system of asset-backed finance, which would take the risk away from the markets by holding every stakeholder responsible to the system. However, the key is adopting such a system globally. A strengthened IFRA is a corollary of a stronger IFL regime embodying enforceable powers in respect of the regulatory standards and practices it advocates.

CHAPTER 2

Cyclic Financial Crises and the Development of IFL[*]

The development of IFL is an evolutionary process[1] characterized by repetitive crises events and the regulatory responses to such events. The powerful economic forces and paramount domestic interests in influential industrialized countries shape the nuances in financial products and services that define financial market.[2] This development of the market itself effects progression of financial law.

The IFIs (such as the G7) and the international financial regulatory standards (such as Basel II) either became redundant or lost effectiveness as they failed in their objectives to enforce financial discipline in the pre-2008 period. Although, the Financial Stability Forum (FSF) initiated its regulatory reform work in 1999, it was the GFC that set to work the G20 and the FSB to undertake the gigantic task of putting in place crisis management and prevention mechanisms to guard against future financial

---

[*] I owe thanks to Prof. Christine Desan and the Writing Group participants at the Institute of global Law & Policy (IGLP) 2012, Harvard Law School, for helpful comments on an earlier version of this chapter. I am also grateful to the IGLP for inviting me to participate in its workshops, once in 2012 and again in 2017. The IGLP 2017 workshop provided invaluable comments and feedback as I was developing the proposal for this book.
1. Proctor approaches the subject from legal aspects of defining law and traces historical development of the concept as it emerges in today's globalized world through technological challenges. Proctor, C. (2005). *Mann on the Legal Aspect of Money* (6th ed.) Oxford University Press. *See*, for a bibliographic account of the development of IFL, Arner, D. & Ashraf, U. (2012). *International Financial Law,* in, Oxford Bibliographies, OUP. NY.
2. To explore IFL as an academic discipline highlighting interaction between domestic laws, domestic conflict rules and international treaties, *See*, Sebastianutti, P. (2009). What Is This Thing Called International Financial Law? *Law and Financial Markets Review*, 3(1), 64-71. Available at http://search.informit.com.au/documentSummary;dn = 710655244810779;res = IELHSS   *See also*, Bellis, M. D. (2010). Public Law and Private Regulators in the Global Legal Space. Jean Monnet WP No. 17/10. Bellis discusses the interrelationship of domestic legal systems and international law regulatory regimes to highlight important issues of accountability and legitimacy by employing different models of private norms as used in public regulation within domestic legal orders.

crises.[3] Primarily, these reforms aimed at redesigning the IFRA to make it resilient to future crises. However, in the overall clamor of impending short-to-medium-term priorities, the development of the broader field of IFL itself could seize but limited attention. The post-GFC reform initiatives and the existing regulatory institutions have all except a legal authority in terms of their scope, functions and the instruments they can employ to achieve their objectives, it demands a review of their scope and the underlying legal instruments to align their objectives and powers. An attempt to answer simple questions like whether establishing the FSB[4] (a soft-law body operating on consensus-based decision-making model) or drafting Basel III regulations (voluntary standards; adoption timeline 2019) would be sufficient to prevent the next financial crisis– compels us to go beyond these *signpost achievements*. We find ourselves asking: What else is required to be accomplished to manage financial stability? The answers lead us to revisit and redefine the structure and functioning of the law itself and the structure and working of the existing IFRA because the current IFL and IFRA both have yet to align with the existing market realities to serve the purpose of maintaining international financial market stability. The GFC exposed major weaknesses in the working and design of IFL and in the governance framework of the IFIs.

Section §2.01 begins by looking at the chronological development of IFL during the gold standard and the Bretton Woods era. Under the controlled regimes of the nineteenth century, the development of IFL followed through the gold standard (considered by some as the most stable financial times) and the Bretton Woods system (based on the precept of *domestic finance*). Section §2.02 makes an analysis of the era of liberalization marked by financial disruptions and global imbalances. This section looks at this drastic transformation of *finance* from a *domestic concept* to an *international phenomenon* under the de-regulatory philosophy of market fundamentalism.

---

3. Immediate responses included, setting up bailout packages in various countries, like the Troubled Assets Relief Programs (TARP, USD 700 billion) in the US, direct government intervention by lowering federal fund rates and providing direct lines of credit, guaranteeing liabilities or orchestrating takeovers (the ECB provided short-term credit lines). The IMF estimated in April 2009 that Western governments in total spent around USD 10 trillion to shore up their financial systems. *See*, Liang, T. L. (2010). The Global Financial Crisis and Policy responses. Civil Services College, Singapore, available at https://www.cscollege.gov.sg/Knowledge/Pages/The-Global-Financial-Crisis-and-Policy-Responses.aspx For a graphical presentation of policy responses in the US, *See*, Reyes, A. (2013). The Financial Crisis Five Years Later: Responses, Reform, and Progress. Retrieved from, http://www.treasury.gov/connect/blog/Pages/The-Financial-Crisis-Five-Years-Later.aspx. For Asia, *See also*, Arner, D. W., & Schou-Zibell, L. (2011). Asian Regulatory Responses to the Global Financial Crisis. *Global Journal of Emerging Market Economies*, 3(1), 135-169. Retrieved from http://hdl.handle.net/10722/139340; For a view at the EU level, *See*, Arroyo, H. T. (2011). The European Union's Fiscal Crisis and Policy Response: Reforming Economic Governance in the EU, http://www.oecd.org/gov/budgetingandpublicexpenditures/48871475.pdf *See also*, FSA (March 2009). The Turner Review: A Regulatory Response to the Global Banking Crisis. Retrieved from http://www.fsa.gov.uk/pubs/other/turner_review.pdf; and, Claessens, S., & Kodres, L. (2014). The Regulatory Responses to the Global Financial Crisis: Some Uncomfortable Questions, IMF WP 14/46. Available at https://www.imf.org/external/pubs/ft/wp/2014/wp1446.pdf.
4. Though the FSB has been described as the *fourth-pillar* of the global economic structure along with the IMF, the WB and the WTO, yet unlike the other three, it is not a multilateral treaty-based organization.

Chapter 2: Cyclic Financial Crises and the Development of IFL   §2.01

This period is dotted with innumerable instances of financial, banking and at times, systemic crises across the globe. Section §2.03 looks at the twenty-first century finance and at the events leading to the GFC. Section §2.04 confronts the GFC and at the current state of IFL and explores its role in the post-crisis regulatory reforms. This leads us to the next chapter, which looks at the development of the IFRA.

§2.01   IFL AND THE CONTROLLED REGIMES

Early twentieth-century financial and monetary procedures underwent a dramatic change. The change was to bring capital controls and enhanced restrictions across financial markets. With a shift from classical liberalism in the nineteenth century to an embedded liberalism in the twentieth century, adult suffrage, democracy, unionism and labor rights (including employment maximization and trade protectionism) took precedence over monetary independence of central banks, which would otherwise adhere to defending capital controls and pegged exchange rates. The global system continued to adopt a very conservative and controlled movement until the end of the Second World War.

However, in the post-War era, countries started emerging from the phenomena like *path dependence, negotiating costs, and network externalities* as some movements in the later part of the twentieth century picked up acceleration (including the Western alliance's formation during the Second World War, the Bretton Woods system).[5] Although, the development of IFL has been remarkable following the various crises and post-crises reforms in the 1870s, 1920s, 1940s, and 1970s and since 2008, yet, IFL remains essentially a work-in-progress. IFL has potential implications for both public international law and municipal law due to overlapping jurisdictions that involve states and non-state actors, international, regional and domestic regulatory standards and their subsequent obligations.[6] Despite this multi-level, multifarious institutional interaction, the basic fabric of IFL itself remains inherently soft and nonbinding.[7]

The global financial system underwent a full-scale transformation in terms of its theoretical underpinnings and physical manifestations in the past century, in the context of the Gold Standard, Bretton Woods system, the WC and NIFA I&II etc. It oscillated from controlled capital to full-scale market-driven financial environment. This transformation came along with a string of financial disruptions (especially the post-1970s) and responses to such crises contoured the development of IFL and its regulatory mechanism.

---

5. Cane & Kritzer have done a classic empirical legal study of the systems and institutions particularly European and American, taking into account not only the normative interpretations of law but also social, political, economic and ethical aspects. *See*, Cane, P. & Kritzer, H. M. (Eds.). (2010). *The Oxford Handbook of Empirical Legal Research*. Oxford University Press.
6. Akehurst debates on the interrelationship of municipal law, international law and international economic law and on the questions of jurisdiction and legal personality of international law itself. *See*, Akehurst, M. B. (1987). *A Modern Introduction to International Law* (7 ed.): Allen & Unwin Ltd. *See also*, Ch. 3 for a detailed discussion.
7. *See*, Ch. 6 discusses the soft-law nature of IFL.

[A] The Classical Gold Standard

Gold standard, in simple terms is a monetary system in which the standard economic unit of account is based on a fixed quantity of gold. It is a controlled capital flow system, distinguishable into three types based on *specie, exchange and bullion*. In the gold specie standard, monetary unit is associated with the value of circulating gold coins or the monetary unit, which possesses the value of a certain circulating gold coin but other coins, may be made of less valuable metal. The gold bullion standard is a system in which gold coins do not circulate, but the authorities agree to sell gold bullion on demand at a fixed price in exchange for the circulating currency. And, the gold exchange standard mostly does not involve circulation of gold coins, rather, a government guarantees a fixed exchange rate for the currency of another country that uses a gold standard (specie or bullion), regardless of what type of notes (or coins) are used as a means of exchange. This exchange standard is a type of *de facto gold standard* where the value of the means of exchange has a fixed external value in terms of gold that is independent of the inherent value of the means of exchange itself.

Under the scope of this chapter, the gold standard era is divided into two periods: the golden period, which according to some historians, started almost a quarter century before the First World War and remained until the War broke out. Most of the literature equates this period as an era of financial stability because of less volatile financial markets.[8] The second era, which lasted until 1930s, is commonly known as a period of reconstructed gold standard.

Scholarly critique on the relationship of gold standard and financial market stability spreads along the full spectrum: ranging from keeping up the financial market stability to bringing down the international monetary system (IMS) completely. In this section, we will review whether it was gold standard that kept the financial system alive or the inter-War reconstructed gold standard,[9] which, led to the gradual deterioration of the financial system, culminating in the Great Depression.[10]

There are two opposing views on the role of the gold standard in maintaining financial system's stability. The conventional view attributes financial stability to the gold standard and holds it in high prestige. Friedman and Schwartz,[11] Temin and Fischer and Eichengreen[12] are critical of the conventional view that the gold standard maintained *sanity* of the system. To them, the gold standard not only brought the

---

8. *See*, Proctor, *supra* n. 1.
9. Bordo in a review of the book, *Golden Fetters: The Gold Standard and the Great Depression* called the inter-war gold standard as *a pale shadow of the pre-World War I gold standard system*, which unlike its predecessor, failed to impart stability. pp. 193-197. FRASER, last accessed May 31, 2017. Available at https://fraser.stlouisfed.org/scribd/?title_id=3595&filepath=/docs/meltzer/borrev94.pdf#scribd-open.
10. The reconstructed gold standard, as records Eichengreen, lacked the credible commitment of the pre-War system as it gradually became evident that the monetary authorities would no longer subsume internal stability to external goals. *See*, Eichengreen, B. (1992). Golden Fetters: The Gold Standard and the Great Depression. Oxford University Press.
11. Friedman, M., & Schwartz, A. J. (1963). *A Monetary History of the United States 1867-1960*. Princeton University Press.
12. Eichengreen, *supra* n. 10.

collapse of financial stability, a decrease in production output and deterioration of prices but also proved an obstacle to speedy recovery from the Great Depression. Not surprising that the history found the United Kingdom (UK) and the Scandinavian countries coming out of the depression sooner than any other countries (France took the longest time to recover) who did not readily opt out of the gold standard.

In a sharp contrast, however, other scholars such as Kindleberger[13] hold that the collapse of the gold standard set the stage for the depression of 1929, which brought financial chaos across the world. Kindleberger thus argues that, the stability of the pre-War gold standard was a result of: First, an effective management by the Bank of England (BoE) and its role as an international lender of last resort (LoLR); and second, the British capital market's ability to inject more investments and liquidity into the international financial markets on demand. However, this provision to inject liquidity could not last long as the UK was too weak to continue providing resources for the stability of the international financial system during and after the War, while the United States (US) was not willing to take over that traditional managerial-role historically played by the UK. As Kindleberger has put it, only a dominant economic *hegemon*[14] could provide required resources much needed for the stability of a financial system during crisis. Eichengreen, however, contradicted the claim that it was London alone that imparted stability to the international financial markets by keeping gold standard intact). London, as he claimed, could be the leading IFC but Berlin and Paris rivaled it.

[1]   *Politicization of the Monetary System (1919-1928)*

The construct of IFL rests upon credibility of commitments made by the Member States and on successful international cooperation. During 1880-1913 policy commitments to uphold the system based on gold standard made by the national government were based on the perception that the gold standard and general domestic prosperity are mutually reinforcing. In an environment, teeming with the spirit of international cooperation any unilateral action would be more damaging for the initiator.[15] Simultaneously, BoE played a leading role in upholding international cooperation, the

---

13. Kindleberger, C. P., & Aliber, R. Z. (2005). *Manias, Panics, and Crashes: A History of Financial Crises* (5ed), John Wiley & Sons.
14. Kohane for the first time presented this theory. *See*, Keohane, R. (1980). The Theory of Hegemonic Stability and Changes in International Economic Regimes. In O. R. Holsti, S. M. Randolph, & G. L. Alexander (Eds.), *Change in the International System* (pp. 131-163). Westview Press.
15. Kenen distinguished between *international economic cooperation* and *international economic policy coordination*. To him, international coordination is one form of cooperation in which governments can agree on taking a coherent policy action which could be beneficial only when taken by all in a coordinated manner, which can be termed as mutually beneficial adjustments in domestic policy consideration. Kenen, P. B. (1990). *The Coordination of Macroeconomic Policies*. In W. H. Branson, J. A. Frenkel, & M. Goldstien (Eds.), *International Policy Coordination and Exchange Rate Fluctuations* (pp. 63-102). University of Chicago Press.

second important pillar in maintaining the gold standard mechanism. It acted as an International LoLR[16] and brought harmonization in monetary policies across states.[17]

The outbreak of the First World War disrupted the so-called *smooth* functioning of the gold-standard-based IMS. Credibility and cooperation, the two pillars of stability, both were politicized under the changed circumstances. As the wartime governments encouraged the spread of unionism to secure labor peace, the erstwhile purely domestic issues of wage rates and employment became part of the broader international discourse.[18] Balance-of-payment differences and employment policies became animated to reflect a clear clash in domestic versus external priorities and led governments to adopt policies influenced by their domestic public opinion. The development of IFL was jeopardized as the central bankers and monetary authorities became the grist for the political mill and were under severe criticism both from the leftist and from the rightist. Rising budget deficits led to printing more money and consequent rise in inflation.

Unfortunately, the new legislative policies aimed at insulating monetary authorities from political pressures, restricted central banks from joining any cooperation arrangements with other central banks. Thus, the legislation intending to stabilize the gold standard had adversely affected cooperation, which was the driving force of the financial system. What politicization of monetary authority did to the international cooperation, the fiscal *war of attrition* and political pressures on distribution of taxes did to the credibility factor – the second pillar supporting the facade of gold standard.[19] The gold standard was not an uncontested monetary system any longer; shifts in domestic policies and political disputes of core countries were shaping it profoundly.

More than ever before, incompatible conceptual frameworks, doctrinal divisions within the countries, and disputes over wartime debts and reparations rendered all attempts aimed at increasing international cooperation to strengthen the crumbling international institutional framework futile. Under such uncertain circumstances, the BIS was established in 1930. The sole purpose of its establishment was to manage reparation settlements from Germany to the allied powers. The War weakened the balance-of-payment position for all countries except the US, which emerged as a strong economy in the post-War era.

Later on, however, the reconstruction of war-torn countries of Europe initiated a reverse capital and gold flow, from the US to Europe. This capital flight mounted pressure on the US Fed resulting into the Federal Reserve's adoption of monetary contraction in 1928. The US policy of monetary contraction coincides with the intensified French demand for gold. This strain between the US and France left the rest

---

16. Note contradiction in scholarship: The BoE was rather the *international borrower of last resort*, particularly during 1890s and in 1907 when the financial system was particularly under distress, and she herself became hostage to international cooperation. *See*, Eichengreen, B. (1996). *Globalizing Capital: A History of the International Monetary System*. Princeton University Press, p. 8.
17. *Conductor of the international orchestra*, as Keynes referred to the BoE, in Keynes, J. M. (1930). *A Treatise on Money* (Vol. 2): London.
18. Eichengreen, *supra* n. 16, at 9.
19. *See*, Alesina, A. F. & Drazen, A. (August 1989). *Why Are Stabilizations Delayed?* NBER WP No. 3053. Available at SSRN: http://ssrn.com/abstract=246871.

of the world, particularly Europe and Latin America in extreme fiscal and economic pressures and set stage for the 1929 great depression. According to Forbes magazine report, gross global foreign investment rose from an estimated 7% of GDP in 1870 to 18% in 1914, while by 1938, it had fallen back to 5%, and maintained there until the 1970s. In 1870, the ratio of world trade to GDP was 10%, which rose to 21% in 1914, and it fell to 9% by 1938.[20]

[2] The Great Depression (1929-1939)

As the War ended, the westward capital flows for repayment of the Wartime US debts were balanced out by US lending to central Europe to rebuild war-ridden economies and industries. Low domestic interest rates in the US, expansionary economic policies and capital flows, including gold, from the US to the Western Europe brought back the pre-War parity of the gold standard, more specifically in the Great Britain.

By 1928 as the Fed realized capital flows dissipating in less productive uses, they tightened the monetary policy and gradually curtailed US foreign lending. This tightening of monetary policy directly affected European countries, which, largely, had become heavily dependent on the inflow of capital and gold from the US. The decrease in gold and capital inflows led to the weakening of payment positions for Europe and in response, they started adopting protectionist trade policies and restrictive monetary policies to maintain payment positions and gold parities with the US. Together with a decreased demand for exports, US internal consumption also declined independently during this time. By 1929, the financial system still under reconstruction from the destruction of the War came under tremendous stress due to augmented restrictions and rising imbalances. Deflation forced countries especially the ones producing primary commodities to depreciate their currencies. The *beggar-thy-neighbor* depreciation policies pursued at home by many countries coupled with suspension of gold convertibility accelerated an economic downturn due to declining foreign investments and disrupted international trade.

In the meanwhile, the expansionist monetary policy along with low interest rates ignited the Wall Street boom that fed on reparation payment inflows to the US. This asymmetry in the surplus and deficit countries aggravated downturn in many countries, which were forced to adopt policies that are more restrictive. No country was ready to give unilateral concessions to any other and there was almost an absolute lack of collective action to have a coordinated monetary or fiscal policy ultimately resulting into adoption of passive monetary policies and contractionary fiscal policies.[21] As Eichengreen said, countries continued to oppose sacrificing gold standard in order to

---

20. *See*, Lewis, N., (January 3, 2013). *The 1870-1914 Gold Standard: The Most Perfect One Ever Created*, Forbes/Opinion. Available at http://www.forbes.com/sites#/sites/nathanlewis/2013/01/03/the-1870-1914-gold-standard-the-most-perfect-one-ever-created/ last accessed 31 May 2017.
21. Coordination failure well explained in, Cooper, R. & John, A. (1988). *Coordinating Coordination Failures in Keynesian Models. Quarterly Journal of Economics*, 103(3), 441-463.

reflate the economy, albeit in an environment dominated by lack of international cooperation.

There are divergent views on the causes of the Great Depression in the US.[22] As the US stock exchange crashed, US lending to Europe totally collapsed, resulting in imbalance of payments and disruption of trade. The first manifestation of the default was in Latin America in 1931. The London Economic Conference held in 1933 to coordinate reflationary initiatives, proved useless as different countries perceived different causes of the same problem hence they were suggesting often contrasting remedies and the conference went without producing a coordinated response. Thus, *the recycling mechanism*,[23] which paved the way for successful international settlements in 1920s, undercut the systemic stability in 1930s.

The final blow to the debilitating international payment system serving under the gold standard came with the banking crisis. Germany and Austria faced bank runs to which both responded by suspending convertibility of their currencies and by imposing exchange controls. National-level responses to the collapse of domestic financial systems particularly the bank runs and collapses were not instantaneous, mainly because gold standards posed insurmountable obstacles to have a unilateral action. In this constraining situation, even the central banks as domestic LoLR could not intervene to inject liquidity, as that interference would risk gold convertibility. The US Fed Reserve did not intervene while the banking system faced shocks both in 1931 and in 1933.[24] Next in queue facing banking disruptions were the Great Britain, the US and France. The former two abandoned gold standard in 1931 and 1933 respectively. During this time more than two dozen countries followed suit, Belgium left in 1934, only France adhered to the gold standard until 1936 and she suffered the worst financial losses. Soon the financial instability and chaos spread widely across states and led the world deeper into the Great Depression.

[3] Death of the Old and the Birth of the New

How did the breakup of the financial system under the gold standard affect the functioning of the international financial system? The biggest change that followed from abandoning the gold standard was the ability for individual countries to have an independent monetary and fiscal policy free from the entanglements of fixed exchange standards.

There are two contrasting views – the conventional and evidence – on the interrelationship of the gold standard and the end of the depression. According to the former view, after abandoning the gold standards some of the countries employed devaluation of currency as an instrument of policy. These devaluations, however,

---

22. According to some opinions, it started off with monetary tightening; however, the drop in the US GNP during 1928-1929 was too severe to be restricted to only this cause. Other factors include: structural problems and imbalances within the US economy, the reduction in internal US consumption, and, the impact from the Wall Street crash on confidence, amongst others.
23. Eichengreen, *supra* n. 16, at 14.
24. *Ibid.* at 18.

failed to bring about the expected gains and rather exacerbated the hard economic conditions.

Contrary to this, the evidence view holds that it was pursuance of depreciation as an instrument of policy in some countries, which, triggered their economic recovery and subsequent to that employment, investments and exports rose quickly. Accordingly, adoption of the gold standard not only meant gold convertibility, but abandoning the gold standard also meant doing away with the rigid system based on orthodox financial principles as well as that orthodox thought working behind the system. It required doing away with the ethos of the gold standard and the system of convertibility. Recovery was fast and visible only in those countries where the financial system underwent complete reformation. Governments could not immediately follow expansionary policies aiming at reflation after suspending gold convertibility and thus the economic recovery and beneficial effects of doing away with the gold standard were less visible. However, slowly and gradually as countries kept coming out of the *ethos* of the gold standard, economic recovery progressed in those states.

[B]   The Bretton Woods and Domestic Finance

The power mechanics at work during the classical and neo-classical era remained predominantly military manifestation of might however the end of the cold war brought economic strength to the driving seat and economics became the standard to gauge relative influence of the various states. The system of controlled capital movement under the gold standard and the Bretton Woods was rooted in an era in which military muscle was used to acquire and secure wealth.[25]

It is useful to see crises and regulatory responses to them in a historical context as after almost every crisis episode, institutional, legislative and supervisory review leads to reforms. And as history unfolds, after the Great Depression, the financial sector particularly in the US was reregulated carefully, most notably by the Glass-Steagall Act (GSA) of 1933. During the next 40 years, the Bretton Woods system closely regulated the financial system and kept capital accounts essentially closed.

The first part of the section below, while distinguishing gold standard from the Bretton Woods system, analyzes formative years of this new monetary arrangement to explore the need for a new system; and, if so, the dynamics as this new system is established. The analysis serves two purposes. First, it highlights the peculiar political system prevalent at that time, which was essentially bipolar and facilitated the making of an institution-based monetary, trade and financial system and maintained stability in the financial world for almost a quarter of a century. Second, it explains that under the existing circumstances, replicating a *consensus-based* system on the pattern of the Bretton Woods is not a possibility any longer as the political and economic map of the world has changed dramatically. This is important to consider in the context of Bretton Woods-II or NIFA-II discussions that especially triggered to reconstruct the financial

---

25. Times have changed. It is now (after the Cold war) economics (or wealth) that provides means to power. *See*, Braithwaite, J. & Drahos, P. (2000). *Global Business Regulation*: Cambridge University Press. p. 475. *See also*, Morgenthau, H. (1948). *Politics Among Nations*. Knopf.

map of the world in the aftermath of the GFC. Helleiner argued that the success of the Bretton Woods Conference was a product of a remarkable combination of concentrated power in the state system, which mustered a transnational expert-consensus under wartime conditions. In the absence of a similar political environment, replicating similar financial plans seems difficult if not altogether impossible.[26] The Bretton Woods system was distinguishable from the gold standard in multiple ways. First, the pegged exchange rates were made adjustable, subject to the presence of some *fundamental disequilibrium*,[27] second, presence of controls for international capital flows, and, finally, creation of the IMF entrusted with the role to monitor national economic policies and to extend finance to countries having trouble with balance-of-payments.

These three elements were not perfect complements to each other and remained conflicting in certain ways. The capital controls were effective in delivering stated objective but the national governments during the 1940s and 1950s did intervene frequently in the domestic financial system to regulate their economies in order to reduce unemployment and to address persisting balance-of-payment deficits. The controlled capital flows and restrictive regulations were subsequently relaxed with the return to current-account convertibility in 1959. During the 1940s and 1950s, capital controls coupled with exchange restrictions enabled governments to regulate imports and exports and thereby fulfilling their commitment towards full employment and growth at home. The controls worked fairly well given the meager resource strength of the IMF, and an absence of conventional adjustment mechanism capable of influencing domestic policies. The section below looks at the formation of the Bretton Woods and consequent effects on the development of IFL.

[1]   The Formation: Keynes and White's Plan

The 44 nations gathering at Bretton Woods were determined to set a new course based on mutual trust and cooperation, on the principle that peace and prosperity flow from the font of cooperation, on the belief that the broad global interest trumps narrow self-interest. This was the *original* multilateral moment 70 years ago,[28] remarked IMF's Managing Director.

The Bretton Woods was an *exception* and not a pattern in the development of IMS – as famously has been said – which otherwise tends to be mostly a product of spontaneous individual choices, constrained by historical inheritance, and is usually

---

26. Helleiner, E. (2010). A Bretton Woods Moment? The 2007-2008 Crisis and the Future of Global Finance. *International Affairs*, 86(3), 619-636.
27. This meaningful term was left undefined. Mikesell says the term was never defined in fewer than 10 pages which imparted an air of ambiguity to the conditions when pegged rates can be adjustable. *See*, Mikesell, R. F. (1994). *The Bretton Woods Debates: A Memoir* (Essays in International Finance Series No 192). Princeton University.
28. Lagarde, C. (2014). *A New Multilateralism for the 21st Century*. Richard Dimbleby Lecture, by the MD of the IMF, February 3. Available at http://www.imf.org/external/np/speeches/2014/020314.htm.

not the result of any conference negotiations.[29] As the GFC entered into an increasingly intense cycle, and the G20 started convening its meetings towards the end of 2008 (and onwards), many analysts over-speculated that it might be a *new Bretton Woods-moment*.[30] However, the processes like the Bretton Woods Conference are complex and demand strenuous work, right political backdrop, and an unwavering commitment to orchestrate such an agreement and its implementation. James' view of the conference held at Bretton Woods in July 1944 was that it was not immediately successful but it was a unique blend of the perspectives and the policies relating to trade, stabilization and capital movements, which meant that prevailing ideas (especially the ideas of John Maynard Keynes) and the interests of the US would merge. Technically, it was a victory for the US in the garb of *benign multilateralism*. The myth of the Bretton Woods was created by a powerful retrospective interpretation of the events and personalities, for example, *the god-like figure of Keynes*[31] *lent a golden halo to the whole exercise at the Bretton Woods* reflects such attributions.

The purpose of the 1944 Conference was not only to reconstruct the debilitating economic order but also to recast the capitalist system in the world. The world was under the influence of German victories and euphoria for a Nazi New Order[32] as the Bretton Woods system was being negotiated. After the defeat of France in 1944, Keynes' proposal (originally, a response to Funk's economic plan) advocated excessive trade liberalization in order to serve two purposes: to inhibit the possibility of a new world dominated by American aspirations, and, to preserve British privileged access to its colonies. Keynes and White had conflicting ideals regarding obligations of creditor countries, exchange rate flexibility and capital mobility. For Keynes, the foremost objective was restoration of full employment. To serve this end, he wanted to allow countries the flexibility not only in fixing their exchange rates but also in opting trade restrictions for the same purpose and to restore full convertibility of pound sterling on current account. White, on the other hand – in alignment with the general US policy – wanted no controls or pegged currencies with the exception of allowing an international overseeing institution with veto power on parity changes. The prime concern for Americans was to get an assurance from the UK for a nondiscriminatory trade policy free of *imperial preferences*,[33] and in return, they were willing to provide financial assistance to the UK on favorable terms. More than anything else, Americans believed

---

29. Eichengreen, B. (2008). *Thirteen Questions about the Subprime Crisis*. Tobin Project Conference Paper, Toward a New Theory of Financial Regulation. February 1-3, White Oak, Florida.
30. Bases, D. (Nov. 6, 2008). *World Faces New Bretton Woods Moment: Stiglitz*. Reuters. Retrieved from http://uk.reuters.com/article/2008/11/06/us-financial-stiglitz-interview-sb-idUKTRE4A58BI20081106.
31. For, Lionel Robbins' description of *the godlike Keynes, See*, Harrod, R. F. (1972). *The Life of John Maynard Keynes*. Penguin, Harmondsworth. p. 740; *See also*, Moggridge, D. (1992). *Maynard Keynes: An Economist's Biography*. Routledge Press.
32. It was Funk who pointed it as Nazi New Order. *See*, Funk, W. (July 1940). *The Economic Reorganization of Europe*. Rath Health Foundation, available at http://www4.dr-rath-foundation.org/brussels_eu/roots/06_economic_reorganization_europe.html last accessed, May 31, 2017. *See also*, Gold, J. (1984). *Legal and Institutional Aspects of the International Monetary System: Selected Essays* (Vol. I): IMF No. 19; and, Moggridge, *supra* n. 31, at 654.
33. The UK discriminated in favor of their ex-colonies for trade terms.

that free trade would be a panacea to most of the European issues including payment deficits, raw material shortages and even for Franco-German politico-economic rivalries.

The creation of a new international financial system under the Bretton Woods was the outcome of a complex historical process resulting from the havocs of the Wars and from the existence of a sharp political bipolarity. The planning for the post-War international financial and monetary system was very much under the British and American consideration even at the Genoa Conference, 1922 (held at the end of the First World War), which failed in achieving any settlement.[34] The memory of the decade of 1920s was a compelling reason to institutionalize international monetary and financial arrangements this time during the post-War settlements. The preparations started since 1940 and 1941 in the UK (under Keynes) and in the US (under White) respectively led to the signing of the Atlantic Charter in August 1941 followed by the Mutual Aid Agreement in February 1942. After going through a series of negotiations and drafts, Keynes and White finally published the Joint Statement, which was inherently, a compromise manifesting the asymmetric bargaining power of the British with the Americans.

The final agreement reached between the two diplomats was to have an *adjustable peg*, which, according to some critics, turned out to be an oxymoron. While the British were also able to secure agreement from the US on scarce currency clause (authorizing controls on imports from countries running persistent payment surpluses and whose currencies become scarce within the Fund), the Americans vehemently opposed Keynes proposals for setting up a Clearing Union (that would require the US to contribute to the tune of USD 23 billion).[35]

[2]   Problems and Consequences (1945-1971)

The IMF, one of the Bretton Woods institutions commenced its operations in 1947 with a modest quota and drawing rights under the Articles of Agreement. It was a time of extreme shortage of dollar in Europe given the scale of reconstruction, demand for food, industry and capital needs. European consolidated fiscal deficit rose from USD 5.8 billion to USD 7.5 billion from 1946 to 1947 rendering the IMF significantly toothless as the sums required to fill the deficit was beyond total capacity of the Fund to finance. In view of that, the US issued the Marshall Plan with USD 13 billion intergovernmental aid to finance Europe's fiscal deficit. Although this plan was put into practice simultaneously with the IMF's agenda during 1948-1951, yet it could not hold together the par system and Europeans had to devalue their currencies in 1949 by an average of 30%.

---

34. *See*, Gardner, R. (1969). *Sterling-Dollar Diplomacy: The Origins and the Prospects of Our International Economic Order* (2 ed.). McGraw-Hill. *See also*, Howson, S., & Moggridge, D. (1991). Review: The Wartime Diaries of Lionel Robbins and James Meade, 1943-1945, in, R. Skidelsky (Ed.). *The Economic Journal 101*, pp. 1289-1291, Wiley. *See also*, Skidelsky, R. (1991). *The Economic Journal, 101*(408), 1289-1291.
35. Similarly, in 1970s while creating the EMS, the German Bundesbank was reluctant to provide unlimited support for weak currency countries.

On the trade front, as discussed above, the Americans dominated the discussions at the Bretton Woods to seek an open and enhanced multilateral trade. They succeeded mostly in achieving an agreement to have an organization in charge of drawing down tariffs to facilitate trade-related objectives. Countries were instructed to substantially remove monetary restrictions on trade within five years under Article XIV of the IMF Agreement. This goal, however, remained unrealized as governments in periphery countries resisted such trade liberalization deteriorating their terms of trade.

Thus, to channelize trade and tariffs, the General Agreement on Tariffs and Trade (GATT) had its first round in 1947 with the US slashing its quotas by one-third. The second round took place at Annecy in 1949 but it involved no significant concession by all 23 members followed by the Third round at Torquay in 1950-1951, which was a complete failure. Primarily, it was due to lack of coordination at almost all levels including an additional ambiguity on areas of mutual coordination between the IMF and the GATT. Arguably, in International Trade Law[36] and International Monetary Law, the WTO, and the IMF and the World Bank (WB) functioned as sole authoritative organizations respectively.

The International Trade Organization (ITO) was entrusted with the task of facilitating trade liberalization through coordinated and simultaneous reduction of tariffs and quotas. However, the US refusal to sign the Havana Charter (under which the ITO was to be created) thwarted these efforts.[37] Fifty-six countries participated in the United Nation's Conference on Trade and Employment in Havana but the agreement failed because the US did not ratify it. It became a tug-of-war between the protectionists opposing liberalization and the perfectionists, who criticized the myriad exceptions claimed by various countries from open trade seeking stability of their domestic economies.

The founders of the Bretton Woods provided schedule for a gradual restoration of current-account convertibility and established the IMF to oversee such transition. It was assumed that a coordinated and simultaneous transformation of all countries would benefit all of the countries. This transformation, however, could not succeed owing to, what Eichengreen called, the *network externalities,* as a series of troubles continued to threaten financial stability. The first one was from the sterling crises in 1947 and then 1949 devaluations, which led to the realization of having a regional entity in Europe, the European Payments Union (EPU). The EPU was established with a view to supplement the IMF's work in trade and payments settlement.

The EPU, originally planned to stay for two years, continued working until 1958. It operated on the model of the Bretton Woods albeit with significant deviations and the BIS was mandated to clear payments. Successive devaluations during 1947 to 1949 and the emerging cold war dynamics (which began with the Soviet's refusal to fulfill its obligations under the IMF) made the US realize for the first time severity of the

---

36. On the role of trade regulation, *See,* Gadbaw, R. M. (2010). Systemic Regulation of Global Trade and Finance: A Tale of Two Systems. *Journal of International Economic Law, 13*(3), 551-574.
37. In a sense called a casualty of cold war as right after the conflict broke out with Soviets, NATO took precedence over the Marshall Plan. *See,* Eichengreen, B. (2009). *Globalizing Capital: A History of the International Monetary System (2 ed).* Princeton University Press.

post-War adjustment issues. The balance-of-payment problem also affected governments' choice between higher interest rate on the one hand, and growth and employment on the other. Many countries could not opt for higher interest rate as they had to expense growth and employment to set off payment deficit therefore, these countries mostly resorted to putting in place exchange controls.

At the same time, another post-War development that brought far-reaching effects on the European horizon was the second wave of democratization and simultaneous rise of leftist labor movements. The arising stirred demands to have even stronger labor unions, higher wages and more taxes on the wealthy and called for elaborate social reforms. The socialist parties deriving these movements for reform would moderate their demands only after getting assurance from their national governments for full employment and growth.[38] The governments had little choice but to make commitments to bring about these changes. However, despite the tall promises made in the UK and France, fragmented labor unions caused huge disruptions to the national growth plans.

The general European outlook at that time was complex and grim[39] as national governments, squeezed of financial resources, were dealing with the humongous task of reconstruction. Domestic strife and protests from socialist leftist were rising. While on the international front, there was a paradigm shift setting in as the big colonial empires were receding while the US rising as the most influential nation having controls on currency, finance, and with an overriding voice in the political affairs. It dominated international negotiations, the formation and operations of the international forums like the IMF and the GATT. In 1948, the US had accumulated more than two-thirds of global monetary reserves.[40] The exorbitant rise of the dollar as the reserve currency was making the IMS asymmetrical. The IMF, created to bring symmetry to the international financial system, was struggling to find its role. The US managed to have greater say even in the domestic policies and affairs of many of the European countries because of its huge reserves of dollars and gold. The Marshall Plan was one such instrument conditioned on the exclusion of these leftist socialist parties who were asking drastic reforms in monetary and fiscal policies from their governments. This was particularly the case in Italy and France.[41]

Iran nationalized British oil holdings in 1951 threatening the United Kingdom's control. Meanwhile, the commodity boom of the Korean War era had slowed down while the American and Canadian loans (raised earlier during the wartimes) became due. Consequently, the UK imposed exchange controls on imports, which together

---

38. Maier, C. (1987). The Two Postwar Eras and the Conditions for Stability in Twentieth-Century Western Europe. *American Historical Review* 86(2): 327-352.
39. For Europe's post war situation, *See*, Balogh, T. (October 1946). The US and the World Economy. *Oxford University Institute of Statistics Bulletin*, 8, 309-323. MacDougall, D. (1957). *The World Dollar Problem: A Study in International Economics*. St. Martin's Press.
40. Eichengreen, *supra* n. 37 at 112.
41. To See the interplay of Marshall Plan (used as a tool) and the domestic policies followed by European countries, Esposito, C. (1994). *America's Feeble Weapon: Funding the Marshall Plan in France and Italy, 1948-1950*. Greenwood Press.

with a reduced unemployment rate, helped Britain regain its pace towards liberalization.

A propos France, the worst situation was on payment deficits. France, since the Genoa Conference in 1922 had persistently criticized special status given to any single currency as it distorts balance in the financial system. Not so surprisingly, Charles de Gaulle[42] intermittently disapproved America's *privilege* because of the US dollar as the leading reserve currency. The French foreign political entanglements – like the war in Indochina, Algeria and the Suez crisis – on the one hand, and its ambitious domestic plans for public investments and deficit spending on the other, led to the imposition of stringent controls by the government. With de Gaulle in power, he kept opting for more devaluations and increased controls. Under his leadership, France, became a surplus country by 1959. Triffin[43] pointed at the distortions, which were because of the dollar's position as the most powerful currency and led to a tug-of-war between major European countries and the US for more influence and control within the Bretton Woods system.

On the German front, presence of large American forces and a continuous inflow of labor from Eastern Germany weakened labor unions' bargaining power yet the industrial progress and growth rates remained moderate. Though briefly, the Korean War during 1950s worsened trade terms for her as Germany was the big importer of raw materials and a huge rise in the prices of raw materials forced her to re-impose exchange controls. However, this imposition helped Germany to maintain a high growth rate throughout that period and finally led her to have a permanent surplus afterwards.

Despite the fact that the three big European powers were again on the center stage of European monetary and financial affairs by the 1960s, the US' persistent surplus – far above the surplus that these Europeans powers could gather with hard struggles – became a perpetual source of threat to its trading partners. In addition to the tight race for surplus, these powers also faced risk of liquidity shortages arising from the asymmetric financial system itself given the Bretton Woods institutions had but only limited capacity to correct such an imbalance. This was the process described by Triffin, which consequently led to a search for alternatives to the US dollar). Naturally, the US was least interested in its appreciation of the *European problem* of finding such alternatives to the dollar as reserve currency.

---

42. France was a large creditor of US Treasury who threatened liquidating its balance. Any such move by the French could trigger classic *bank-run* like situation (the US had typical maturity mismatch in its assets and liabilities). Charles Kindleberger and Emile Depres ignored this aspect of US imbalances, *See*, Eichengreen, *supra* n. 37 at 115.
43. Triffin was the main architect of the EPU. Triffin's dilemma, pointed out that the Bretton Woods' tendency for growth of foreign dollar reserves was inherently unstable and could trigger a bank-run like situation. Under such situations, if depositors, in anticipation of dollar devaluation, queue for converting their dollar reserves, a bank-run becomes most likely outcome. *See*, Triffin, R. (September 1947). National Central Banking and the International Economy. In L. A. Metzler, R. Triffin, & G. Haberler (Eds.), *International Monetary Policies*. Federal Reserve System, Washington. Also, Kenen, P. B. (1960). *British Monetary Policy and the Balance of Payments 1951-1957*. Harvard University Press.

It was quieter at the Bretton Woods' front in the beginning. The IMF's quota was kept stagnant at USD 9.2 billion until 1958 (original quota was USD 8.8 billion at its inception in 1944) against the initial commitment of Member States to increase quotas by 50% by 1959. Despite the expansion of the world economy and inclusion of many emerging countries in the IMF, its quotas were not correspondingly increased so to limit its influence and sphere. The US persistently opposed any increase in quotas throughout this time. In 1961, 10 industrialized countries agreed to add USD 6 billion of their currencies into the IMF's supplies of these particular currencies through the General Agreement to Borrow (GAB). The Group of Ten (G10), a club of industrialized countries, formed a Group of Deputies in 1963, which recommended an increase in IMF quotas and initiated negotiations for finding an alternative to the dollar as reserve currency.[44] This move could not receive much appreciation from the Third-World-developing countries that hardly participated in proceedings at the formation of the Bretton Woods system. The developing countries were deeply occupied in handling their extraordinary balance of payment challenges[45] and felt that their financial needs were as important and grave as those of the industrialized countries. They did not perceive G10 as a forum capable to represent their issues, most importantly the quota increase and its fairer distributions.

These apprehensive circumstances and the need to look for an alternative reserve asset led to the First Amendment to the Articles of Agreement of the IMF and thereby, to the creation of Special Drawing Rights (SDRs). The US vehemently opposed the idea of the SDRs in the beginning, however, as de Gaulle proposed returning to gold standard (which he saw as the only way to bring back symmetry in the system), and the Bank of France actually started increasing its conversion of dollars into gold, this move immediately transformed the US official stance on SDRs. At the Fund's meeting in Rio in 1967, the details on SDRs were mapped out and finalized.

The first SDR allocation was disbursed in 1970 with new challenges at hand. The US by this time had restored current-account convertibility with a surplus in payments balance and in order to pursue liberal policies, lowered the trade restrictions, which weakened enforcement of capital controls. Simultaneously a rapid growth of Multinational Corporations (MNCs), increased usage of over and under-invoicing strategies, and lax controls on banking transactions in Europe significantly transformed the financial equation. The biggest threat in achieving monetary goals was not emanating from liquidity shortages anymore rather from the inflation policies being replicated all around in an expansionary move. In such situation, adding SDRs could only intensify the already inflationary environment.

Meanwhile, the politico-economic policy shifts marked by the US involvement in the Vietnam War and the consequent tightening of capital controls through the Interest

---

44. Fund's quotas were increased for the first time in 1964 by only 25% (France, Belgium, Italy and the Netherlands objected to larger increases), and third time in 1970 by another 30%.
45. Excessive devaluations: almost sixty-nine substantial devaluations from 1954-1971 in fifty developing countries were made). *See*, Edwards, S., & Santaella, J. (1993). Devaluation Controversies in the Developing Countries: Lessons from the Bretton Woods Era. In, M. D. Bordo & B. Eichengreen (Eds.), *A Retrospective on the Bretton Woods System: Lessons for International Monetary Reform* (pp. 405-460). NBER, University of Chicago Press.

Equalization Tax (was enacted in September 1964), significantly raised the cost of maintaining dollar reserves for the central banks. This rickety financial environment, dreaded by most of the countries, called for revaluation of parity and devaluation of currencies. The IMF linked extension of credit conditional to adoption of deflationary policies but the British government refused to adopt it and instead devalued sterling by 17% in November 1967. These devaluations were strongly associated with the failure of the respective currency as well as with overall strength of financial management being exercised in that country. In sharp contrast, however, in developing countries, the finance ministers in most of the cases, had to resign in the event of any currency devaluation.[46]

Now, there was need for a coordinated action and an effective adjustment mechanism that could revalue currencies and ensure long-term stability. The policy makers as well as institutions of international financial governance realized the severity of the *dollar problem* but were not ready to address the real causes, as that would involve a call for complete reformation of the international financial system. Such a reform would have moderated dollar's reserve currency privilege; not surprisingly, the US was most unwilling to make it an agenda item.[47] Ultimately, the failure to follow a coordinated approach to devalue national currencies in a proportionate manner to address external imbalances triggered the end of the Bretton Woods in 1971.

The year 1971 brought not only massive volatility of capital flows but also an endemic instability in the financial system. An enormous conversion of dollars into deutsche mark scared Germany and she immediately floated the mark in anticipation of rising inflation. The Netherlands joined the club. Other European countries also made prompt revaluations. France and the UK announced to convert their dollars into gold by mid-August when the Nixon administration abruptly closed the gold window on August 13, kicking off a whirlpool in the financial system, which over the next four months kept industrialized countries struggling to sort out a reform agenda for the international financial system. Consequently, an agreement was reached at the Smithsonian Conference in Washington, whereby the dollar was modestly devalued and other currencies were devalued in a way to effect adjustments.

The Smithsonian Conference however changed nothing fundamental.[48] On the financial horizon, Triffin's dilemma[49] still loomed large. The dollar value of global gold reserves could increase only marginally. By 1972, the UK had to float its currency out of the Smithsonian band due to inflationary policies of the government, followed by Switzerland in early 1973. After that, all other countries joined the race to fall out from the Smithsonian band.[50] The Smithsonian conference produced only fleeting gains and

---

46. Cooper, R. N. (1971). Currency Devaluation in Developing Countries. *Princeton Essays in International Finance*, Vol. 86, Princeton University.
47. *Supra* n. 37 at 127.
48. The Smithsonian Agreement (December 1971) adjusted the fixed exchange rates established at the Bretton Woods Conference of 1944.
49. Triffin, *supra* n. 43.
50. Although the Smithsonian Agreement was hailed by President Nixon as fundamental reorganization of international monetary affairs, the dollar price in the gold free market continued to

the Bretton Woods system ceased to exist.[51] The gold reserves were held in significant quantity by many countries to defend their currency and hedge against the US dollar. Both gold coins and gold bars were traded in liquid markets and served as a private store of wealth. In 1999, the European Central Bank (ECB) and 11 European national banks signed the Washington Agreement on Gold declaring that gold *will* remain an important element of global monetary reserves. The formation of a system like the Bretton Woods was an exception and not a pattern in the story of creating financial market mechanisms. A look at the successor financial market mechanisms, that is, the neo-liberal globalized financial regimes (or the ones pre-1945), reveal that most of these financial mechanisms were established in a different politico-economic context than the Bretton Woods.

Opinions, on the *efficacy* of the Bretton Woods system are a mixed bag. More often, it is celebrated as a pillar of stability in the post-War *golden age* of exchange rate stability, prosperity and growth. Accordingly, this growth and prosperity came through tremendous expansion of trade, that is, a direct outcome of the GATT/WTO. However, critics have pointed that the post-War growth and prosperity led to financial market stability and increased trade despite the fact that the governments throughout this time restricted capital movement across borders. The IMF more often than not capitulated to US influence and failed to deliver the promises it was meant to fulfill, namely, to oversee the operation of convertible currencies and to support financing in an instance of temporary payment imbalance. Inversely, the Marshall Plan instead took the task of providing the financial support mechanism and the IMF absented its help to countries dependent upon Marshall Aid, undermining the institution's authority. Three important lessons can be drawn from the breakdown of Bretton Woods:[52] first, the realization that the available adjustment mechanism was inadequate, and that operating a system of pegged exchange rates in the presence of highly mobile capital is too difficult to ensure. Second, that international cooperation and coordinated responses to serious issues can effectively set to work an otherwise ineffective framework; and, finally, cooperation in support of a system of pegged currencies can be most effective when made a part of an interlocking web of political and economic transactions.

§2.02 THE ERA OF INTERNATIONAL FINANCE (1970-1993)

The 1970s was marked mostly by floating exchange rates, lax capital controls and a relaxed monetary policy, in particular adopted by the US. During that time, the Committee of Twenty (C20) took on the task of reforming the par value system through their *grand-design* aimed at maintaining the 2¼% currency exchange fluctuation band as delineated under the Smithsonian Agreement. This mechanism worked fairly well

---

cause pressure on its official rate; soon after 10% devaluation was announced on Feb. 14, 1973, Japan and the EEC countries decided to let their currencies float. A decade later, all industrialized nations followed the suit.
51. For timeline of the fixed exchange rate system (*See* appendix I).
52. *See* also, Eichengreen, *supra* n.37.

despite the inability of many member countries to stick to the Smithsonian arrangements.[53]

The Smithsonian arrangements couldn't survive the stress that the mid-1970s brought in. The main factors behind its failure included the missing political and institutional preconditions, lack of implementation framework and accountability back up necessary for survival of any regulatory mechanism. The absence of an enabling mechanism to translate these international agreements into domestic laws for their onward implementation was missing. The 1973 oil crisis added to poorer enforcement of the snake mechanism and led to its ultimate breakdown. Although, the Werner report in 1969 laid out institutional reform package aimed at irrevocable exchange rates and the adoption of a single currency in a decade's time, it was not implemented. ; It lacked recommendation for the establishment of a central bank responsible and accountable to carry out the necessary function and more importantly, because of the US opposition to the idea.

Thus most of the domestic and international monetary mechanisms followed during the 1970s led to rampant inflation. The Western European economies and Japan who always preferred exchange rate stability set to the pursuit of mechanisms for currency pegs. After the Bretton Woods collapse, and by the 1980s, these countries decided to manage and control huge currency fluctuations. To serve this end, the European Monetary System (EMS) was created. The US under Volcker's influence[54] profoundly upheld floating exchanges. Volcker put into practice Milton Friedman's postulation of rate mechanisms,[55] which materialized through the Second Amendment to the IMF Articles of Agreement in 1978, making it the present version of the Article IV.[56] The Article IV thus provided a new code of conduct for exchange arrangements as the old system based on par value collapsed.[57] It legalized a member's freedom to choose whatever exchange arrangement it wished to adopt (including floating) and eliminated the special status given to gold. The second amendment presented a complete departure from the original par value system mainly due to: first the recognition of the need for a Member State not to resist an adjustment to its exchange

---

53. The EEC countries agreed in 1972 to maintain stable exchange rates and created the *snake-in-the-tunnel mechanism* for managing currency fluctuations (the snake) inside narrow limits against the dollar (tunnel). However, within two years the snake lost many components due to issues including oil hits, and was reduced to just a *German-mark zone* comprising Germany, Denmark and the Benelux countries.
54. Paul Adolph Volcker, an American economist was Chairman of the Federal Reserve under Presidents Jimmy Carter and Ronald Reagan from August 1979 to August 1987.
55. Friedman, M. (1953). *Essays in Positive Economics*, University of Chicago Press.
56. Second Amendment entered into force on Apr. 1, 1978, established the right of members to adopt exchange rate arrangements of their choice.
57. Under the old par value system, a member's choice as to how it valued its currency against the currency of other members was very limited as the value had to be expressed in terms of gold, either directly or through the U.S. dollar. A member's ability to modify the value of its currency against this common denominator was also limited beyond a specified limit and a member that changed the par value of its currency without the concurrence of the Fund became ineligible to use the Fund's resources, and the Fund would concur only if it was satisfied that the change was necessary to correct a *fundamental disequilibrium. See,* Hagan, S. (2006). Article IV of the Fund's Articles of Agreement: An Overview of the Legal Framework Retrieved from https://www.imf.org/external/np/pp/eng/2006/062806.pdf.

rates if that is required to address some underlying conditions. Second, recognition of the fact that the stability of the overall system of exchange rates is enhanced by pursuit of domestic policies by a member country that create underlying conditions for economic and financial stability (because of the important nexus that exists between member's domestic policies and its exchange rate). Last, the assumption that members would avoid following exchange rate policies designed to undermine or interfere with the adjustment process.[58]

By 1979, the European Economic Community (EEC)[59] countries resorted to another mechanism, which also paved the way to the establishment of the European Monetary Union (EMU). In this Union, the EMU states irrevocably pegged their exchange rates by replacing national monies with a single European currency. This was the first strong step towards harmonization realized by devising an integrated mechanism albeit at regional level. With these developments, the era of informally pegged or pegged-but-adjustable exchange rates was over.

Under the EMS, Germany, the strong-currency-country, assumed the role that the US played at the Bretton Woods institutions in 1944. France, on the other hand, faced intermittent problems during that time. She, after devaluing the French Franc for the third time against the Deutsche Mark in March 1983, seriously started contemplating withdrawal not only from the EMS but also from the European Community (EC). After Mitterrand failed, France however revised its monetary policy in the direction of currency stabilization. Meanwhile, the European economy also picked up pace and Europe made serious attempts at strengthening its *regional Bretton Woods*.

The first step in this regard for a European single market (leading to the establishment of the EU) was the Delors Report that came in 1989, followed by the Maastricht blueprint in 1991. The Delors Report focused on complete centralization of monetary authority. Previously, the Werner Report findings had only referred to a mechanism whereby all the central banks would join in a way to form a monetary federation, now the Delors Report delineated establishment of the ECB in 1991.

The path adopted under the Maastricht Treaty[60] was based on three stages. The transitional framework under the treaty provided inherent flexibility for *the-weak-currency-countries* to catch up with *the strong-currency-countries*. The three-stage adoption of the Maastricht Treaty involved four criteria for convergence. It was decided that only those countries would enter the mechanism who truly qualify the criterion. In 1991, it seemed an easy task to apply the criterion but by 1999 – which was the date set for the commencement of the third stage integration – the situation arising at that time made it hard to stick with the original deadlines.

In 1992, the Soviet collapse came as a hard set back to the European economies so much so that Italy and Britain left the ERM and the rest of the European economies were struggling to shoulder the pressure by tightening capital controls. The removal of

---

58. *Ibid.*
59. The EEC has historically contrived to forge a complicated web of economic agreements, particularly aiming at Franco-German hostilities. The purpose was to design an intertwined web of alliances, which would not allow any country to opt out (and not to cooperate with) of the EEC policies.
60. It was signed on Feb. 7, 1992 by the members of the EC.

capital control mechanism by the end of 1980s, made it difficult for countries to keep up with the EMS. By the early 1990s, international cooperation between monetary authorities almost vanished. By 1993, this hapless state of monetary coordination pushed for a larger adjustment band (originally planned at 2¼ in 1970s) between the members of the EC up to a whopping 15%.

Outside Europe, a group of smaller countries established currency boards through constitutional amendments and thereby pegged their currencies to one of their larger trading partner. The statutory action under the constitution provided necessary insulation required by the monetary authorities to maintain a pegged exchange rate free from political manipulations and pressures. But this system was not feasible for big countries where currency boards were not allowed to perform the LoLR function. In retrospect, as we can see now that the countries who maintained pegged exchange rates remained better off comparative to the ones who opted floating exchange rates, especially in terms of putting in place adequate controls to contain inflation.[61]

In the developing world, the monetary policies followed liberalization and opted for flexible exchange rates mainly after 1960s due to large-scale cross-border mobility of capital. Most of the developing world before the Second World War based their economic policies on two pillars: import substitution and financial repression.[62] Suddenly, this wave of liberal financial controls and free market operations resulted in repetitive currency fluctuations and exchange rate variations, which altogether disrupted their trade balances. Not surprisingly, grafting of these new liberal policies in their old repressed structures was bound to bring recurring crises. The first episode in this long string of crises was the debt crises of 1980s.

[A]   Systemic Risk Episodes (1983-2000)

A massive movement of petrodollars coming from oil producing countries fueled the debt crises in 1983. International banks used these huge deposits in extending massive loans to developing countries. At the same time, inflation kept crawling up throughout the 1970s, which ultimately led to interest-rate hike in the US. The frenzied interest-rate hikes surpassed the capacity of the borrowing developing countries to service their loans resulting into spread of system-wide risks. It was the first major systemic risk[63] instance in the globally interconnected financial markets though this time it did not

---

61. For effects and causes of inflation in the developing economies, *See*, Edwards & Santaella, *supra* n. 45.
62. *See*, Kenen, P. B. (1994). *The International Economy* (4 ed.). Cambridge University Press.
63. Systemic risk has been defined as arising from mispricing of risk in financial markets, which often means that risk is underpriced in relation to its cost and that the underpricing of risk results in too much of it being created in financial markets. For details, *See*, Alexander, K., Dhumale, R., & Eatwell, J. (2006). *Global Governance of Financial Systems: The International Regulation of Systemic Risk*. Oxford University Press. p. 24. The G10. Report defines systemic risk as an event triggering a loss of economic value with significant adverse effects on the real economy. The adverse real economic effects from systemic problems are generally seen as arising from disruptions to the payment system, to credit flows and from the destruction of asset values. G10. (January 2001). *Report on Consolidation in the Financial Sector*. Retrieved from BIS http://www.bis.org/publ/gten05.pdf.

threaten system-wide financial stability.[64] It was Mexico in 1995 for the first time that kick-started the decade-long contagion of serious financial crises in Asia,[65] up in the north to Russia in 1998, reaching Latin America to Brazil in 1999, to Turkey in 2000 and back to Argentina in 2001 and Brazil in 2002. Financial disruptions, extreme exchange rate fluctuations, and deep recessionary periods marked these crises. Before the onset of the financial crisis in 2008, the need to reform the international financial system was already there, however, it was not as compelling as has become today.

[1]   The 1980s Debt Crisis: Mexico and Brazil

The new oil discoveries brought opportunities for economic growth and sooner its economy was growing at more than 8% a year during 1978-1981. Employment rates increased tremendously but this growth also brought inflation with it that rose to more than 28% and soon its current-account deficit doubled to 15% of GDP. Mexico's cumulative foreign debt reached almost USD 70 billion with an USD 18 billion due by August of that year. Since Mexico did not put in place any exchange controls, therefore, following the inflation hike and the huge current-account deficit, a tremendous capital flight took place. This resulted in a 40% decrease in the Peso's value within a few days as the Bank of Mexico stopped supporting peso. The government, in August, imposed exchange controls as capital continued to fly out and all dollar-denominated pesos were converted at 20% less than the market rate. On August 13, the Mexican government announced a default, two days before its debts were due.[66]

The task at hand was to keep the financial system working. Letting Mexico default on its payments was in nobody's interest as foreign debts to Mexico involved a

---

64. *See*, Arner, D. W. (2009). The Global Credit Crisis of 2008: Causes and Consequences. *The International Lawyer, 43*, 91-136. Retrieved from http://ssrn.com/paper = 1400623 p. 99.
65. Financial troubles started from early 1980s in the emerging markets of Asia, Russia and Latin America but came to the fore only in the 1990s. Buckley provides one of the pioneer analyses on the subject and traces history of the debt markets from 1980s to understand financial turbulence of the late 1990s. *See*, Buckley, R. (1999). *Emerging Markets Debt: An Analysis of the Secondary Market, 8.* Kluwer Law International. For a more recent analysis of trade and finance relations in the regional market context, *See*, Buckley, R. P., Hu, R. W. & Arner, D. W. (Eds.). (2011). *East Asian Economic Integration: Law, Trade and Finance.* Edward Elgar Publishing. *See also*, Azis, I. J. & Shin, H. S. (2014). *Global Shock, Risks, and Asian Financial Reform,* Edward Elgar Publishing. Malaysia was the only Asian country who despite suffering serious financial losses during 1990s refused the IMF bailout plan, and instead, implemented domestic unorthodox policies, which brought myriad advantages especially for the poorer class. *See*, Buckley, R., & Fitzgerald, S. M. (2004). *An Assessment of Malaysia's Response to the IMF During the Asian Economic Crisis.* Singapore Journal of Legal Studies, 96; *See also*, Arner, D. W. & Schou-Zibell, L. (2011). Asian Regulatory Responses to the Global Financial Crisis. *Global Journal of Emerging Market Economies, 3*(1), 135-169. *See*, for a broader history of crises eruption, Kindleberger & Aliber, *supra* n. 13. For a rigorous analysis and a fact-based assessment of current practices and regulations in Asia's financial institutions and markets, Liu, Q., Lejot, P., & Arner, D. A. (2013). *Finance in Asia: Institutions, Regulation and Policy,* Routledge Press.
66. *See*, Kaminsky, G. L., & Reinhart, C. M. (1998). *Financial Crises in Asia and Latin America: Then and Now.* Paper Presented at the 110th Meeting of the American Economic Association. Vol. 88, No. 2.

complex web of reciprocal guarantees and participating loans.[67] The Mexican peso was pegged to the US dollar when it sought balance-of-payment support from the IMF during the 1970s crunch (the IMF fund came with stringent conditionality). This time in the 1980s, Mexico was determined not to subscribe to any IMF resources. However, the US and the BIS intervened to inject dollars in the form of advance payments extending lines of credit. Later on, the IMF put in place a standby arrangement following request from the Mexican government. Not too far away, Brazil shared an almost similar situation and interestingly received similar international responses.

Both of these crises throw light on the vulnerabilities of an integrated financial market and underscore the provision of collective responsibility in order to maintain global financial stability. It was not in the interest of the US and other creditors to let Mexico default because of the fear of triggering cross defaults. It was a costly decade. Altogether 39 countries rescheduled around USD 140 billion in commercial bank debts during 1980s. The IMF's role in stabilizing various economies during crises had substantially transformed from what was originally designed by Keynes and White in the 1940s.[68]

[2] *Russia 1996-1999*

The IMF significantly took a hit when it took sides for Boris Yeltsin[69] in a bid to promote democracy during the elections in Russia. In this regard, the IMF (and western countries) supported Russia by significantly relaxing its policies, conditionality and compliance requirements under the standby arrangements. In fact, it offered a tailor-made Systemic Transformation Facility (STF) exclusively for the states emerging after the Soviet disintegration.

Russia and 13 other states of the former Soviet Union joined the IMF and the WB in May 1992.[70] The US and other western countries particularly Germany wanted Russian integration into the international system and they pooled resources together to help stabilize Russia as well as the Ruble. Although generous financing facilities were made available in Russia, it could not fight the extreme inflation, which ran upwards of 1000% during 1993. The Fund kept its on-again/off-again disbursements under various arrangements until 1996 when serious reports of funds constantly flowing out of Russia to Cayman Islands and the Isle of Man surfaced out. These monies included the funds, which were provided through various Fund arrangements. This was alarming. The Fund withheld its disbursements for a year. Meanwhile the Ruble was allowed to float and it fell almost 30% further. Russia imposed a 90-day moratorium on foreign commercial debt.[71] By 1999, Russia came to the IMF again but this time the IMF issued SDRs, to set off Fund's prior payments and issued a press release indicative of

---

67. Lowenfeld, A. F., (2010). The International Monetary System: A Look Back Over Seven Decades. *Journal of International Economic Law. 13*(3), at 588.
68. *Ibid.* at 589.
69. Boris Yeltsin led Russia out of Soviet Union and offered hard resistance to anti-democratic forces.
70. Russia became member of the WTO in August 2012.
71. Lowenfeld, *supra* n. 67, at 591.

its strong disapproval of the funds being transferred out of Russia to offshore places. Stanley Fischer while disapproving this view, appreciated Russian efforts at reviving domestic economy. According to him, being a member of the international financial system, Russia enjoys the right to IMF assistance package. About the misappropriation reports, Mr. Fisher, who was First Deputy Managing Director of the Fund on the Russian Federation, said, the FIMACO[72] report shows that there is no evidence of large-scale misappropriation of money, but only instances of misreporting to the IMF. For example, around the time of the election in 1996, there was a huge transaction that was not accurately reported thereby resulted into an exaggerated account of Russia's reserves.[73] We know that later on, in this context, the Pricewaterhouse Coopers published a full report on FIMACO misappropriation.[74]

[3] IFL Through the 1990s

During this tumultuous decade of chaos and crises, the European Exchange Rate Mechanism (ERM) crisis in 1992 epitomized coordination failure in maintaining a structure of fixed but changeable parities.[75] By 1992-1993, troubles in the ERM had cost the German government about USD 1 billion, and to the Swedish government, a hefty USD 26 billion.[76] On the other hand, some (notably George Soros) made fortunes betting against the pound sterling.[77] The Mexican peso crisis devastated emerging economies not only in Latin America but affected as far as Canadian economy and Philippines – due to the subsequent *tequila-effect*.[78] From 1997-1999 crises in East Asia brought down Suharto's government in Indonesia and encompassed several Asian tigers including Thailand, Indonesia, Singapore, Korea and Malaysia triggering financial panic, which coincided with the Long-Term Capital Management (LTCM) collapse.[79] Both of these episodes pointed at the weaknesses in the NIFA and highlighted potential for self-destruction latent within the architecture. Once again the string of

---

72. Financial Management Company Ltd (FIMACO), a Jersey company (1990) whose existence was disclosed by Russia's chief prosecutor, Yuri Skuratov in 1999. It followed official denials as well many scandals.
73. Press conference call with Stanley Fischer on Russian Federation, Jul. 29, 1999, available at: http://www.imf.org/external/np/tr/1999/tr990729.htm (last accessed, Jun. 1, 2017).
74. The PricewaterhouseCoopers report was published on the IMF website on Aug. 5, 1999. Available at http://www.imf.org/external/country/rus/fimaco/index.htm.
75. *See*, Obstfeld, M. (1995). *The Logic of Currency Crises*. In B. Eichengreen, J. Frieden, & J. von Hagen (Eds.), *Monetary and Fiscal Policy in an Integrated Europe* (pp. 62-90). Springer Press.
76. *See*, for a theoretical and policy analysis of the causes and consequences of the EMS, Buiter, W. H., Corsetti, G. & Pesenti, P. A. (2001). *Financial Markets and European Monetary Cooperation: The Lessons of the 1992-93 Exchange Rate Mechanism Crisis*.Cambridge University Press.
77. In a setting of purposeful action by the authorities, the possibility of self-fulfilling crises becomes important. In such a situation, an arbitrary expectational shift can turn a fairly credible exchange rate peg into a fragile one, as Maurice proclaims. *See*, Obstfeld, *supra* n. 75.
78. *See*, Frankel, J. A. (2003). *Experience of and Lessons from Exchange Rate Regime in Emerging Economies*. NBER WP No. 10032. Available at http://www.nber.org/papers/w10032.pdf.
79. For a more recent look at LCTM, Lowenstein, R. (Sep. 7, 2008). LTCM: It's a Short-Term Memory. *New York Times*. Retrieved from http://www.nytimes.com/2008/09/07/business/worldbusiness/07iht-07ltcm.15941880.html?_r=0 last accessed Aug. 2, 2016. *See also*, Edwards, F. R. (1999). Hedge Funds and the Collapse of LTCM. *Journal of Economic Perspectives*,

crises ran from Brazil in 1999 and 2002, to Latin America, to Turkey in 2000 and finally back to Argentina in 2001. In the derivative market, the Barings crisis laid bare volatility of this market and reflected on the disability of regulators to deal with such fast-paced developments taking place in the financial industry.

In the developed world, however, financial crisis during this era remained much less visible. The crisis in Japan (the second biggest economy of the world) spanned over a prolonged period of time (1980s to 1990s). Despite the unusually long expanse of crisis, Japanese financial market issues attracted but only fringe attention from both the economists and global policy makers.[80] Even the crises in Scandinavia and in Asia in 1990s though were severe one-off events yet these remained devoid of substantial policy reform at the international level.[81] Since the Asian crises were viewed as currency crisis so the responses were essentially narrow in scope. The scholarship on macroeconomic reform measures, transnational regulatory regimes or international supervisory networks could hardly produce substantial developments that could alter significantly the nature of the prevalent IFL regime. Arner and Buckley argue for a powerful indictment of the repeated failures on the part of regulatory authorities and call for strengthening of IFL and its underlying principles.[82]

[4]   The Asian Crisis 1997-1998

Global conditions have played a significant role in bringing about financial crisis in the emerging economies.[83] The decade of 1990s was not an exception. Between 1992-1995, Indonesia, Malaysia, Singapore, South Korea and Thailand grew at a rate of over 7%, and Chinese economy had a steady growth rate in double digits.

Asian economies were marked with tremendous growth coupled with low interest rates in major financial centers, increased capital mobility in the form of foreign investments, macroeconomic stability, strong fiscal positions and thriving export sectors with high yield. However, the domestic political and even economic

---

13(2), 189-210. Available at www180.gsb.columbia.edu/faculty/fedwards/papers/Hedge_Funds_&_the_Collapse_of_LTCM.pdf.

80. The ADB report points out that the Japanese government's much delayed response increased the severity of the crisis. *See*, Fujii, M., & Masahiro, K. (2010). *Lessons from Japan's Banking Crisis: 1991-2005.* Retrieved from the ADBI WP 222. http://www.adb.org/sites/default/files/publication/156077/adbi-wp222.pdf. For an overall assessment of the causes of crisis, *see* IMF's report that identifies weak corporate governance and lack of regulatory forbearance as the two main causes of the crisis. *See*, Kanaya, A. & Woo, D. (2000). *The Japanese Banking Crisis of the 1990s: Sources and Lessons.* Retrieved from https://www.imf.org/external/pubs/ft/wp/2000/wp0007.pdf.

81. *See*, Soederberg, S. (2002). On the Contradictions of the New International Financial Architecture: Another Procrustean Bed for Emerging Markets? *Third World Quarterly*, 23(4), 607-620.

82. Following an historical approach, the authors compare various financial crises of the twentieth century to show that how misconceived economic policy responses paved way for the next crash. *See*, Buckley, R. P. & Arner, D. W. (2011). *From Crisis to Crisis: The Global Financial System and Regulatory Failure*. Kluwer Law International.

83. *See*, Beim, D. & Calomiris, C. (2001). *Emerging Financial Markets*, McGraw-Hill.

policies were inconsistent in most of these economies.[84] Opting for some less thoughtful policies like availability of substantial foreign funds at extremely low interest rates resulted into stocks and real estate boom in the broader macroeconomic context of weaker banking systems, poor corporate governance and effectively fixed exchange rates led to piling up of dollar-denominated debt. Against this backdrop, the region was hit hard by a series of crises triggered by: low export demand, massive short-term debts, repeated devaluations and sudden upsurge in capital outflows. Some of the characteristic features of the Asian crises were:[85] first, the crises started off as *speculative-panics* that triggered massive exodus of short-term funds from these economies and the financial panic, as it gained momentum, led to currency crisis. ; Second, the presence of defective foreign exchange policies, which resulted directly from the post-Bretton Woods tremendous exchange instability and resultant privatization of foreign exchange risk. Asian economies opted for informal pegs with the US dollar, and a quest for exchange rate stabilization caused serious current-account deficits.[86] Third, the 1980s was an era of petrodollars fueling debt markets, and an absence of capital controls[87] in the emerging economies provided the necessary momentum to short-term speculative investments finding their way into these economies, leading to formation of enormous asset bubbles. The financial markets of that time in emerging economies were not sophisticated enough to put in place necessary regulatory mechanisms,[88] transparent and strong institutional norms and stringent financial codes of conduct; (d) highly liquid short-term debt structure in these economies was used to finance illiquid assets[89] hence, in a way, making it vulnerable to liquidity shocks.

Starting with Thailand, the Bangkok Bank of Commerce went bust in 1996 and shortly after that the crisis spread to the Philippines within 10 days and Peso was floated following Thai baht. The crises continued to Indonesia and Malaysia who initially tried to resist currency fluctuations but could not sustain longer. Only Hong Kong was able to rebuff the contagion however Taiwan could not stop its onward march and it reached Korea (the 11th largest economy of the world at that time). Instantly it grabbed not only regional focus but also from around the world and the Group of Seven (G7) had to intervene to urge international banks to extend short-term

---

84. The post-1990s scholarship emphasizes lack of efforts on Asian regional market development, which would benefit all. *See* for example, ADB. (2008). *Emerging Asian Regionalism: A Partnership for Shared Prosperity*. The ADB. aric.adb.org/emergingasianregionalism/pdfs/Final_ear_chapters/final%20report.pdf.
85. *See*, Kindleberger & Aliber, *supra* n. 13.
86. Avgouleas, E. (2012). *Governance of Global Financial Markets: The Law, the Economics, the Politics*. Cambridge University Press. p. 73.
87. Capital controls were gradually eliminated as part of the Washington Consensus and later NIEO underlined similar principle especially for these economies. *See* for example, Soederberg, *supra* n. 81.
88. *See*, Eichengreen, B. & Portes, R. (1997). *Managing Financial Crises in Emerging Markets*. Paper presented at the Federal Reserve Bank of Kansas City's Annual Economics Conference, Aug 28-30, Wyoming. *See also*, Lejot, P. L., et al. (2003). *Asia's Debt Capital Markets: Appraisal and Agenda for Policy Reform*. HKIMR Working Papers, *See also*, Buckley, *supra* n. 65.
89. *See*, Radelet, S., et al. (1998). *The East Asian Financial Crisis: Diagnosis, Remedies, Prospects*. Brookings Papers on Economic Activity, 1, 1-90.

loans to Korea. Indonesia witnessed same bank runs in 1998 and the entire banking system was shut down unlocking a deep recession. There are alternative views on how much reform was needed, nonetheless, Asia confidently continued with the export-led growth model.

One striking development initiated as part of the responses to the financial crisis in Asia, was the Chiang Mai Initiative (CMI) established in 2000.[90] It was a swap and a credit line extension of short-term and very-short-term Financing Facilities at regional level in Asian countries, which was agreed by the central banks. The CMI was initiated in the background of EMS and another Japanese proposal[91] forwarded during the Asian crisis to establish for Asian Monetary Fund (AMF) on the lines of the IMF in order to avoid the intruding conditionality associated with IMF funding (this has drawn criticism by most of Member States who used IMF funds).[92] The CMI initiative aimed at providing a regional mechanism for Asian countries that in times of crisis could float their currencies jointly rather than separately, and without having to adopt IMF conditions.[93] It did not take too long to establish the CMI on the footprints of the EMU once the AMF idea rolled out. However, unlike European arrangements, the Asian integration efforts are always economics-driven rather than based on grand political ideals.

[5]   Argentinian Crises 2000-2007

During the second half of the 1990s, Argentinean economic expansion based on privatization proceeds and the parity of the US dollar and Argentine peso by law (adopted by Carlos Menem in 1989) stopped working. Argentina sought both commercial loans as well as the IMF support. Consequently, the IMF approved the first tranche in March 2000 and extended another in November 2000, however, both of these funding based on incorrectly reported projections. Despite the deceptive projection, the IMF extended yet another facility in 2001.

The panic started almost right away. President de la Rua declared a state of siege in consequence to massive withdrawals of monies, closures and riots. Later on, as Adolfo Rodriguez Saa was elected as President on December 23, he declared a default

---

90. *See* for the context, ADB, *supra* n. 84. *See also*, ADB. (2009). *Emerging East Asia: A Regional Economic Update*. Asia Economic Monitor: http://aric.adb.org/pdf/aem/dec09/Dec_AEM_complete.pdf. *See*, for reforms to the Asian Bond Market, Lejot, P. L., Arner, D. W. & Liu, Q. (2004). Asia's Bond Market: Reforms to Promote Activity and Lessen Financial Contagion. *HIEBS Working Papers*. And, Lejot, P. L., Arner, D. W., & Chan, M. K. C. (2003). Nine Steps to Strengthen Asia's Bond Markets. *International Financial Law Review*. 43, pp. 43-44.
91. Overall Asian governments were very suspicious of a Japanese dominant AMF as Japan was the only country in Asia with enormous financial resources to set up.
92. *See*, for a broader understanding of the Asian Bond Fund establishment, Lejot, P. L., & Arner, D. W. (2004*)*. Well-Intentioned Asian Bond Fund Won't Work. *International Financial Law Review*, pp. 23-24. *See also*, Lejot, P., Arner, D. & Liu, Q. (2006). Missing Links: Regional Reforms for Asia's Bond Markets. *Asia-Pacific Business Review*, 12(3), 309-331.
93. *Asian way implies* minimal conditionality, non-interference in the sovereign affairs of other countries and also minimal lending. Also, the CMI could not rescue Indonesian rupiah fall in 2005, and Thai baht crash in 2006 rendering the initiative rather a *hollow shell. See*, Eichengreen, *supra* n. 37.

on Argentina's public debts. By then, the cumulative GDP had declined by 20% since 1998. Unemployment was at 20% and more than half of Argentinians were living below the poverty line. Finally, after the elections in 2003 when Nestor Kirchner came into power, he declared that he would not pay back any of the IMF loans until the Fund agreed to new standby arrangements. The IMF did not extend new loans resulting into an Argentinian default on payments on September 9, 2003. Surprisingly, the IMF soon after caved in, and announced a new three-year arrangement for Argentina the next day. On September 11, Argentina paid back USD 2.9 billion loan to the Fund and President Kirchner announced that Argentina would pay back all its debts (approximately USD 9.9 billion) to the IMF by the end of 2005. Interestingly, President Lula da Silva of Brazil had also made a similar announcement on December 14, saying, Brazil would pay all its outstanding debts two years earlier than the scheduled date.

Argentina was the most conspicuous case where the IMF faced unique challenges. President Kirchner of Argentina, Chavez of Venezuela and Lula da Silva of Brazil declared in 2007 that the Bretton Woods institutions had become irrelevant. For Lowenfeld, writing at the end of 2007, these institutions despite being in a role-transformation phase remain indispensable as organizations to deliver the essential tasks of coordination, rule making and crisis management.[94] In retrospect as we see, the IMF continued to perform its lending functions as recently as in resolving the SDC in Europe.

[B] New Millennium and the Global Finance

Financial markets by this time have become largely global with prevalent floating exchange rates and some exceptions with pegged exchanges. Under the NIFA principles, global connectedness, deregulation and liberalization had made way for market-driven regulatory standards.[95] The emerging economies in Asia only half-heartedly adhered to a flexible currency policy and remained highly skeptical in letting their currencies appreciate particularly against Renminbi. Asian economies adopted largely the export-led growth model and were directly hit by the Chinese spectacular economic growth. China successfully kept in place strict capital controls and stable exchange rates due to its peculiar domestic political set up. Furthermore, the confluence of the Chinese and the US policies, which reinforce each other's benefit, work to the disadvantage of other Asian economies.[96] The Chinese export of manufactured goods and merchandise competing with the US exports of financial products and services led to define the former as a *saver and producer*, while the latter to a *consumption economy*. This *'consumption v. production' duo* appeared appealing to the rest of the emerging Asian economies who tried to copycat Chinese policy. This

---

94. Lowenfeld, *supra* n. 67 at 595; and, Lowenfeld, A. F. (2008). *International Economic Law*, Oxford University Press.
95. *See* for NIFA, Norton, J. J. (2010). NIFA-II or Bretton Woods-II: The G20 (Leaders) Summit Process on Managing Global Financial Markets and the World Economy – quo Vadis. *J Bank Regul, 11*(4), 261-301. Retrieved from http://dx.doi.org/10.1057/jbr.2010.17.
96. *See*, Caballero, R. J., Farhi, E. & Gourinchas, P. O. (2008). An Equilibrium Model of Global Imbalances and Low Interest Rates. *American Economic Review, 98*(1), 358-393.

Chapter 2: Cyclic Financial Crises and the Development of IFL §2.03[A]

excessive capital availability in the market sowed seeds for the mortgage bubble, which exploded in 2008. Excessive deregulation without consolidating risk management practices and lack of appropriate protection mechanism against foreign exchange risk has inevitably led to financial disruptions.[97] The striking feature of this era was the astounding scandals that broke out in the developed world including the Enron (2001) and the WorldCom (2001-2002) in the US. Both of these episodes highlighted a lack of transparency in the regulatory standards. The extent of fraud and manipulation demonstrated by these episodes illustrated potential fallouts on the financial market environment from incomplete information disclosures and imperfect enforcement of approved regulatory standards. The next part sketches the role and development of IFL in its recent attempts at redefining and redesigning the regulatory structures.

§2.03 THE GFC

[A] The Context, Course and the Destruction

Contextualizing financial crises and regulatory responses from a historical context provides a perspective to a regulatory reforms agenda.[98] From mid-1990s to mid-2000s, the decade remained speckled with sporadic episodes of crises primarily in the emerging economies. Abolition of capital controls in the post-Bretton Woods era facilitated transition to free float of currencies, which further led to inevitable privatization of foreign exchange risk. This new development in globalized financial markets obligated banks on the one hand to opt for riskier products and on the other hand, hemmed in governments to constantly liberalizing capital controls and deregulation of banking industry.

Each crisis incidents in one way or the other sensitized the markets as well as regulators of the latent risks on a rise. For example, the Franklin National in 1974 (the first banking crisis after the Bretton Woods) imperiled not only the US banks but also the entire Eurodollar market. The US Fed had to play an international LoLR role to manage this Bank as it threatened its clearance system (this signifies an end of the era of national monetary policy). The collapse of the British–Israel Bank of London highlighted issues in insolvency regimes. The Debt crises in 1983 posed the first major systemic risk shock to the global financial markets. The BoE and the Fed signed a bilateral agreement for holding up an 8% capital adequacy (later, 8% was adopted by all other states under Basel regulation). From 1980-1995, 5,182 commercial and savings banks, savings and loans, and credit unions failed. These institutions held almost USD 910 billion in assets and imposed losses on the three federal insurance funds (on US taxpayers USD 192 billion).[99] International banks in the developed

---

97. Taylor, L. & Eatwell, J. (2000). *Global Finance at Risk: The Case for International Regulation*. The New Press.
98. *See*, Buckley, & Arner, *supra* n. 82.
99. Barth, J. R. & Brumbaugh, R. D. (1997). *Development and Evolution of National Financial Systems: An International Perspective*. Paper presented at the Latin American Studies Association, 1997, Mexico. April 17-19, p. 17.

countries used these huge deposits to extend massive lending to developing countries. The Stock-market crash in 1987 brought *contagion* concept and its repercussions into the financial world.

A critical look at the turn of the century financial disruptions shows global imbalances, financial practices rife with accounting manipulations compromising transparency and incomplete disclosures. We also saw a deluge of innovative financial products at a tremendous speed finding their way into the financial markets which far exceeded the comprehension of regulators (the capital flows by the end of the twentieth century outweighed trade flows by a factor of over 60 to 1).[100] These developments were taking place in an overly euphoric context holding the belief that financial markets have since long *graduated*[101] and would not repeat follies of the past.

[1]   Phase I: Nascent Shocks, Fledgling Responses

Before the 2008 crisis broke out, the horizon of IFL echoed what Reinhart's captioned book termed, *this time is different*.[102] Market optimism resonated almost as high as it was the night before the 1929 crash. Just a day before the Lehman Brothers filed bankruptcy, Donald Luskin remarked, [s]*ure, there are trouble spots in the economy...but none of this is cause for depression...Anyone who says we're in a recession, or heading into one (especially the worst one since the Great Depression) is making up his own private definition of recession.*[103]

Retrospectively, the GFC revealed that the IFL experts overlooked the new context of the present era and its technological advancements and interconnectedness. If it were stock speculations that brought the great market crash in 1929, the US home mortgage boom triggered the 2008 GFC. The financial markets ricocheted same optimism in 1929 that we reckon dominated the Jackson Hole in 2005,[104] where Rajan's concerns were slammed by the more optimistic voices. Rajan brought to discussion that the shift from depository intermediation to professional asset management has multiplied tail risks but he was turned down along with his critique on Greenspan. In short, policy makers and private sector bankers found that this diversification of risks and available resources of credit funding (where even most illiquid assets can generate liquidity through securitization, constant flow and availability of funds through alternative sources) have helped building *firewalls* around economy. An absence of apparent price bubbles despite huge volatility[105] in the financial sector over the past 25 years augmented this line of thinking. At the Northern Rock, when crisis erupted in

---

100. Sutherland, P. D. (1998). *Managing the International Economy in an Age of Globalization.* The 1998 Per Jacobsson Lecture, available at http://www.imf.org/external/am/1998/perj.htm.
101. Reinhart, C. M. & Rogoff, K. S. (2009). *This Time Is Different: Eight Centuries of Financial Folly.* Princeton University Press.
102. Ibid.
103. Washington Post referenced this quote in September 14 op-ed. By Donald Luskin.
104. Jackson Hole Conference, (2005), *The Greenspan Era: Lessons for the Future.* Papers and comments available at http://www.kc.frb.org/publications/research/escp/escp-2005.cfm.
105. The term *manias* has been replaced by *bubbles* in recent financial history.

2007 authorities as well as markets took considerable time before realizing the gravity of the situation.

Financial market governance regimes and regulatory mechanisms in force at that time that fell short of not only predicting the crisis-bubble but also the governance structures fell down as a house of cards at the first blow of crisis.[106] The section below is sketching the process, causes and consequences of the GFC. The financial markets in 2007 started disseminating alarm from the steep fall in housing prices. The first significant distress came with the collapse of Northern Rock, a fully solvent, medium sized mortgage bank in England. Unfortunately, the run on the Rock was taken merely as a false alarm.[107] Although, the Treasury and the BoE responded almost instantly – within three days – yet it was too late. The bank run triggered almost instantly. This was the first run on a UK deposit-taking institution after almost 150 years.[108] Northern Rock collapse was a momentary liquidity crunch at a solitary institution and was perceived as a *supervisory failure*.[109] The next signal came in March 2008 when Bear Stearns, the fifth largest US investment bank faced huge losses in its securities portfolio. Bear Stearns' rescue package was based on the assumptions that financial markets are stable and these are one-off spin-offs of bad supervision and very limited in scope. The Federal Reserve bought ill-performing portfolio of the bank at USD 28 billion and the rest of the bank was taken over by JP Morgan and the crisis got *resolved*.

It was not until September when the US Treasury bailed out the Fannie Mae (Federal National Mortgage Association) and the Freddie Mac (Federal Home Loan Mortgage Corporation), two Government Sponsored Enterprises (GSEs). The bailout and eventual nationalization of both of these GSEs by the US government in September 2008 was intended to save the *collateral damage* and didn't surprise many.[110] It did not take long when Lehman Brothers, a major investment bank in the US filed bankruptcy on September 15, after making a desperate effort to find a buyer, or be bailed out by the government. As we saw, the Lehman fall was detrimental to the financial market stability. Lehman triggered the collapse of the confidence in the US markets just as the Northern Rock did in the UK. The crisis soon became global by shifting from the US

---

106. For a good analysis of how crisis exposed regulatory failings, *See*, Goodhart, C. A. E. (2008). The Regulatory Response to the Financial Crisis. *Journal of Financial Stability*, 4(4), 351-358. *See also*, Buiter, W. H. (2007). *Lessons from the 2007 Financial Crisis*. CEPR No. DP6596. Available at http://ssrn.com/abstract=1140525.
107. *See* for a background on causes and initial course, *See*, Bruni, F. & Llewellyn, D. T. (Eds.). (2009). *The Failure of the Northern Rock: A Multi-dimensional Case Study*. SUERF – The European Money and Finance Forum. *See also*, FSA. (2009). *The Turner Review: A Regulatory Response to the Global Banking Crisis*. Retrieved from http://www.fsa.gov.uk/pubs/other/turner_review.pdf *See also*, Walker, G. A. (2010). Financial Crisis: U.K. Policy and Regulatory Response. *The International Lawyer*, 44(2), 751-789. And, Arner, *supra* n. 64.
108. For a thorough study of Northern Rock and how its failure ushered in the GFC, *See*, Shin, H. S. (2009). Reflections on Northern Rock: The Bank Run that Heralded the Global Financial Crisis. *The Journal of Economic Perspectives*, 23(1), 101-119.
109. Blundell-Wignall, A., & Atkinson, P. (2008). *The Sub-Prime Crisis: Casual Distortions and Regulatory Reforms*. July 14-15, paper presented at the Reserve Bank of Australia, available at http://www.rba.gov.au/publications/confs/2008/index.html.
110. *See*, on the origins of crisis and initial responses, Blundell-Wignall, A., & Atkinson, P. (2009). Origins of the Financial Crisis and Requirements for Reform. *Journal of Asian Economics*, 20(5), 536-548.

subprime mortgage into a general credit crunch in the European markets due to the interdependence of banking institutions as was reflected by the American International Group's (AIG) Credit Default Swaps (CDS). Failure of the AIG would have affected European markets directly (as AIG and Goldman Sachs had provided CDS cover to plenty of European banks) thus the AIG got a USD 85 billion support on September 18, 2008 from the US Treasury – one day after the Lehman was allowed to collapse. The chaos has set in by then.

Financial institutions were unprepared to handle risks of this magnitude. The existing risk management mechanisms proved largely insufficient and ineffective. Merrill Lynch was bought by Bank of America to fend off the impending bankruptcy. Morgan Stanley and Goldman Sachs availed bailout funds on September 22, 2008. Meanwhile, the AIG default threatened the financial markets both in the US and in Europe, particularly in England. Washington Mutual (Wa Mu), one of the biggest US savings and loans bank was taken over by the Federal Deposit Insurance Corporation (FDIC) and was declared bankrupt on September 26, 2008. JP Morgan Chase bought the bank assets for just USD 1.6 billion from the FDIC. The domino did not stop there. On September 29, 2008, Wachovia, a major US commercial bank went bust (and negotiations started with Citigroup for a possible takeover) and it was bought by Wells Fargo in October. The US immediately announced the rescue package, known as the Troubled Assets Relief Program (TARP)[111] to inject money into the system. In London, the Treasury got Lloyds TSB to buy Halifax Bank of Scotland (HBOS) after a tense bargain.

By this time, the financial institutions around the Anglo-American world were reeling from the financial tremors. Elsewhere, a number of more sophisticated banks including but not limited to Royal Bank of Scotland, Citigroup, Fortis (in Benelux), ING (the Netherlands) were facing major threats. Most of the developed countries had to announce TARP-like rescue packages to inject monies into their banking system. Particularly, major disruptions in the Icelandic banks arrested much attention and resources from the UK and other European countries to put out a total collapse due to cross-border linkages involved in these financial transactions.

[2] Phase II: The Onslaught of the Crisis

The monetary policy that aggressively promoted home-ownership and government-sponsored enterprises like Fannie Made, amplified by private sector lending practice, amassed an unsustainable subprime mortgages through the government-sponsored shadow banking sub-system.[112] Resultantly, the subprime bust in March 2007 was not only chaotic but it also triggered a system-wide liquidity crunch. Furthermore, too low

---

111. After the collapse of Lehman, the Congress passed the Emergency Economic Stabilization Act of 2008 authorizing the Treasury to spend up to USD 700 billion by purchasing troubled assets and by injecting capital into nation's banking system under the TARP. *See*, Braithwaite & Drahos, *supra* n. 25.
112. Yergin, D. (Oct. 20, 2009). *A Crisis in Search of a Narrative*. Financial Times, p. 11. Retrieved from http://www.ft.com/intl/cms/s/0/8a82d274-bda9-11de-9f6a-00144feab49a.html#axzz3k9jds77m.

interest rates for too long stimulated the formation of a credit bubble and at the same time a boost in property values incentivized financial institutions to develop innovative financial instruments to resell mortgage-backed securities. Opacity of this financial innovation created *repricing* of Credit Risk.[113] Basically, there are three factors to explain why the subprime crisis became contagious and brought strong spillovers: First, the Security and Exchange Commission (SEC) failed to deliver on its gatekeeper role by permitting investment banks to avoid SEC net capital rule. It offered an option to elect more relaxed alternative. This enabled banks to engage in massive off-balance sheet leverage through engaging in a lot of property trading and lending to hedge funds and private equity groups.[114] Moreover, the US investments banks as well as commercial banks were exempt from European oversight. Second, the SEC introduced a system in which each investment bank developed its own individualized Credit Risk model outside of the Basel II (which was not implemented). This created discrepancies and gaps in evaluating risks for cross-border transactions. Third, dominance of a few big commercial banks (like Lehman Brothers, Bear Stearns and Merrill Lynch) amalgamated insurance and reinsurance functions for CDS, which gave rise to the phenomenon of *too interconnected to fail*.[115]

[B]   A Probe into the Origins

[1]   Why the GFC?

The GFC[116] had complex causes, ranging from long-term to short-term financial, ideological, conceptual, technological and economic reasons.[117] This section analyses

---

113. Tett, G. (Aug. 4, 2008). *The Big Freeze Part 1: A Year that Shook Faith in Finance.* Financial Times, p. 9. Tett, G. (2009). *Fool's Gold: How the Bold Dream of a Small Tribe at J.P. Morgan was corrupted by Wall Street Greed and Unleashed a Catastrophe.* Free Press.
114. *See*, Gapper, J. (Aug. 4, 2008). *Big Freeze Part 2: Banking.* Financial Times. Retrieved from http://www.ft.com/intl/cms/s/0/cc160f46-624f-11dd-9ff9-000077b07658.html#axzz3k9jds77m.
115. *See*, Markose, S., et al. (2010). *Too Interconnected To Fail: Financial Contagion and Systemic Risk* in Network Model of CDS and Other Credit Enhancement Obligations of US Banks. Retrieved from http://repository.essex.ac.uk/3716/ last accessed Jun. 1, 2017.
116. The term *GFC* refers to the crisis that triggered in 2008. There are other terms also including *liquidity crisis, credit crisis, great recession, sub-prime crisis* etc. The GFC in this regard was a banking crisis, caused by capital shortage. To expand it further, there are two types of crises: banking crises (which affect the money stock and thus threaten an economy), and financial crises (which may destroy wealth but do not endanger an economy as a whole). Banking crises can be precipitated by a shortage of capital or by a shortage of liquidity. *See*, Lastra, R. M. & G. Wood (2010). The Crisis of 2007-09: Nature, Causes, and Reactions. *Journal of International Economic Law*, 13(3): 531-550.
117. There is a huge (and ever-growing) literature on the causes of the GFC. For an official analysis of the US, *See*, *The Financial Crisis Inquiry Report* (2011), at http://www.gpoaccess.gov/fcic/fcic.pdf. For a leading discussion on the UK, *See*, The Turner Review: A Regulatory Response to the Global Banking Crisis (2009), *available at* http://www.fsa.gov.uk/pubs/other/turner_review.pdf. For the EU context, *See*, The High-Level Group On Financial Supervision, The EU Report (2009), *available at* http://ec.europa.eu/internal_market/finances/docs/de_larosiere_report_en.pdf. For book-length treatments: *See*, Cassidy, J. (2009). *How Markets Fail: The Logic of Economic Calamities*. Farrar, Straus and Giroux. See also, Kolb, R. W. (2011). *The Financial*

the causes of the GFC and the regulatory responses directly associated with the development (transformation) of IFL in the context of the following issues: first, whether there was a lack in theoretical conceptualization (or in policy direction) and its translation in adopting a liberal regime in financial markets; second, on the lack of enforcement mechanisms in IFL structures; third, that the crises are recurring, regular (and perhaps normal?) feature of international financial system; and, finally, what implications, can be drawn in improving IFL's response mechanisms for future crises?

The progression of the GFC involved an extremely rapid financial expansion without responsible risk assessments, rapid asset price appreciation and failure to notice bubble-formation, and rapid growth of structured credit products whose return relied heavily on continued favorable economic conditions, for example, CDOs. Other factors included a widespread rise of household leverage and subsequent defaults (as opposed to real estate boom and bust of the past in commercial properties only), sliced-and-diced collateralized products (securitization) that increased dependency of many classes of borrowers on the system (which created not only systemic vulnerabilities but also sharply transformed liquidity crisis into an insolvency crisis). Finally, it involved opacity and complexity of the financial system resulting from derivatives, shadow banking operations and other sophisticated financial instruments.[118] Main causes of the GFC, as widely discussed include:

At the macroeconomic level, following issues were of concern: First, financial innovation and technological engineering created complex financial products that produced excess liquidity in the market leading to rapid credit expansion. Low inflation and low interest rate over an extended period gave another impetus to credit expansion. At the same time, loose monetary policies facilitated a rise in asset prices and in countries like the US abetted a spike in mortgage (residential) properties. On the other hand, supervisory controls and regulatory capital requirements for these mortgage providers remained lukewarm at the most. Insufficient oversight over US GSEs and a political motivation to provide low-priced housing (No-Income No-Job Assets – NINJA policies) caused glut of irresponsible lending. Eichengreen and Park wrote that the traditional separation of macroeconomic and financial policies (the Tinbergen principle) caused the crisis, the development of a synthesis points the way to solution. Second, risk management failures: Mode-based risk assessments and inappropriate risk-management tools rendered it hard to gauge precisely the risk exposure for many lending institutions. Their stress-testing failed to take account of not only tail events (black swans) like total freezing of the inter-bank or commercial paper market.

Third, securitization,[119] multi-layered CDOs, exponential growth in Over-the-Counter (OTC) derivative market, and originate-to-distribute models created perverse incentives for the market. Most of these instruments were created with a view to *decentralize risk* but due to the nature of financial markets, inability of *watch-dogs* and

---

Crisis of Our Time. Oxford University Press; Sorkin, A. R. (2009). *Too Big to Fail: The Inside Story of How Wall Street and Washington Fought to Save the Financial System from Crisis – and Themselves*. Viking Press.
118. *See*, Claessens & Kodres, *supra* n. 3.
119. Simply put, it is the transformation of assets (that are difficult to value) into tradable securities.

insufficient supervision (and ineffective regulation) made risks *invisible* and obscured credit worthiness of counter-parties. In fact, Basel I encouraged risk taking off-balance sheet which (only partly corrected under the Basel II) led to a drastic deterioration in mortgage-lending standards and other regulatory risk management practices. This clean up of balance sheet was done by selling off loans to other banks or purpose-built legal bodies including Special Investment Vehicles (SIVs), Special Purpose Vehicles (SPVs) and hedge funds.[120] The assets on the bank's balance sheet converted into securities and sold out to these vehicles through securitization, which gained exponential momentum throughout 2000s and resulted into dried up markets (ultimately crashed in 2007). Certain forms of financial innovation (such as securitization of subprime mortgages or those relating to Credit Risk modeling) were actually backed by the Basel rules.[121] These innovations accentuated information asymmetry problems in the financial sector, whereas the increased complexity made risk-assessment harder and thus risk management more difficult.

In the run up to the GFC, the US had already switched from the Glass-Steagall demarcations. Originally, GSA in 1930s separated commercial banks from investment banks to stop risks flowing from investment banking businesses to commercial banks. The boundaries between both investment and commercial banking were blurred without making a provision for an independent prudential regulatory authority that could enforce tougher regulations including stringent capital requirements.[122]

[2] *The Controversial Gramm-Leach-Bliley Act (GLBA) 1999*

The enactment of the GLBA in 1999 seemed a revolutionary event as it marked the end of the regulations specifically enforced for the perceived defects in the banking system, which caused the Great Depression of 1929. Furthermore, the GLBA was also implemented to address the financial innovations (in product line), the financial services industry has introduced since the 1930s. It came out as a commonly held belief that now is the time for the market forces to define firewalls, hence no need for the obsolete arbitrary regulations.

The enactment of GLBA in 1999 in the US was a monumental piece of deregulation and this legislation left profound effects on the design and operation of major transactions in the modern international debt markets and on commercial behavior of prominent banks. The implications included: (a) GLBA empowered the Fed to be an umbrella supervisor for financial holding companies, and federal agencies such as the

---

120. Brealey explored *why do investment banks continue to invent and successfully sell complex new securities that outstrip our ability to value them*? *See*, Brealey, R. A., C. Myers, S., & Allen, F. (2006). *Principles of Corporate Finance* (8 ed.). McGraw Hill.
121. Scheicher, M., & David, M.-I. (2012). *Securitization: Instruments and Implications*. In A. N. Berger, P. Molyneux, & J. O. S. Wilson (Eds.), *Handbook of Banking*. Oxford University Press. Available at http://ssrn.com/abstract=1405882 p. 601.
122. *See* for example, Benston, G. (1990). *The Separation of Commercial and Investment Banking: The Glass-Steagall Act Revisited and Reconsidered*. Oxford University Press. For historical evidence, *See*, Kroszner, R. S., & Rajan, R. G. (1994). Is the Glass-Steagall Act Justified? A Study of the US Experience with Universal Banking before 1933. *The American Economic Review*, *84*(4), 810-833.

Office of the Comptroller of the Currency (OCC), SEC and Commodity Futures Trading Commission (CFTC). For the state banking and insurance agencies, a *functional regulator* of various holding companies subsidiaries and affiliates.[123] However, the Fed's umbrella supervision under the GLBA was flawed because regulation of financial markets and firms was fragmented at the firm level.[124] Despite law cemented the Fed as the top regulator for giant firms, it hardly empowered the regulator with sufficient powers over investment banks such as Lehman Brothers, Bear Stearns or AIG Inc.[125] and, (b) the enactment of the GLBA signified liberalization of US banking and financial activities. It repealed the restrictions against the combining of banking, securities and insurance operations for financial institutions.[126] It provided impetus to the growth of shadow banking activities while substantially changing the nature of financial intermediation in the US from a traditional bank's credit intermediation process to securitization-based credit intermediation process. A New York Fed working paper classified transformation of banks within the legal framework of financial holding companies under the GLBA as internal shadow banking sub-system. In this way, it allowed large banks to transform their traditional process of *hold-to-maturity, and spread banking* to a more profitable process of *originate-to-distribute, and free-banking* respectively.[127]

There are contrasting views on GLBA's role in bringing the subprime mortgage crisis of 2007 followed by the financial crisis of 2008. Among the proponents of the Act, Bill Clinton (under whose era, the act was passed), as well as economists Brad DeLong and Tyler Cowen have argued that the GLBA softened the impact of the crisis. Atlantic Monthly columnist, Megan McArdle, has argued that *if* the Act was part of the problem, it would have been commercial banks (and not the investment banks) in trouble and its repeal would not have helped the situation. Former Senator Phil Gramm also defended his bill: if GLBA was the problem, the crisis would have been expected to originate in Europe where they never had Glass-Steagall requirements to begin with. Financial firms that failed during this crisis, like the Lehman Brothers, were the least diversified and the ones that survived like the J.P. Morgan were the most diversified. Moreover, GLBA did not deregulate anything. It came out as a commonly held belief that instead of obsolete arbitrary regulations, market or increasing market competition can itself define where Chinese walls need to be placed. Critics have varied opinions on the role of the market however. Wood thinks that markets are more efficient in making decisions and in imposing discipline rather than the governments. The costs of regulation should be borne by the stakeholders and not by taxpayers. Randall also

---

123. *See*, Olive, C. D., & Arner, D. W. (2002). *Sectoral Regulation in the United States: Financial Services Modernization in the US and the GLBA of 1999*. Sweet & Maxwell. pp. 121-122.
124. *See*, Haubrich, J. G., & Thomson, J. B. (2008). Umbrella Supervision and the Role of the Central Bank. *Journal of Banking Regulation*, *10*(1), 17-27. p. 25.
125. *See*, Paletta, D., & Scannell, K. (Mar. 11, 2010). The Financial Crisis: Some Questions for Those Fixing the Mess. *The Wall Street Journal*, p. 20.
126. *See*, Olive & Arner, *supra* n. 123.
127. Shadow banks are defined as *financial intermediaries that conduct maturity, credit, and liquidity transformation without access to central bank liquidity or public sector credit guarantees*. *See*, Pozsar, Z., et al. (July 2010). *Shadow Banking*. Retrieved from Federal Reserve Bank of New York, Staff Report No. 458 http://ssrn.com/paper = 1645337 p. 3.

Chapter 2: Cyclic Financial Crises and the Development of IFL §2.03[C]

supported efficient market view and welcomed the GLBA enactment. To him, regulations play contrary effect and that the regulatory safety net has often had the unfortunate impact of undermining rather than promoting financial stability. Santos called it a *costly-cat-and-mouse-game* between banks and their regulators. This perspective views banks and their regulators as competitors to each other and not *partners-in-business* with mutual stakes in ensuring systemic stability.

On the other side however, there is strong criticism on the role of the GLBA in bringing on the recent crisis. According to some, it contributed significantly to the GFC[128] by allowing excessive deregulation that, among other things, allowed for the establishment of giant financial supermarkets (that could own investment banks, commercial banks and insurance firms), something that was banned since the Great Depression. Its passage, critics pointed, cleared the way for companies that were too big and intertwined to fail.

[C] IFL in Action

In October 2007, the FSF reported to the G7 Ministers and Governors at their April 2008 meeting in Washington. By now, the G20 has assumed the lead from the G7 as the agenda setter for international finance. The FSB and the BCBS provided a supervisory forum for regular cooperation to design universal risk-based management mechanism. The Washington Summit declaration[129] contained a detailed action plan based in part on the principle that all financial markets, products and participants – including shadow banking institutions – must be subject to prudential regulation. The Action Plan affirmed amongst others:[130]

> In order to avoid new systemic risks, we reaffirm our commitment to common global standards by pursuing the financial regulatory reform agenda according to our agreed timetable in an internationally consistent and non-discriminatory manner. We will monitor its full and timely implementation in all jurisdictions through the FSB Coordination Framework for Implementation Monitoring.

This agenda was inclusive of Basel II, II.5 and III and the OTC derivative market, policy measures to address systemically important financial institutions (SIFIs), the Key Attributes for Effective Resolution Regimes and the principles and standards for sound compensation practices to boost work on systemic financial market infrastructures.[131] In 2009, the G20 published a Leaders Statement[132] that went a step forward by committing to undertake whatever it may require to strengthen global financial

---

128. *See*, Sherman, M. (2009). *A Short History of Financial Deregulation in the United States*. CEPR. Retrieved from http://www.cepr.net/documents/publications/dereg-timeline-2009-07.pdf.
129. Commitment to the following reform principles pledged: (1) strengthening transparency and accountability, (2) enhancing sound regulation, (3) promoting integrity in financial markets, (4) reinforcing international financial markets, and, (5) reforming international financial institutions. *See*, G20. (November 2008). *Declaration Summit on Financial Markets and the World Economy*. Retrieved from http://www.un.org/ga/president/63/commission/declarationG20.pdf.
130. *Ibid.*
131. *Ibid.*

supervision and regulation. The work in the wake of these two summits continued in Pittsburgh (2009)[133] and Seoul (2010)[134] to cover not only financial regulatory matters but also trade, currency and monetary affairs.

The most significant step in the series came in the G7 comprehensive statement in October 2008, endorsed by the full membership of the IMF, the WB and the EU.[135] It focused on five major regulatory areas.[136] The findings drew on a large body of coordinated work from: the BCBS, the International Organization of Securities Commissions (IOSCO), the International Association of Insurance Supervisors (IAIS), Joint Forum, the International Accounting Standards Board (IASB), the Committee on Payment and Settlement Systems (CPSS), the Committee on the Global Financial System (CGFS), the IMF, the BIS, and national authorities and important private players in key financial centers.[137] Later on, the G20 Declaration to support an open global economy by laying foundations for reform in the Action Plan[138] was to ensure that a global crisis, such as this one, does not happen again. The basic principles agreed were:[139] (a) market principles of open trade and investment regimes foster dynamism, innovation and entrepreneurship which are essential for economic growth, employment and poverty reduction; (b) IFIs can provide critical support to global economy and (c) to implement reforms that will strengthen financial markets and regulatory regimes so as to avoid future crises.

---

132. In London, the leaders pledged to: (1) restore confidence, growth and jobs, (2) strengthen financial supervision and regulation, (3) strengthen global financial institutions, (4) resist protectionism and promote global trade and investment, (5) ensure a substantial and fair recovery for all, and, (6) deliver their commitments. *See*, G20. (Apr. 2, 2009). *London Summit: Leaders' Statement*. Retrieved from https://www.imf.org/external/np/sec/pr/2009/pdf/g20_040209.pdf.
133. At Pittsburgh, the leaders pledged to: (1) strong, sustainable and balanced growth, (2) strengthen the international financial regulatory system, (3) modernize global institutions with specific reforms at the IMF and other Development banks and (4) an open global economy. *See*, G20 Framework for Strong, Sustainable, and Balanced Growth *See*, G20. (September 2009). *G20 Leaders Statement: Pittsburgh*. Retrieved from http://www.g20.utoronto.ca/2009/2009 communique0925.html.
134. At the Seoul Summit, the nine-point Multi-Year Action Plan on Development (MYAP) was spelled out. The leaders tasked the OECD countries with five out of the total nine pillars: (1) human resource development, (2) private investment and job creation, (3) food security, (4) domestic resource mobilization, and, (5) knowledge sharing. The leaders also committed to continue the work of the G20 on: (1) preventing corruption through the Anti-Corruption Action Plan, (2) to rationalize and phase-out over the medium-term inefficient fossil fuel subsidies, (3) to safeguard the global marine environment, and, (4) to combat the challenges of climate change. *See*, G20. (November 2010). The G20 Seoul Summit Leader's Declaration. Retrieved from https://www.oecd.org/g20/summits/seoul/G20-Seoul-Summit-Leaders-Declaration.pdf.
135. *See*, FSF. (April 2008). *Report of the FSF on Enhancing Market and Institutional Resilience*. Retrieved from http://www.financialstabilityboard.org/wp-content/uploads/r_0804.pdf?page _moved=1.
136. Five major regulatory areas included: (1) strengthened prudential oversight of capital, liquidity and risk management; (2) enhancing transparency and valuation; (3) changes in the role and uses of credit ratings; (4) strengthening the authorities' responsiveness to risks; and, (5) robust arrangements for dealing with stress in the financial system. *See, Ibid.*
137. *See,* for an analysis on the areas, Arner, *supra* n. 64.
138. G20, *supra* n. 129.
139. *Ibid.*

Chapter 2: Cyclic Financial Crises and the Development of IFL §2.03[C]

The G20 and the FSB made coordinated regulation of the cross-border OTC derivative market a top priority. National regulators, including the US SEC and the Australian Securities and Investments Commission (ASIC), reviewed national regulation for identifying any missing areas, conflicts or overlaps. However, despite these coordinated efforts, a number of potential issues specifically those involving multilateral or internationally coordinated responses remained unaddressed.

These political commitments supplemented with technical reports resulted in the formation of standards, which were to be adopted by national jurisdictions around the world. In the US, Henry Paulson succeeded in announcing a rescue package, the TARP[140] for USD 700 billion on September 17, 2008 which aimed at: (a) instant support to stabilize the financial markets which were collapsing like a house of cards, and, (b) to buy troubled assets from these *troubled* institutions to resell them after revising at their current values.[141]

In the US, an emergency order restricting short selling was promulgated on September 18, 2008 to address sudden and excessive fluctuation of securities prices, which was disrupting orderly functioning of markets. At European horizon, the AIG's almost collapse sparked the threat. The UK was under the direct heat of the crisis, and the Financial Services Authority (FSA) and the SEC restricted short sales in the financial sector stocks on September 21, 2008.[142] The FSA adopted Short-Selling Instrument[143] on September 18, 2008, prohibiting any transactions that may create a net short position in a UK financial sector company, or increase any net short position in a UK financial sector company that the person had immediately before September 19, 2008.

---

140. The US Treasury established several programs under TARP to help stabilize the US financial system, restart economic growth and prevent avoidable foreclosures. Although Congress initially authorized USD 700 billion for TARP in October 2008, that authority was reduced to USD 475 billion by the Dodd-Frank Act. See, https://www.treasury.gov/initiatives/financial-stability/TARP-Programs/Pages/default.aspx#.
141. Out of a total of USD 700 billion, the following amounts were committed for TARP's five program areas: (1) around USD 250 billion was committed in programs to stabilize banking institutions (USD 5 billion of which was ultimately cancelled); (2) approximately USD 27 billion was committed through programs to restart credit markets; (3) approximately USD 82 billion was committed to stabilize the U.S. auto industry (USD 2 billion of which was ultimately cancelled); (4) approx. USD 70 billion was committed to stabilize AIG (USD 2 billion of which was ultimately cancelled); (5) approximately USD 46 billion was committed for programs to help struggling families avoid foreclosure, with these expenditures being made over time. *See, Ibid.*
142. The FSA (UK markets regulator) on September 19 revealed a list of twenty-nine (later expanded to thirty-two) financial services companies it was seeking to protect from short-selling to combat the GFC. The ban was aimed to prevent investors from creating or adding to short positions in banks, insurers and other financial companies. Short sellers (particularly hedge funds) who profited from falling prices were blamed for the plunging shares of HBOS and other banks. *See,* Larsen, P. T., Mackintosh, J., & Hughes, J. (Sep. 19, 2008). *FSA Bans Short-Selling of Banks.* Financial Times. Retrieved from https://www.ft.com/content/16102460-85a0-11dd-a1ac-0000779fd18c.
143. *See,* for an overview of existing financial situation, *The UK and the EU.* (2008). Capital Markets Law Journal, 3(4), 500-524. *See also,* Short Selling (No. 5) Instrument, FSA 2009/1. Available at http://www.bankofengland.co.uk/pra/Documents/policy/inst2009.pdf.

Any such financial move was to be treated as *misleading behavior* tantamount to market abuse.[144]

Retrospectively, studies on the September 2008 ban in the US and the UK show that these prohibitions did not yield any concrete welfare benefits, especially in terms of reduction of price volatility.[145] On the contrary, it had an adverse impact on liquidity. Avgouleas wrote that the best way to regulate short sales could have been through a dual strategy of disclosure and short trading halts, rather than prohibition, and this could have served three important objectives.[146] First, it could preserve liquidity-enhancing short sales and the valuable information that these trades carry. Second, it could check downward price pressures egged on by herd-mentality and market irrationality. Third, it would lead to rather compatible national regulatory regimes setting down the foundations of a new global framework for short-sale regulation.[147] The UK issued two rescue packages: one worth GBP 500 billion on October 8, 2008 and another in January 2009 for GBP 50 billion.[148] These support and relief packages issued after 2008 crisis implied not only extensive extension of government guarantees but also bought their toxic loans from the banks to avoid their imminent collapse.[149]

Amongst further reforms, Basel III introduced *bail-in* measures (which would force creditors to share the cost of propping up large banks before taxpayers have to foot the bill). It is expected that the combination of a stronger definition of capital, higher minimum capital requirements, and introduction of new capital buffer will ensure that the banks are able to withstand periods of economic and financial stress.

In the US the Dodd-Frank legislation in contrast, addressed systemic-wide issues by incorporating the idea of *living-wills* making winding up easier in case of an eventual collapse.[150] This Act has broadened the Fed's regulatory and supervisory power to monitor *systematically important* banking organizations and designated non-bank financial institutions. In contrast, narrow banking does not really resolve systemic-wide problems. Nonetheless, the Dodd-Frank legislation is not considered a

---

144. *See*, Willmott, N., & James, P. (December 2008). FSLA Update: The FSA's Ban on Short-Selling of Financial Stocks: Regulation by Smoke and Mirrors? *Butterworths Journal of International Banking and Financial Law*, 622-624.
145. *See*, SEC Halts Short Selling of Financial Stocks to Protect Investors and Markets. Available at https://www.sec.gov/news/press/2008/2008-211.htm https://www.sec.gov/rules/other/2008/34-58592.pdf.
146. *See*, Avgouleas, E. (2010). A New Framework for the Global Regulation of Short Sales: Why Prohibition Is Inefficient and Disclosure Insufficient. *Stanford Journal of Law, Business, and Finance*, 16(2). Retrieved from http://ssrn.com/abstract=1411615.
147. Avgouleas, *supra* n. 146.
148. *See*, Rescue Plan for UK Banks Unveiled. (Oct. 8, 2008). BBC News: Business. Retrieved from http://news.bbc.co.uk/2/hi/business/7658277.stm *See*, EC. (2009). *Economic Crisis in Europe: Causes, Consequences and Responses*. European Economy No. 7 Available at http://ec.europa.eu/economy_finance/publications/publication15887_en.pdf.
149. FSB (October 2008). Issue No 24. Available at BoE's website, last accessed Jun. 1, 2017 http://www.bankofengland.co.uk/publications/Documents/fsr/2008/fsrfull0810.pdf.
150. *See* FSA (2009). *The Turner Review*: A Regulatory Response to the Global Banking Crisis, *available at* http://www.fsa.gov.uk/pubs/other/turner_review.pdf at 93-94. Lord Turner advocated use of new capital and liquidity requirements rather than a proposing a *structured* solution – such as clear institutional separation between classic bank services to the real economy (narrow banking or utility banking) and risky propriety trading activities (investment banking or casino banking).

Chapter 2: Cyclic Financial Crises and the Development of IFL §2.04

panacea to address too-big-to-fail issues, and has been criticized heavily for the additional costs that financial institutions will incur in order to comply with the regulation.

The Dodd-Frank Act brought a sweeping set of changes mainly focused on putting limitations on proprietary trading, enhanced consumer protection laws, and to provide for establishment of a body to manage systemic risk. Volcker's package on the other hand, was the part of the legal reforms that were to be implemented in the US through the Dodd-Frank legislation. There are concerns that these country-specific legal reforms in addition to Basel III requirements are likely to push these highly risk-oriented products from regulated banking sector to the other sectors of the economy (which are either loosely regulated or do not fall under the restrictive regulatory preview). These sectors comprise hedge funds, private equity firms, trading houses, speculative arbitrage and the newest being the energy companies. Also, arbitrage possibilities cannot be ruled out as risk would shift from heavily regulated jurisdictions to the *light-touch* jurisdictions. Final regulations for implementation of the Volcker Rule[151] were issued by five US Federal agencies in December 2013.[152] The Volcker Rule restricts banking entities from engaging in proprietary trading and from investing in or sponsoring private equity and hedge funds (covered funds), absent an applicable exemption. The Volcker Rule's restrictions also apply to Foreign Banking Organizations (FBOs), i.e., non-U.S. banks that maintain a bank branch, agency office or subsidiary in the US, including all branches of such FBO globally and all 25% affiliates of the global FBO.[153]

§2.04 CONCLUSION

To sum up, challenging financial crises are as old as the history of financial markets. They have shaped the development of IFL and its regulatory architecture both in constructive and, at times, in a way rendering it vulnerable and feeble.[154] Arguably, the concept of financial deregulation is closely associated with Adam Smith's free-market philosophy,[155] also reflected by the Efficient Market Theory (EMT).[156] Under the laissez faire economy, it is a widely held belief that financial regulations largely base on the

---

151. The Volcker Rule (in the Dodd-Frank Act) prohibits banks from proprietary trading and restricts investment in hedge funds and private equity by commercial banks and their affiliates.
152. *See*, US SEC website, Responses to FAQs, Regarding the Commission's Rule under section 13 of the Bank Holding Company Act (the Volcker Rule), available at https://www.sec.gov/divisions/marketreg/faq-volcker-rule-section13.htm, last accessed, Aug. 8, 2016.
153. *See*, SIFMA website, Volcker Rule Resource Centre, available at http://www.sifma.org/issues/regulatory-reform/volcker-rule/overview/ *See also*, *The Volcker Rule: Impact of the Final Rule on Foreign Banking Organizations* (December 2013). Morrison Foreseter. Retrieved from http://media.mofo.com/files/Uploads/Images/131211-Volcker-Rule.pdf.
154. Reinhart & Rogoff, *supra* n. 101.
155. *See* Mankiw, N. G. (2015). *Principles of Economics* (7 ed.). CenGage Learning. (9-10); Smith, A. (1904). *An Inquiry into the Nature and Causes of the Wealth of Nations* (E. Cannan Ed. 5 ed.). Methuen & Co., where he noted that *Every individual…neither intends to promote the public interest, nor knows how much he is promoting it…He intends only his own gain, and he is in this, as in many other cases, led by an invisible hand to promote an end, which was no part of his intention. Nor is it always the worse for the society that it was no part of it. By pursuing his*

theory of rational and self-correcting market principles,[157] however, risks inherent in the markets create procyclicality, which keeps the cycle of booms and busts running.

In any post-crisis period, reforms are aggressively followed with loud commitments but as recovery sets in, the momentum for reforms almost always slows down. Earlier, during the 1990s crises, the British Chancellor of the Exchequer recognized that the *need is not only for proper national supervision but also for a fundamental reform of global financial regulation.*[158] This research points at a corollary of the reforms and regulation processes by emphasizing the need for an enforcement mechanism in the realm of IFL.

This chapter has looked at the chronological development of IFL under the controlled regimes of the twentieth century and at the transformation of financial regimes under the liberalization and de-regulatory periods. It examined the various crises episodes, how these shaped the development of IFL, and at the drastic transformation of *finance* from a *domestic concept* to an *international phenomenon* (under the de-regulatory philosophy of market fundamentalism). It examined the current state of IFL by analyzing the GFC and the way IFL and its regulatory institutions responded to the crisis and took up the post-crisis reform agenda.

---

own interest the frequently promotes that of the society more effectually than when he really intends to promote it. Available at http://www.econlib.org/library/Smith/smWN.html.
156. *See*, Fama, E. F. (1970). Efficient Capital Markets: A Review of Theory and Empirical Work. *The Journal of Finance*, 25(2), pp. 383-417. Paper available at http://www.e-m-h.org/Fama70.pdf.
157. *See*, Larsen, P. T. (2009, March 31). A Lot to be Straightened Out. *Financial Times*. Retrieved from http://www.ft.com/intl/cms/s/0/5f5b2200-1d8a-11de-9eb3-00144feabdc0.html#axzz3 jYyHDR8Z.
158. Gordon Brown (1999). Speeches before the CFR, NY, September 16, as quoted by Alexander, et al. *supra* n. 63. *See also*, Brown, G., King, M., & McCarthy, C. (2006). Memorandum of Understanding between HM Treasury, the BoA and the FSA. http://www.bankofengland.co.uk/financialstability/Documents/mou.pdf.

CHAPTER 3
IFL and the Development of Its Regulatory Architecture*

The twentieth century was marked by controlled financial regimes however once the Bretton Woods system of fixed exchange rates eroded, the financial markets after the 1980s underwent quite dramatic changes. For example, finance was no longer a domestic subject. Old restrictive financial regimes were replaced by the de-regulatory and liberal philosophies, which diminished national boundaries and thereby made finance a subject of international attention. This was happening under the umbrella of the WC, and later under the NIFA, essentially reversing neo-Keynesian economics with neoliberal philosophies. In one opinion, this market fundamentalism dominated until 2008 when the GFC set a new order in the financial markets – sometimes referred to as the NIFA II or *Bretton Woods II*.

Chapter 2 has reviewed the development of IFL by employing historical analysis. This Chapter addresses two distinct streams: the first stream focuses on ideological and political ethos underpinning the development of financial markets and how this development contoured the formation of the regulatory practices. Stream II focuses on the regulatory architecture – the various bodies and institutional network – that was established mostly in response to various crises. In exploring these structural manifestations of IFL, section§ 3.01 starts by looking at the institutional heritage that financial markets carried from the post-War and later from the post-Bretton Woods time and analyze the interplay of the role of law and institutional underpinnings in the development of international financial markets. The section then analyzes the interplay of liberalization and deregulation under the ethos of the WC and the NIFA. Section §3.02 looks at the structure, role and functions of the most important pillars of the IFRA

---

* This chapter builds on a paper, *The Need for Consolidating International Financial Regulatory Architecture: Case for a Global Supervisor*, presented at the 13th Finance and Banking Conference on *Lessons Learned from the Financial Crisis at the* Silesian University in October 2011. The Participation to the conference was funded by a grant from RGC's project, Enhancing Hong Kong's Future as a Leading IFC.

and highlights what essentially has undermined these institutions in times of crisis. It further identifies the factors why reforms are still pending. Section §3.03 evaluates the existing IFRA, and raises the question whether the existing regulatory architecture has become resilient enough to prevent future financial disruptions? The answer would summarize what the reforms have achieved so far and whether the existing IFRA presents the ideals that post-2008 reform envisioned?

§3.01 FINANCIAL MARKET DEVELOPMENT

This section analyzes theories of the development of financial markets, of law and of institutions and how these interact to shape the IFRA.

[A] The Institutional Heritage

[1] The Post-War Controlled Financial Markets

The post-War regulatory architecture was founded on formal arrangements where economic cooperation and coordination was to be carried through the offices of the United Nations and was characterized by (a) trade flows, (b) international support for reconstruction and development, (c) limited capital flows, (d) treaty-based international institutions and (e) fixed exchange rates.[1]

Under the Bretton Woods design, the ITO, (, which was never established as such but evolved from as the GATT), was meant to be established to oversee trade and investment liberalization; the IMF was created to manage monetary arrangements; and the International Bank for Reconstruction and Development (IBRD, the World Bank) was to supervise reconstruction and development finance. One noticeable point here – will be discussed in detail under the section on post-Bretton Woods institution – is that since this structure was based on restricted capital flows until 1970 hence there was no need for a treaty-based structure to regulate finance. This regulatory philosophy was embedded in the assumption that free capital flows across jurisdictions and exchange rate fluctuations were the main risk factors, whereas international trade and investments were regarded as necessary drivers of economic growth and developments. Hence, elaborate institutional arrangements were defined for trade with an intended omission on regulating capital flows. These arrangements worked fairly well but only up to 1971.

[2] The Post-Bretton Woods and the Emergence of Risk

Whilst it was a different financial world after the Bretton Woods IMS collapsed yet the regulatory architecture was kept unchanged. The emerging financial horizon was characterized by – floating currencies, liberalized markets and finance becoming

---

1. *See*, Arner, D. W., & Buckley, R. (2011). Redesigning the Architecture of the Global Financial System. *Melbourne Journal of International Law*, 11(2), 185-239.

increasingly global, and trade and investments with enormous cross-border institutional linkages. Owing to free capital flows and floating exchange rates, several developments occurred in the international financial markets that brought an array of risks unknown to financial markets previously.

Finance was essentially domestic under the Bretton Wood system hence the risk in the financial markets was borne by the public sector. However, after the collapse of the Bretton Wood, the risk in the financial market got privatized. Earlier, it was for the governments to maintain fixed exchange rates, therefore, the private sector remained free from most of the risks and there was not a pressing need to develop internal risk management systems. With the breakdown of the Bretton Woods, virtually the big reserve currencies went floating against the US dollar, and with this came the inevitable privatization of the foreign exchange risk. The banks, finding themselves exposed to a multitude of risks, adopted strategies hedging their risks. They diversified their portfolios into multiple currencies in offshore jurisdictions. This brought the foreign exchange risk into the private sector, resulting in enormous pressure on governments to liberalize national controls on cross-border capital flows and to deregulate banking practices. This privatization of risk puts a lot of strain on domestic and international systems. However, with the liberalization of markets and risk privatization, the financial system, both national and international, at once was exposed to huge stress as capital controls were loosened. Extreme volatility of financial markets, which became a permanent feature of the international financial markets. The post-1971 architecture was characterized by: (a) continued liberalization of trade and investment, (b) international support for reconstruction and development, (c) series of treaty-based international institutions and (d) free-floating currency regimes/exchange rates.

The failure of the formal treaty-based mechanisms for capital controls strengthened the belief that the global financial markets have *graduated* and are ready to enter into binding arrangements. The BIS (once dysfunctional under the Bretton Woods regime of domestic finance and restricted capital movements) got another life especially its reserve committees (particularly BCBS) became actively involved in shaping the post-Bretton Woods regulatory architecture.[2]

The IMF also tried to cope with the emerging realities and through the Second Amendment, the Articles of Agreement[3] were rewritten to take into account the new international monetary circumstances (gold was written out of the system and member countries were allowed to peg their currencies to any external reference except gold.[4] This era was primarily characterized by the LDCs debt crises as financial markets in the

---

2. *See*, for details on the activities of the committees, Ch. 2.
3. Signed and entered into force on Dec. 27, 1945, as amended in 1976 by the Board of Governors' Resolution (31-34). Second Amendment to the IMF's Articles of Agreement can be found at https://www.gold.org/sites/default/files/documents/after-the-gold-standard/1976apr30.pdf and the Articles at http://www.imf.org/external/pubs/ft/aa/index.htm.
4. *See*, Giovanoli, M., & Devos, D. (Eds.). (2010). *International Monetary and Financial Law: The Global Crisis*. Oxford University Press. *See also*, Weber, R. H. (2001). Challenges for the New Financial Architecture. *Hong Kong Law Journal, 31*(2), Retrieved from http://ssrn.com/paper=926662.

emerging economies' were far less sophisticated to handle enormous amounts of capital flows and huge influx in interest rate hikes. International cooperation, on the other hand was taking place through the G5 and the G7. In Europe, EU was still an evolving regional organization working along with other international financial organizations like the Basel Committee. The WC was the dominating economic philosophy of the time and a spirit of deregulation prevailed over policy formulation processes albeit with a hint of prudential regulations.

[3]   Graduated Financial Markets

Since the dawn of the twenty-first century, a dominant perception was that the financial markets and market institutions have *graduated* since long and in consequent to this recognition, the concept of market fundamentalism received much applause. It was commonly believed that further research for forecasting financial risks or economic crises is not imminent. The study of financial institutions was regarded by many economists as unimportant.[5] Petersmann wrote that many constitutional problems of IEL remained *under-theorized*:

> [e]conomic analyses of market failures and public choice analyses of governance failures must be supplemented by constitutional choice analyses of constitutional failures and by comparative institutional economics evaluating alternative decision-making processes like citizen-driven market processes, political processes and judicial procedures.[6]

An absence of theoretical underpinnings has not been limited to financial market development only, historically, scholarship especially economists have almost deliberately conferred a weaker emphasis on the role of the institutions and of law in economic and financial development. The interconnection between the law (in establishing clear rules of business, issues of governance, protection of property rights, corporate governance laws, taxation systems, enforcement of contracts, resolution regimes for commercial disputes and rule of law) and financial market stability (and economic development) remained obscure for long time. At best, it flourished only in fits and bounds.

Although financial markets were seriously affected during the crisis episodes of 1990s and early 2000s but due to the limited geographic reach (mostly in developing countries only), these issues could not attract much attention from the mainstream economists in the industrialized economies. Even the crisis in Japan – the second

---

5. Allen, F. (2001). Do Financial Institutions Matter? Centre for Financial Institutions, University of Pennsylvania, WP No. 01-04. Available at http://fic.wharton.upenn.edu/fic/papers/01/0104.pdf.
6. Petersmann, Ernst-Ulrich., (2012). *International Economic Law in the 21st Century. Constitutional Pluralism and Multilevel Governance of Interdependent Public Goods*. Hart Publishing, Oxford.

largest economy of the world (in 1990s and 2000s), and Scandinavian crisis (of 1990s) could hardly attract much attention from the main stream macroeconomists.[7]

[B] Theories of Institutional Development

[1] Where Stands the Law?

The pace of institution building and development varied vastly between the developed and the developing economies; the former deliberately cultivated strong institutional norms while the latter remained behind in achieving institutional sophistication. The industrialized world, however, paid very little attention to the widening gap in theorizing financial standards and in their tangible implementation, which led to this disconnect between theorizing the financial law and its correlation with stability and development. Efforts at law and development have failed for decades.[8] Though the development theory functioned at its best only in fits and bounds, yet, four distinct phases can be identified:

(1) The first wave (1950-1965) was after the decolonization in the context of newly independent states and focused on building indigenous legal systems in tandem with economic and political developments within those countries. Thomas Heller, while taking stock of international experiences in legal and judicial reform in Latin America, Europe, India and China, raised some key questions on the debate. The questions included: What are the common assumptions about the role of the courts in improving economic growth and democratic politics? Do we expect too much from the formal legal system? Is investing in judicial reform projects a good strategy for addressing the problems of governance that beset many developing countries? If not, what are we missing?[9] The standard development formula, then known as *modernization*, called for enhancing four societal features, namely: bureaucratic governmental apparatus; capitalist market system; generalized universalistic legal system; and, democratic political system.[10]

---

7. Allen and Carletti note five specific areas of financial system in want of appropriate theories: banking regulation, global imbalances, asset price bubbles, central bank checks and balances and, competition in financial services. See, Allen, F., & Carletti, E. (2013). New Theories to Underpin Financial Reform. *Journal of Financial Stability*, 9 pp. 242-249. %20theories%20to%20underpin%20published.pdf.
8. Tamanaha, B. Z. (2011). The Primacy of Society and the Failures of Law and Development. *Cornell International Law Journal*, 44. Available at http://www.lawschool.cornell.edu/research/ilj/upload/tamanaha-final.pdf.
9. Jensen, E., & Heller, T. C. (Eds.). (2005). *Beyond Common Knowledge: Empirical Approaches to the Rule of Law*. Stanford University Press. Available at http://cddrl.stanford.edu/publications/beyond_common_knowledge_empirical_approaches_to_the_rule_of_law/.
10. Talcott Parsons. (1964). Evolutionary Universals in Society. *American Sociological Review*, 29(3), pp. 339-356. Available at http://www.d.umn.edu/cla/faculty/jhamlin/4111/Readings/ParsonsUniversals.pdf.

However, extraordinary politico-economic changes took place in many countries since the 1960s. Enormous economic strides were made in a few decades by Asian tigers including, Hong Kong, Singapore, South Korea, followed by China and India among others, which gave a technological boost and marked the second wave of the *law and development theory*.

(2) The second phase stretched from 1965-1975. This wave of democratization around the world began in the mid-1960s – ironically, not long after political scientists explained that many countries lacked civic culture essential to democracy.[11] The late twentieth century ushered in an era of *global diffusion of markets and democracy*. However, some important variables –, which were not taken into account in making projections for the role of legal institutions in economic development and growth – came to the forefront. These factors included for example, population growth (, which far exceeds the economic growth in reality). These failures resulted in little value except to a few, thereby, favoring a corrupt elite group in those societies only, while the masses at large, suffered. By the end of the 1970s, this second wave was in gradual erosion and lacked clear ideas about what could be done to facilitate economic and political development.

(3) Meanwhile, against this pessimistic background, the third wave, spanning from 1985-2000, highlighted issues regarding constitutionalism and human rights. During this era, it was expected that the law would provide the legal infrastructure required for development. It was recognized that law has the capacity to bring about the social, economic and political changes (including requisite cultural attitudes) conducive to development.[12]

(4) Then, the fourth wave based on a new approach to *law and development* came around mid-1990s. This shifts in perceptions resulted in elevating the rule of law[13] from a *development policy tool to a development policy objective*.[14] This phase was founded upon Max Weber's concept of legal certainty.[15] However, Weber's conception has been challenged by the modern

---

11. Huntington, S. P. (1965). Political Development and Political Decay, World Politics,17(3). Pp. 386-430. Out of 150 states only 41 were democracies in 1974 in contrast to three-fifths nation-states today. *See*,. http://www.la.utexas.edu/users/chenry/core/Course%20Materials/SPH1965/0.pdf last accessed Oct 18, 2017
12. *See*, Trubek, D. M., & Santos, A. (2006). The Third Moment in Law and Development Theory and the Emergence of a New Critical Practice. In D. M. Trubek & A. Santos (Eds.), *The New Law and Economic Development: A Critical Appraisal*. CUP. Available at http://law.wisc.edu/gls/dtttm.pdf.
13. *See*, for discourse on the rule of law, Ohnesorge, J. K. M. (2007). Developing Development Theory: Law and Development Orthodoxies and the Northeast Asian Experience. *University of Pennsylvania Journal of International Economic Law, 28*(2), 219-308. Available at https://www.law.upenn.edu/journals/jil/articles/volume28/issue22/Ohnesorge28U.Pa.J.Int'lEcon.L.219(2007).pdf. To read about how the IFIs played a role in highlighting importance of rule of law, *see*, Ohnesorge, J. K. M. (2007). The Rule of Law. Annual Review of Law and Social Science, 3, 99-114. Available at http://www.annualreviews.org/doi/pdf/110.1146/annurev.lawsocsci.1143.011207.080748.
14. Trubek & Santos, *supra* n. 12.
15. Douglass North, and Mancur Olson are regarded contemporary proponents. *See*, Posner, E. (1997). Standards, Rules, and Social Norms. *Harvard Journal of Law & Public Policy, 21*. *See also*,

day globalization processes and by the capitalist system where economies are driven by huge multinational corporations and whose interests are shielded under the precept of legal uncertainty and not through formal and abstract rational law. Some contest the idea that *bright-line rules* are superior to vague standards in regard to certainty and predictability termed as *fallacy of legal certainty*.[16] This theme will be hammered out in Chapter 6 with regard to the nature of the regulatory architecture based on not so bright-line rules.

IFIs now recognize the importance of predictable and calculable law for markets. In some respects, they are revisiting the 1960s *law-and-development movement* but with lessons learnt from the shift from socialism to capitalism (and from the AFC).[17] Although contemporary capitalism is global, the commercial laws that undergird it are not. Even if the IMF or the World Bank (WB) could devise *one best* bankruptcy law, it would be unrealistic to suppose that other countries would simply adopt it. The neoliberal agenda strongly dominates international policy making, and those who embrace it have learned it the hard way that markets are not always self-sustaining.[18] Superior belief on market's disciplining ability led to light-touch regulation of financial entities. Markets require institutional back-stop and here the IFIs distinguish the prominence of law.

[2] Institutions Matter

Institutions are important. The development of financial institutions is directly associated with the development of financial markets, financial system and ultimately, economic growth and development of an economy. This research raises questions on the inadequacy of both the core and support institutions responsible to carry out financial market regulation. The ineffectiveness of the existing institutional architecture was laid bare by the prostrated global financial markets following the 2008 crisis, which also reflected on the inadequacy crisis resolution mechanisms.

Friedrich A. Hayek, The Road to Serfdom (1944). Available at http://cnqzu.com/library/Philosophy/neoreaction/Friedrich%20August%20Hayek/Friedrich_Hayek%20-%20The_road_to_serfdom.pdf Hayek undergoes a full transformation, visible from his later works like in *Law, Legislation and Liberty: A New Statement of the Liberal principles of Justice and Political Economy (1973)*. Routledge, accessible at https://libsa.files.wordpress.com/2015/01/hayek-law-legislation-and-liberty.pdf last accessed Oct 08, 2017

16. Raban, O. (2010). The Fallacy of Legal Certainty: Why Vague Legal Standards May Be Better for Capitalism and Liberalism. *Boston University Public Interest Law Journal*, 19(175). Available at http://papers.ssrn.com/sol3/papers.cfm?abstract_id=1419683.
17. *See* for example, the writings of Tamanaha, *supra* n. 8.
18. Carruthers, B. G., & Halliday, T. C. (2007). Law, Economy, and Globalization: Max Weber and How International Financial Institutions Understand Law. In N., Victor & R., Swedberg (Ed.), *On Capitalism*. Stanford University Press. *See also*, Krever, T. (2011). The Legal Turn in Late Development Theory: The Rule of Law and the World Bank's Development Model. *Harvard International Law Journal*, 52(1). Available at http://www.harvardilj.org/wp-content/uploads/2011/02/HILJ_52-1_Krever.pdf last accessed October 9, 2017.

The post-Bretton Woods world in 1980s, unbridled new forces of free market economy, which weakened a states' control mechanisms significantly. In particular, with the fall of communism and failure of policy-based approaches, the foremost question that came to prominence (and was blown out of proportion by the followers of Friedrich Hayek, Milton Friedman) was: how to facilitate transition from total state-owned controls to a functioning market economy in the former Soviet Bloc countries.[19] These hasty liberalization policies did not work very well in the long run and the subsequent events added new dimensions to the role of institutions in economic development (e.g., a need for support-providing legal institutions in securing property rights in the transition economies).[20]

Attempts at defining the correlation between *law and development* in the pursuit of modernization have now spanned more than half a century. The nomenclature though has changed over time: in the fifties, sixties and seventies, it was named as the *law and development movement*; in the eighties, nineties and through the turn of the century, it meta-morphed from *good governance programs* to *rule of law and development*. However, the prospects are sloppier for law and development than for other elements of the modernization package. The past 30 years have demonstrated that components of capitalism (market fundamentalism, securing financing, establishing factories leading to production chains) and democracy (instituting periodic elections) can be implemented through new institutional arrangements that can function effectively, although they may not transcend similar legacy in developing societies as it did in the West.[21]

The movement for international liberalization brought benefits, but liberal markets remain efficient only if these are regulated efficiently.[22] The New Institutional

---

19. Arner, D.W. (2007). *Financial Stability, Economic Growth and the Role of Law*. Cambridge University Press. p. 16.
20. *See*, Williamson, O. E. (2000). The New Institutional Economics: Taking Stock, Looking Ahead. *Journal of Economic Literature, 38*(3), 595-613.
21. Tamanaha, *supra* n. 8.
22. Maynard Keynes's quote stated in 1941, also quoted by Eichengreen (2009) in Ch. 4 p. 143 where he regards existence of an automatic balance-of-payment adjustment mechanism as a *doctrinaire delusion*. Wood also endorses the view that markets are efficient in enforcing discipline than the governments; *see*, Wood, P. R. (2008). *Law and Practice of International Finance*. Sweet and Maxwell. Kaufman believes that *markets know best and that those who compete well will prosper, while those who do not will fail. See*, Kaufman, H. (Apr. 28, 2009). How Libertarian Dogma Led the Fed Astray. *Financial Times*. At http://economistsview.typepad.com/economistsview/2009/04/libertarian-dogma-and-the-fed.html. Post-GFC scholarship in particular reflects on the reasons why market forces failed to effectively regulate nuances of products; during the 2008-2010 markets disappointed mostly in offering symmetric information and cast a doubt on if these always act rationally. *See*, Blundell-Wignall, A., Atkinson, P., & Lee, S. H. (2008). The Current Financial Crisis: Causes and Policy Issues. *Financial Market Trends – OECD*. Retrieved from http://www.oecd.org/finance/financial-markets/41942872.pdf, also shared in Akerlof, G. A., & Shiller, R. J. (2009). *Animal Spirits: How Human Psychology Drives the Economy, and Why it Matters for Global Capitalism*. Princeton University Press. *See also*, Paletta, D., & Scannell, K. (Mar. 11, 2010). The Financial Crisis: Some Questions for Those Fixing the Mess. *The Wall Street Journal*.

Economics[23] (NIE) thus was revived into literature, for example by Douglas North.[24] NIE extends economics by focusing on the socio-legal norms and rules that inspire economic activity and builds upon the analysis, which earlier institutional economics and neoclassical economics provided.[25] Most scholars doing research under the NIE's methodological principles followed Douglas North's demarcation between institutions and organizations. Institutions are the *rules of the game*, as North expands the term *what institutions mean*, or, more formally, *are the humanly devised constraints, consisting of both the formal legal rules and the informal social norms* that govern individual behavior and structure social interactions (institutional frameworks).[26] He further expands on the role of the institutions, which provide the basic structure on which human beings throughout the history have created order and attempted to reduce uncertainty in exchange...they connect the past with the present and the future so that history is largely an incremental story of institutional evolution in which the historical performance of economics can only be understood as part of a sequential story.[27]

In the past, normative rules governing the international economic system were being exclusively created by the states under their domestic laws or under certain situations under the public international law. However, in the light of the profoundly flaccid mechanism of lawmaking and law realization, it is becoming more and more apparent that the traditional three-pronged distinction between the domestic law,

---

23. The NIE looks at how institutions play a role in shaping economic behavior and views market as a result of the complex interaction of these various institutions (e.g., individuals, firms, states, social norms). The earlier tradition continues today as a leading heterodox approach to economics. Originally, Thorstein Veblen's instinct-oriented dichotomy between technology on the one side and the *ceremonial sphere* of society on the other, brought to focus institutional economics. Its name and core elements trace back to a 1919 American Economic Review article by Walton H. Hamilton. However, from late twentieth century a new variant, that is, the *new institutional economics* integrated later developments of neoclassical economics including economic theory of organization, information and property rights into the broader analysis of mainstream economics. See, for example, Coase, R. (1998). The New Institutional Economics. *American Economic Review, 88*(2), 72-74. See also, Coase, R. (1991). *The Institutional Structure of Production*. Paper presented at the Nobel Prize Lecture, reprinted in 1992. American Economic Review, available at http://www.nobelprize.org/nobel_prizes/economics/laureates/1991/coase-lecture.html.
24. Douglass C. North (1997). The New Institutional Economics and Third World Development. In J. Harriss, J. Hunter, and C. M. Lewis (Ed.), *The New Institutional Economics and Third World Development* (pp. 17-26) Routledge.
25. Rutherford, M. (2001). Institutional Economics: Then and Now. *Journal of Economic Perspectives, 15*(3), 185-194.
26. Douglass C. North, (1990). *Institutions, Institutional Change and Economic Performance*. Cambridge University Press. p. 3.
27. *Ibid.* p. 118.

public international law and the *lex mercatoria*[28] is an inadequate conceptual approach to define transnational market relations.[29]

[C] FML and Institutional Correlations

Whilst the Bretton Woods system in 1940s was based on global trade and fixed exchange rates with finance being regulated domestically, international regulations for finance were never required. However, after the Bretton Woods system was abandoned in 1970s, finance became international and the financial markets interconnected. The financial institutions operating across jurisdictions involved multiple legal systems in complex transactions. This new transition necessitated appropriate rules and standards governing such transactions international in design, scope and application. The interconnectedness and interdependency of banking and nonbanking firms and the adoption of the universal banking models made the whole system intensively risk-sensitive.[30] This necessitated the need to have common rules and standards and code of conduct to be devised through coordination and cooperation among national authorities.

Financial liberalization brings inevitable financial fragility in its wake, which the recent history has reflected.[31] The link between the banking crisis and systemic crisis has already been established in the scholarship.[32] It is prudent to contrast and weigh relative benefits in the form of financial and market efficiency to be achieved through deregulations with the costs of financial fragility, banking risk and closely linked systemic threats. Over the past three decades, there were 42 systemic banking crises from 37 countries and there were at least nine major financial crises started from 1990s

---

28. Lex mercatoria or *law merchant* is an autonomous body of regulations created independently and enforced by private economic actors to govern international trade relations without the involvement of nation-states. *See*, Michaels, R. (2007). The True Lex Mercatoria: Law Beyond the State. *Indiana Journal of Global Legal Studies*, 14(2). Available at http://www.repository.law.indiana.edu/cgi/viewcontent.cgi?article=1359&context=ijgls.
29. Nowrot, K. (2014). Evolving Hierarchies in Transnational Financial Networked Governance: The Relationship between the International Accounting Standards Board, the FSB and the G20. In M. Fenwick, S. Van Uytsel, & S. Wrbka (Eds.), *Networked Governance, Transnational Business and the Law* (pp. 231-256). Springer.
30. *See*, on universal banking and changing role of banks, Krosner, R. S. (1998). Rethinking Bank Regulation: A Review of the Historical Evidence. *Journal of Applied Corporate Finance*, 11(2). Retrieved from http://ssrn.com/paper=138820.
31. *See*, McKinnon, R. I. (1973). *Money and Capital in Economic Development*. Brookings Institution. Shaw, E. S. (1973). *Financial Deepening in Economic Development*. Oxford University Press. And, King, R., & Levine, R. (1993). Finance and Growth: Schumpeter Might Be Right. *Quarterly Journal of Economics: MIT Press*, 108(3), 717-737.
32. *See*, Taylor, L., & Eatwell, J. (2001). *Global Finance at Risk: The Case for International Regulation*. Polity Press. *See also*, Lastra, R. M. (2006). *Legal Foundations of International Monetary Stability*. Oxford University Press., and, Garicano, L., & Lastra, R. M. (2010). Towards a New Architecture for Financial Stability: Seven Principles. *Journal of International Economic Law*, 13(3), 597-621. Alexander, K., Eatwell, J., Persaud, A., & Reoch, R. (2007). New Crisis Management Measures to Avoid Future Bank Bail-Outs. (Jun. 6, 2012): EC Press Release No IP/12/570, available at http://europa.eu/rapid/press-release_IP-12-570_en.htm?locale=en. FCIC. (January 2011).

to 2000s in emerging market economies (EMEs).[33] The whole narrative of instability revolves around the frequency and the volume of capital moving across jurisdictions at a point in time. It bears direct effects on the monetary, financial and banking policies, domestically as well internationally.

The volume and frequency of capital mobility during Keynes' time bear no comparison to transactions taking place after the globalization of financial markets and financial services. Had Keynes and White any idea of the volume of capital inflows and outflows in the globalized world, their reconstruction plans for an international financial system comprising Bretton Woods must have embodied three basic components, as pointed by Ross[34] The dilemma is that no IFRA institution represents truly any of these three functions, namely: a bankruptcy regime; a global financial regulator (GFReg) with enforcement powers; and, a global lender of the last resort (LoLR).

In this backdrop, states form IFIs to address collective problems by employing coordinated tools of cooperation like information sharing, contributing to a collective pool of sums needed in case of any financial disruption etc. Because financial markets are imperfect, consumers of financial products do not have full access to information. Here, IFIs are needed to resolve the limitations caused by market imperfections. They accept funds from surplus units and channel the funds to deficit units. Without financial institutions, the information and transaction costs of financial market transactions would be enormous.[35]

The IFIs demand its Member States to observe certain rules, standards and agreements that have been consented to by such Member States. The Member States are thus required to respond positively to such rules and regulations for collective financial stability. On the part of the IFIs, the global governance mandate they enjoy requires transparency, legitimacy and universality on the one hand, and demand accountability and compliance, both procedurally and substantively, on the other. Common set of rules, standards and regulatory practices are defined and agreed to by the national regulators and as this agreement involves political and economic sovereignty of the participating states, it is necessary that the organizational structures and decision-making processes satisfy core principles of global governance.[36] The IFIs' financial standards are deliberated by its members and are adopted through agreements. These standards are generally of three types:[37] (1) model contracts or agreements to facilitate cross-border financial transactions (e.g., International Swaps and Derivatives Association (ISDA); (2) interstate agreements to promote cross-border competition in banking and financial services (e.g., in trade law, the WTO; and, (3)

---

33. *See*, Luc Laeven & Fabian Valencia. (2002). Systemic Banking Crises: A New Database (IMF WP/08/224), p. 3; and Masahiro Kawai, (2010) Reform of the International Financial Architecture: An Asian Perspective. *The Singapore Economic Review* 5(1), 207, p. 207.
34. Buckley, R. P. (2008). *International Financial System: Policy and Regulation*. Kluwer Law International. p. 14.
35. Madura, J. (2012). *Financial Markets and Institutions*. South-Western Cengage Learning. 10th ed.
36. Alexander, K., Dhumale, R., & Eatwell, J. (2006). *Global Governance of Financial Systems: The International Regulation of Systemic Risk*: Oxford University Press. p. 34.
37. *Ibid*. p. 35.

agreements to enhance and maintain financial stability through efficient financial risk management (e.g., the Basel process, which will be discussed in the next chapter).

Recently, the G20 has been engaged in the complex task of developing a comprehensive analysis of the experiences its members have had with the globalization and de-regulatory processes. It took on its agenda to analyze the specific role of globalization in economic growth and on institution building in the financial sector. Recent events have proven that in order to fully profit from globalization, governments must undertake sound economic policies, implement appropriate supervision and regulation frameworks and consolidate robust institutions, including the development of social safety nets to protect the most vulnerable segments of society.[38] States used to compete for power as a means to wealth; they now compete for wealth as a means to power.[39] It would be therefore, relevant at this stage to look at the theoretical underpinnings of global regulatory philosophy at the turn of the century and how it influenced the institution-building processes in the financial market operations.

[1]   The WC (the Consensus)

The Consensus refers to a *set of economic policy reforms* postulated in 1989 by a former IMF advisor, John Williamson. These reform principles originally formulated to deal with the Latin American debt crisis were extended later on to other jurisdictions. The term *Washington* connoted an affirmation of the economic agencies of the US government, the IFIs (mostly based in Washington DC) and the Federal Reserve Board (FRB) and other policy think tanks. The Consensus envisioned an increased economic growth, reduced inflation, and, a viable balance of payments and equitable income distribution system. The consensus in simple terms can be summarized into:[40] (a) fiscal discipline: implying an operational deficit of less than 1% to 2% of GDP to be enforced; (b) deficits reduction: mainly through expenditure reduction or by redirecting spending, for example, from subsidies towards services those are *proper objects of government expenditure*, such as basic health and education; (c) broadened tax regime: sufficient to produce tax revenue required by the government; (d) market-based real interest rates; and, (e) competitive exchange rates: to foster an *outward orientation* and export growth.

The Consensus, formulated amongst the members of the IMF, the WB and the US Treasury pronounced three main tenets of macro-stability, liberalization (that implied low tariffs and deregulation) and privatization. This development philosophy was

---

38. G20. (2002). *Globalization: The Role of Institution Building in the Financial Sector*. Mexico Summit. Available at http://www.g20.utoronto.ca/docs/institutionbuilding-report.pdf last accessed Jul. 30, 2017.
39. Braithwaite, J., & Drahos, P., *Global Business Regulation*, Cambridge University Press, 2000. p. 475.
40. *See*, Williamson, *supra* n. 20 and, Williamson, J., (2004). The Strange History of the Washington Consensus. *Journal of Post Keynesian Economics, 27*(2), pp. 195-206. *See*, for current analysis, Williamson, J., (January 2014). The Washington Consensus as Policy Prescription for Development. A lecture in the series, *Practitioners of Development*, delivered at the World Bank. Available at https://piie.com/publications/papers/williamson0204.pdf.

passed on to the debtor countries in Latin America, Asia and Africa through the means of conditionality[41] and by strongly encouraging governments to lift trade barriers and tariffs to outside investment and foreign currency transactions to achieve full expansion.[42] Thus, market capitalism and deregulation of the international financial markets became prevalent economic philosophy under the WC. The capital market liberalization was the key precept of the Consensus from the beginning but the nature of the capital flows to the global south underwent a dramatic shift in early 1990s on account of ongoing global deregulation and counter-recessionary policies followed by the Organization for Economic Cooperation and Development (OECD) countries. The financial inflows to emerging economies became more short-term and speculative in nature. Interestingly, just before the Asian crisis erupted, the Interim Committee of the IMF was deliberating to modify IMF's Charter to impose upon its members a legal obligation to further open up capital accounts.

The WC philosophy survived well beyond the 1980s, most notably in the structural adjustment policies applied by the IMF and WB in Asia and in Latin America. But after two decades of application, the external debt crisis that the WC was supposed to resolve had only grown deeper. Only the East Asians were able to significantly reduce poverty and could maintain higher growth during that time. It is to be noted that this was precisely the region that refused to follow the Consensus policies.[43] By early 2000s, the failure of the Consensus policies was widely acknowledged. The Consensus also attracted criticism for its *boiler-plate* approach to development policy and practice of *conditionality,* which helped diffuse the consensus around the world but terribly ignored national peculiarities in its haste to apply universalistic recipes.[44] Later, we had what became to be known as *Augmented WC* by Dani Rodrik,[45] which in addition to the items given by Williamsons adds, corporate governance, anti-corruption, flexible labor markets, WTO agreements, financial codes and standards, *prudent* capital-account opening, non-intermediate exchange rate regimes, independent central banks/inflation targeting, social safety nets, and, targeted poverty reduction in the expanded version of the Consensus.

---

41. Conditionality is a policy condition imposed by the IMF/WB in exchange for its loans. In political economy terminology, it is the use of conditions attached to the provision of benefits such as a loan, debt relief or bilateral aid. Conditionality is typically employed by the IMF or a donor country with respect to loans, debt relief and financial aid. It may involve relatively uncontroversial requirements to enhance effectiveness, such as anti-corruption measures, but they may involve highly controversial clauses like austerity or the privatization of key public services, which has traditionally provoked strong political opposition in the recipient country, recently for example in the case of Greece.
42. Soederberg, S. (2001). The Emperor's New Suit: The New International Financial Architecture as a Reinvention of the Washington Consensus. *Global Governance, 7,* 453-467. p. 454.
43. Williamson, J. (2002). What Washington Means by Policy Reform. *Peterson Institute for International Economics.* Retrieved from http://www.iie.com/publications/papers/paper.cfm?researchid=486.
44. Babb, S. (2012). The Washington Consensus as Transnational Policy Paradigm: Its Origins, Trajectory and Likely Successor. *Review of International Political Economy, 20*(2), 268-297, p. 5.
45. *See* for example, Rodrik on the Augmented Washington Consensus, (Jan. 27, 2006). New Economist. Available at http://neweconomist.blogs.com/new_economist/2006/01/rodrik_on_the_a.html last accessed, Jul. 21, 2017.

[2] The NIFA

A risk-based international standards conception in the 1990s came out as a compromise between financial market stability and reregulation.[46] Apparently, it originated to address the growing instability in EMEs due to high capital flows yet it reserved most of the features of its predecessor, more notably it kept intact the free flow of capital. Critics called it an instrument to perpetuate US political hegemony in the geography of global financial reform[47] since the US vehemently opposed any ideas for universal capital controls.

Primarily driven by the G7/8 Leaders and Finance Ministers, NIFA-I[48] remained largely concerned with crisis prevention and financial stability through enhanced surveillance, transparency, information sharing and rigorous formulation and adoption of international standard. In this context in 1999 following initiatives took off: (i) establishment of the FSF as an umbrella oversight-coordination network of the international financial standard-setters by the G7/8 members, (ii) the creation of joint FSAP and the Reports on the Observance of Standards and Codes (ROSC) program by the WB/IMF respectively at the encouragement of the G7, (iii) the G7's continuing efforts to effect IMF reforms and (iv) establishing a broader body of the G20 Finance Ministers, which ultimately provided the foundations for NIFA-II in 2008.[49]

The international financial standard-setting or the global financial governance (GFG) therefore signifies a broad fabric of rules and procedures by which internationally active financial institutions have been governed. The architectural elements of the *governance concept* refer to public mechanisms by which authoritative decisions about these rules and procedures are adopted.[50] In the section below we look at the functional as well as procedural elements of this global governance architecture.

§3.02 THE PILLARS OF IFRA

The regulatory institutions framework for the international financial markets during the first decade of the twenty-first century remained loosely bonded with a lack of coherence and political legitimacy.[51] The G10[52] resorted to an informal and secretive decision-making mechanism, which remained successful until its decisions were applicable to the G10 members only. The WB not only recognized G10 standards but

---

46. See, for NIFA, Norton, J. J. (2010). NIFA-II or Bretton Woods-II: The G20 (Leaders) Summit Process on Managing Global Financial Markets and the World Economy – quo Vadis. *Journal of Banking Regulation*, 11(4), 261-301. Retrieved from http://dx.doi.org/10.1057/jbr.2010.17.
47. Armijo, L. E. (2001). The Political Geography of the World Financial Reforms: Who Wants What and Why? *Global Governance*, 7, 379-396. p. 392.
48. More commonly known as NIFA-I, see for details amongst others, Soederberg, S. (2005). *The Politics of the New International Financial Architecture*. Zed Books.
49. Norton, *supra* n. 46.
50. Germain, R., (2001). Global Financial Governance and the Problem of Inclusion. *Global Governance*. p. 411.
51. Alexander, et al. *supra* n. 36, p. 23.
52. Belgium, Canada, France, Germany, Italy, Japan, Luxembourg, Netherlands, United Kingdom, United States, Sweden, Spain and Switzerland (in 1974, last three were not members).

Chapter 3: IFL and the Development of Its Regulatory Architecture   §3.02[A]

also appended it with the IMF conditionality and surveillance programs. The most significant institutions established after the Second World War to ensure broader systemic stability included the Bretton Woods institutions in 1944 and, the BIS[53] – with its various committees: the Basel Committee on Banking supervision (BCBS)[54] – which gave Basel Capital Accords I,[55] the Basel Capital Accord II (2003) and Basel III[56] – International Organization of Securities Commissions (IOSCO) for securities regulation, IAIS for insurance and IASB for global accounting standards. In the post-GFC phase, the work was carried out by the FSB in collaboration with G20 and Basel Committees. The section below is looking at structural, procedural and functional aspects of these various institutions.

[A]   The BIS

The BIS[57] was the first major international economic organization established in 1930 by a few Member States and private shareholders primarily to help manage war reparation payments from the German government to the allied powers as per the Treaty of Versailles 1919.[58] The second important function it meant to perform was to hold gold reserves of the major powers of that time. After the War, it started facilitating cross-border currency payments across Europe. Interestingly, it continued to play an important role after the breakdown of the Bretton Woods and in particular during the transition to eventually become the meeting place for technical discussions on central bank cooperation and financial stability. As its customers are central banks and international organizations (IOs), the BIS do not accept deposits from or provides financial services to private individuals or corporate entities.

The BIS is the world's oldest IFI and remains the principal center for international central bank cooperation. It occupies a very critical position vis-à-vis providing a blueprint for the development of any global central bank, an international financial regulatory body or even for a multilateral cooperation mechanism for international monetary cooperation to assess historical development of the BIS and gradual transformation of its role in order to provide a perspective on the recent efforts at

---

53. The BIS established on May 17, 1930 in Basel, Switzerland comprising of members from central banks and IOs. Originally, it was made trustee to receive reparation payments from Germany but soon it shifted its focus. The Bank used to provide emergency and crisis support to central banks (1930s to 1990s) now coordinates cooperation among central banks and conducts economic analysis and research.
54. BCBS was established in 1974 by the G10 Central Bank Governors after the collapse of Bankhaus Herstatt of Germany and Franklin National Bank of the US to promote monetary and financial stability.
55. Basel Accord I (1988) the members: Belgium, Canada, France, Germany, Italy, Luxembourg, the Netherlands, the UK and the US central banks.
56. In 2010, Basel III proposals have been forwarded by BCBS for discussion and adoption by 2014, while implementation begins 2019, accessible at http://www.bis.org/press/p100912.pdf.
57. Most of the dates and figures in this section are from the BIS website, *see*, tabs: history/activities; at https://www.bis.org/about/index.htm and the report at 75, *see*, https://www.bis.org/about/thisisthebiz.pdf.
58. WWI reparations: Belgium, France, Germany, Japan, UK, Switzerland (and the US via JP Morgan).

harmonizing global regulatory reforms. The BIS's most important decision-making bodies include General Meeting of member central banks, Board of Directors, and, a General Manager, assisted by the Executive Committee. The BIS was established in the context of the Young Plan (1930), which dealt with the issue of reparation payments imposed on Germany under the Treaty of Versailles following the First World War. The new bank was established to perform functions of: collection, administration and distribution of the annuities payable as reparations. The BIS was to act as a trustee for the Dawes and Young Loans and to promote central bank cooperation. The reparations function was finished in almost no time and it then concentrated entirely on the coordination of monetary and financial stability. Under this new role, it was functioning as the bank to central banks and IOs.

[1] The Second World War: Of Justifying Continued Existence

With the outbreak of the War in 1939, it was no longer possible for representatives of belligerent countries to attend the BIS meetings even in a neutral country like Switzerland. To provide for the BIS's survival given its existence was indispensable in the post-War reconstruction of the monetary order, the Board decided to suspend all Board meetings until the end of the War. It adopted a neutrality declaration. Throughout the war, the BIS continued to collect interest payments due by Germany in respect of the investments the BIS had made in the German economy in 1930/1931. Investigations after the War revealed that the German Reichs Bank had used large quantities of gold stolen from central banks in the occupied territories to make wartime payments to a number of institutions including the Swiss National Bank and the BIS. During the war, the BIS received by way of German interest payments, 3.7 tons of such gold, which had been taken from the central banks of Belgium and the Netherlands.[59] The BIS cooperated fully with the post-war investigations and returned all this gold to those countries by 1948.

[2] The Post-War Period: Of Building Strengths

The Bretton Woods Agreement of 1944 called for abolition of the BIS. This was partly because of a widespread suspicion about the BIS' wartime activities and partly because apparently there was little scope for the BIS to play a useful role within the Bretton Woods framework. However, in response to these calls, the central banks, particularly European came out strongly in favor of keeping the institution intact – it was, after all, *their institution*.

---

59. *See*, Foundation and Crisis (1930-1939), BIS website http://www.bis.org/about/history_1 foundation.htm.

[3] The Bretton Woods Era: Of Faltering Convertibility and Strengthening Cooperation

Central bank cooperation at the BIS between 1940s and early 1970s was dominated by the Bretton Woods system based on freely convertible currencies at fixed but adjustable exchange rates. In the 1950s, the BIS played an important technical role in assisting European countries in making their currencies fully convertible. It was successful to an extent that by the end of 1958, full convertibility was restored across Europe and the EPU was rolled back.

After 1958, the Bretton Woods system of freely convertible currencies at fixed exchange rates was fully operational. The BIS began to play an important part in coordinating crisis management among central banks whenever monetary, commodity or other imbalances threatened to undermine the IMS. These efforts (in maintaining gold pool, swaps network, sterling support arrangements) were coordinated at the BIS in the context of the newly established G10, which abetted in spinning out the lifespan of the Bretton Woods system during a period of otherwise unprecedented economic growth (i.e., during the *silver fifties and the golden sixties*) but could not prevent its eventual breakdown. By the early 1970s the value of the dollar was being determined virtually by the markets, marking the end of the Bretton Woods system, and triggering an era of floating currency system had already begun. Despite this lack of enduring success, the prized endowment was the sustained presence of the Bretton Woods system through those years, which institutionalized cooperation among central banks. Much of this took place in the informal and discreet environment of the BIS, enhancing its role as a forum for central bank cooperation.

Back in 1964, the Committee of Governors of the EEC began to meet regularly at the BIS to discuss integration of monetary policy at EEC level. In the early 1970s, when the Bretton Woods system was falling off, the Committee of Governors agreed to put limits on exchange rate fluctuations between participating European currencies. This was hailed as a first step towards closer integration (the so-called *Snake mechanism*).[60] A European Monetary Cooperation Fund was set up in 1973 to support the operation of the *Snake mechanism* and the BIS was appointed an agent for it. Over time, the Committee of EEC Central Bank Governors, supported by the BIS Secretariat, developed into a cohesive body for policy exchange and coordination. In 1988-1989 some of its members served in personal capacity on the Delors Committee, which issued a report in 1989 setting out a model for an independent central bank committed to price stability. Their recommendations decisively influenced the framework for European EMU set out in the Maastricht Treaty of 1992. The European Monetary Institute (EMI) – the precursor of the ECB – was located at the BIS until it moved to Frankfurt in 1994. Currently, the BIS is housing the FSB and is providing logistics and other legal support to augment FSB's role, and functioning. This ability to transform its role according to the issues and needs of time gave an inherently organic character to the BIS.

---

60. *See* Ch. 5 for the development of the EU integrated market.

[4] The BIS, Banking Supervision and Financial Stability

The collapse of the Bankhaus Herstatt in 1974 in Germany and of the Franklin National Bank in the US prompted the G10 countries to pledge various informal initiatives including the 1974 landmark event when the BCBS was established. It was to devise regulations and best practices for monetary and financial matters through an informal but consensus-based approach. It was also to act as trustee in regard to international financial settlements entrusted to it under agreements by its members. The decisions were to be implemented through voluntary adoption and were kept legally nonbinding.

In 1988, the Committee issued the Basel Capital Accord to introduce 'Credit Risk' measurement framework for internationally active banks, which later on, became a globally accepted standard. Besides the BCBS, other BIS-based committees included the CGFS (since 1971), the CPSS (since 1990), and the Markets Committee (since 1964). The sub-committees of Basel Committee are Standards Implementation, Policy Development, Accounting Taskforce and the Basel Consultative Group. In 1999, the FSI was created to promote dissemination of the work undertaken by the supervisory community, and to provide practical training for financial sector supervisors worldwide.

[5] The Changing Role of the BIS

Since 1930, central bank cooperation has taken place at Basel through regular meetings of the Central Bank Governors, experts and other agencies. In support of this cooperation, the BIS developed its own research in financial and monetary economics and make an important contribution to the collection, compilation and dissemination of economic and financial statistics.

In the 1970s and 1980s, the focus was on managing cross-border capital flows. The disruption came in capital flows following the oil crises and the international debt crisis. The 1970s crisis brought the issue of regulatory supervision of internationally active banks to the fore, resulting in the *1988 Basel Capital Accord* and its *Basel II revision* of 2001-2006. The issue of financial stability in the wake of economic integration and globalization, as highlighted by the 1997 Asian crisis received a lot of attention. The crisis in 2008 has brought forward Basel III (*see*, Chapter 4) along with a massive revamp of the whole system (*see*, Chapters 5 and 6).

The BIS has played a critical role in housing the FSF and later helping it transform into the FSB. The role and position of both of these bodies is discussed in the next section under the FSB. The BIS has been sensitive to the shared criticisms levied on the regulatory institutions for being devoid of legitimacy due to poor representation from the emerging markets and the developing world.[61] In response to the criticism and

---

61. Sixty central banks represent and have voting rights at the BIS: Algeria, Argentina, Australia, Austria, Belgium, Bosnia and Herzegovina, Brazil, Bulgaria, Canada, Chile, China, Colombia, Croatia, the Czech Republic, Denmark, Estonia, Finland, France, Germany, Greece, Hong Kong SAR, Hungary, Iceland, India, Indonesia, Ireland, Israel, Italy, Japan, Korea, Latvia, Lithuania, Luxembourg, the Republic of Macedonia, Malaysia, Mexico, the Netherlands, New Zealand,

general inclusive reforms, it expanded its central bank membership in 2006 and also included on its Board of Directors, bank governors from Mexico and China.[62]

[B] Securities Regulation

Financial liberalization during the late twentieth century brought a fusion of functions and activities between the banking and nonbanking sector. Some scholars claim that this fusion of activities between the two sectors dates back to the great depression (1929-1933) in the US when more than 9000 banks were closed, and another almost 2000 had to merge.[63] Gradually, various banks commenced operations and started dealing in securities.[64] However, it bourgeoned after the GSA was done away and universal banking model started flourishing.

More recently, most of the financial markets, banks and nonbanking financial institutions including securities, finance and insurance companies have joined the intermediation process. This changed not only the traditional concepts of risk assessment, risk management and risk measurement but also the variables employed by the industry for assessment and managing those risks giving rise to the debate between institutional regulation and functional regulation.

The traditionalists viewed the securities industry more resilient than the banking sector because of the funding structure, which is more liquid and consisted of tradable assets with higher level of collateralization. Also, in case of default, there would be but limited losses hence the negative externality to the financial sector was confined with leaving little need for an LoLR. Therefore, prudential regulation for the security industry only involved making rules for the conduct of the business e.g., anti-fraud or consumer protections standards and not for capital adequacy requirements or for the function of payment settlements.[65]

Norway, Peru, the Philippines, Poland, Portugal, Romania, Russia, Saudi Arabia, Serbia, Singapore, Slovakia, Slovenia, South Africa, Spain, Sweden, Switzerland, Thailand, Turkey, the United Arab Emirates, the UK the US and the ECB.
62. Agustín Carstens, was appointed chairman on Jan. 10, 2011. See, Griffith-Jones, S., & Young, K. (2009). *Institutional Incentives and Geopolitical Representation in Global Financial Governance: Explaining the Puzzle of Regulatory Forbearance before the Crisis*. At www.policydialogue.org.
63. Dale, R. (1992), *International Banking Deregulation: The Great Banking Experiment*. Blackwell. See also, Herring, R. J., (1993). International Banking Deregulation: The Great Banking Experiment. *The Journal of Finance*, 48(4), pp. 1553-1556. Retrieved from http://www.jstor.org/stable/2329052.
64. Some absolve banks fully, see, Benston, G. (1990). *The Separation of Commercial and Investment Banking: The Glass-Steagall Act Revisited and Reconsidered*. Oxford University Press. Benston concludes that the evidence from the pre-Glass-Steagall period is totally inconsistent with the belief that banks' securities activities or investments caused them to fail or caused the financial system to collapse. See also, White, E. N. (1983). *The Regulation and Reform of the American Banking System, 1900-1929*. Princeton University Press., and Kroszner and Rajan (1994) supports Benston's view that the Glass-Steagall Act was justified on the public interest argument, which does not hold true as the evidence testifies, see, Is the Glass-Steagall Act Justified? A Study of the U.S. Experience with Universal Banking before 1933. American Economic Review, 1994, vol. 84 (4), 810-832.
65. Alexander et al. *Supra* n. 36 p. 56.

However, this traditional view underwent a paradigm shift as liberalization swept its way in the late 1980s, fading away the *wall of separation* in the US and Japan.[66] The US stock market crash in 1987 followed by the Russian debt default in 1998 and the LTCM collapse triggered enhanced securities regulation precisely because of the discovery of its close association to systemic risk. The underlying threat emanated from derivative market as big securities firms were taking large exposures in portfolios of derivative markets in which the underlying assets had significant maturity mismatches with the firm's liabilities. This could very much bring in systemic implication in case of a sell-off or a refusal by wholesale investors to provide more capital. This happened in the case of Barings Bank despite the fact that the Barings' portfolio of derivatives contained instruments with uniform or standard terms only.[67] This systemic risk had latent potential for contagion because trading books of many banks had substantial exposure to other securities firms through repurchase and foreign exchange markets. In turn, many of the investment banks were members of clearing and settlement – thus linking the risk in securities to the banking institutions, and as Alexander called it, the *Herstatt risk*.[68] In this context, IOSCO was set up in 1983[69] to address systemic risk in securities market. IOSCO is the most broadly representative forum that serves to formulate regulatory standards for more than 95% of the global securities markets and it regulates more than 100 jurisdictions.[70] And, precisely because of this, it is relevant to explore the structure and function of IOSCO for any study involving enforcement of IFL.

---

66. Lowenfeld, A. F. (2008). *International Economic Law*. Oxford University Press.
67. Ibid.
68. Alexander et al. *supra* n. 36.
69. Eleven securities regulatory agencies from North and South America changed this organization from an inter-American regional association (1974) to a global body in April 1983 at a meeting in Quito, Ecuador.
70. Note that the membership to the Technical Committee, which is most influential, is restricted to the OECD only. Other Signatories include: Albania, Alberta, Australia, Austria, Bahrain, Belgium, Bermuda, Brazil, British Columbia, British Virgin Islands, Bulgaria, Cayman Islands, China, Croatia, Cyprus, Czech Republic, Denmark, Dubai, Finland, France, Germany, Greece, Guernsey, Hong Kong, Hungary, India, Isle of Man, Israel, Italy, Japan, Jersey, Jordan, Kenya, Lithuania, Luxembourg, Malaysia, Malta, Mexico, Montenegro, Morocco, Netherlands, New Zealand, Nigeria, Norway, Ontario, Poland, Portugal, Québec, Romania, Serbia, Singapore, Slovak Republic, Slovenia, South Africa, Spain, Sri Lanka, Switzerland, Thailand, Tunisia, Turkey, United Kingdom, United States, West African Monetary Union, Tunisia. And pending signatories include: Algeria, Argentina, Bahamas, Bangladesh, Barbados, Bosnia and Herzegovina, Chile, Colombia, Costa Rica, Dominican Republic, Egypt, El Salvador, Estonia, Macedonia, Ghana, Gibraltar, Indonesia, Ireland, Jamaica, Kazakhstan, Korea, Labuan, Malawi, Mongolia, Pakistan, Panama, Papua New Guinea, Peru, Philippines, Armenia, Russia, Oman, Sweden, Chinese Taipei, Tanzania, Trinidad and Tobago, Uganda, Uruguay.

Chapter 3: IFL and the Development of Its Regulatory Architecture §3.02[B]

[1]   International Organization of Securities Commissions (IOSCO)

Originally established as an informal nonprofit organization, IOSCO's objectives included[71] protecting investors (including customers of financial services); ensuring that markets are fair, efficient and transparent; and, reducing systemic risk.[72]

The Preamble to IOSCO's By-Laws states that securities authorities resolve to: (a) cooperate in developing, implementing and promoting adherence to internationally recognized and consistent standards of regulation, oversight and enforcement in order to protect investors and to maintain fair, efficient and transparent market and to address systemic risks; (b) enhance investor protection and promote investor confidence in the integrity of securities market, through strengthened information exchange and cooperation in enforcement against misconduct and in supervision of markets and market intermediaries; and, (c) exchange information at both global and regional levels on their respective experiences in order to assist the development of markets, strengthen market infrastructure and implement appropriate regulation.[73]

IOSCO By-Laws clearly manifest international dimension of coordination in order to develop market regulations. Even the first resolution passed in 1986 underscored need for international coordination and domestic protection of each nation for any fraudulent securities transactions.[74]

Its ordinary members exercise one vote each at the general meetings and on the respective committees they serve. Associate members do not have right to vote and nor they represent on the committees except for the President's Committee. The affiliate members are self-regulatory organizations (SROs) and neither have the right to vote nor can they represent or serve on any of the important committees.[75]

IOSCO's Executive Committee meets periodically and is constituted of 19 agency representatives elected for two years. It includes the Chairmen of the Technical[76] and Emerging Market committees, one ordinary member from each of IOSCO's regional committees and nine ordinary members elected by the President's Committee, and is subject to the bylaws of the organization. The Executive Committee has membership from only the most developed securities markets and has emerged as the most

---

71. Based on the three objectives of securities regulation, the IOSCO issued thirty-eight Principles governing securities regulation, in June 2010, available at http://www.iosco.org/library/pubdocs/pdf/IOSCOPD323.pdf.
72. *See*, IOSCO. (May 2003). Objectives and Principles of Securities Regulation: IOSCO available at http://www.iosco.org/library/pubdocs/pdf/IOSCOPD154.pdf.
73. IOSCO. (September 2011). Methodology: For Assessing Implementation of IOSCO Objectives and Principles of Securities Regulation: The IOSCO; Basel, Switzerland. p. 9 www.iosco.org IOSCO has adopted various resolutions and memorandums in the past to a variety of issues concerning international regulation of securities markets. For example, in 1986, it adopted a resolution concerning Mutual assistance for reciprocal exchange of information. IOSCO. (1986). A Resolution Concerning Mutual Assistance *Rio Declaration*: IOSCO. In 1991, a Memoranda of Understanding (MOU) was signed containing principles for information exchange and disclosure requirements between regulators.
74. IOSCO (1986), available at http://www.iosco.org/library/resolutions/pdf/IOSCORES1.pdf
75. The Membership as at Jan. 5, 2012: Ordinary: 115; Associate: 11; Affiliate: 75.
76. Established on 1987 with fifteen members: Australia, Brazil, Canada (Ontario, Quebec), China, France, Germany, Hong Kong, India, Italy, Japan, Mexico, Netherlands, Spain, Switzerland, the UK and the US.

influential forum to propose standards. The Technical Committee comprises of the G10 regulators proposes key standards that affect global securities markets. Although, all the members have the opportunity to comment on and suggest changes to all the proposals forwarded by the Technical Committee that are passed on from the Emerging Markets Committee to the Executive Committee and finally to the President's Committee, but practically, it is the Technical Committee's membership (only limited to OECD countries) that shapes all the issues and play a principal role in the formulation of standards and exerts a *disproportionate influence* over the development of securities regulations. The Technical Committee expanded its membership first time in 2009 to include China, Brazil and India as the only developing countries other than Mexico in its membership. Furthermore, IOSCO has four Regional Standing Committees, namely: the Africa/Middle-East Regional Committee, the Asia-Pacific Regional Committee, the European Regional Committee and the Inter-American Regional Committee to discuss specific regional problems of the members of the constituting organizations.[77]

This exclusive decision-making mechanism at IOSCO has attracted major criticism. When IOSCO was established, it aimed primarily for the G10 countries having large sophisticated and developed financial markets. Emerging markets and regions other than North America and Central Europe were passive participants. The decision-making process also lacked transparency as the meetings were not open to even those IOSCO members not on a particular committee allowing them access in addition to outside observers. Thus, the influence exerted by the Technical Committee within IOSCO was under heavy criticism on grounds of legitimacy and accountability.[78]

In one area, however, IOSCO has developed a particularly innovative approach to implementation, monitoring and enforcement on the basis of soft-law mechanisms modeled on self-regulatory systems: the IOSCO Multilateral Memorandum of Understanding (MMoU). As a self-regulatory system, the IOSCO MMoU contains three main levels: implementation of pre-established standards via pre-commitment, monitoring via peer review and enforcement.

At the first level, the MMoU contains a range of specific obligations to which signatories both agree and commit to, having the authority and legal backing necessary for compliance and performance of obligations. Signature is open to securities regulators but only on the basis of an evaluation by IOSCO and the existing signatories that the potential signatory meets the necessary requirements.[79] Potential signatories thus have to apply for permission to join (as in a traditional SRO) and must be vetted by the

---

77. IOSCO website, for example for details on African Regional Committee, *see*, https://www.iosco.org/about/?subsection = display_committee&cmtid = 7.
78. *See* Ch. 6 for details on legitimacy issue.
79. Current signatories are: Australia, Bahrain, Belgium, Bermuda, the British Virgin Islands, Canada (Alberta, British Columbia, Quebec, Ontario), China, the Czech Republic, Denmark, Dubai, Finland, France, Germany, Greece, Hong Kong, Hungary, India, the Isle of Man, Israel, Italy, Japan, Jersey, Jordan, Lithuania, Luxembourg, Malaysia, Malta, Mexico, Morocco, the Netherlands, New Zealand, Nigeria, Norway, Poland, Portugal, Romania, Singapore, the Slovak Republic, South Africa, Spain, Sri Lanka, Thailand, Turkey, the United Kingdom and the United States.

organization and its existing membership for suitability and compliance.[80] As a second level, peer review is undertaken in the context of actual implementation, with the failure to perform according to obligations being subject to investigation and potential enforcement (up to and including expulsion, once again, similar to an SRO) by the organization. While certain problems have emerged with jurisdictions and noncompliance, the IOSCO MMoU nonetheless provides an interesting example of a possible soft-law- based self-regulatory model for IFL.

[C] International Association of Insurance Supervisors

Insurance market poses a special challenge to regulators due to asymmetry of information between the purchaser and the seller of insurance products. These asymmetries are not limited to spectrum of risk lying with the buyer rather encompass the limited liability structure of the insurance companies, which makes them susceptible to excessive risk taking without paying due attention to risk management measures. Information asymmetries cause a moral hazard problem that undermines the capacity of the insurance company to properly calculate and hedge underlying risks.[81] Another inherent risk in insurance industry is the investment structure of the insurance companies, which is usually excessively leveraged out.

Adding to the inherently susceptible structure of the investment companies is the nature of investment businesses itself apart from other *externalities*. Regulatory arbitrage creates opportunities for some but it leads to systemic threat at the same time. This in combination with the above two factors encourage insurance companies to pick riskier investment policies. This necessitated adoption of standardized procedures and transparent regulatory practices for insurance sector through increased information exchange and better standardization, which can discourage regulatory arbitrage on the one hand while confining the financial risk on the other.

The increasing interconnectedness of financial markets amplified the systemic risk, which made regulators and policy makers to design a New International Economic Order (NIEO). It was in that background when Hans Tietmeyer[82] suggested for the establishment of the FSF in his famous proposals. Tietmeyer proposals stated that the primary role of the IAIS should be of a supervisory rule-setting body and that there should be intensified cooperation and coordination with national authorities, international financial organizations charged with the function of monitoring and fostering the implementation of standards.[83] The IFRA is in want of a single set of rules or standards and a central body to oversee consequent adoption and implementation of such standards. IAIS was established in 1994 as a private nonprofit organization to help exchange views on regulatory practices in the insurance industry. IAIS, though initially

---

80. Pending signatories include: Austria, Bulgaria, Chile, Costa Rica, Cyprus, El Salvador, Ghana, Indonesia, Panama, Peru, Philippines, Russia, South Korea, Switzerland, Taiwan and Tunisia.
81. Alexander et al. *supra* n. 36.
82. *See*, Tietmeyer, H. (Feb. 11, 1999). Report on the International Co-operation and Co-ordination in the Area of Financial Market Supervision and Surveillance, Speech Retrieved from http://www.financialstabilityboard.org/wp-content/uploads/r_9902.pdf?page_moved=1.
83. Alexander et al. *supra* n. 36 p. 62.

created to coordinate exchange of information[84] across jurisdictions only but soon it became an important IFI and assumed functions to formulate minimum regulatory standards and adequate best practices for adoption by national regulators and global supervisors.[85]

[1] Organizational Structure of IAIS and Nature of Insurance Markets

IAIS' membership, unlike Basel Committee and IOSCO, expanded quickly. It included national regulators and supervisors from more than 160 jurisdictions and another 70 plus observers from the insurance and professional sectors. IAIS, like IOSCO, conducts an Annual General Meeting where major decisions are taken and the proposed principles and standards are approved for adoption. All members of IAIS are entitled to vote – and voting is one member, one vote except the annual budget approval, amendments to bylaws, relocation of the secretariat and election of the Executive Committee where one country, one vote practice is adopted – and to attend the annual session (Unlike IOSCO where all members do not have voting rights).Composed of 15 members, the committee is elected at the Annual General Meeting for two years representing the world. The IAIS operates in secret and its deliberations are not usually made public unless with two-third votes of the members at a General Meeting. It gets financed through the membership fees. The Association's work is conducted through an elaborate committee system comprising of the Technical Committee, the Budget Committee and the Emerging Markets Committee.

The Technical Committee is further composed of various technical working groups and this committee is responsible to develop standards on all relevant issues. Another significant difference in the working of IAIS from IOSCO is that a private person including law firms, insurance firms or even some government bodies or anyone nominated by the Executive Committee having interest in insurance can be an IAIS member as an observer. However, the observer members neither have voting rights nor they can serve on the Executive Committee.

[2] The IAIS Standards

IAIS much like BCBS and IOSCO do not impose binding legal obligations on its member countries. It is operated under a set of bylaws, which can be amended by majority vote.[86] However, in comparison to IOSCO and Basel Committee, IAIS is *more accountable* to its members and its standards enjoy more legitimacy than the other two sister organization owing to the broad representation of all developed and developing

---

84. IAIS. (1997). Memorandum of Understanding on Mutual Assistance and the Exchange of Information between the Authority/Jurisdiction and the Authority/Jurisdiction. *Report from the IAIS Exchange of Information Sub Committee Insurance Supervisory Principles*, approved on Sep. 3, 1997.
85. IAIS. (February 2007). IAIS Multilateral Memorandum of Understanding on Cooperation and Information Exchange (IAIS MMoU).
86. IAIS. (2010). By-Laws: (2010 edition): International Association of Insurance Supervisors. http://www.iaisweb.org/By-laws-45.

Chapter 3: IFL and the Development of Its Regulatory Architecture §3.02[C]

countries to its membership. The one member, one vote principle and the openness of its proceedings of the working groups provide an equal opportunity to all the members to contribute significantly in standard formulation processes. Even the observers can suggest revisions to the proposals before these are submitted to the Technical Committee, which approves the proposals before sending to the Executive Committee for its final endorsement. Here, the standard formulation process provides an opportunity to all the regulators from developed and emerging economy countries through the dialogue process, which helps in better implementation and adoption of these standards in their respective jurisdictions.

The first supervisory principles by the IAIS were issued in 1997 and were revised in 2000 after a criticism from the IMF and the WB on account of providing an inadequate framework of insurance regulation and supervision for most of the countries.[87] The next sets of standards known as the Insurance Core Principles (ICP) were immediately incorporated by the IMF and the WB as reference points in their FSAP. However, these ICPs underwent a comprehensive study as the WB/IMF surveillance revealed major omissions and weaknesses. After substantial changes and revisions and seeking feedback from both developing and developed countries, 28 ICPs for a comprehensive supervision of insurance framework were reissued in 2003.[88]

The revised ICPs brought three important changes: it delineated solvency limits, capital adequacy standards and regulation of reinsurance companies. Insurers that are inadequately capitalized can threaten financial and systemic stability. Solvency limits and capital adequacy requirements for insurance companies are not as determinable as in the case of banking businesses because major risks lay on both sides of the balance sheet i.e., on the assets and the liabilities. Capital adequacy requirements for insurance companies only form a part of the solvency regimes and there is no internationally agreed upon minimum standards to assess capital adequacy requirements and solvency limits of the insurance firms. There is a huge mismatch in respective maturities of assets and liabilities. Unlike the banking sector, the assets side of the balance sheet of insurance companies is shorter while its liabilities are uncertain and disproportionate to the assets due to information asymmetries. There are different solvency requirements under various jurisdictions, for instance, the US follows risk-based approach, which is different from solvency margins being taken in Japan, while the EU follows solvency ratios, which are again different from both the US and Japan. This difference in minimum requirements, however, breeds grounds for regulatory arbitrage in the case of reinsurance, which makes financial markets more susceptible to

---

87. These principles were first approved in September 1997, were amended in December 1999 after incorporating feedback from IMF and WB. These were extended to insurance business conducted on a services basis without any foreign establishment. These aimed to improve the supervision of internationally active insurance companies, stating that all insurance establishments should be subject to effective supervision, that authorization involving cross-border activities should be subject to consultation between the relevant supervisors. See, IAIS. (December 1999). Principles Applicable to the Supervision of International Insurers and Insurance Groups and their Cross-border Business Operations (Insurance Concordat): Revised from 1997 Principles: International Association of Insurance Supervisors.
88. IAIS. (October 2003). Insurance Core Principles and Methodology: IAIS.

risk. Therefore, IAIS standard-setting development is organic so to respond to such differences and new developments.[89]

The IAIS has been working together with IOSCO and Basel Committee to bring convergence in the regulatory standards for the global financial markets (the Joint Forum).[90] The IAIS is also coordinating its efforts with other forums including the EC, the WB, the IMF, the FSB and G20 committees.[91] In 2001 multidisciplinary working group was established to assess the feasibility of public disclosures. IAIS supports the three-pillar approach under the Basel regulations and it works under common frameworks for solvency requirements.[92]

[D]   Reinsurance

As the credit-risk transfer market is expanding so are its implications for systemic financial stability.[93] The requirements for supervision of reinsurers are different from direct insurers (in terms of liquidity, investments, corporate governance and for exchange of information), the IAIS has issued separate standards for supervision of reinsurers in October 2003.[94] The standards were based on two principles: home country control and evaluation of reinsurance cover.

For home country control, the IAIS adopted from the 2002 principles that all reinsurers should be subject to supervision and regulation from their home country authorities, and that each home country regulator should be evaluated and subject to some form of accreditation for its supervisory practices.[95] For the second principle, the IAIS set standards for evaluation of reinsurance cover and for reinsurance companies. Standard setting for reinsurance cover applies to the reinsurance cover of primary insurers and covers the policies and procedures that primary insurers should maintain and the supervisory approaches for assessing the adequacy of reinsurance cover.[96] The passing of the Dodd-Frank Act in the USA included the Non-admitted and Reinsurance Reform Act (NRRA), establishment of the FSOC and the Federal Insurance Office (FIO). Also, within the OECD continued development of the Global Insurance Statistics (GIS)

---

89. See the recent report on ICPs, IAIS. (October 2011). Insurance Core Principles: Standards, Guidance and Assessment Methodology.
90. See, for details IOSCO joint forum, section above.
91. See, for report on improving public disclosure practices of financial intermediaries. IAIS. (April 2001). Multidisciplinary Working Group on Enhanced Disclosure: Final Report to BCBS, CGFS, IAIS, and IOSCO.
92. See for common framework on solvency, where IAIS will closely consider developments within BIS, BCBS, IASB, the International Actuarial Association (IAA), the International Federation of Accountants (IFAC), the IMF, IOSCO, the Organization for Economic Cooperation and Development (OECD) and the World Bank. IAIS. (2005). A New Framework for Insurance Supervision: Towards a Common Structure and Common Standards for the Assessment of Insurer Solvency.
93. See for details, IAIS. (March 2003). IAIS Paper on Credit Risk Transfer between Insurance, Banking and Other Financial Sectors: Presented to Financial Stability Forum.
94. IAIS. (2002). Principles on Minimum Requirements for Supervision of Reinsurers.
95. Alexander., et al. *supra* n. 36.
96. In 2003 IAIS issued the supervisory standards for reinsurer first time.

project underscored the OECD's efforts towards expanding their monitoring tools and strengthening its insurance statistics framework.[97]

[E] The Joint Forum and Mutual Assistance

In 1996, Joint Forum[98] was created as a cross-sector cooperative group by the Basel Committee, IOSCO and IAIS.[99] The purpose for the creation of Joint Forum was to help facilitate exchange of information across these three interconnected sectors including the financial conglomerates. The joint forum is represented in equal number by all the three institutions and the members meet thrice a year.[100]

Issues of Common Interest to the Committees include: (a) risk assessment and management, internal controls and capital requirements; (b) the use of audit and actuarial functions in the supervision of regulated entities and corporate groups containing regulated entities; (c) corporate governance, including fit and proper tests; (d) outsourcing of functions and activities by regulated firms; (e) different definitions of banking, insurance and securities activities and the potential for regulatory arbitrage; and, (f) identifying the core common principles of banking, insurance and securities sectors articulating the differences as these arise.[101]

The September 11 terrorist attacks and the GFC constituted as the biggest events transforming most of the regulatory practices making them more responsive to integrated risk across all three areas of finance. G20 requested Joint Forum to identify key risk areas, which have not been covered fully under the existing regulatory framework and to make adequate recommendations accordingly. The Joint Forum highlighted five key areas in the report that may pose a systemic threat to the stability of the international financial architecture[102] and include: key regulatory differences across banking, insurance and securities sectors; supervision and regulation of financial groups; mortgage origination; hedge funds; and, credit-risk transfer products.

The 1999 IOSCO principles were updated and expanded in a 2009 report. Joint Forum Review of the Differentiated Nature and Scope of Financial Regulation (the DNSR Report)[103] recommended reviewing and updating the 1999 Principles. The DNSR Report was later on endorsed by the FSB also. This DNSR Report contained not only a review on the implementation of the original 1999 principles but also it took into

---

97. IAIS. (2010). Global Reinsurance Market Report (GRMR).
98. The Joint Forum was initially referred to as *The Joint Forum on Financial Conglomerates*. During 1999 its name was shortened to The Joint Forum in recognition of the fact that its new mandate went beyond issues related to financial conglomerates, but also extended to issues of common interest to all three sectors. *See* https://www.iosco.org/about/?subSection = joint _forum&subSection1 = history /.
99. IOSCO. (December 2011). Principles for the supervision of financial conglomerates: Consultative report: The Joint Forum: BCBS, IOSCO and IAIS; Basel, Switzerland.
100. Main Sub-groups include: Risk Assessment and Capital; Conglomerate Supervision; and, Customer Suitability.
101. IOSCO. (January 2010). Review of the Differentiated Nature and Scope of Financial Regulation – Key Issues and Recommendations, (IOSCO, BCBS and IAIS): Joint Forum. (The DNSR Report).
102. IOSCO. *Supra* n. 101.
103. *Ibid.*

account the lessons learnt from the 2008 crisis and it highlighted supervisory and regulatory gaps.

IOSCO has overall performed well particularly in mapping capital adequacy standards for the firms offering securities through value at risk model.[104] IOSCO recognized in a report published in 1989 that the regulatory capital for securities firms should be determined depending upon the type of activities a firm is involved in.[105] The Joint Forum has achieved far more success than its counterparts, BCBS and the Financial Action Task Force (FATF) in reaching an agreement on the usage of IAS for security offerings, despite the fact that both of those committees are far more popular than IOSCO. From the very outset, one of the IAIS's objectives was to enhance information exchange between relevant organizations. In this direction, it approved Recommendation Concerning Mutual Assistance, Cooperation and Sharing of Information (IAIS 1995), which outlined cooperative efforts for mutual information exchange. In this sense, it built upon the IAIS bylaws to cooperate. The recommendations were based on the mutual assistance and reciprocal basis and the signatories committed themselves to implement these recommendations. Later on, in 1997, these recommendations were incorporated into a model Memorandum of Understanding approved by the IAIS in 1997. The MOU and the revised ICPs have been significant contributions from IAIS underscoring its position as an international financial supervisor.[106]

[F] International Accounting Standards (IAS)

Financial products travel across jurisdictions, which necessitate convergence of accounting standards for fair treatment of the value of these products. One of the objectives of Basel II was to bring about this convergence in the application of these accounting standards. This was to be achieved by bringing together accounting, economic and regulatory capital through uniform standards. G20 reiterated its commitment to the development of a single set of accounting standards but despite these strong commitments by the Basel Committee and the G20, there are predominantly two sets of accounting standards: the IASB reporting standards called the International Financial Reporting standards (IFRS) and the US' Generally Accepted Accounting Principles (GAAP).

The recent financial crisis in 2008 has unfolded a critical role of the choice of accounting standards as well. Accordingly, market-based accounting for financial instruments (marked-to-market) was central in deteriorating the crisis, as financial institutions were forced to continuously revalue their assets where the market was constantly plummeting. This multiplied the solvency-threat manifold. However, other side of the argument says that financial assets can only be valued at current market

---

104. IOSCO. (May 1998). Methodologies for Determining Minimum Capital Standards for Internationally Active Securities Firms, which Permit the Use of Models under Prescribed Conditions: A Report by the Technical Committee of IOSCO.
105. IOSCO. (1989). Capital Adequacy Standards for Securities Firms: A Report of the Technical Committee of IOSCO.
106. IAIS. (2010). Joint Forum Press Release of Review of the Differentiated Nature and Scope of Financial Regulation: Key Issues and Recommendations; January 8: Joint Forum.

price and any alternative method applied may hide real financial condition of the company or that institution. Despite an agreement to have transparency, the difference on the choice of single set of standards remains unsettled.[107] The IFRS Foundation is a nonprofit organization, working in public interest through its trustees who are responsible to safeguard independence of the standard-setting processes. The trustees are accountable to a Monitoring Board comprising of public authorities. The IASB is the standard-setting body of the IFRS Foundation. The IFRS Interpretation Committee (formerly called IFRIC) consists of 14 voting members appointed by the trustees representing diverse countries and professional expertise. The mandate of the committee includes reviewing the contested accounting issues to give authoritative guidance on regular basis. For this purpose, the Interpretation Committee adopts an open, transparent and thorough process while working in close coordination with similar national committees. The IFRS Foundation was established with objectives to: (a) develop a single set of high quality, understandable, enforceable and globally accepted IFRSs through its standard-setting body, the IASB; (b) promote the use and rigorous application of those standards; (c) take account of financial reporting needs of emerging economies and SMEs; and, (d) bring about convergence of national accounting standards and IFRS to high quality solutions.[108]

The IASB expanded its membership from 14 to 16 members on their Board focusing on developing-country representation. It required four members from each Asia/Oceania, Europe, North America and one each from Africa, South America and two others to reflect a geographical representation. However, the membership distribution remains same with regard to small countries.

This disproportionate representation has also been a common theme of critique particularly in the BIS and the BCBS – though to a lesser extent in IOSCO and IAIS. The recent expansions in the membership has also raised some issues as to the transparency in the expansion process as it was carried out particularly with reference to the selection of new members. The membership structure of these organizations inherently favors the viewpoints of the stronger countries who dominate policies. This bears direct implications on the inherent soft-law-based nature of IFL on the one hand, and on the other hand, the consensus-based decision-making mode enables a cherry-picking approach to be available to the Member States whose interests are not served best by any of the rules and standards formulated. Hence, IFL remains at best porous in adoption of standards and weaker in enforcement. Disparities between domestic legislation and regulatory standards hinder the development of a *global prospectus* or *international passport prospectus*.[109] The need remains for harmonization and

---

107. Arner, D. W. (2011). Adaptation and Resilience in Global Financial Regulation. *North Carolina Law Review*, 89, 101-148.
108. *See* IFRS website, visited on Jan. 16, 2012. IFRS. (2011).
109. Arner, D. W. (2002). Globalization of Financial Markets: An International Passport for Securities Offerings? *International Lawyer*. Retrieved from http://hdl.handle.net/10722/74853.

coordination between the international securities market, in accounting standards and the role of the IASC on the one hand and the relationship between IOSCO and IASC on the other.

[G] Credit Rating Agencies (CRA)

In the backdrop of the development of nonbanking sector, it is pertinent to analyze what went wrong with the securitization,[110] notably when all the financial products available in the market were diligently rated[111] by the sacrosanct credit rating agencies (CRAs).[112] The ratings made many investments appear safer than they actually were and thus had a hand in bringing about the crisis.[113]

In the aftermath of the GFC, rating agencies drew significant criticism on a number of issues. The first relates to the conflict of interest as CRA's compensation is being met by the issuer whose securities are being rated by the agencies. There was an inherent conflict between their status as private, profit-seeking entities and the status of a quasi-public regulator to begin with. To make matters worse, as Cervone points in her recent work, these not only continued to operate with little government regulation, but have also been largely exempted from established legal standards (applicable to traditional forms of investment advice in the USA and the EU).[114] Another relates to the possibility of CRA's may manipulate issuers for benefits, financial or otherwise. And, to exacerbate the *accountability gap*, as Cervone points out, market discipline such as reputation did not provide sufficient restraint during the crisis.[115]

However, one important conflict inherent in the origination process for structured transactions was the risk arising from the quasi-origination function undertaken by the leading rating agencies in complex financial transactions.[116] Simon Johnson, former chief economist at the IMF, suggested that the boom discouraged a close inspection of flaws in the system. The ratings agencies were unable to play a neutral

---

110. IOSCO. (June 2009). Stocktaking on the Use of Credit Ratings: IOSCO, BCBS and IAIS: Joint Forum.
111. CRAs are major players in today's financial markets, with ratings having a direct impact on the actions of investors, borrowers, issuers and governments. The *Big Three* CRAs with global presence are: the US-based Standard & Poor's; Moody's; and, the Fitch Ratings.
112. Caprio, G., Demirgüç-Kunt, A., & Kane, E. J. (2010). The 2007 Meltdown in Structured Securitization: Searching for Lessons, Not Scapegoats. *World Bank Research Observer:* Oxford Journals, 25(1), 125-155. Retrieved from http://ssrn.com/paper = 1293169.
113. Andrew Ross Sorkin, Mary Williams Walsh, U.S. Accuses S.&P. of Fraud in Suit on Loan Bundles. (Feb. 4, 2013). International New York Times, available at http://dealbook.nytimes.com/2013/02/04/u-s-and-states-prepare-to-sue-s-p-over-mortgage-ratings/?_php = true&_type = blogs&smid = fb-share&_r = 0 last accessed Feb. 22, 2014.
114. *See*, Cervone, E. (2015). Credit Rating Agencies: The Development of Global Standards. In C. L. Lim & B. Mercurio (Eds.), *International Economic Law after the Global Crisis: A Tale of Fragmented Disciplines.* Cambridge University Press.
115. *Ibid.* p. 49.
116. Arner, D. (2009). The Global Credit Crisis of 2008: Causes and Implications for Financial Regulation. *The International Lawyer,* 43(1). p. 108.

role and were infected by conflicts of interest and simply could not afford to alienate the institutions whose securities they were rating. Another criticism on the role of credit ratings agencies is on the sovereign ratings when political pressures influence their ratings.[117] This criticism was levied strongly in the 2008 crisis in context of the US as well as eurozone countries.[118] The post-crisis regulation albeit fragmented regulation in various parts of the world treating CRAs differently has intensified this issue many fold. In particular, the EU regulation and the US regulations differ in many aspects including in discipline CRA liability. As mentioned earlier, the big three CRAs though are located in the US but their presence is across the globe. This cross-border nature of the function of CRAs therefore, necessitates harmonization in the development of regulatory standards via extraterritoriality and private-sector governance in the CRAs industry as has been well analyzed in Cervone's recent work, which also refers to the current fragmentation of the regime[119] as well as the actors involved in rule-making.[120]

[H] The FSF

As part of the NIFA, the FSF was the only new institution that was created in the aftermath of the AFC[121] under the patronage of the G7 in 1999. It was established to continue the development of international financial and regulatory standards and to promote international financial stability, improve the functioning of financial markets, and, to reduce systemic risk through enhanced information exchange and international cooperation in financial market supervision and surveillance.[122] The new body, the FSF (FSB in 2009) included five different types of members: national authorities (including

---

117. Charles A.E., Goodhart. (Oct. 20, 2011). Europe after the Crisis, Institute for New Economic Thinking, p. 10. last accessed Feb. 22, 2014 at http://inetceconomics.org/sites/inet.civicactions.net/files/goodhart-europe-after-crisis-v10.pdf.
118. During the 2012, in a major blow to the ratings industry, the Federal Court of Australia ruled that Standard & Poor misled investors by giving its most trusted rating to instruments that S&P knew to be faulty in 2012. An appeal court ruled again in 2014 and Standard & Poor was held liable for investment losses on securities bought by Australian towns. See for news coverage, The Australian, Sydney Morning Herald *(Australia)*, Les Echos *(France); Wall Street Journal (USA); Worldcrunch (11 May, 2012), available at* http://www.worldcrunch.com/business-finance/australian-court-in-landmark-ruling-against-ratings-agency/federal-court-sydney-abn-amro-s-amp-p/c2s10053/#.UwiuNWPNtdg .
119. *Fragmentation continues to be a persistent feature of international economic law*, remarked Lim and Mercurio in their work while talking about the ever-changing nature of the international economic law. *See*, Lim, C. L., & Mercurio, B. (Eds.). (2015). *International Economic Law after the Global Crisis: A Tale of Fragmented Disciplines*. Cambridge University Press.
120. *See*, Cervone, *supra* n. 114.
121. Transformed into the FSB, April 2009 in the aftermath of the GFC.
122. *See*, the FSB website, *Our History*, available at http://www.financialstabilityboard.org/about/history/.

the G7 and the ECB),[123] IFIs, other IOs,[124] international regulatory and supervisory organizations and committees of central bank experts.[125] The BIS played important role of providing secretariat services to the FSF, BCBS, IAIS, G10, CPSS and CGFS. The FSF created a number of specialist ad hoc *working groups* focusing on specialized areas and making recommendations relating to the development and implementation of respective standards for those particular areas.[126]

In October 2007, the FSF coordinated a consultative process inclusive of the IMF and others and recommended establishment of a single body to harmonize regulatory practices in the financial markets. The FSF consulted BCBS, IOSCO, IAIS, IASB, CPSS, CGFS, BIS and IMF, national authorities in key financial centers including insights sought from private-sector market participants and was transformed into the FSB. With this, its membership also underwent a huge expansion to reflect equitable representation of both, the countries having world savings and the countries in possession of world reserves.[127]

[I] The FSB

In this context, the FSB was formed to develop and promote implementation of effective regulatory, supervisory and financial sector policies at the international level. At the April 2009 London Summit the G20 placed the FSB at the center of intensified international regulatory cooperation in the wake of the GFC. Its mandate grew into an extensive list of functions and activities, broadly grouped into three main areas: (a) to assess vulnerabilities affecting the financial system and identify and oversee actions

---

123. National authorities include: Argentina (Banco Central de la República Argentina), Australia (Reserve Bank of Australia), Brazil (Banco Central do Brasil, Comissão de Valores Mobiliários, and Ministério da Fazenda), Canada (Bank of Canada and Office of the Superintendent of financial Institutions, and Department of Finance), China (People's Bank of China, China Banking Regulatory Commission, Ministry of Finance), France (Banquet de France and Autorite des Marches Financiers and Ministere de lEconomie), Germany (Deutsche Bundesbank, Bundesanstalt für Finanzdienstleistungsaufsicht, and Bundesministerium der Finanzen), Hong Kong SAR (Hong Kong Monetary Authority), India (Reserve Bank of India, Securities and Exchange Board of India and Ministry of Finance); Indonesia (Bank Indonesia), Italy (Banca d'Italia, Commissione Nazionale per le Società e la Borsa, Ministero dell'Economia e delle Finanze), Japan (Bank of Japan, Financial Services Agency and Ministry of Finance), Mexico (Banco de Mexico, Secretaría de Hacienda y Crédito Público de México), the Netherlands (De Nederlandsche Bank, Ministry of Finance), Republic of Korea (Bank of Korea, Financial Services Commission), Russia (Central Bank of the Russian Federation, Federal Financial Markets Service and Ministry of Finance), Saudi Arabia (Saudi Arabian Monetary Agency), Singapore (Monetary Authority of Singapore), South Africa (Ministry of Finance), Spain (Banco de Espana, Ministerio de Economía y Hacienda), Switzerland (Swiss National Bank, Swiss Federal Department of Finance), Turkey (Central Bank of the Republic of Turkey), the UK (Bank of England, FSA and HM Treasury), the USA (Board of the Federal Reserve, Securities & Exchange Commission, U.S. Treasury).
124. The IOs include: BIS, ECB, EC, IMF, OECD, WB and international-standard-setting bodies and other groupings like the BCBS, CGFS, CPSS, IAIS, IASB and IOSCO.
125. *See*, the FSB website, http://www.financialstabilityboard.org/about/fsb_members.htm.
126. The ad hoc groups included: Highly leveraged institutions, Capital flows, Offshore financial centers, Implementation of standards, Incentives to foster implementation of standards, Deposit insurance, e-Finance.
127. Griffith-Jones & Young, *supra* n. 62.

needed to address them; (b) to develop policy, either directly or through coordinating the activities of the international-standard-setting bodies; and, (c) to ensure effective implementation of international standards.

[1] The Transformation

The G20 leaders who reconstituted the FSF as the FSB made a series of changes. The first step was to expand its membership to encompass, in addition to its original members, all G20 nations, Spain, Singapore, Hong Kong, Switzerland and the European Union (EU). The result was a new body, which included representatives of economies that accounted for approximately 85% of global economic output and regulators of the main international financial centers, as well as the international-standard-setting bodies (such as the BCBS) and relevant IFIs (the IMF, WB and OECD).The decision to reconstitute the FSF as the FSB opened up questions on its future status as part of the international financial architecture. There were two scenarios: (1) should the FSB be regarded primarily as a crisis-management body brought to life in crisis emergencies? or, (2) is it heading to become a permanent part of the global financial architecture? In the former scenario, the FSB might be mothballed between financial crises, only to be reactivated as and when needed for a more coordinated international effort for crisis planning and crisis management. It could be managed in the interim by a small Secretariat on a *care and maintenance* basis, although clear criteria for determining when the body should be activated need to be spelled out vividly. The alternative would be to put the FSB on a permanent footing as an international agency, in which case it would have a large permanent staff, a dedicated funding source and separate legal personality.

Stressing the importance of the newly established FSB in the global economic governance architecture, US Treasury Secretary, Tim Geithner stated[128] that after the Second World War, we came together and established the IMF, the WB and the GATT, but the FSB is, in effect, a *fourth pillar* of that architecture.[129]

[2] Membership

The FSF coordinated a consultative process inclusive of the BCBS, IOSCO, IAIS, IASB, CPSS, CGFS, BIS, the IMF and various national authorities[130] in key financial centers to

---

128. *See*, the Press Conference, the G20 Pittsburgh (September 2009). Available at http://www.whitehouse.gov/the_press_office/Press-Briefingby-Treasury-Secretary-Geithner-on-the-G20-Meetings accessed Feb. 26, 2014.
129. FSF is the predecessor institution, transformed into the FSB in 2009. *See*, for historical details section above on the FSF. *See also*, http://www.financialstabilityboard.org/about/overview.htm Arner, D. W., & Taylor, M. W. (2010). The Global Credit Crisis and the Financial Stability Board: Hardening the Soft Law of International Financial Regulation? *University of New South Wales Law Journal, 32*, 488-513.
130. National authorities: Argentina (Banco Central de la República Argentina), Australia (Reserve Bank of Australia), Brazil (Banco Central do Brasil, Comissão de Valores Mobiliários, and Ministério da Fazenda), Canada (Bank of Canada and Office of the Superintendent of financial

seek insights from private sector market participants, to report to the G7 Ministers and Governors at the April 2008 Washington meeting. The report recommended transforming the FSF into the FSB, a single body to harmonize regulatory practices in the financial markets.

Like other international coordinating bodies the FSB had to strike a balance between an inclusive membership and an effective decision-making. The FSB membership also underwent a huge expansion to reflect equitable representation of both, the countries having world savings and the countries in possession of world reserves.[131] Although the FSB's expanded membership includes ministries of finance, central banks and regulatory agencies, an unequal allocation of seats among the member countries has helped to keep its size to more manageable limits. Nonetheless, the expansion in the membership potentially raised the number of people around the table from about 42 in the days of the FSF, to its current 70 leading to fears that the body might be too large for effective decision-making. The FSB's first chairman, Mario Draghi, attempted to address this concern by establishing a Steering Committee in the spring of 2009, which provided a mechanism for a smaller *Directoire* of members, mainly drawn from the former FSF membership, to set the FSB's agenda and monitor progress. This move was not, however, uncontroversial, resulting in the G20 leaders intervening in 2011 in their Cannes Summit Declaration to request that the FSB Steering Committee should include the executive branch of governments of the G20 Chair and the larger financial systems as well as the geographic regions and financial centers not currently represented in a balanced manner consistent with the FSB Charter. In other words, it would appear that both the finance ministries and the emerging economies newly represented on the FSB were feeling excluded from its decision-making process and the Steering Committee's membership were expanded to accommodate these

---

Institutions, and Department of Finance), China (People's Bank of China, China Banking regulatory Commission, Ministry of Finance), France (Banque de France and Autorite des Marches Financiers, and Ministere de lEconomie), Germany (Deutsche Bundesbank, Bundesanstalt für Finanzdienstleistungsaufsicht and Bundesministerium der Finanzen), Hong Kong SAR (Hong Kong Monetary Authority), India (Reserve Bank of India, Securities and Exchange Board of India and Ministry of Finance), Indonesia (Bank Indonesia), Italy (Banca d'Italia, Commissione Nazionale per le Società e la Borsa, Ministero dell'Economia e delle Finanze), Japan (Bank of Japan, Financial Services Agency and Ministry of Finance), Mexico (Banco de Mexico, Secretaría de Hacienda y Crédito Público de México), the Netherlands (De Nederlandsche Bank, Ministry of Finance), Republic of Korea (Bank of Korea, Financial Services Commission), Russia (Central Bank of the Russian Federation, Federal Financial Markets Service and Ministry of Finance), Saudi Arabia (Saudi Arabian Monetary Agency), Singapore (Monetary Authority of Singapore), South Africa (Ministry of Finance), Spain (Banco de Espana, Ministerio de Economía y Hacienda), Switzerland (Swiss National Bank, Swiss Federal Department of Finance), Turkey (Central Bank of the Republic of Turkey), United Kingdom (Bank of England, Financial Services Authority and HM Treasury), the United States of America (Board of Governors of the Federal Reserve System, U.S. Securities & Exchange Commission (SEC), U.S. Department of Treasury). For further details *see*, http://www.financialstabilityboard.org/about/fsb_members.htm.

131. Griffith-Jones & Young, *supra* n. 62.

concerns. The recomposition led to an increase of 11 seats on the Steering Committee.[132]

In respect of membership, there are certain concerns regarding whether or not it has the right composition, given the diversity of developed and emerging economies involved. At the same time, politically, while it may (and perhaps should) be possible to add (demonstration of compliance) or remove members (e.g., noncompliance), politically it is unlikely that the basic structure can be changed in the short-term. Nonetheless, the balance of members remains a concern given the variance in the number of seats across members.

In response to criticisms from some emerging economies that they were disadvantaged by its membership structure, the FSB undertook a review of its representation and presented its recommendations to the G20 heads of government at their November 2014 summit in Brisbane. An April 2014 progress report to the G20 finance ministers and central bank governors had indicated that this review was unlikely to result in fundamental changes in representation, given that the FSB regards its current membership of 70 as *the upper limit* consistent with representativeness and effectiveness, and it declared that there was no appetite either for moving towards a *constituency-based* form of representation or for reducing the countries represented on the FSB.[133] The final report reflected these interim findings and concluded that five emerging markets – Argentina, Indonesia, Saudi Arabia, South Africa and Turkey – should be assigned a second seat on the Plenary. To ensure no expansion in the overall size of the Plenary, the IMF, World Bank and three standard-setting bodies – IOSCO, the Basel Committee and IAIS – agreed to give up their second seat.[134] The extent to which this move may make the FSB a less effective coordinator of standard-setting activities remains to be seen.

However, the review did not address an arguably serious issue of membership bias, the over-representation of the EU Member States at the expense of the rest of the world. Not only do the larger EU economies (Germany, France, the UK and Italy) each have three seats on the FSB, but European institutions – namely the European Commission (EC) and the ECB – also have their own seats. With the Eurozone member countries having now agreed to hand over the supervision of the largest, most systemically important banks to the ECB, and with regulations increasingly written at the EU level by the EC and its specialist agencies (EBA, EIOPA and ESMA), there would seem to be a strong case for scaling down the representation of a number of EU Member

---

132. *See*, the FSB Report to the G20 Los Cabos Summit on Strengthening FSB Capacity, Resources and Governance Jun. 18-19, 2012, p. 4 http://www.financialstabilityboard.org/publications/r_120619c.pdf.
133. Chairman's letter to the G20 Finance Ministers and Central Bank Governors, April 2014, available at http://www.financialstabilityboard.org/publications/r_140411.pdf.
134. *See*, Report to the G20 Brisbane Summit on the FSB's review of the structure of its representation, November 2014, available at http://www.financialstabilityboard.org/wp-content/uploads/Report-to-the-G20-Brisbane-Summit-on-the-FSB's-Review-of-the-Structure-of-its-Representation.pdf.

States. In the monetary policy field similar arguments have existed since the introduction of the euro in 1999 resulting in diminished representation of the relevant states in bodies such as the IMF's Executive Board.

One clear benefit from the membership review was the agreement to *enable* non-member authorities (either from or beyond the Member jurisdictions) to be involved in the work of the FSB's Committees and working groups, either through membership of these bodies or attendance at individual meetings. This agreement permits the FSB to offer greater flexibility for institutions other than those that formally represent their countries to take part in Standing Committees and working groups. An example is allowing agencies, which are not formally represented, such as the US CFTC or the Hong Kong Securities and Futures Commission (SFC), to take part in some working groups that are relevant.

[3]   Internal Structure

The FSB's internal structure largely mirrors the threefold set of responsibilities that we outlined earlier. In addition to the Plenary and the Steering Committee the FSB has established three Standing Committees that are responsible for conducting vulnerabilities assessments, supervisory and regulatory cooperation and implementation monitoring respectively. In addition, one change resulting from the 2012 revision to the Charter was the creation of a Standing Committee on budget and resources that reflected growing institutionalization of the FSB (*see* section below).

The functions of each of the Standing Committees are set out in the FSB Charter. Article 14 provides that the Standing Committee on Vulnerabilities Assessment (SCAV) shall have the following functions: (1), monitor and assess vulnerabilities affecting the global financial system and propose to the Plenary actions needed to address them; (2) monitor and advise on market and systemic developments, and their implications for regulatory policy; (3) provide input for the early warning exercise conducted in collaboration with the IMF.

Article 15 describes the functions of the Standing Committee on Supervisory and Regulatory Cooperation (SCSRC). It requires to: (a) address key financial stability issues relating to the development of supervisory and regulatory policy, identify relative priorities, and seek to ensure that the different policy initiatives fit together into a coherent whole; (b) assist in managing the coordination issues that arise among supervisors and regulators on issues that have cross-sector implications and raise any need for policy development required to close regulatory gaps that pose risk to financial stability; (c) set guidelines for and oversee the establishment and effective functioning of supervisory colleges; and, (d) advise on and monitor best practice in meeting regulatory standards with a view to ensure consistency, cooperation and a level playing field across jurisdictions.

Article 16 sets out the functions of the Standing Committee on Standards Implementation (SCSI), which aim to: (a) ensure comprehensive and rigorous implementation monitoring of international financial standards, agreed G20 and FSB commitments, recommendations and other initiatives in consultation and coordination with other relevant bodies, through mechanisms such as the Coordination Framework for Implementation Monitoring (CFIM); (b) undertake peer reviews amongst its members; (c) report to the Plenary on members' commitments and progress in implementing international financial standards, agreed G20 and FSB commitments, recommendations and other initiatives; and, (d) encourage global adherence to prudential regulatory and supervisory standards, such as through the FSB's Framework for Strengthening Adherence to International Standards.

In addition to these three Standing Committees, the 2013 revision to the FSB's Charter resulted in the creation of a Budget and Resources Committee, which is responsible for assessing the resource needs of the FSB Secretariat and developing a medium-term budget and resource framework as well as approving an annual budget. This Committee is also empowered to make recommendations to the Plenary for ways of enhancing the sources of the FSB's revenue.[135]

A final tier of FSB committees are the Regional Consultative Groups that bring together FSB and non-FSB members from six geographical regions (the Americas, Asia, Europe, Middle East, Africa and the Confederation of Independent States). The function of these Groups, as revealed through the relatively terse press releases issued by the FSB after each meeting, seem to be mainly an opportunity for the FSB to explain its policies and initiatives to non-member countries. It is unclear to what extent these bodies facilitate a genuine dialogue between members and non-members.

[4]   Functions

The FSB's present governance structure consists of the Plenary, a Steering Committee, a Chairperson and the FSB Secretariat:

- FSB Plenary is the decision-making organ. The Steering Committee provides operational guidance between plenary meetings to carryforward the directions of the FSB. A full-time Secretary General and an enlarged Secretariat based in Basel provides logistics support to the FSB.
- Jurisdictions eligible for plenary membership included the existing FSF membership plus the rest of the G20, Spain and the European Commission. Eligibility for new members was decided to be reviewed periodically.
- The Plenary representation both – the country and regional – was to be drawn from authorities responsible for maintaining financial stability. Plenary members also included the chairs of the main SSBs and central bank committees, and representatives of the IMF, the WB, the BIS and OECD.
- The Steering Committee's composition is decided by the FSB Chair in a manner that ensures maximum effectiveness in taking forward the FSB's work. The Steering Committee ensures effective information flow to the full membership.
- The FSB Chair could extend ad hoc invitations to non-members to attend plenary meetings.

---

135. FSB, *infra* n. 143, Art. 17.

- To support the FSB's role, Standing Committees were created. There are three Standing Committees: the Standing Committee for Vulnerabilities Assessment, the Standing Committee for Supervisory and Regulatory Cooperation, and the Standing Committee for Standards Implementation. There are four working groups: Cross-border Crisis Management Working Group under the Standing Committee for Supervisory and Regulatory Cooperation, Expert Group on Non-Cooperation Jurisdictions under the Standing Committee for Standards Implementation, and Working Group on Compensation and the Working Group for Over-the-Counter (OTC) Derivatives under the Steering Committee. The Steering Committee may establish faster acting ad hoc work streams as needed, which may comprise non-FSB member countries.[136]

The FSB's functions included:

- Over time, promote and coordinate alignment of international standard-setting activities to address overlaps or alternatively tap in the regulatory gaps and clarify demarcations in the light of changes in national regulatory structures relating to prudential and systemic risk, market integrity and consumer protection, infrastructure and accounting and auditing.
- Step up its regional outreach activities to broaden the range of countries engaged to promote international financial stability, and to raise visibility of its work through stronger public relations exercise.
- The FSB and the IMF to intensify their collaboration, each complementing the other's role in conducting Early Warning Exercises, joint presentation to the IMFC on financial risks and vulnerabilities and policy recommendations to mitigate such risks and vulnerabilities.
- At the G20 Cannes Summit in November 2011, the G20 leaders called for *the establishment of the FSB on an enduring organizational footing*. Noting that they had given the FSB a strong political mandate, the leaders recognized the need *to give it a corresponding institutional standing, with legal personality and greater financial autonomy*, while preserving the existing and well-functioning strong links with the BIS.[137] This commitment pointed in the direction of the second of the two possible models, although it should be noted that a formal treaty would normally be needed to establish a body with these characteristics and the G20 leaders displayed no appetite for engaging in a round of treaty negotiations on financial stability and regulation.

The reference to maintain strong links with the BIS was another indication that the leaders did not – at least at that juncture – envisage creating a fully fledged part of the international financial architecture. And the BIS played an important role of

---

136. *See*, Organizational Structure and Governance. Available at http://www.financialstabilityboard.org/about/organisation-and-governance/.
137. *See*, G20 (November 2011). Cannes Summit Declaration, Para 38. Available at https://www.oecd.org/g20/summits/cannes/Cannes%20Leaders%20Communiqu%C3%A9%204%20%20November%202011.pdf last accessed October 09, 2017 f.

providing secretariat services to the FSF, BCBS, IAIS, G10, CPSS and CGFS. The FSF created a number of specialist ad hoc working groups focusing on specialized areas and making recommendations relating to development and implementation of respective standards for those particular areas.[138] In this context, the FSB was shaped to develop and promote implementation of effective regulatory, supervisory and other financial sector policies at the international level by bringing together national authorities responsible for maintaining financial stability and the BIS facilitated.

Perhaps not surprisingly, the promised enhancements to the FSB's institutional standing turned out to be relatively modest. The G20 at its St. Petersburg summit in September 2013 welcomed the establishment of the FSB as a legal entity with greater financial autonomy and an enhanced capacity to coordinate the development and implementation of financial regulatory policies[139] however, in practice, very little had appeared to have changed. The FSB itself informed the G20 leaders that it considers a treaty-based inter-governmental organization not to be an appropriate legal form at this juncture[140] – without offering any explanation of its reasons for having drawn this conclusion. A *lack of consensus* among the members about the role the FSB should play in the international financial architecture could be the most likely explanation for the FSB having invoked *the doctrine of the unripe time.*[141]

The FSB was established as *an association by the name of Financial Stability Board* (hereinafter *the Association*) ... pursuant to Article 60 of the Swiss Civil Code.[142] Article 60 provides that Associations with a political, religious, scientific, cultural, charitable, social or other noncommercial purpose acquire legal personality as soon as their intention to exist as a corporate body is apparent from their Articles of Association.

A similar compromise appears to have been at work in determining the FSB's funding. Unlike the IMF for example, the FSB has no independent source of revenue, to fund its operations. The option of introducing a membership fee was considered but rejected as the FSB informed the G20 leaders not to introduce a membership fee at this stage for augmenting the resource pool.[143] As with the recommendation concerning a treaty-based institution, the rationale for the FSB having taken this position of funding was not explained either. Instead, as Article 7 of the Articles of Association makes clear that the Association will be funded by the BIS on the basis of and in accordance with

---

138. Ad hoc groups included: highly leveraged institutions, capital flows, offshore financial centers, implementation of standards, incentives to foster implementation of standards, deposit insurance, e-finance.
139. *See*, G20. (September 2013). St. Petersburg Summit Declaration, para. 64. Available at http://www.g20.utoronto.ca/2013/2013-0906-declaration.html#finreg.
140. *See*, the FSB Report to the G20: Los Cabos Summit on Strengthening FSB Capacity, Resources and Governance, para. 11.
141. As named in, F. M. Cornford (1908), Microcosmographia Academica. Bowes & Bowes, available at http://www.maths.ed.ac.uk/~aar/baked/micro.pdf.
142. *See*, the FSB, Articles of Association of the Financial Stability Board, (of Jan. 28, 2013), *see* Art. 1, at http://www.financialstabilityboard.org/wp-content/uploads/AoA-26-March-2015-FINAL.pdf.
143. *See*, the FSB Report, *supra* n. 140. para. 14.

the terms of a renewable *Multi-Year Funding Agreement* and by voluntary contributions from members.[144] One clear implication of this arrangement is that the members could not agree on an alternative funding source, such as a membership fee, which would have provided the FSB with independent funds of its own.

The FSB became a separate legal entity in the form of an association (Verein) under Swiss law on January 28, 2013 as its Articles of Association were adopted by the Plenary. However, it continues to receive funding and services support from the BIS under a January 2013 agreement executed between the FSB and the BIS.[145] Ideally an organization like the FSB needs to raises its own resources. As an Association under Swiss law the FSB is not entitled to the same privileges and immunities normally granted to IOs by their founding treaties, and to obtain them it would need to enter into a separate agreement with the Swiss authorities. In consequence, the FSB remains beholden to the BIS to obtain the needed immunities by operating as an association under the BIS Headquarters Agreement. The FSB submission to the G20 leaders at their Los Cabos meeting did, however, propose that this arrangement should be revisited after the elapse of five years, holding out the possibility of the FSB negotiating a separate Headquarters Agreement of its own. Separation from the BIS will serve to differentiate its role from that of traditional central banks and thereby be capable of speaking to a wider audience and coordinating with a broader range of participants in financial regulatory matters.

[5] Decision-Making

The effectiveness of decision-making in international forums is in part a function of the level of representation of the member institutions: ideally, the representatives on a body like the FSB should be empowered to give binding commitments on behalf of their institutions without the need to refer back to head office (a practice that would result in substantial delays in achieving agreement on key policy initiatives). Members are obligated to maintain financial stability, openness and transparency of the financial sector, implement international financial standards (including the 12 key International Standards/Codes), and, undergo periodic peer reviews, using amongst other evidence, the IMF/WB public FSAP reports.

And, the members have been reaffirming their commitments and obligations during the successive gatherings and deliberations, for example, at G20 meeting in 2012, the membership in order to avoid additional systemic risks in the financial system, committed to:

> [w]e reaffirm our commitment to consolidate and implement the international agenda on reforms to financial regulation. During the session, we made a comprehensive review of all the work that has been made on financial regulation. Additionally, it was planned to develop a series of proposals to strengthen the

---

144. The FSB, *supra* n. 143, Art. 7.
145. The FSB (2015). First Annual Report, Jan. 28, 2013-Mar. 31, 2014, published on Jan. 29, 2015. Available at http://www.financialstabilityboard.org/wp-content/uploads/First-FSB-Annual-Report.pdf.

capacities, resources and governance of the Financial Stability Council to adequately fulfill its mandate.[146]

The need for its members to be sufficiently empowered to commit their respective institutions is reflected in the FSB's Articles of Association, which states that the *representation at the Plenary shall be at the level of central bank governor or immediate deputy; head or immediate deputy of the main supervisory/regulatory agency; and deputy finance minister or deputy head of finance ministry.*

The Articles of Association further state that the FSB's Plenary, its chief decision-making body, operates by *consensus*.[147] This implies that agreement of all members is required for major policy decisions, with the result that the FSB is obliged to find common ground among its members before it is able to adopt new policy initiatives. This contrasts with the majority or qualified majority voting processes of other, treaty-based international bodies.[148] Moreover, as Article 3(3) of the Articles of Association makes clear, a member's domestic legal and policy framework has precedence over any decisions or obligations arising from FSB membership, while Article 10 provides an all-encompassing opt-out should any member choose to utilize it:

> The policy making and related activities of the [FSB] shall be governed by the FSB Charter. These activities, including any decisions reached in their context, shall not be binding or give rise to any legal rights or obligations under the present Articles. Members can recuse themselves at any time from these activities or decision-making where such activities or decision-making are not consistent with their legal or policy frameworks.[149]

Thus it would appear that the FSB has *no ability* to impose binding obligations on its members should it seek to adopt any policies without reaching full consensus (an approach that is sometimes described as *practical consensus* as it avoids the need for complete unanimity and thus prevents any one member from preventing a decision from being reached) and should a dissenting member choose to ignore its decisions. The G20 leaders rejected the notion of establishing the FSB as a formal IO based on a multilateral treaty, a move considered not to be an appropriate legal form at this juncture.[150] The FSB Charter, however, has been continuously changed and adapted by the G20, and this feature of flexibility in adaptation – otherwise is a source of diverse

---

146. Jose Antonio Meade Kuribreña, (Feb. 26, 2012), G20 Finance Ministers and Central Banks Governors meeting, Mexico City, Available at http://www.g20mexico.org/en/news-room/speeches/236-palabras-iniciales-del-secretario-jose-antonio-meade-kuribrena-durante-la-conferencia-de-prensa-sobre-reunion-de-ministros-de-finanzas-y-gobernadores-de-bancos-centrales-del-g20, last accessed, January 2015.
147. FSB, *supra* n. 143, Art. 6.
148. For example, decisions in the EU's Council of Ministers are taken by qualified majority (same as at the IMF's Executive Board).
149. FSB, *supra* n. 143, Art. 10.
150. *See*, FSB Report, *supra* n. 140, point 11.

policy confrontations – is in contrast to a formal treaty, which, once drafted, is difficult to amend – and hence, harder to violate.[151]

However, this informality and lack of legal authority represents a major limitation on the FSB's ability to discharge the responsibilities placed on it by the G20 leaders, especially when dealing with potentially highly politically sensitive issues such as the distribution of losses in a cross-border bank resolution.

[6] *Enforcement*

FSB is founded by the Article 16 of the Charter, which specifically states that this body does not intend to create any legal rights or obligations. The mandate of the FSB is to: (a) assess vulnerabilities affecting financial system and identify and oversee actions needed to address them; (b) promote coordination and information exchange among authorities responsible for financial stability; (c) monitor and advise on market developments and their implications for regulatory policy; (d) advise on and monitor best practices in meeting regulatory standards; (e) undertake joint strategic reviews of policy development work of the international standard-setting bodies to ensure their work is timely, coordinated, focused on priorities and addressing policy gaps; (f) set guidelines for and support the establishment of supervisory colleges; (g) manage contingency planning for cross-border crisis management, particularly with respect to systemically important firms; and, (h) collaborate with the IMF to conduct Early Warning Exercises.[152]

The FSB and the BCBS provides a supervisory forum for regular cooperation in designing a universal risk-based regulatory mechanism,[153] fair treatment of consumer's financial services and products, and financial soundness, stability and integrity of financial markets and institutions. However, the enforcement of the standards has been the source of discontent. Thus, in addition to simple surveillance, the FSB has stepped up four new mechanisms to encourage compliance with international standards.[154] First, the member jurisdictions commit to implement international financial standards. However, as with other regulatory bodies, the consequences of noncompliance are not made clear in the Charter.[155] Second, review under the IMF/WB FSAP was made mandatory for member countries. Third, member jurisdictions commit to undergo periodic peer reviews, comprising both the thematic and country peer reviews. Fourth, the FSB will finalize procedures by identifying noncooperative

---

151. Wouters, J., & Odermatt, J. (2014). Comparing the 'Four Pillars' of Global Economic Governance: A Critical Analysis of the Institutional Design of the FSB, IMF, World Bank, and WTO. *Journal of International Economic Law.* 17(1). pp. 49-76.
152. *See, the Mandate*, accessible at http://www.financialstabilityboard.org/about/mandate/.
153. Following the G30 report, risk was categorized into credit risk, market risk, operational or strategic risk, and liquidity or payment and legal risk. The framework of risk-based supervision and risk management involves four levels: identification, measurement, disclosure and internal risk management.
154. *See*, Jeong, Y.-C. (2010). 2010 Seoul Summit and Future of Financial Supervisory Board (FSB) as the Fourth Pillar. *Korea University Law Review*, 7(17).
155. *See*, FSB, *supra* n. 143.

jurisdictions and assisting them to improve their adherence, especially in the prudential regulations, tax and Anti-Money Laundering (AML)/Combating the Financing of Terrorism (CFT) areas.

[7] The Role of the FSB in Post-crisis Financial Reforms

During a relatively short period of its existence the FSB has pursued an ambitious policy agenda, first under the Chairmanship of Mario Draghi (at the time the Governor of the Banca d'Italia) and currently under Mark Carney (who was, when appointed, the Governor of the Bank of Canada and became the Governor of the BoE part way through his first term). To a substantial degree the agenda followed by the FSB during this period reflected on the priorities established under the Draghi Chairmanship, with Carney aiming to bring these initiatives to a conclusion. Relatively few new initiatives have been commenced under the latter's Chairmanship.

The FSB's work program over the past five years was neatly encapsulated in the Communique issued by the G20 leaders following their summit in St. Petersburg. The program over the past five years has implemented internationally consistent reform to financial systems where major jurisdictions, in part or in full, have: (a) implemented new global capital standards (Basel III); (b) completed the necessary frameworks for OTC derivatives to be traded on exchanges or electronic trading platforms, centrally cleared, and reported; (c) identified global systemically important banks and insurers, and agreed to subject them to heightened prudential standards to mitigate the risks they pose; (d) implemented agreed tools and procedures for the orderly resolution of large, complex financial institutions without taxpayer loss; and, (e) progressed in addressing potential systemic risks to financial stability emanating from the shadow-banking system.[156]

With the exception of the first point, the FSB has taken the lead in all of the above points, either directly or through the coordination of other standard-setting bodies. Even with respect to the first of these, the FSB has played a prominent role in ensuring the implementation of Basel 3 through its implementation monitoring efforts, specifically the CFIM and its peer reviews of individual members. The FSB has recently launched a peer review on the implementation of its policy framework for financial stability risks.

The fundamental issue in assessing the FSB's effectiveness as a coordinating body is the extent to which progress has been made in achieving the agenda. In this respect, progress appears to have been patchy. For example, although many jurisdictions have adopted the framework for the central clearing of OTC derivative, there remain a number of unresolved jurisdictional conflicts, despite the FSB's best endeavors. The fundamental issue concerns whether derivatives rules for clearing houses in other jurisdictions are equivalent to those in the host jurisdiction and therefore can be substituted for those of either the EU or the US, avoiding the need for parties to a

---

156. *See*, G20 Declaration, St. Petersburg (September 2013). Paragraph 61, at http://www.g20.utoronto.ca/2013/2013-0906-declaration.html#finreg.

derivatives transaction to comply with two overlapping, but not necessarily mutually consistent, sets of rules. At the FSB's behest, the EC and CFTC agreed to a *path forward* in June 2013, but a year later, as Reuters reported, differences in margining rules were still inhibiting the EC from finding US rules equivalent to its own.[157] While it would be unfair to blame the FSB for this ongoing jurisdictional dispute, the fact that it lacks the power to impose a solution on its members to ensure that the international financial system does not become fragmented by conflicting regulations indicates a fundamental weakness in the soft-law framework.

Devising a framework for resolution of cross-border banking groups points to another weakness in the FSB's ability to make such decisions that bind its members. The FSB can encourage member countries to adopt the Key Attributes, which are a set of international standards for bank resolution regimes. Nonetheless, adoption of the Key Attributes in their entirety remains patchy, as the FSB's own peer review revealed. The degree of commitment of some members – especially those in Asia – to the new bank resolution framework remains in question.

This patchy adoption of the Key Attributes does not bode well for another major component of the FSB's cross-border resolution regime: the willingness of the authorities in multiple countries to defer to the resolution approach adopted by the authorities in a G-SIFI's home country. This so-called *Single Point of Entry* approach has been promoted by the FDIC, and the BoE, but notwithstanding their principle agreement on this resolution approach, considerable doubts remain about how it will be used in practice. Meanwhile, authorities in other countries have fewer incentives to cooperate than the authorities in the UK and the US, thus bringing into question how widely this resolution approach will be adopted. But without agreeing to binding rules in advance the temptation will be for authorities to adopt the same *sauvé qui peut* strategies that prevailed during the GFC and brought about, in part, the establishment of the FSB to address to.

These policy issues illustrate the challenges in one of the FSB's core mandates: implementation and monitoring. While monitoring (through the FSB itself, the G20, the various standard-setting organizations and the IMF FSAP process) appears to be functioning remarkably well in terms of both participation and identification of issues, without enforcement mechanisms there are limits to the effectiveness of peer pressure and transparency. In addition, the various review processes are constant taxes on the resources of both the FSB and its members (of all sorts).

For the FSB as and where it stands now, it needs to come up with an appropriate self-evaluation mechanism to avoid inertia in reforms as the IMF's governance reforms issue has been facing for long. Though on FSB's website, policy frameworks, progress reports and other documents are available yet there is criticism on lack of information

---

157. Huw Jones, (Jun. 27, 2014), Reuters. EU throws down gauntlet to U.S. over derivatives, available at http://www.reuters.com/article/2014/06/27/eu-regulations-clearing-idUSL6N0P 83L720140627.

about the internal workings of the FSB and its decision-making processes.[158] Ultimately, the FSB will be judged by its performance, which will be determined by whether the institution is able to put in place the structures and early warning systems to prevent or alleviate the next major crisis or its effect as the case may be. Therefore, if FSB is to remain at the center of global economic governance and financial stability, questions will arise about whether its design equips it to deal adequately with the many challenges in future. To promote global compliance with its financial standards, its legitimacy will likely be challenged by the non-member jurisdictions as long as it remains skewed and its decision-making mechanisms remain less transparent.

[J] The G's Group and the G20

Although this chapter will be focusing only on the role of the G20 in the reform of the IFRA in the post-2008 era, yet it is important to refer to the myriad grouping that Gs' constitute today. This is to underline two aspects: (1) the repetitiveness of a small group of core countries, which have been part of almost all G-groupings (except the Group of Seventy-Seven (G77); and (2) the nature of the work these governmental organizations have assumed follows the pattern reflected in their membership.

The G10 refers to the group of countries that have agreed to participate in the General Arrangements to Borrow (GAB). The GAB was established in 1962, when the governments of the eight IMF members – Belgium, Canada, France, Italy, Japan, the Netherlands, the UK and the US – and the central banks of two others, Germany and Sweden, agreed to make resources available to the IMF for drawings by participants, and, under certain circumstances, for drawings by non-participants.[159] The G10 was strengthened in 1964 by the association of the 11th member, Switzerland, then a non-member of the Fund, but the name of the G10 remained the same. The following IOs are official observers of the activities of the G10 and include: the BIS, EC, IMF and OECD.[160] The Group of Ten signed the Smithsonian Agreement in December 1971, replacing the world's fixed exchange rate regime with a floating exchange rate regime.

The Group of Seventy-Seven (G77) 1964: At the end of the first session of the United Nations Conference on Trade and Development (UNCTAD), 77 developing countries formulated this giant but *loose group* on June 15, 1964, under the *Joint Declaration of the Seventy-Seven Countries* issued at the UNCTAD session. The objective was to promote its members' collective economic interests and create an enhanced joint negotiating capacity in the UN. The first major meeting was held in Algiers in

---

158. The BIS website https://www.bis.org/about/orggov.htm?m=1|2 and, Wouters & Odermatt, *supra* n. 156.
159. *See*, G10, available at the BIS web, https://www.bis.org/list/g10publications/index.htm.
160. The Smithsonian Agreement reestablished an international system of fixed exchange rates without the backing of silver or gold, and allowed for devaluation of the U.S. dollar. This was the first time when under an agreement, currency exchange rates were negotiated. Though the agreement was praised by the then-US President, Richard Nixon as *the most significant monetary agreement in world history* yet the par value system began to wane by 1972-1975. *See* Ch. 2 for details.

1967, where the Charter of Algiers[161] was adopted and the basis for permanent institutional structures began. By November 2013 the organization had since expanded to 133 member countries.[162]

The Group of Eight (G8) came into existence in 1997 by the powerful economic democracies of the world. It brought together eight countries: France, Germany, Italy, Japan, UK, US, Canada and Russia. Before G8, in 1975, the Group of Six (G6) was in existence leaving Canada and Russia, then in 1976 Canada joined followed by Russia in 1997 making it G8. G7 and G8 emerged as the most significant forums for economic and financial cooperation by 1998. Not surprisingly until 1998, the international financial architecture was primarily determined by the G7/G8/the BIS/IMF and IOs (IOSCO 1983, IASB 1973 and IAIS 1994).[163]

The Group of Thirty (G30): The Bellagio Group, formed by Austrian economist Fritz Machlup, was the immediate predecessor to the Group of Thirty, which is an international body of leading financiers and academics. The Group was founded in 1978 by Geoffrey Bell at the initiative of the Rockefeller Foundation, which also provided initial funding for the body. The objective of the G30 was to inspire understanding of economic and financial issues and to examine consequences of decisions made in the public interest on foreign exchange, currency, international capital markets, IFIs, central banks and supervision of financial services and markets and macroeconomic issues.[164]

[1] The Group of Twenty (G20)

In the aftermath of Asian crisis, one of the most significant developments was the establishment of the G20 forum[165] in September 1999 as a global policy forum by the G7. G20 along with the FSF (since 2009 the FSB) have been dealing with a series of emerging market crises occurred during the 1990s and other global issues affecting the international financial system and financial stability. The G20 comprises 19 countries and other members: Argentina, Australia, Brazil, Canada, China, France, Germany, India, Indonesia, Italy, Japan, Mexico, Russia, Saudi Arabia, South Africa, the Republic of Korea, Turkey, the UK and the USA with the EU represented by the rotating Council

---

161. The Charter of Algiers (1967), available at http://www.g77.org/doc/algier~1.htmlast accessed October 9, 2017.
162. For membership details, see, www.g77.org.
163. To Summarize: The G5 (the Library group – 1974): US, UK, West Germany, Japan and France. The G6 (1975): US, UK, West Germany, Japan and France, Italy. The G7 (1976): G6 + Canada. The G8 (1997-1999): G7 + Russia + EU. The G22 (1997): G8 + 14 (Argentina, Australia, Brazil, China, Hong Kong, Indonesia, India, Malaysia, Mexico, Poland, Singapore, South Africa, South Korea, Thailand. The G33 (1999): G22 + 11 (Belgium, Chile, Cote'd Ivoire, Egypt, Morocco, Netherlands, Saudi Arabia, Sweden, Spain, Switzerland, Turkey).
164. See for details, http://group30.org/about . The Group published several reports and projects. See for example, for work on supervisory approaches, G30. (2008). The structure of Financial Supervision Approaches and Challenges in a Global Marketplace. Available at http://group30.org/images/uploads/publications/G30_StructureFinancialSupervision2008.pdf f
165. Some of the facts for this section have been taken from G20 meeting websites under respective presidencies. See, for example, G20 information Centre at http://www.g20.utoronto.ca/ https://en.wikipedia.org/wiki/G-20_major_economies, https://g20.org/.

Chapter 3: IFL and the Development of Its Regulatory Architecture §3.02[J]

presidency and the ECB as the 20th member of the G20. In addition, there are three ex officio representatives from the IMF and one from the WB. These meetings are set around a year-long program, which is implemented through senior officials and working groups. It works closely with IOs, including the FSB, International Labor Organization (ILO), IMF, OECD, UN, WB and WTO.[166]

The first G20 Leaders' Summit on *Financial Markets and the World Economy* was hosted by former President George Bush, November 14-15, 2008 in Washington, DC.[167] The 2008 crisis was the worst crisis since the Great Depression, which made French President Nicolas Sarkozy and British Prime Minister, Gordon Brown held out the hope of a *new Bretton Woods* in the lead-up to the first G20 leaders' summit in November 2008.[168] The G20 heads of government came into being in 2008 because economic catastrophe loomed, and the existing global governance organizations and institutions had insufficient capacity to address the disruption.

The Second Leaders' Summit held in London on April 2, 2009 resulted in the transformation of a *Global Plan for Recovery and Reform*.[169] On September 24-25, 2009, President Obama hosted a third G20 (Leaders) Summit in Pittsburgh on *Creating a 21st Century International Economic Architecture*. This Summit launched the new G20 Global Growth Framework mentioned below.[170] The Fourth G20 (Leaders) Summit was held in Toronto from June 26-27, 2010 on Recovery and New Beginnings. A Fifth G20 (Leaders) Summit was held in Seoul from November 11-12, 2010, and the sixth summit was held in 2011 in France, the seventh in 2012 in Mexico followed by the eighth G20 summit of the G20 heads of government held in September 2013, St. Petersburg, Russia.

In September 2013, G20 Leaders met in St. Petersburg and committed to develop comprehensive growth strategies by the Brisbane summit in 2014.[171] These commitments were to be encapsulated in a Brisbane Action Plan. The challenge for 2014 was to transform that commitment into results. To be effective, these growth strategies will need to include practical actions to improve productivity and competitiveness, strengthen investment in infrastructure, encourage trade, make it easier to do business and boost employment. Individual country reforms will need to be complemented and strengthened by similar actions by all G20 members. The ninth G20 heads-of-government meeting took place on November 15-16, 2014 in Brisbane, Australia. The agenda[172] required to: (a) provide strategic priority for growth, financial rebalancing and emerging economies, investment and infrastructure, and employment and labor mobility; (b) support the recovery as the global economy moves beyond the GFC; and,

---

166. *See*, for example, https://g20.org/about-g20/g20-members/.
167. G20. (November 2008). *Declaration Summit on Financial Markets and the World Economy*. Retrieved from http://www.un.org/ga/president/63/commission/declarationG20.pdf.
168. *See*, Waterfield, J. K., (Oct. 15, 2008). Gordon Brown's Bretton Woods Summit Call Risks Spat with Nicholas Sarkozy. *The Telegraph*. Retrieved from http://www.telegraph.co.uk/news/worldnews/europe/france/3205033/Gordon-Browns-Bretton-Woods-summit-call-risks-spat-with-Nicholas-Sarkozy.html last accessed Aug. 28, 2015.
169. G20. *Supra* n. 128 (2009).
170. *Ibid.*
171. FSB Report, *supra* n. 132.
172. *Ibid.*

(c) coordinated growth strategies as well as finalizing agreements on core financial reforms, and actions on tax and anti-corruption.

The 10th G20 Summit was held in Turkey on November 15-16, 2015[173] and for the 11th Summit, China hosted in 2016.[174] The most recent was hosted by Germany in July 2017, which apart from having the highest priority on strong, sustainable, balanced and inclusive growth, the theme of the summit was *shaping an interconnected world*. In this context, the Leaders adopted a declaration focusing on sharing the benefits of globalization; building resilience; improving sustainable livelihood; and, assuming responsibility.[175] The first G20 in South America will be in Buenos Aires in 2018.

The G20 raised high hopes in the beginning and especially when the heads of states summits started taking place regularly[176] bringing much needed credibility to the forum. Many questions arise in the context of the role and position of the G20 vis-à-vis resolving financial crisis: If the G20 is succeeding in achieving its aspirations and goals? Presuming that it endures at the leaders' level: will the G20 stick to a largely economic and financial agenda? Will this agenda complement or rather fall in conflict with the G8, the IMF, the UN and other global institutions economic and security vocations?[177]

Over the past five years, the G20 members have agreed and are implementing a broad range of policy reforms to promote financial stability and support strong, sustainable and balanced growth. The G20's financial regulatory reform agenda is coordinated by the FSB, which reports to the G20 on its progress in developing and implementing reforms. In 2014, the G20 focused four core areas:[178] building resilient financial institutions, to end too-big-to-fail, shadow-banking risks, and, making derivative markets safer.

In recent decades, emerging and developing countries have become bigger players in the global economic horizon. However, their representation at the IMF has not kept pace with these changes (Chapter 6 discusses these issues in detail). The G20 continues to pursue reforms to the IMF's governance structure to ensure that country representation better reflect the economic weight of its members. These changes will build greater confidence in the IMF's ability to respond to global economic instability. The G20's approach beyond the Brisbane Summit will determine the openness of the

---

173. The focus of the Anatalya summit was the grave security and political concerns regarding Syria and the refugees' crisis in Europe. Here, political issues took primacy over the economic and financial market concerns. The deadly Paris attacks and absence of an imminent financial threat transformed the agenda to security and political issues. *See, G20 Leaders' Communique, Antalya Summit, 15-16 Nov 2015*. Retrieved from http://www.mofa.go.jp/files/000111117.pdf.
174. The G20 summit 2016 was held on Sep. 4-5, 2016 in Hangzhou, China. The twelfth G20 was recently concluded in Hamburg, Jul. 7-8, 2017.
175. G20 (Jul. 7-8, 2017). Leader's Declaration: Shaping an Interconnected World. Hamburg. Available at https://www.g20.org/Content/EN/_Anlagen/G20/G20-leaders-declaration.pdf?_blob=publicationFile&v=11 last accessed Aug. 1, 2017. *See also*, http://www.consilium.europa.eu/en/meetings/international-summit/2017/07/07-08/.
176. Heads of State G20 meetings started from the 2008 Washington Summit.
177. *See*, Heinbecker, P. (2011). The Future of the G20 and its Place in Global Governance. *CIGI G20 Paper, 5*. Retrieved from https://www.cigionline.org/sites/default/files/g20no5.pdf last accessed August 27.
178. *See*, G20 (2014). A G20 Agenda for Growth and Resilience. Available at https://www.g20.org/g20_priorities/g20_2014_agenda last accessed Feb. 25, 2014.

Chapter 3: IFL and the Development of Its Regulatory Architecture §3.03

global financial system and consequently the strength and sustainability of global growth. The FSB recommends that the G20 commit to an approach characterized by:[179] (a) global standards for the resolution of global systemically important institutions to ensure failure of cross-border institutions to be handled fairly, predictably and smoothly; (b) deferring each other's market regulatory regimes where they achieve equivalent outcomes; (c) peer reviews and impact assessments to ensure consistent implementation when we get standards right and refinement of standards when we get them wrong; and, (d) enhanced cooperation to avoid domestic measures that fragment the global system.

§3.03 EVALUATING THE EXISTING FINANCIAL ARCHITECTURE

International institutions vary according to the type of the instrument used to bring them to life as that defines the mode of operation, agenda and its effectiveness. Under the current regulatory structure, countries are only answerable to their treaty-based commitments. In IFL sphere however, the international regulatory standards are based on voluntary adoption by individual countries. However, the losses and lessons from the GFC led many to question the adequacy of this system based on the assumption of individual responsibility.[180] Much time has been spent in exploring possibilities to have international regulatory institutions dedicated to risk prevention (with permanent presence and mandate) and risk management (in case of eruption of a crisis). Clearly, IFL requires establishment of a permanent body addressing both crisis prevention as well as crisis-management system if financial market stability remains a public good and governments remain committed to provide their respective publics this global public good. Nonetheless, this is a major agenda for IFL and its regulatory structures. There are possibilities where an institution like the FSB with the help of support institutions can discharge both of the functions in future that is, crisis prevention and crisis management by adopting dynamic variations to its soft-law-based structure.

The present regulatory architecture of international financial governance can be marked broadly by three institutional pillars: the core pillars, the emerging pillars and the support pillars. The core pillars comprise of the G7 and the IMF, the G20 and the IMF as the emerging pillars, while the support pillars extend facilitation to the overall regulatory institutional structure, which forms a complex web of different technical committees under the BIS, the WB and the OECD. These committees range from insurance to banking supervision to securities regulations, payment mechanism to accounting standards etc. The interesting feature is to look at the web of overlapping mechanisms, influence of control and supervision and coordination amongst all these

---

179. *See*, Carney, M. (Feb. 24, 2014). *Financial Reforms: Progress and Challenges. Letter to the G20 Finance Ministers and Central Bank Governors*, FSB. Retrieved from https://www.financialstabilityboard.org/publications/r_140222.pdf.
180. Arner & Taylor, *supra* n. 129.

bodies. The G7 sets the direction for the market trends and the supervisory models to be adopted, while the IMF ensures how much compliance is being made by various state and non-state actors (core pillars). The relationship between these two domineering bodies is based on moral suasion while these bodies exert influence relationship with almost all the other actors of the architecture.

Figure 3.1 The Current IFRA: Depicting Interaction Relationship Between Various International Financial Actors[181]

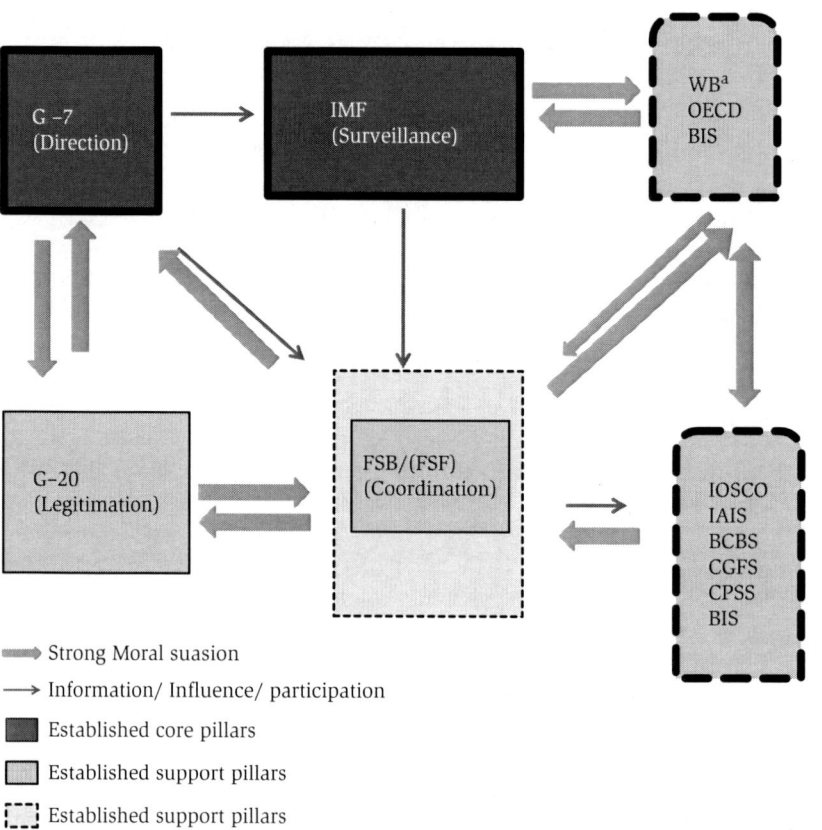

More interesting is the position and role being played by the emergent pillars in the post-2008 crisis where the G20 and the FSB are occupying central position in terms

---

[181]. *See*, Ashraf, U. (Jun. 21, 2012). The Reform of the International Financial Regulatory Architecture: Addressing Legitimacy Issues. Paper presented at the 4th Conference on Global Financial Markets, Martin Luther University Halle-Wittenberg.

Chapter 3: IFL and the Development of Its Regulatory Architecture §3.03

of expanded memberships and therefore legitimizing its authority.[182] The nature of the interaction taking place between the core pillars and emerging pillars is of strong moral suasion; however, G7 and G20 interaction relation is more of influence as their representative membership overlaps. The support pillars, which are primarily technical bodies (under the BIS and the WB) are sharing information between themselves apart from coordinating linkages with the core and emerging pillars. Recently, the FSB has taken over the charge of coordination between various offshoots of supervisory structure. Although, the G20 is perceived to be a direction-setting platform, recent scholarship has been alluding to the FSB assuming a pivotal role in regulating global finance.[183]

Despite significant progress made recently towards stabilizing future financial transactions, the existing IFRA clearly attracts criticism for want of legitimacy, proper representation of the countries in the decision-making processes and a lack of institutional accountability. This has been recognized in literature and some effort is being made to bring about governance reforms in regulatory institutions in the wake of mounting criticism. The G20 leaders, in their November 2008 statement stated:

> [E]merging and developing countries, including the poorest ones, should have greater voice and representation. The FSF must expand urgently to a broader membership of emerging economies and other major standard setting bodies should promptly review their membership.[184]

From 2008 to 2017, a number of financial institutions have made progress in adopting new reforms and transforming their role like the FSB, however, significant others have yet to implement and adopt new roles like the IMF. It was agreed by over 50 Heads of States and two hundred Finance Ministers that the global regulatory institutions including the BIS, the BCBS and the FSF should *enhance their outreach and consultation with developing countries.*[185] In 2015, the G20 Finance and Central Bank Deputies met in Istanbul and agreed on (a) full, consistent and prompt implementation of agreed reforms; (b) the design of remaining post-crisis reforms; and, (c) addressing new risks and vulnerabilities as top priorities for the FSB's G20 financial regulation agenda.[186]

The plenary agreed to report an annual consolidated report on the implementation of the regulator reforms and their effects to the G20. The idea is to use these reports

---

182. See Ch. 6 for details on these representation and legitimation issues.
183. See for perspectives on Consolidation of regulatory structures, Ashraf, U., & Arner, D. W. (October 2011). *The Need for Consolidating International Financial Regulatory Architecture: Case for a Global Supervisor.* Presented at *the Lessons Learned from the Financial Crisis*, Proceedings of 13th International Conference on Finance and Banking. Karviná: Silesian University.
184. G20. (November 2008). *Supra* n. 174. *See also*, Griffith-Jones and Young, *supra* n. 62.
185. *See*, Addressing systemic issues: enhancing the coherence and consistency of the international monetary, financial and trading systems in support of development in UN. (2003). Monterrey Consensus of the International Conference on Financing for Development. Mar. 18-22, 2002, Monterrey, Mexico: Department of Economic and Social Affairs, UN p. 19.
186. FSB, (Apr. 9, 2015). Financial Reforms: Progress on the Work Plan for the Antalya Summit. The letter available at http://www.financialstabilityboard.org/wp-content/uploads/FSB-Chairs-letter-to-G20-April-2015.pdf.

(inclusive of the FSB's peer reviews) to enable the G20 to evaluate reforms if are meeting their intended objectives and to highlight good practices and shortcomings. The second priority area is finalizing the remaining post-crisis reform agenda. In this regard, the emphasis is on three issue areas: completion of the capital framework for banks, measures to help end too-big-to-fail and putting in place appropriate safe guards against potential risks from derivatives market. And finally, the third priority for the FSB is to address new risks and vulnerabilities, which it has identified as: market-based finance and misconduct or moral hazard issue. The moral hazard or the misconduct issue in the financial institutions has risen to a level having the potential to create systemic risk. Therefore, the work plan that the FSB has gathered includes working together with other institutions like the World Bank to benchmark and monitor the reforms on incentives and compensation practices.[187]

§3.04 CONCLUSION

To conclude, this chapter addressed two distinct streams: the first stream focused on ideological and political ethos underpinning the development of the financial markets and how these contoured the formation of the regulatory institutions. Stream II rigorously studied structural manifestations of IFL thought its regulatory network and considered its institutional heritage, which was influenced from the post-War and the post-Bretton Woods time to evaluate the role of law in the development of international financial markets. In the process, it surveyed the ethos of the WC and the NIFA, and has analyzed the structure, role and functions of the most important pillars of the IFRA to identify main obstacles to reform. It questioned the resilience of the prevalent regulatory architecture in the wake of next crisis.

The next three chapters appraise whether *an enforcement mechanism* in the realm of IFL is crucial in the post-crisis reconstruction of the regulatory architecture by asking a set of questions: What have the reforms since 2008 achieved so far. Has financial system become safer and fairer than it used to be before the crises? If the regulatory architecture as it exists today has become resilient enough to prevent future financial disruptions? The answers to these questions would summarize what the reforms have achieved so far and whether the existing IFRA presents the ideals that post-2008 regulatory reform envisioned. These questions are important to answer in order to adjust and align the reforms underway. The next three chapters are looking at these questions in order to evaluate whether *an enforcement mechanism* in the realm of IFL is indispensable in the post-crisis reconstruction of the regulatory architecture.

---

187. The FSB in its Frankfurt meeting included five new institutions as plenary members: the ministries of finance/treasuries for Argentina, Indonesia, Saudi Arabia and Turkey and the South African at the Reserve Bank.

CHAPTER 4
Regulatory Regimes and IFL*

The IFRA was shaped mainly by sporadic financial crises and haphazard regulatory responses from Bretton Woods to WC to the so-called NIFA as discussed in the previous chapter. The GFC exposed the various dimensions of the then financial architecture, essentially its non-legal, noncommittal and transient nature. The post-GFC responses iterate the noncommittal nature of the new regulations (such as Basel). And yet the SDC exposed weaknesses within a legal, committal and intransient framework of the European single market.[1] The crisis in the European Union (EU) exposed not only the weaker theoretical and conceptual foundations of the treaty-based binding structure but also brought to light the fragility and incompleteness of the integration mechanics embraced during the development of the single market. Informal International Lawmaking (IN-LAW) scholarship as well as the Global Administrative Law (GAL)'s compensatory approach claimed much praise by providing alternative perspectives to seek compliance, however, the most recent populist-cum-nationalist trend discredit the utility of IN-LAW as well as GAL in policy debate. The conflict between pursuing pure national interest versus adopting obscure, uncertain and at times irrelevant standards is complex. The conflicts raise an extremely simple yet hard-to-answer question: what could be an optimum regulatory regime, if any?

Right after the 2008 crisis, many academic and policy forums raised the question that if Basel II were implemented globally, would it still result in the 2008 meltdown. *The answer was a simple resounding no.* In the midst of the reforms, another question frequented the debate: if Basel II could not stop the GFC, would Basel III (or IV) be a bulwark against a future one? As simplistic as it may sound, the question has ignited a controversial debate on the accountability and legitimacy of not only the Basel regime

---

* This chapter has benefitted from an earlier research conducted for a 2012 publication: Conceptual Challenges under Basel II and Basel III, London, Munich: LAP. I am grateful to Prof. George Walker, and Prof. David Southern, who, at a time when the financial crisis just started, invoked in me a great interest to study Basel regulatory process.
1. *See*, Ch. 5 for details.

but also of the processes through which these international regimes are negotiated and implemented.

Regulatory institutions make the core of the pyramid of international financial system and its various pillars render support to the functioning of economic globalism. The most revolutionary and ambitious of this regulatory effort at an international level has been the Basel regime. Though Basel I came with a much simpler script, it's Basel II and beyond that has enlarged the canvass in order to develop a comprehensive approach aimed at globally harmonized regulations. Given the consensus-based decision-making model, voluntary adoption and complexity of international finance under the NIFA, the supersession of Basel II even before its universal adoption hardly surprised many. Now, we are already on to Basel III, for which adoption time line has been continuously shifting forward since 2011. The question is less of enforcement per se of a regulatory regime but the issue is of the outcomes of such enforcement.

This chapter compares and contrasts the pre- and post-2008 Basel Regulatory regimes to evaluate for its effectiveness as a risk prevention tool. This focused *substance and process* analysis reviews transnational regulatory goals against the prevalent national priorities and practices. The pre-2008 period analyzes the development of the capital adequacy regulation (the Basel I, II and III) and emergence of various risks especially the Operational Risk (OR). The capital buffers prescribed under the Basel II (the pre-2008 scenario) were scant, while the Basel III framework is yet to be judged against future financial flare-ups. The post-2008 phase focuses on Basel III critique in terms of the question raised above: if Basel III would be strong enough to stop another global financial meltdown?

In line with this book's primary question – whether the newly evolving soft-law-based regulatory architecture is resilient enough against future crises – this chapter probes two issues: (1) relevancy of the regulatory substance: that is, if implementing the regulatory standards meet the intended objective of providing financial stability; and, (2) whether the standards are implemented in practice, and if not, then the gap between the expected outcomes and actual outcomes.[2] Section §4.02 introduces us to what regulation implies, the definitional aspects of regulation, supervision in the context of regulatory risk management and the various approaches to it. Section §4.03 provides substantial analysis on the pre-2008 period capital standards – formation, development and impact assessment. Section §4.04 looks at the post-2008 regulatory reform, primarily Basel III and its impact assessment. Section §4.05 critically looks collectively at the resilience of the post-2008 regulatory initiatives and how these are shaping the future of IFL.

---

2. This subject is in want of quantitative studies. Limited analysis can be found in FSAPs and ROSC by the IMF.

§4.01 REGULATION AND RISK MANAGEMENT

[A] Some Distinctions

[1] Regulation and Supervision

Despite the fact that regulation and supervision are sometimes used interchangeably, there are some important conceptual distinctions between both of these terms. Regulations can be defined as: *a set of rules and standards that govern financial institutions and their main objective is to foster financial stability and to protect the customers of financial services.*[3] A correlated second term is supervision, which can be defined as: *a process designed to oversee financial institutions in order to ensure that the rules and standards are properly applied.*[4] Note the terms, govern versus oversee, for regulation and supervision respectively.

Regulation and supervision are related yet distinct terms and cannot be held apart. In a technical sense, regulation refers to the *substance*, actual rules and structure of the institutions, while supervision refers to the *process* of monitoring of compliance to these rules, which is ensuring enforcement of regulatory standards to meet the objective of protecting financial market participants.[5] These two bodies, one assigned the task of rule-making and the other with a mandate to monitor the enforcement of those rules may work separately but they cannot work independent of each other in any jurisdiction. An accomplished supervision would not let absolute failures in the regulatory policy, though not the vice versa. It is the substance of the rules that holds primacy and steers the regulatory terrain of financial landscape in any jurisdiction.

Supervision has two dimensions, micro and macro. Both dimensions complement each other, and a compromise on either of the two would be detrimental to the other. The objective of the micro-supervision is to oversee and limit the distress of individual financial institutions i.e., a protection extended to the individual customers of a particular bank or a financial institution. On the other hand, macro-supervision has a system-wide focus, with a discernible objective of the protection of the economy as a whole, including overall performance of state institutions.

[2] Key Regulatory Structures

To formulate key standards, the FSB has devised a criterion for a sound financial system comprising of: relevant and objective, universality in applicability, flexible in implementation (given unique special circumstances of member countries), broadly

---

3. Larosiere, J. d. (February 2009). Report of the High Level Group on Financial Supervision in the EU. Brussels. Available at http://ec.europa.eu/internal_market/finances/docs/de_larosiere_report_en.pdf.
4. As above, (Larosiere 2009).
5. FCIC. (January 2011). *The Financial Crisis Inquiry Report: Final Report of the National Commission on the Causes of the Financial and Economic Crisis in the United States.* Retrieved from, http://www.gpo.gov/fdsys/pkg/GPO-FCIC/pdf/GPO-FCIC.pdf, p.xviii, last accessed, Aug. 22, 2015.

endorsed (i.e., such standards to be issued by an internationally recognized body in the relevant area and may include a public consultation process. This criterion would also be satisfied when endorsed by IFIs, such as the IMF and the World Bank (WB), and finally, assessable by national authorities or by third parties such as the IFIs.[6]

Crises and reform processes also trigger debate on defining regulatory domain. Specifically, whether the domain of the regulator should be *function-specific,* and if so, then in that instance, whether it is appropriate to incorporate provisions for multiple regulators. On the other hand, if the domain is not function-specific, then, whether to have institutional regulators whose regulatory ambit is delineated by institutional typology? It is necessary to comprehend these distinctions as different models are being pursued in various jurisdictions. This is almost critical because international regulatory standards are adopted by individual Member States only through domestic legislation. Four common financial regulatory structures have been identified by the Group of Thirty (G30) described briefly as below: In a functional regulatory structure, the supervisory oversight is determined by the business that is being transacted by the entity, without regard to its legal status. Each type of business may have its own functional regulator.[7]

Regulation of a particular financial institution or a bank generally depends on the kind of business it does, and if regulation depends upon a particular business trait of the institution, it would be functional regulation. The prime example is the system being followed in the UK, Italy and France. The G30 defines the institutional structure as: [O]ne in which a firm's legal status (e.g., a bank, broker-dealer, or insurance company) determines, which regulator is tasked with overseeing its activity from both a safety and soundness and a business conduct perspective.[8]

That is, if an institution performs some of the functions of a universal bank, it will be subject to bank regulations under the institutional structure of regulation. It is adopted in Germany, China and Mexico.

The G30 defines the single integrated structure as: [O]ne in which a single universal regulator conducts safety and soundness, and oversight and conduct-of-business for all the sectors of financial services business.[9] From 1998 to 2012 the UK operated under a single integrated structure. The Financial Services Authority (FSA)'s responsibilities included, *inter alia*: prudential supervision of banks, building societies, investment

---

6. Key standards come under various policy areas and the criteria is provided at the FSB website, and includes standards on: Macroeconomic Policy and Data Transparency, Financial Regulation and Supervision and Institutional and Market Infrastructure. FSB. *Key Standards for Sound Financial Systems*. Retrieved from http://www.financialstabilityboard.org/what-we-do/about-the-compendium-of-standards/key_standards/?page_moved = 1 last accessed Aug. 21, 2015. See also, G30 (2008). The Structure of Financial Supervision: Approaches and Challenges in a Global Marketplace. Available at http://group30.org/images/uploads/publications/G30_Structure FinancialSupervision2008.pdf, last accessed, May 5, 2017. Hereinafter noted as G30 (2008).
7. G30 (2008).
8. *Ibid.* p. 13.
9. *Ibid.*

Chapter 4: Regulatory Regimes and IFL　　　　　　　　　　　　　　　　§4.01[A]

firms, insurance companies; securities firms, and, clearing and settlement systems.[10] Whereas monetary policy is held separately, and in the case of the UK, was dispensed by the BoE.

[3]　Twin-Peak Structure

Twin peak structure is adopted by Australia and the Netherlands. The G30 defines the twin-peak structure as: [A] form of regulation by objective is one in which there is a separation of regulatory functions between two regulators: one that performs the safety and soundness supervision function and the other that focuses on conduct-of-business regulation.[11]

The US has adopted an exceptional structure to any of the above, possibly because of the GLBA,[12] which repealed parts of the GSA of 1933, removing barriers in the market among banking companies, securities companies and insurance companies. The GSA prohibited any combination of an investment bank, a commercial bank or an insurance company functions to be exercised by any one institution. The GSA aimed *to enhance competition* in the financial services industry by providing a prudential framework for the affiliation of banks, securities firms, and other financial service providers, and for other purposes.

This diversity of financial markets in its structures as well as processing of functions makes it challenging to have a standardized international regulatory framework especially for cross-border financial transactions. Each of the regulatory approaches has its own merits and demerits. For example, functional regulation is more specialized it is therefore, generally viewed as more sensitive to particular features of a specific kind of business and is likely to pose lower barriers to entry to new businesses. Since new entrants are often an important source of innovation, this may contribute to the dynamic efficiency of the financial system. Moreover, since functions tend to be more stable over time and across countries than the institutions which perform them, functional regulation may provide a more stable regulatory framework than institutional regulation. However, this does not hold true when some specialized financial institution assumes multiple functions. This complexity then may lead to fragmented supervision jeopardizing stability of the market system.[13] Regulating diverse and competing institutions complicates the choice of regulatory framework by restraining flexibility to accommodate the distinct needs of individual institutions. It

---

10. Brown, G., King, M., & McCarthy, C. (2006). Memorandum of Understanding between HM Treasury, the Bank of England and the Financial Services Authority, March 2006. Available at http://www.bankofengland.co.uk/financialstability/Documents/mou.pdf, last accessed, Feb. 26, 2014.
11. G30 (2008).
12. Known as the Financial Services Modernization Act (FSMA), the US Congress enacted Nov. 12, 1999.
13. Herring, R. J. (1993). International Banking Deregulation: The Great Banking Experiment. *The Journal of Finance, 48*(4), 1553-1556.

not only creates arbitrage opportunities for some but also further complicates regulatory design as well as implementation. The financial market is competitive, innovative and fast while the regulators lag mostly behind in this race.[14]

[4]   Regulatory Risk Management

I made a mistake in presuming that the self-interests of organizations, specifically banks and others were such that they were best capable of protecting their own shareholders and their equity in the firms. Further, on the continuum of crisis he said, [T]is modern risk management paradigm held sway for decades...the whole intellectual edifice collapsed in the summer of last year. (Allen Greenspan's confession)[15]

Stability and efficiency in financial system and welfare of market participants is usually sought through a combination of rules and standards set by the law and the discipline imposed by market players themselves. The sheer number of transactions in the financial sector and huge volume of money involved render financial markets vulnerable to huge risk exposures. Over the past three decades 147 banking crises have been counted, of which 13 were reported as borderline events with deeper implications on the financial system.[16] According to a range of reviews, there have been at least 42 systemic banking crises in 37 countries. There have been at least nine major financial crises during the 1990s and 2000s in EMEs.[17] Banking crises have become more frequent in the post-Bretton Woods period, occurring on an average after every 20 to 25 years in both industrial and emerging market countries with the annual probability of crisis about 4%-5% according to an analysis.[18] Unemployment rates in industrialized countries remain 50% higher than 2008. One hundred million more people live in extreme poverty than there were before the 2008 crisis.

It is safe to make an assumption from the frequency of repetitive crisis episodes that if regulators remain unable to address basic systemic problems swiftly and effectively, the world may continue to be traumatized by shocks from recurring

---

14. Coats, D. (Ed.) (2011). Exiting From the Crisis: Towards a Model of more Equitable and Sustainable Growth. Report of a Trade Union Task Force, European Trade Union Institute (ETUI), Brussels. Available at http://www.ituc-csi.org/IMG/pdf/Exiting_from_the_crisis_Washington.pdf p. 130.
15. The former Chairman of the Fed in a testimony concedes on errors of regulation and judgment by the market, *see*, *The Financial Crisis and the Role of Federal Regulators*, Hearing before the Committee on Oversight and Government Reform House of Representatives, House Hearing, 110 Congress, Oct. 23, 2008. Available at http://www.gpo.gov/fdsys/pkg/CHRG-110hhrg55764/html/CHRG-110hhrg55764.htm last accessed Aug. 23, 2015.
16. *See*, Laeven, L., & Valencia, F. (2012). Systemic Banking Crises Database: An Update (Vol. WP/12/163): IMF. Available at http://www.imf.org/external/pubs/ft/wp/2012/wp12163.pdf.
17. *See*, Laeven, L. & F. Valencia, Systemic Banking Crises: A New Database. International Monetary Fund, Washington, D.C.(IMF Working Paper WP/08/224), 2002 at 3 and Kawai, M. Reform of the International Financial Architecture: An Asian Perspective, *The Singapore Economic Review*, 5(1), 207, (2010) at 207.
18. Walter, S. (2011). Basel III: Stronger Banks and a More Resilient Financial System. Speech by the Secretary-General, BCBS at the Financial Stability Institute, *see*, http://www.bis.org/speeches/sp110406.htm last accessed Aug. 23, 2015.

Chapter 4: Regulatory Regimes and IFL

§4.01[A]

episodes of crises. Traditionally costly banking crises were associated with emerging economies but the 2008 crisis has changed this thesis. It raises questions on the regulatory substance and the processes, which are mainly directed and designed by advanced economies.

Take the case of Basel regulation for an instance. Both Basel I and II included a risk-weighted capital adequacy framework. However, for the last 20 years banks' balance sheets have ballooned while their equity failed to take off. For example, from 1993 to 2008 the total assets of a sample of G-SIFIs saw a 12-fold increase (increasing from USD 2.6 trillion to just over USD 30 trillion). But the capital funding of these assets only increased sevenfold, (from USD 125 billion to USD 890 billion).[19] In risk terms, the average risk weight declined from 70% to below 40%. However, the real issue is that this reduction does not represent a genuine reduction of risk in the banking system.[20]

Haldane by drawing a simple analogy between catching a Frisbee and catching a financial crisis narrates the real problem why risk assessment and management in the financial sector often remain far from the grasp of regulators and supervisors. Catching a Frisbee is difficult in particular, by animals like a dog given the complexity of calculating various parameters like speed, angle and distance however catching a Frisbee is remarkably common. It follows the simplest of rule of thumb: *running at a speed so that the angle of gaze to the Frisbee remains roughly constant.* For humans (regulators) however, catching a crisis like catching a Frisbee is difficult. Making it efficacious requires the regulator to weigh in a complex array of financial and psychological parameters, like allowing innovation while grasping risk appetite of the market can be challenging. Reflecting on the reasons behind a watchdogs' failure, writes Haldane, that the causes are simple. It is rather a *hesitation to restrain and to play a balancing act between innovation, independence and stability*. His paper explores sub-optimal, overly complex regulations that are being developed in the aftermath of the crisis and are costly and cumbersome. In financial regulation, *less can serve more*, however optimum effectiveness of rules is a must.[21] The Secretary-General of the Organization for Economic Co-operation and Development (OECD), Angel Gurría[22] said that the crisis reflected *massive failures of financial regulation, supervision and governance. Ambitious financial innovation has more or less always caused regulatory ambition.*[23] Since the heavily regulated entities are constantly looking for ways to circumvent regulation, therefore, catching a crisis Frisbee can be formidable in the financial sector.[24] Most often than not, regulators remain in dilemma whether to act

---

19. *Ibid.*
20. *Ibid.*
21. Haldane, A.G. (2012). The Dog and the Frisbee. The Federal Reserve Bank of Kansas City's 36th Economic Symposium, *The Changing Policy Landscape*, Jackson Hole, Aug. 31, 2012. Wyoming.
22. Coats, *Supra* n. 14. p. 14.
23. *See*, for example, Merton H. Miller, Financial Innovation: The Last Twenty Years and the Next, *Journal of Financial and Quantitative Analysis*, 21 (1986) 459.
24. Generally referred to as *regulatory dialectics* where questions regarding ex-ante or ex-post regulation pose a dilemma to initiate any action.

ex-ante or in the event of a crisis follow a reactionary approach[25] given the costs that a delayed response to crisis can bring on a financial system. Consequently, the modern approach to handling risk management in financial markets ideally requires regulatory authority engagement with industry consultation to derive a general agreement on enforceable standards.

Currently, significant developments are taking place especially as the Basel III regulations have been rolled out for implementation and adoption. There is a tough balance between ensuing financial stability and not to overburden market participants with increased compliance costs. Usually, the perceived short-term costs from increased regulation are easier to sell politically, compared to the abstract benefits of lowering the risks through these regulations to the future generations,[26] however, over-regulation can hamper financial markets' independence by restraining the markets to open and competitive allocation of resources (as new regulations can increase the costs of compliance in the immediate future). Unfortunately, despite having this debate on finding the perfect balance between expensive crises and rising costs of compliance to the various regulatory regimes, the institutional development context remains in want of new theories on preventing contagion and systemic risk.[27] Systemic crises almost always redefine and redirect the course of market developments. Events like the collapse of Bankhaus Herstatt redefined the concept of *interconnectedness* of international markets. The history of financial crisis is as old as the market itself[28] and the regulation of financial markets is a continuing task. As financial markets expand, new and innovative products will continue to develop, making it therefore, impossible to apply a *one-size-fits-all* formula for effective regulation and supervision of international financial markets and institutions. The market shows patterns in its behavior as it responds to crisis.

[5]   The Regulatory Objective

Under the laissez faire economy, it is generally believed that the financial regulations are largely based on the theory of rational and self-correcting market principles.[29]

---

25. *See*, Kane, E. (1987). Competitive Financial Reregulation: An International Perspective. In R. Portes & A. Swoboda (Eds.), *Threats to International Financial Stability*, Cambridge University Press, p. 114.
26. *See*, Ingves, S. (November 2014). Implementing the Regulatory Reform Agenda: The Pitfall of Myopia, Paper presented at the Federal Reserve Bank of Chicago, by the Chairman, BCBS and Governor of the Sveriges Riksbank, available at http://www.financialstabilityboard.org/wp-content/uploads/Stefan-Ingves-Implementing-the-regulatory-reform-agenda-the-pitfall-of-myopia.pdf.
27. Allen, F., & Carletti, E. (2013). New Theories to Underpin Financial Reform. *Journal of Financial Stability*, 9, 242-249. *See* also, Ch. 3.
28. Kindleberger, C. P., & Aliber, R. Z. (2005). *Manias, Panics, and Crashes: A History of Financial Crises* (5 ed.). Hoboken, N.J. John Wiley & Sons.
29. *See*, Fama, E. F. (1970). Efficient Capital Markets: A Review of Theory and Empirical Work. *The Journal of Finance*, 25(2), 383-417. Paper presented at the Twenty-Eighth Annual Meetings of the American Finance Association New York, Dec. 28-30, 1969. Available at http://www.e-m-h.org/Fama70.pdf and, Larsen, P. T. (2009, March 31). A Lot to be Straightened Out. Financial Times, available at http://www.ft.com/intl/cms/s/0/5f5b2200-1d8a-11de-9eb3-00144feabdc0.

Similarly, at the heart of the libertarian dogma is the belief that markets know best and that *those who compete well will prosper, while those who do not will fail.*[30] Regulations, over the past few decades before the GFC rested on the notion that markets are rational and highly efficient at allocating resources besides being capable of exercising a good self-policing and self-correcting mechanism.[31] On the other hand, from the time of Maynard Keynes to the GFC, the necessity of having a *steady-hand-of-government* in managing those *animal spirits*[32] has also been underlined in scholarship mainly as the result of repetitive financial crisis in Latin America and East Asia. These crises challenge the perception that markets offer symmetric information and hence can always act rationally.[33] Many instances of crises brought to light risks posed by under-regulated or unregulated financial sectors to the financial system.[34]

Talking of the incapacity of regulatory regimes and misaligned regulatory objectives, Schooner and Taylor criticize Basel capital regulations, which remain by large, the most comprehensive set of regulatory policies on capital requirements so far. They note, first, that Basel I was unable to differentiate Credit Risk under the formula for risk-weighting categories as risk was evaluated on loan-by-loan basis rather than at the portfolio level at that time. Second, the OECD/non-OECD distinction was arbitrary and mostly politically driven. One of the major criticisms of Basel I, they identified, was the failure to recognize the risk being created through diversification.[35] In relation to Basel II, due to procyclicality trends Basel II underestimated the risks in good times while overestimated for bad times.[36] The system of banking regulation thus requires a thorough overhaul.[37] Ideally, financial regulation should aim at: (a) maintaining stability by ensuring solvency of market actors, (b) implementing procedures that allow for orderly winding up of failed institutions, (c) limiting taxpayers' exposure to risks and limiting future bailouts[38] (d) protecting, in particular, small investors against fraud, and, (e) ensuring capital availability, its appropriate allocation, if as long as it doesn't distort the balance of market forces.

---

html#axzz3jYyHDR8Z, p. 9, last accessed Aug. 23, 2015. *See* also, Kaufman, H. (Apr. 28, 2009). How Libertarian Dogma Led the Fed Astray. *Financial Times. See*, http://economistsview.typepad.com/economistsview/2009/04/libertarian-dogma-and-the-fed.html, p. 11.

30. Kaufman, H. (Apr. 28, 2009).
31. Schooner, H. M., & Taylor, M. W. (2010). *Global Bank Regulations: Principles and Policies.* Academic Press, USA.
32. Akerlof, G. A., & Shiller, R. J. (2009). *Animal Spirits: How Human Psychology Drives the Economy, and Why it Matters for Global Capitalism,* Princeton University Press.
33. *See,* Blundell-Wignall, A., & Atkinson, P. (2008). The Sub-Prime Crisis: Casual Distortions and Regulatory Reforms. Paper presented at the Lessons from Financial Turmoil of 2007 & 2008, Jul. 14-15, 2008, Reserve Bank of Australia, available at http://www.rba.gov.au/publications/confs/2008/index.html, and, Blundell-Wignall, A., Atkinson, P., & Lee, S. H. (2008). The Current Financial Crisis: Causes and Policy Issues. Financial Market Trends – OECD. Retrieved from http://www.oecd.org/finance/financial-markets/41942872.pdf.
34. Paletta, D., & Scannell, K. (Mar. 11, 2010). The Financial Crisis: Some Questions for Those Fixing the Mess. *The Wall Street Journal*, p. 20.
35. Schooner, H. M., & Taylor, M. W. (2010).
36. Blundell-Wignall, A., & Atkinson, P. (2008). pp. 55-100.
37. Hellwig, M. (2010). Capital Regulations after the Crisis: Business as Usual. Max Planck Institute for Research on Collective Goods, p. 31.
38. Habbard, P., Coats, D., & Watt, A., The Regulation of Financial Markets. In Coats, D. (2011), p. 131, *supra* n. 14.

§4.02 THE BASEL: INCEPTION AND DEVELOPMENT

Following the collapse of fixed exchange rate system and rapid liberalization of capital flows in the West, international financial markets were exposed to new uncertainties arising out of hybrid transactions and new capital and interest rate risks, which emanated from floating exchange rates and increased cross-border capital flows. This rapid liberalization, excessive borrowing and lending fueled by massive amounts of petrodollars, and interest rate hikes in the US laid bare the causal link between systemic risk and systemic crisis. The situation was aggravated further with the collapse of a number of big financial institutions such as the Franklin National Bank in the US and Bankhaus Herstatt in Germany resulting in the very first set of regulatory recommendations, known as Capital Accords.

[A] Historical Evidence I: Basel I and II

The Basel Committee began its journey with the issuance of initial recommendations in 1975 commonly called the *First Concordat*. The first concordat, for the first time in the history of international financial regulation (IFR), acknowledged and established the principle of joint responsibility between home and host supervisors for supervision of foreign banking establishments. It was stated that the provision of *liquidity* shall be the responsibility of host supervisors and the degree of *solvency* of foreign branches shall be the responsibility of home-supervisors. The Concordat placed strong emphasis on information sharing and cooperation between home and host authorities. Following the collapse of Banco Ambrosiano in 1982, and keeping in view the problems identified in regulation of holding companies and mixed activity groups, the Basel issued *the Revised Concordat in 1983* wherein, in addition to earlier principles, it was stated that the authorities should adopt the principle of *consolidated supervision* and that the health of financial institutions should be judged on both stand-alone and consolidated-basis. The Revised Concordat further made an important recommendation that the home and host authorities should monitor the effectiveness of supervision conducted by the other and should step in to extend supervision or to take necessary action if the supervision being done by the other is less satisfactory. The 1983 Revised Concordat was subsequently examined by the Basel Committee to issue an *Information Supplement*

The year 1988 marked an important milestone in the history of international financial market's regulation. The Basel Committee was successful in creating an agreement among supervisory authorities on the application of minimum capital rules, commonly called *the Basel Capital Accord or Basel I*. The Basel I fixed a minimum capital ratio of 8% to total risk-adjusted assets and provided a tiered definition of capital, and divided bank assets into different risk buckets on the basis of underlying risks involved.[39] Surprisingly, the Basel I faced minimal resistance. The factors behind

---

39. Alexander, K., Dhumale, R., & Eatwell, J. (2006). *Global Governance of Financial Systems: The International Regulation of Systemic Risk*. Oxford University Press.

its universal acceptance and application were its *relative simplicity of the regime and minimum regulatory compliance costs.*

However, subsequently, it became the subject of increased criticism as the focus of these rules was only counterparty default, that is, it encompassed factors relating to only credit risk. Market and operational risk were not weighed in for calculating minimum capital ratios for banks.[40] Another point that worked to its disadvantage was its failure to create a level-playing field for all IFIs through its classification system as it assigned a 0% risk figure for the OECD Governments and central bank credits, while a 100% risk figure for all other claims irrespective of the credit standing of the counterparty concerned.[41]

The next significant gain on the regulatory consolidation was the establishment of the *Minimum Standards* in 1992, followed by the adoption of the *Core Principles* for effective banking supervision in 1997. Though a *Market Risk* charge was also included in Basel I through the Market Risk Amendment in 1996 (following the failure of the Barings Bank), however, due to its crude classification system and failure to adjust to subsequent changes in the structure and the operation of financial markets, the single measurement mechanism became outdated. It became eminent to overhaul the whole system. The Basel Committee thus started working to devise a more risk sensitive and adaptable-to-change mechanism.

After extensive consultations, a new capital framework, commonly called *Basel II*, was introduced in 2004. The purpose of this framework was to improve safety and soundness of the financial system through a *three-pillar structure*, comprising of: (i) capital adequacy, (ii) supervisory review and (iii) market discipline through necessary disclosures.[42]

This new system under Basel II was considered to be highly risk sensitive as additional risk buckets were incorporated for calculating minimum capital requirements. A new operational risk charge was added for losses triggered by failure of internal control systems, processes and staff corruption. This effort to reinforce internal controls and systems was accompanied by new supervisory-review mechanisms and market-disclosure requirements. Largely, the new system was kept flexible, innovative and adjustable to varying banking structures, operations and products. The Basel Committee offered banks a choice between two broad methodologies for calculating their capital requirements for credit risk including: (a) the Standardized Approach (TSA), to measure credit risk in a standardized manner supported by external credit assessments; and, (b) the Internal Ratings-based Approach (IRA), which subject to explicit approval of the bank's supervisors, would allow banks to use their internal rating system for credit risk.[43]

Unfortunately, this new framework also failed to prevent the next crisis. Notably, the Basel Committee had limited participation with no formal status to seek compliance to its regulatory framework. The structure was weak in the sense that it remained

---

40. Walker, G. A. (2001). *International Banking Regulation: Law, Policy and Practice*. Kluwer Law.
41. Walker, G. A. (1999). So Close but So Far. FT (FRR), pp. 1-3.
42. Walker, G. A. (2001). *Supra* n. 40.
43. Valdez, S., & Molyneux, P. (2010). *An Introduction to Global Financial Markets* (6 ed.): Palgrave.

ineffective in devising binding international standards in regulating financial markets and financial institutions. Surprisingly, it worked remarkably well in developing a consensus on application of minimum standards in the supervision of financial markets and in formulating common standards. However, many member countries remained unable to adopt the Basel regulation into their domestic laws for implementation.

[1]   An Assessment

Basel I and Basel II employed the strategy to transfer risk management on to banks and hold them accountable through transparency of their actions. Banks – large ones in particular – were entrusted with the responsibility of setting up risk assessment models for their organizations, instituting changes to transform their organizational culture, and to implement internal control models. Accountability, in this regard was based on transparent compliance to capital adequacy requirements for credit, market and operational risk, whereas transparency in this case rested on disclosure by the market participants and monitoring by the regulator.

Under the Basel regime, based on the realization that one size would not fit all variants of risk, different models were designed to measure each category of risk. For example, to measure credit risk, standardized, foundation and advanced models were developed. With reference to market risk, the building blocks approach or standardized method and value at risk (VAR) model were used. Likewise, for operational risk, basic indicator approach (BIA), standardized approach and advanced measurement approaches (AMAs) are employed. Of these approaches, the more sophisticated models became the pre-reserve of the larger banks as these involved higher expertise and costs to employ. This in turn, created a fear of the emergence of a two-tier banking system, big and small banks with lower costs to big banks – as the bigger banks would have complex systems in place needed to employ the advance methods to measure risk. The caveat however was that the these new models could lead to a flurry of new hybrid products issued by the large banks as they replace tier I capital with hybrids. It could provide banks with capital relief while at the same time keeping rating agencies satisfied with the overall level of capital, which would remain unchanged.[44] Thus, a divergence in the rules applicable to big and small banks here seemed unavoidable. On the other hand, requiring all banks to comply with a single standard was in a way self-defeating as it would stifle developments in risk management techniques by removing the incentives needed to develop such measures.

Several flaws were identified with the Basel Accords I and II. Here, only a few are being discussed with a view to assess vulnerabilities in the framework. One of the basic problems with Basel Accords, which has not been addressed even in the proposed Basel III, is its failure to establish a regulatory system that would treat similar promises

---

44. Sappideen, R. (2004). The Regulation of Credit, Market and Operational Risk Management under the Basel Accords, *The Journal of Business Law*, 2004 (January) 59-93.

in the financial system in the same way.[45] This differential treatment of promises not only provides arbitrage opportunities but also makes it very easy for banks to transfer financial promises to a less regulated sector enabling banks to hold less capital against actual risks.

Second issue is of procyclicality with Basel II which determined capital requirements in relation to liabilities for banks: demanding low capital requirement during a boom and a higher provisioning in the balance sheets under financial duress.[46] Procyclicality is one of the biggest factors hampering effectiveness of the Basel II framework.[47] Many analysts have been voicing their concerns on its procyclical potential.[48] The recent crisis has shown that this propensity for procyclicality further exacerbates a deteriorating financial situation.

A survey by the Financial Stability Institute in 2006 suggested that only about 100 countries were planning to adopt and apply Basel II over the next few years. Despite the fact that most of the European countries implemented Basel II before the 2007 crisis,[49] the adoption of the standards by less than 100 members raises questions as to the universality and legitimacy of these regulations on the one hand, and, raises concerns on the regulatory content and appeal on the other.

[B] Historical Evidence II: Newly Emergent Operational Risk

Until the last quarter of the twentieth century, operational loss events were frequent happenings though smaller in magnitude. This frequent visitation to the financial markets made them predictable and often preventable.[50] The high magnitude operational loss events used to be rare and would include tax noncompliance, disruption of business due to terrorism or natural disasters, major internal frauds and unauthorized business activities. The gigantic growth of the financial markets over the last two decades has rendered banking activities (investment banking) complex and operational risk events, once rare under segregated commercial banking activities, have become frequent (with selling loans, CDOs, securitization and subprime mortgages).

---

45. Blundell-Wignall, A., & Atkinson, P. (2010). Thinking Beyond Basel III: Necessary Solutions for Capital and Liquidity. *OECD Journal: Financial Market Trends*, 2010(1).
46. Habbard, P., Coats, D., & Watt, A. (2011). *Supra* n. 38.
47. *See*, United Nation, Report of the Commission of Experts of the President of the UN General Assembly on Reforms of the International Monetary and Financial System, known as the Stieglitz Commission Report, Sep. 21, 2009. Available at www.un.org/ga/econcrisissummit/docs/FinalReport_CoE.pdf.
48. Taylor, A. & C. Goodhart (2006), Procyclicality and Volatility in the Financial System: The Implementation of Basel II and IAS 39. In S. Gerlach & P. Gruenwald (Eds.), *Procyclicality of Financial Systems in Asia, Palgrave Macmillan, see also*, Burton, D., Ryback, W. A., & Vinals, J. (2006).Comments on Procyclicality and Volatility in the Financial System: The Implementation of Basel II and IAS 39. In S. Gerlach & P. Gruenwald (Eds.), *Procyclicality and Volatility in the Financial System*. Palgrave Macmillan.
49. Jesús Saurina, (June 2008), Banking on the Right Path, Finance & Development, available at https://www.imf.org/external/pubs/ft/fandd/2008/06/pdf/saurina.pdf, last accessed, Mar. 3, 2014.
50. For example in commercial banking, the loss events would range from minor accounting errors to small credit card frauds or equipment failure.

Now these events involve not only huge costs for one particular institution but also pose a threat to systemic stability in an integrated financial world. A credit crunch in the US subprime market can affect banking activities across the Atlantic overnight. This robust growth in financial activities and its global integration has made operational risk as one of the key objectives in devising regulations for the banking industry. As operational risk is positively correlated with income size and dispersion of business units so prior to its tremendous growth in banking activities and business volume it had little effect on management's decision-making and capital allocations. In contrast, credit and market risk variables[51] were of utmost significance because of the sheer volume of losses those risks were associated with.

The modern approach to minimize risks in the financial markets is therefore, based on accurate measurement and efficient management of risks and it recognizes the need for regulatory compatibility with the ever-changing nature of the markets.[52] The strategy adopted in this regard has been fourfold. First, recognizing risks categories – an evolving category as newer risks are being continuously added to the list. Second, requirement of a mandatory cushion often referenced as Capital Adequacy Requirements against possibility of bank failures due to these risks. Third, adoption of recognized models for computation of various risks and disclosure of these risks along with required financial information to regulatory authorities. And, fourth, creating awareness within the organizations (the industry and among employees of the financial institutions) of the need to accustom themselves with new dimensions of accountability.

Operational risk (OR) emerged as a volatile area offering potential threats while at the same time it remained the most difficult to measure.[53] Since the end of 1980s, more than 100 operational loss events exceeding USD 100 million in value each, and a number of losses exceeding USD 1 billon have impacted global financial markets. It is no more a constituent item in the basket of *other risks* category in fact Basel III focuses especially on the management and control of OR due to its interlinkages with almost all the other prevalent forms of financial industry risks. Its unique orientation has made OR an absolute subject of analysis. This is precisely why this chapter is focusing a good deal on how OR has emerged as an important potential area. The next section first dwells on the definitional aspects, then historical processes and finally the more complex issues of approaches measurement.

---

51. Hernobai, A. S., T. Rachev, S., & Fabozzi, F. J. (2007). *Operational Risk- A Guide to Basel II Capital Requirements, Models and Analysis.* Wiley & Sons Inc.
52. For arguments on securitization as a technique in innovative financial products, *see,* Dam, K. (2010). The Subprime Crisis and Financial Regulation: International and Comparative Perspectives, *Chicago Journal of International Law,* 10 p. 1.
53. There has been strong criticism on Basel Committee on the issue of measurement and management of OR. While the management part did work, it overlooked the measurement aspect of OR. Due to its rare occurrence and unpredictability, OR is undoubtedly difficult to measure, nonetheless, for effective management, precise measurement is a prerequisite.

Chapter 4: Regulatory Regimes and IFL §4.02[B]

[1] Defining Operational Risk

The European Commission (EC) defines OR as *the risk of a change in value caused by the fact that actual losses, incurred for inadequate or failed internal processes, people, and systems, or from external events (including legal risk), differ from the expected losses*.[54] Basel II defines OR under Article 4(52) of Regulation (EU) No 575/2013 as, *risk of loss resulting from inadequate or failed processes, people and systems or from external events*.[55] This definition includes legal risk, but excludes strategic and reputational risk. Legal risk includes, but is not limited to, exposure to fines, penalties or punitive damages resulting from supervisory actions, as well as private settlements. Power observes this *rapid emergence of OR from this low epistemic status to its institutionalization* as a key component of global banking regulation.[56] He further contends that the meaning and implications of the Basel proposals have been fiercely contested by international banks and three key domains of policy controversy remain particularly visible around: definitional issues, data collection, and limits of quantification.

Operational risk is harder to quantify and model than market and credit risk as the former can include classes of risks (such as fraud, security, and privacy protection, legal and physical or environmental risks). Operational risk events are increasing as a result of ever more stringent regulatory compliance requirements, increased outsourcing and fast-paced technological advancements. All of these factors can dramatically affect an organization's overall risk profile.[57] A good loss-capture process is required to ensure losses are identified, assessed, managed and reported as a part of sound organizational governance.[58]

How Basel I and II treated OR? It was largely a residual category for miscellaneous and unable-to-be-categorized risks along with legal risk. Especially the crisis in the early 2000s such as rogue trading losses at Société Générale, Barings, Allied Irish Bank (AIB), Daiwa, UBS, Orange County and National Australia Bank highlighted the severe losses brought by this unable-to-be-categorized OR. Episodes like Enron added another dimension to the sphere while the addition of disasters like the September 11 terrorist attacks, and Hurricane Andrew and Katrina broadened the scope of OR manyfolds. The

---

54. EC. (Feb. 9, 2012). New European rules on Over-the-Counter Derivatives and Market infrastructures, European Commission, MEMO/12/91, available at http://europa.eu/rapid/press-release _MEMO-12-91_en.htm [Press release].
55. EBA. (Jun. 12, 2014). Draft Regulatory Technical Standards on Assessment Methodologies for the Advanced Measurement Approaches for Operational Risk under Art. 312 of Regulation (EU) No 575/2013. EBA/CP/2014/08. Retrieved from https://www.eba.europa.eu/documents/1018 0/724762/EBA-CP-2014-08 + CP + on + draft + RTS + on + AMA + assesment.pdf.
56. Power, M. (2005). The Invention of Operational Risk. *Review of International Political Economy*, 12(4), 577-599. Routledge, available at http://dx.doi.org/10.1080/09692290500240271.
57. *See*, Lopez, J. A. (2002). What Is Operational Risk. Retrieved from FRBSF Economic Letter No. No. 2002-02: January 25. Federal Reserve Bank of San Franciso: http://www.frbsf.org/economic-research/publications/economic-letter/2002/january/what-is-operational-risk/, last accessed, Aug. 23, 2015.
58. Drury, N. (2009). Why has Operational Risk Returned to the Limelight? *The Market Magazine*, pp. 60-64. Retrieved from http://www.markit.com/assets/en/docs/markit-magazine/issue-6/MM06_RandD.pdf.

following section draws on the historical process of how OR emerged as an *agenda-forming* category under Basel II policy process.

[2]   Historical Recognition

The new guidelines on the International Convergence of Capital Measurements and Capital Standards defined new capital rules.[59] In the meanwhile, the Basel Committee had initiated work on OR in September 1998[60] by publishing results in an informal industry survey. The committee proposed to develop either uniform capital charge for OR based on a measure of business activities such as revenues, costs, total assets or internal measurement systems or differentiated charge for businesses with high ORs based on measures commonly used to evaluate those business lines. The major work in this regard was conceived through a series of consultative impact studies.

In January 2001, *first consultative document* was released, which initiated a debate but attracted criticism. It was finalized during the Second Quantitative Impact Study (QIS-2)[61] May 2001- January 2002[62] (representing the second round of industry consultations) amid regulatory efforts to reexamine industry's exposure to OR. Its target was on information concerning loss events, the bank's quarterly aggregate operational risk loss experience, and a wider range of potential exposure indicators tied to specific business lines.

QIS-3 (October 2002 to May 2003) ushered in the third and final round of consultations. Basel Committee presented three approaches to calculate OR capital charge along a continuum of increasing sophistication and risk sensitivity: BIA, TSA and AMA, to encourage banks to move along the spectrum of more sophisticated measurement systems and practices. The inclusion of advanced approach illustrated Basel Committee's propensity to accept partial use of advanced methods for operational risk, which operate in a similar way for credit risk analyses.[63]

---

59. BCBS. (2006). International Convergence of Capital Measurement and Capital Standards: A Revised Framework, available at http://www.bis.org/publ/bcbs128.pdf. This document is a combined version of two earlier standards on the issue: the comprehensive version of International Convergence of Capital Measurement and Capital Standards: A Revised Framework, including the elements of the 1988 Accord that were not revised during the Basel II process, the 1996 Amendment to the Capital Accord to Incorporate Market Risks, and the 2005 paper on The Application of Basel II to Trading Activities and the Treatment of Double Default Effects. *See,* BCBS. (2004). Basel II: International Convergence of Capital Measurement and Capital Standards: A Revised Framework, http://www.bis.org/publ/bcbs107.pdf and, BCBS. (1988). International Convergence of Capital Measurement and Capital Standards (Basel Capital Accord I), at http://www.bis.org/publ/bcbsc111.pdf.
60. BCBS. (1998). Operational Risk Management. Available at http://www.bis.org/publ/bcbs42.pdf No. 42.
61. The impact study assesses whether the Committee has met goals set in the New Basel Accord. The study gathers data necessary to allow the Committee to gauge the impact of the current proposals across a wide range of banks in the G10 and beyond, given the differing risk profiles of banks and the extent to which credit risk mitigation is used. *See,* BCBS. (2005). Fifth Quantitative Impact Study: Instructions for QIS 5: BCBS, available at http://www.bis.org/bcbs/qis/qis5.htm last accessed, Aug. 23, 2015.
62. QIS 2 is available at http://www.bis.org/bcbs/qis/qishist.htm.
63. To adopt AMA, institutions will have to capture a significant part of the institution's OR.

In April 2003, the *third Consultative Paper (CP-3)* made further modifications to the proposed revision of the existing rules on global banking standards. It included Alternative Standardized Approach (ASA), which is based on a measure of lending volume rather than gross income as exposure indicator of capital charge for retail and commercial banking. Furthermore, compliance with the rollout provisions for OR was made substantially more complex through enhanced qualifying criteria for standardized approach. Commentators asserted that significant hardening of the qualitative criteria may shift the cost-benefit analysis in favor of a cruder approach given little difference between TSA and BIA in terms of pure regulatory capital charge generated.[64]

The multiplicity in approaches to OR capital charge reflected on Basel Committee's need for flexibility in implementation of the Accords. National regulators were expected to exercise judgment in the implementation and adoption of these broader regulatory rules in their local financial systems. The scope and timeline of implementation varied significantly across countries but it was not meant to distort the fundamental objective of consistency. Some national regulators reserved their right of supervisory review (pillar II of Basel II) by selecting certain types of measurement approaches. To address these issues, the Basel Committee issued a technical paper in January 2004 on the home-host recognition of AMA and proposed a *hybrid approach* about how banking organizations that calculate group-wide AMA capital requirements might estimate OR capital requirements of their international subsidiaries.[65]

In June 2004, the Basel Committee released first definitive rules on the regulatory treatment of OR as an integral part of the risk-adjusted capital requirements under pillar I of its revised framework. The Committee stressed the importance of qualitative and quantitative standards for banks that wished to apply AMA for Operational Risk Management (ORM), especially with respect to analysis of internal data, exogenous control factors for OR exposures and construction of internal measurement models to estimate unexpected OR losses to the 99.9th percentile.[66]

The Basel Committee completed its final QIS-5[67] between September 2005 and June 2006 after several amendments to its earlier versions of Basel Capital Accord. The banks with partial AMA estimate were asked to report the fraction of the AMA Capital Charge calculated according to the Standardized or BIA. Finally, the Committee defined the Treatment of Expected Losses by Banks by employing the AMA under the Basel II framework. As opposed to the quantitative impact analysis, this report rather focused on the bank itself, and not on the supervisory practices.

Basel II capital rules stipulated by the Basel Committee Accord Implementation Group (AIGOR) defined three different quantitative measurement approaches in a continuum of increasing sophistication and risk sensitivity based on eight *Business*

---

64. Jobst, A. A. (2007). The Regulation of Operational Risk under New Basel Capital Accord- Critical Issues. *Journal of International Banking Law and Regulation*, 22(5), 249-273.
65. BCBS, Principles for Home-Host Recognition of AMA Operational Risk Capital, January 2004, BCBS No. 106. Available at www.bis.org/publ/bcbs/106.htm.
66. Jobst, A. A. (2007). *Supra* n. 64.
67. BCBS. (2005). *Supra* n. 61. p. 34.

Lines (BL) and seven *Event Types* as units of measures.[68] In the meanwhile, the EU Capital Requirement Directive (CRD) introduced risk management and capital standards for OR. This Directive since January 2008 has been in effect through FSA rules and guidance.[69] Subsequent firm-wide surveys were conducted to support the implementation of the CRD.[70]

[3] The Three Pillars and a Critical Assessment

The origin of these pillars is traceable to the formation of BIS Committee on Banking Regulations and Supervisory Practices for the Central Bank Governors of the G10 countries in 1974. Initially set up to regulate banks in the G10 countries,[71] its scope was later on extended to include nonbank financial institutions. The Committee released its first Accord in 1988, which was adopted, albeit gradually, by numerous countries by 1992. Its important feature was the introduction of minimum capital requirements to forestall probability of a commercial bank failure through excessive credit exposure risk. This was followed by a series of amendments brought in 1996, which recognized market or position risk, and also requiring capital adequacy safeguards. In 2001, further proposals with respect to Credit Risk were mooted. In 2003, Basel Accord II proposed the extension of capital adequacy requirements to safeguard against OR. The new Basel Accord is based on three complementary pillars: minimum capital requirements (Pillar I), the supervisory-review process (Pillar II) and the enhancement of market discipline (Pillar III). In the paragraphs below, we draw a critique of the three pillars. A number of high-profile OR losses, like Barings and BCCI,[72] AIB,[73] led the Basel Committee to come up with an overt approach, where banks were expected to hold separately identified regulatory capital for operational risk events. This provisioning was termed as the Pillar 1. Numerous issues arose while calibrating a scale for the measurement of regulatory capital required under the new Capital Accord. The

---

68. The eight business lines are:(i) corporate finance 18%; (ii) trading & sales 18%; (iii) retail banking 12%; (iv) payment & settlements 18%; (v) agency services 15%; (vi) commercial banking 15%; (vii) asset management 12%; (viii) retail brokerage 12%. The seven loss events are: (i) internal fraud; (ii) external fraud; (iii) employment practices and workplace safety; (iv) clients, products and business practices; (v) damage to physical assets; (vi) business disruptions and system failures; (vii) execution, delivery and process management. *See*, BCBS. (2003). Operational Risk Transfer Across Financial Sectors BIS, available at http://www.bis.org/publ/joint06.htm.
69. *See*, Ch. 6 of the Prudential Sourcebook for Banks, Building Societies and Investment Firms (BIPRU) and in Senior Management Arrangements, Systems and Controls (SYSC), www.fsahandbook.info/FSA/html/handbook; and, https://fshandbook.info/FS/html/FCA/SYSC.
70. FSA. (2007). Operational Risk Management Practices: Feedback from a Thematic Review. Retrieved from FSA Survey, www.fsa.gov.uk/pubs/international/or_practices.pdf.
71. The Herstatt's collapse underscored vulnerabilities in cross-border transactions involving payments and delivery mismatches.
72. The Barings Bank (1995) involved high trading risk, while the BCCI (1992) in illegal transaction risk.
73. A US subsidiary of Allied Irish had huge losses due to a fraudulent trading in 2002. *See*, Portanger, E., Sesitt, M. R., & Galloni, A. (Feb. 7, 2002). Allied Irish Bank Say a Rogue Trader Lost $750 Million in Unauthorized Deals. *The Wall Street Journal*, European Business News. Available at http://www.wsj.com/articles/SB1012991042190203640.

Committee suggested – based on the evidence for those few banks that were able to provide some data – an allocation of 15% of internal economic capital for OR and equated this internal capital figure with 12% of the then existing minimum regulatory capital across the system (Current RWA*8% *12%). The next task for the Committee was to develop a mechanism to access regulatory capital charge. To assess this, the committee prescribed a number of approaches of varying complexity and increasing sophistication to assess regulatory capital for operational risk. The committee added guidelines in the paper, Sound Practices and the Management and Supervision of operational risk,[74] which included issues of identification, assessment, monitoring and control. The pillar 2 framework revolved around four key concepts:

(1) that banks should have mechanisms to assess their risk (the capital adequacy);
(2) that supervisors should review banks' internal capital adequacy assessments and should take appropriate actions, if necessary;
(3) that supervisors should expect banks to operate above their minimum regulatory capital requirements and in case of noncompliance, the supervisor should intervene;
(4) that supervisor should require fast remedial measures if capital is not maintained.

The key issue in pillar II was whether processing for OR would result in additional regulatory capital charge, and if so, then how much capital must be allocated especially where such risk could not be quantified. For those banks using simpler approaches (BIA), capital charge was to be calculated on the basis of an accounting figure (gross income) without any specific reference to the real size of risk within an individual bank. It was difficult for supervisors to justify any additional capital charge in the absence of any quantification of real risk size involved. Adopted this way, the pillar II charge was presumed as a threat from the supervisors. However, in case of banks employing AMA, Pillar II might not pose a serious problem as the risk would be already identified and measured. It would also provide supervisors a tool to encourage improvements in internal risk management systems within banks.

Pillar III came up as the most succinct element of the new framework requiring a bank to disclose: (a) strategies and processes for managing operational risk, (b) the structure and organization for the risk management function, and, (c) the scope and nature of risk reporting and risk measurement systems, policies for hedging and mitigating risk, and strategies for monitoring the effectiveness of hedges. Furthermore, a bank is also needed to disclose: its approach employed to assess regulatory capital that it qualifies for, (b) OR capital charge as to its BL, if any, and, (c) if it employs AMA, an elaboration of that approach.

---

74. *See*, BCBS, No. 86, December (2001) and the revised document at, BCBS. (2003). Sound Practices for the Management and Supervision of Operational Risk. *See* at http://www.bis.org/publ/bcbs96.htm.

The most critical of these disclosures for a bank are the amount of the capital charge and the technique employed for its calibration. The capital charge is the only comparable measure of exposure whereas the disclosure of the technique used to calculate it throws light on the level of sophistication of the bank's risk management systems. Banks are required to document and run Information Technology (IT) systems to record significant events in their risk management system. The pillar III disclosure requirements could be critical for most banks but those banks achieving AMA status, would be indicative of their level of sophistication in risk management. This may increase peer pressure and competition in finance industry to pull other players attaining the same or almost comparable level of risk management.

[4] Operation Risk Approaches

The Basel I capital adequacy rules did not require firms to hold capital cover for operational risk;[75] however, the Basel II made it essential for limited license and limited activity investment firms to meet OR management standards in Senior Management Arrangement, Systems and Controls (SYSC). They are exempt from the mandatory requirement of OR Capital Requirement (ORCR) and firms are free to choose different methods to calculate their ORCR.

The Basic Indicator or the BIA is the simplest method of determining a firm's ORCR, and uses income as an indicator. The ORCR is calculated by taking 15% of the three years' average of the sum of net-interest income and net noninterest income. This three years' average must be calculated using the financial year-end data. It provides an exception to those firms that do not have sufficient income data and where, a firm's yearly income is zero or negative. A firm using the BIA must meet the general risk management standards in the SYSC module of the Handbook. These require a firm to have robust governance arrangements, effective risk management processes and adequate internal control mechanisms suitable to its size, nature, scale and complexity. Prudential Sourcebook for Banks, Building Societies and Investment Firms (BIPRU) 6.3[76] has all the rules and guidance on the BIA.

The BIA based its capital charge upon a fixed percentage (proposed at 15%) of gross income.[77] The Committee chose gross income on the basis that it reflected business volume and therefore would be closer to reflect actual the risk exposure.

---

75. Western banks hold their capital but the capital is rolled over in pledging security for composite deals. When they lend part of their regulatory capital via short-term money market to Lehman Brothers who went into bankruptcy, huge problems ensued. On the other hand, in China, the regulator requires banks to lodge regulatory capital with the Government because banks cannot be trusted to curb lending practices when they have control over the regulatory capital.
76. BIPRU 6 of the FSA Handbook of rules contains detailed rules and guidance on ORCR which are prescribed in SYSC 4 and 7. For BIPRU 6, see, https://fshandbook.info/FS/html/handbook/BIPRU/6, and for SYSC, see, https://fshandbook.info/FS/html/FCA/SYSC.
77. The definition of gross income under the Basel doesn't constitute as a standard accounting definition. It includes: (i) net-interest income (ii) net noninterest income (iii) net trading income and other incomes. It is gross of provisions and it excludes: (i) extraordinary or irregular income (ii) gains/losses in positions in banking book (iii) income from insurance (iv) operating expenses.

Critics, however, argue that gross income is about the past while risk is about the future and it may not reflect quality of OR management. Thus with this indicator, banks would prefer to cut down on operating expenses to inflate their profits than by increasing their gross incomes to have more profits. Instead, selecting a few months of operating expenses as an indicator could be a better measure, offering disincentive neither to the banks to increase their gross incomes nor to the supervisors as capital requirements could be adjusted downward immediately if needed. In case of any bank in terminal difficulties, the capital charge would have been related very strongly to the expenses during liquidation.[78]

The Standardized Approach or TSA bases regulatory capital charge on gross income, but it sets different percentages points (betas) for different predefined business lines,[79] and banks are expected to map their own activities and associated gross income to this structure. Previously, the approach employed different indicators for different business lines but due to difficulty in defining and measuring OR, the committee opted to choose one indicator only. Nonetheless, it faced problems in setting different percentages of one indicator for different business lines.

TSA is more risk sensitive than the BIA as each business line attracts a different percentage charge (risk weighting). The BIA on the other hand applies a single percentage to the relevant indicator. The ORCR is the average of over three years of risk-weighted indicators calculated each year across these business lines. The capital charge for each business line is the net-interest income and net noninterest income for that business line, multiplied by factor (beta). The respective gross income of each business line is taken as to represent the scale of business operations within that business. Thus, it highlights the scale of risk exposure across each business line within a particular firm. The ASA is an alternative approach available to TSA,[80] where a firm using TSA may use alternative indicators for retail banking and commercial banking business lines subject to compliance with certain BIPRU[81] requirements. However, it is required from firms using TSA or ASA to comply with the general risk management standards in SYSC. There is a mixed criticism on applying TSA as it neither offers any advantage in terms of lower capital charge nor provides any incentive for better risk management. On the face of it, some banks resist adopting this approach despite the flexibility it offers to modulate their choice of indicators according to their business lines.

The Advance Measurement Approach (AMA) is the most sophisticated measurement of ORCR designed to provide banks with a range of options. Under this approach, a firm's ORCR is calculated using the firm's personalized OR measurement system.[82] It

---

78. Pezier, J. (2003). A Constructive Review of the Basel Proposals on Operational Risk. In A. Carol (Ed.), *Operational Risk: Regulation, Analysis and Management London*, Financial Times Prentice Hall.
79. The Committee has proposed eight business lines. *See*, BCBS. (2003). *Supra* n. 68.
80. TSA or the ASA were made available from Jan. 1, 2007.
81. *See*, BIPRU 6.4 in Prudential Sourcebook for Banks, Building Societies and Investment Firms, available at http://www.banccentraldecatalunya.ch/wordpress/wp-content/uploads/2013/06/15062013/UK_FSA_BIPRU.pdf.
82. Qualitative and quantitative requirements are set out in BIPRU 6.5, and in SYSC module of the handbook which is made available to the firms from January 2008.

allows banks a framework in which their own internal assessments of OR may be verified and accepted for supervisory purposes. As currently structured, the AMA provides for a *laboratory* in which banks can test and develop their own approach to OR quantification. It is expected, as famously said, that a *thousand flowers* might bloom in this laboratory where all will be roses though of different colors, fragrance, shape or sizes.[83]

However, while opting for this approach, a bank will have to demonstrate to its Central Bank supervisor that its chosen approach captures potentially severe tail losses. As Basel process required operational loss levels not less than 0.1% probability of being exceeded over a one-year horizon, estimating loss event over a period of two years reliably at a 99.9% confidence level would be a miraculous task to achieve. Banks have to meet specific conditions to be eligible to adopt an advanced treatment.[84] It included a general criteria, and qualitative standards covering their OR management structure, processes and environment and quantitative standards governing internal estimates used for the AMA calculations. Under the general criteria, the supervisory authority needs to be satisfied that (a) the bank's risk management system is conceptually sound, and is implemented with integrity, (b) there are adequate staff resources to ensure this, (c) the AMA is based on a rigorous analysis of internal and external data, and, (d) the bank regularly conducts *scenario analysis*.

While all the banks could theoretically opt for the BIA, the Working Paper on the Regulatory Treatment of OR (September 2001) stated that banks would be encouraged to move along the spectrum of available approaches as they develop more sophisticated OR measurement and management systems and practices. Banks that are internally active or have significant OR exposure are required to use a more sophisticated approach than the BIA for this purpose, banks would also be allowed to use TSA for some of the business lines and AMA for other lines, which is subject to a *materiality requirement* that at least a minimum percentage of the bank's business falls under the AMA. To prevent capital charge arbitrage, however, banks would not be allowed to revert to simpler approaches once they have been approved for advanced approaches. A combination of the BIA and the AMA is available to firms with further conditions to be met by the firms opting for such combination.[85] TSA can be combined under very restrictive circumstances (such as the acquisition of new business), which may require a transitional period to roll out of TSA.

The aim was to harmonize processes regarding supervisory approval of such changes and to assist institutions using AMA to further develop their AMA models. The Guidelines[86] provide institutions direction on how to communicate AMA extensions

---

83. Nash, R. A. (2003). The Three Pillars of Operational Risk. In A. Carol (Ed.), *Operational Risk: Regulation, Analysis and Management*. Financial Times Prentice Hall.
84. *See*, for a detailed discussion on AMA, Moosa, I. A. (2008). A Critique of the Advanced Measurement Approach to Regulatory Capital against Operational Risk. *Journal of Banking Regulation*, 9(3), 151-164.
85. BIPRU 6.2 sets out the conditions for combining approaches.
86. Guidelines are an important tool for fostering convergence of supervisory practices across the EU. Although, these are not legally binding, yet supervisory authorities and institutions around Europe must make every effort to comply with them. *See*, EBA, Implementing Basel III in

and changes to the competent authorities. The Guidelines do not contain requirements regarding modeling or risk management of institutions. Changes to the AMA have to be categorized according to their severity as significant, major or minor change, while extensions and significant changes require a prior approval, major and minor changes need to be only notified to the competent authority. Supervisors will review the AMA change policies and ultimately approve or object to any proposed change or extension. Article 105 paragraph 1 of Directive 2006/48/EC and Article 20 paragraph 1 of Directive 2006/49/EC allow institutions and investment firms to use within AMA their internal risk models to determine regulatory capital charge for OR provided these internal models are expressly approved by the competent Authorities. An AMA, including the internal risk model, risk management and control policies and procedures should, at all times, be tailored to the specific characteristics of the institution, so that it's actual OR profile is effectively covered. Both AMA extensions and changes may have a considerable impact on the quality and reliability of the AMA framework and on the level of regulatory capital.[87]

[5] An Assessment

There is a twofold criticism on the AMA modeling of operational risk. First, the internal risk factor, usually identified by banks is the typical measure of internal performance, such as internal audit ratings, volume, turnover, error rates and income volatility. While the second is the external risk factor, which may include market price movements and changes in a borrower's condition etc. The internal performance measures do not necessarily reflect a direct mathematical or statistical link between individual risk factors and the probability and size of future operational risk losses. As large losses are infrequent, so banks usually lack a time series of historical data on the size and frequency of their own operational losses and the causes. This is in sharp contrast to market risk, where changes in the market have a visible impact on the value of bank's trading portfolio. This is also in sharp contrast with credit risk, where changes in the borrower's credit quality are often associated with changes in interest rate spread of the borrower's obligations over a risk-free rate. However, research on the correlation of OR factors and OR loss experiences is still to produce concrete conclusions.

Measuring OR requires both estimating the probability of an OR loss event and the potential size of the loss with most approaches relying on the risk factors that provide an indication of the likelihood of an operational loss event occurring. This lack of prescription and specification element makes available a gamut of approaches to OR quantification for banks where an absence of prescription places a huge burden on the regulator to verify the data as it is provided by the banks. This required expertise and

---

Europe: CRD IV package, accessed Jul. 20, 2015, at http://www.eba.europa.eu/regulation-and-policy/implementing-basel-iii-europe.
87. IARCP. (2012). Results of the Basel III monitoring exercise Top 10 risk and compliance management related news stories and world events that (for better or for worse) shaped the week's agenda, and what is next. International Association of Risk and Compliance Professionals (IARCP). *See*, http://www.risk-compliance-association.com/Monday_October_1_2012_Top_10_Risk_Compliance_News_Events.pdf.

resources, not sufficiently available currently. So Basel stepped back from imposing Internal Measurement Approaches (IMA) that it had put forward earlier for adoption, though it preserved some elements of IMA as minimum quantifying requirements.[88] Due to a number of modern financial market trends like contract outsourcing, job-cuts, and development of online banking, the level, frequency and risk from operational risk events has been on a rise – and expected to rise further.[89]

[C] Spineless Regulation: Past Failures, Future Bets

Thus far, despite the complexity of the Basel II process, it failed miserably in preventing the GFC. Rather, right after 2008, we saw G20, the FSB and other Basel Committees set to the task of Basel III. The question is: if Basel II didn't or couldn't prevent the GFC, would Basel III be able to perform in the wake of another crisis? Before attempting to evaluate this question, the next section is briefly looking at why Basel II didn't work and what Basel III regulatory framework has in common with the Basel II. A few related causes that added to Basel II's failure include: (a) dragged negotiation, adoption and implementation timelines; (b) over-reliance on so-called *impartial* CRAs to rate poor financial products (the Australian Federal Court was the first jurisdiction to charge a Ratings Agency negligent, the Rembrandt Constant Proportion Debt Obligations (CP-DOs) were not capable of AAA performance); (c) the banks' excessive freedom to change and amend various ratios. The scandal involving HSBC's involvement in money-laundering was a case in point of such misuse of authority and influence. Lord Green, former CEO and Chair of HSBC (Trade Minister in David Cameron's cabinet), was informed of *significant risk of financial penalty* as the transactions were in clear breach of prudential banking regulations; (d) laxity in supervisory controls turned Basel II standards into a *free lunch* for the banking industry. There was a strong criticism on the BoE and the US Fed for lack of supervision and enforcement of prudential regulation after the GFC; and, (e) Basel II financial adequacy standard was faulty. The cost of capital should match the risk premium of the capital being invested, and not to work as a penalty system or future perceived risks (risk premium of projects may be 15% but penalty system of perceived risks may be 8%, so there is an operational risk arbitrage of 7%).

These regulatory gaps and loopholes in implementation weekend the international financial system. Just before the 2007 crisis, the US banks typically held about USD 30 for each USD 1 of their equity, whereas in Europe, balance sheets of some of the banks held up to 80 times more loan assets than per dollar of equity. These were the undesirable outcomes of weaker Basel I and Basel II framework. Basel III document faced resistance not only from banks and market-proponents but also from governments who want specific regulations to be modified to suit their domestic interests. Interestingly, some jurisdictions like Switzerland went beyond what Basel III has

---

88. BCBS. (2002). QIS 3, Technical Guidance. *See*, https://www.bis.org/bcbs/qis/qis3tech.pdf accessed Aug. 23, 2015.
89. Baker, P. & Boyd, T. APRA Opposes Big Four on Over Capital Rules. *The Australian Financial Review*, May 2003.

recommended. The Federal Council there has appointed a commission of experts who suggested an additional capital buffer of 9% of their risk weighted assets in the form of contingent convertibles, over and above a 10% regular tier I capital charge to be set aside by big Swiss banks.

§4.03   POST-2008 REFORM INITIATIVES

[A]   A Look at the Inner Thresholds

Bank-runs of whatever form are always serious events. That Lehman's collapse presented a classic case of not only regulatory failure but epitomized a precedential loss. Likewise, the Northern Rock in the UK rocked the confidence on financial markets and on the regulator to bottom prior to Lehman. The post-GFC reform of the international regulatory architecture was the most important task in front of the policy makers, regulators and heads of G20. The most comprehensive global regulatory framework for capital and liquidity risk management for financial institutions including for the Global-Systemically Important Financial Institutions (G-SIFIs) came to be known as Basel III was forwarded by the BCBS.[90] Basel III is a comprehensive set of reform involving prudential regulation to strengthen financial regulation, supervision and risk management of the banking sector. These measures aim at: improving the banking sector's ability to absorb shocks arising from financial and economic stress; improving risk management and governance; and, strengthening banks' transparency and disclosures practices.

The regulation targets two levels, micro-prudential (bank level): help raise the resilience of individual banking institutions, and, macro-prudential (system-wide): risks that can build up across the banking sector as well as the procyclical amplification of these risks over time. These two methods to supervision complement each other as greater resilience at the individual bank level reduces the risk of system-wide shocks.[91]

The Basel Committee issued Basel III in September 2010. The regulation aimed at increasing minimum capital (common equity) requirements from 2% to 4.5% and an additional conservation buffer of 2.5%. These capital enhancements are to be supplemented by a non-risk based leverage ratio. To address procyclical concerns, Basel III proposed to introduce new measures, which included long-term calibration of the probability of default in modeling of risk, forward-looking provisioning and holding buffers of capital above the regulatory minimum[92] and is expected to be enforced up to the maximum of 2.5%.

---

90. *See*, Compilation of documents that form the global regulatory framework for capital and liquidity, at the BIS website, documents reflecting the status of new regulations, implementation time line, reports to the G20 and feedbacks from 2008 onwards accessible at http://www.bis.org/bcbs/basel3/compilation.htm.
91. EBA Website, What is Basel III, *see*, http://www.eba.europa.eu/regulation-and-policy/implementing-basel-iii-europe, and, http://www.bis.org/bcbs/basel3.htm.
92. Blundell-Wignall & Atkinson, *supra* n. 45.

For the purposes of capital buffers, the methodology for determining risk weightings of trading assets has been stiffened. The regulators shifted the focus from risk weighting (the denominator in the ratio) to the capital requirements themselves (the numerator in the ratio), and then to the ratio itself. Under the Basel III, the banks are required to hold three times as much capital on reserve comparing with pre-2008 thresholds. Not only this, but in order to make banks hold larger cushion for safety, it requires banks to hold more tier I capital, such as common equity that must be held to 7% of assets from 2% by 2015. An additional *conservation buffer* of 2.5% is to be maintained by banks in times of strong economic growth, meaning in effect that a bank will need 7% common equity, 8.5% tier 1 capital and 10.5% tier 2 capital to meet its capital requirements, if a bank cannot meet this threshold, it will not be able to pay dividends.[93]

[1] Impact Studies

Basel Committee conducted a Comprehensive Quantitative Impact Studies (C-QIS) on December 31, 2011 to review implications of Basel III standards for financial markets. This study took a sample size of 209 banks, which were divided into Group I comprising of 102 internationally active banks (those having tier I capital in excess of €3 billion). The Group II included all other 107 banks. This monitoring exercise assumed full adoption and implementation of the final Basel III standards based on data as at December 31, 2011.[94] The results (published in April of 2012), amongst others, found the average Common Equity Tier I Capital ratio (CET1) of Group I banks at 7.7% while Basel III minimum requirements call for 4.5%. Group I banks were found to be in want of €11.9 billion to meet Basel III minimum standard requirement of 4.5%. This rises €374.1 billion for a CET I target level of 7.0% including the capital conservation buffer. For the Group II, average CET 1 ratio was 8.8% and to meet Basel III requirements, these banks needed an additional capital of €7.6 billion.[95] The full range of participants (users and providers of disclosures, auditors, regulators and standard setters) agreed that going forward it would be important for investors, financial institutions and auditors to develop principles and formats for better risk disclosures with input from standard setters and regulators.

[2] The European Situation

In 2013, the EU replaced the CRD (2006/48 and 2006/49) with a Directive and a Regulation. The Regulation contained the detailed prudential requirements for credit institutions and investment firms while the new Directive covered areas of the existing CRD where EU provisions need to be transposed by Member States in their domestic

---

93. Salmon, F. (Sep. 12, 2010). Basel III Arrives. Reuters. Available at http://blogs.reuters.com/felix-salmon/2010/2009/2012/basel-iii-arrives/.
94. This study did not take into account the transitional arrangements that Basel III allows otherwise for adoption of standards such as phase-in of deductions.
95. IARCP. (2012). *Supra* n. 87.

jurisdictions. The adoption took effect from January 1, 2014 while some of the new provisions would be phased in from 2014 to 2019.

The EBA has been monitoring and assessing the impact of the Basel III rules on a sample of EU banks since June 2011. This exercise is performed on a semiannual basis with end-December and end-June reporting dates following on C-QIS conducted by the Committee of European Banking Supervisors (CEBS), December 2010. Participation from financial institutions is voluntary and data is only reported on an aggregate basis in order to guarantee anonymity and confidentiality of credit institutions. This exercise monitors to assess various aspects of Basel III implementation, including: (a) changes to banks' capital ratios under Basel III, (b) the level of capital shortfalls including, where applicable, capital surcharges for global systemically important banks,[96] (c) impact on capital ratios and shortfall, resulting from changes in the definition of capital stemming from the new standard, referred to as CET1. The changes include modified rules on capital deductions and the eligibility criteria for Tier 1 and total capital, (d) impact on capital ratios and shortfall, resulting from changes in the calculation of RWAs stemming from the new definition of capital, securitization, trading book and counterparty credit risk requirements, (e) impact from the implementation of the capital conservation buffer, (f) the adequacy of leverage ratio, (g) the adequacy of two liquidity standards – the Liquidity Coverage Ratio (LCR) and the Net Stable Funding Ratio (NSFR),[97] (h) The EBA plays a key role in the implementation of the Basel III framework in the EU and is now mandated to produce a number of Binding Technical Standards (BTS), Guidelines and Reports[98] for the implementation of the CRD IV/CRR package.[99]

After the finalization of CRD IV, Basel III monitoring exercise will assess the impact from the implementation of CRD IV.[100] In addition to this, a semiannual monitoring framework has been set up by Basel Committee to assess risk-based capital ratio, leverage ratio and liquidity metrics using data collected by national supervisors on a representative sample of institutions. The estimates presented assume full

---

96. Global – Systemically Important Banks.
97. Basel III Monitoring Exercise, available at http://www.eba.europa.eu/risk-analysis-and-data/quantitative-impact-study/basel-iii-monitoring-exercise, last accessed, May 4, 2017.
98. The EBA has mandate to produce reports aimed at evaluating the impact of several provisions included in the legislative text, such as the implementation of a leverage ratio in Europe. *Supra* n. 86.
99. BTS are legal acts which specify particular aspects of an EU legislative text (Directive or Regulation) and aim at ensuring consistent harmonization in specific areas. BTS are always adopted by the EC by means of Regulations or Decisions. According to the EU law, the regulations are legally binding and directly applicable in all Member States. This means that, on the date of their entry into force, they become part of the national law of the Member States and their implementation into national law is not only unnecessary but also prohibited. *See*, EBA website, at http://www.eba.europa.eu/regulation-and-policy/implementing-basel-iii-europe *Supra* n. 86.
100. To access older Progress Reports on Basel III implementation, *see* the reports at the BIS page, www.bis.org/publ/bcbs232.htm, last visited Mar. 5, 2014. *See* also, for FSI Survey – Basel II, 2.5 and III Implementation, July 2013, www.bis.org/fsi/fsiop2013.htm.

implementation of the final Basel III requirements based on the data as of June 30, 2013 (the date of data collected for the latest report, March 2014).[101]

Although, the Basel III has a long implementation continuum (until 2019) however, the pace of adoption seems slower than the timelines agreed by the members. Also, the draft regulations in the US and the EU materially differ from the BCBS proposals in areas such as the definition of capital, securitization and the internal ratings-based approach.[102] The BCBS called on the US and EU regulators to revise their proposals. The US FDIC, the OCC and the FRB confirmed that revised capital rules will not now be coming into force on January 1, 2013. The proposed rules[103] were released for comment in June covering the implementation of Basel III capital standards for regulatory capital and the changes made to the methods of calculating risk-weighted assets and risk-weighted capital.

[B] Basel III: Adoption and Implementation Timeline

The Basel III adoption and implementation schedule is a step-wise program. The latest updates on Basel implementation program towards the targeted 2019 timeline are positive and affirmative. As of now, the world's 224 major international banks meet the risk-based capital requirements under Basel III banking regulations and have further narrowed the shortfall in capital required to meet targets for 2019.[104] The aggregate shortfall for the 98 largest internationally active banks relative to the 7% target for common equity (CET 1) in 2019 amounted to €3.9 billion as of June 30, 2014, down from a shortfall of €15.1 billion as of end-2013 and from a shortfall of €485.6 billion on June 30, 2011. In comparison, these 98 banks (known as Group 1 banks with Tier 1 capital in excess of €3 billion) had total after-tax profits prior to distributions of €210.1 billion in the six months ending June 30, 2014. The shortfall for the smaller Group 2 banks, which have Tier 1 capital below €3 billion, narrowed to a mere €0.1 billion relative to the minimum level of 4.5% and was €1.8 billion relative to the 7.0% target, down from shortfalls of €2.0 billion and €9.4 billion, respectively from the previous survey in September last year.[105]

---

101. BCBS. (March 2014). Basel III Monitoring Report, available at http://www.bis.org/publ/bcbs278.pdf.
102. BCBS (October 2012), Report to G20 Finance Ministers and Central Bank Governors on Basel III Implementation, available at http://www.bis.org/publ/bcbs234.pdf.
103. For comments, *see*, Agencies Seek Comment on Regulatory Capital Rules and Finalize Market Risk Rule, at www.federalreserve.gov/newsevents/press/bcreg/20120612a.htm and, Timely & Comprehensive Compliance Information and Insights from the FDIC, at, www.fdic.gov/news/news/press/2012/pr1 21 30.html.
104. *See*, BCBS. (March 2014). *Supra* n. 101. *See also*, BCBS. (November 2014). Implementation of Basel Standards: A Report to G20 Leaders on Implementation of the Basel III Regulatory Reforms. BIS Publications; from http://www.bis.org/bcbs/publ/d299.pdf, and, BCBS. (2015). Basel III Monitoring Report. BIS website http://www.bis.org/bcbs/publ/d312.pdf.
105. All major global banks now meet Basel III requirements. (Aug. 18, 2015). *See*, *Central Bank News*. Retrieved from http://www.centralbanknews.info/2015/03/all-major-global-banks-meet-basel-iii.html. *See also*, a revised report published in September 2014, available at http://www.bis.org/publ/bcbs289.htm; for assessment of *resilience* in Basel III and the effects of its timeline. BCBS, *Supra* n. 101.

The Basel I was released in 1988 and was to be adopted by the G10 countries by 1992. Basel II was released in 2004 and was due to be implemented from year-end 2006.[106] Basel 2.5 was agreed in July 2009 (in consequence to the GFC) introduced stringent measures to assess risk related to securitization and trading book exposures,[107] while Basel 2.5 was scheduled to be adopted and implemented no later than December 31, 2011. However, due to the continuing severity of the crisis, the Committee released Basel III[108] in December 2011, which set higher levels for capital requirements[109] and introduced a new global liquidity framework.[110] In January 2013, the Basel Committee issued the full text of the revised LCR. The LCR underpins the short-term resilience of a bank's liquidity risk profile.[111] The LCR was introduced from January 1, 2015 subject to a transitional arrangement before reaching full implementation by January 1, 2019.[112] Not to forget that the Basel II regulations have not been adopted fully by the US, Russia and Argentina.[113]

The implementation schedule for Basel III was set to commence from January 1, 2013, subject to transitional and phase-in arrangements. The implementation and adoption plan is a step-wise process culminating on January 2019. The latest progress report in this regard was published in April 2016 that maps the adoption and implementation milestones for various countries. The report, based on the information provided by the individual Member States as part of the Committee's Regulatory Consistency Program (RCAP), focuses to ensure that the Basel Standards are transformed into national laws or regulation according to the internationally agreed upon framework.[114] However, several milestones have been marked to ensure gradual compliance and timely implementation of the whole framework.

To serve this purpose, national jurisdictions have committed to implement official regulation and legislation that establishes the reporting and disclosure requirements from January 1, 2014. The Basel Committee in June 2013 issued a consultative

---

106. BCBS. (2006). International Convergence of Capital Measurement and Capital Standards: A Revised Framework (June 2006). BCBS at, http://www.bis.org/publ/bcbs128.pdf, last accessed, Aug. 23, 2015.
107. BCBS. (2009). Enhancement to the Basel III Framework BIS. BIS, July 2009, available at http://www.bis.org/publ/bcbs157.htm.
108. BCBS, (2011). *Basel* III: A Global Regulatory Framework for more Resilient Banks and Banking Systems. (Revised June 2011), available at www.bis.org/publ/bcbs189.pdf.
109. *Ibid.*
110. *See*, Pruzin, D. (Dec. 17, 2010). Basel Panel Issues Final Basel III Package; Version Contains New Liquidity Rule Details, International Business & Finance, Daily Online, BNA.
111. Gu, B., & Liu, T. (2014). Enforcing International Financial Regulatory Reforms. *Journal of International Economic Law. 17*(1), 139-176.
112. *See,* BCBS, Basel III: The Liquidity Coverage Ratio and Liquidity Risk Monitoring Tools, January 2013, available at www.bis.org/publ/bcbs238.pdf. The implementation of Basel III has generally been timely, for example, final rules on liquidity (LCR) have been issued in all but two jurisdictions, and are in force in 22 jurisdictions (98% of the market). *See*, the Basel III implementation tab on FSB website, http://www.fsb.org/basel-iii/ last accessed, Aug. 10, 2016.
113. The BCBS, Report to G20 Financial Ministers and Central Bank Governors on monitoring implementation of Basel III regulatory reform, April 2013, at 15-19.
114. *See*, BCBS. (April 2016). *Tenth Progress Report on Adoption of the Basel Regulatory Framework.* Retrieved from https://www.bis.org/bcbs/publ/d366.pdf last accessed, Aug. 10, 2016.

paper on the revised leverage ratio framework[115] along with public disclosure requirements starting from January 1, 2015. From 2012, the BCBS initiated the Regulatory Consistency Assessment Program (RCAP) to monitor progress in introducing domestic regulations, assessing their consistency and analyzing regulatory outcomes. This monitoring was I initially focused on the Basel III risk-based capital requirements however, now it has been extended to cover all aspects of the Basel III standards. The Basel Committee began phasing in its Basel standards from 2013. As of March 2017: all 27 members jurisdictions have final risk-based capital rules, LCR regulation and capital conservation buffers; 25 of them have issued final rules for countercyclical capital buffers; 25 have issued final or draft rules for domestic systemically Important Banks (D-SIBs); 20 have issued final or draft rules for margin requirements for non-centrally cleared derivatives; 20 have issued final or draft rules for monitoring tools for intraday liquidity management.[116] And, with regard to the global systemically important banks (G-SIBs) framework, all members that are home jurisdictions to G-SIBs have final rules in force. The Committee aims to have assessed the consistency of LCR standards in all 27 member jurisdictions by end-2017.

Five years after the finalization of Basel III, the effects of the new capital rules are being felt by banks. But some of the most significant changes are still to be implemented, meaning the overall impact is unknown. The implementation status of Basel III standards as at April 2017 is:

(a) Risk-based capital standards are still being implemented with:
- Countercyclical buffer: in parallel to the capital conservation buffer is expected to be fully operational on January 1, 2019.
- TLAC holdings: it was issued in 2016 and will take effect from January 1, 2019.
- Minimum capital requirements for market risk: In January 2017, the Committee has issued the revised minimum capital requirements for market risk and is expected to take full effect from January 1, 2019.
- Capital requirements for equity investment in funds: took effect from January 1, 2017.
- SA-CCR: The committee issued Standardized Approach for measuring Counterparty Credit Risk in 2014 and it took effect from January 2017.
- Securitization framework: The Committee issued revisions in December 2014 and July 2016. Expected to take effect from January 2018.
- Margin requirements for non-centrally cleared derivatives: After revisions, the framework started from September 2016.

---

115. BCBS. Basel III: Leverage Ratio Framework and Disclosure Requirements. January 2014, available at www.bis.org/publ/bcbs270.htm. *See also*, BCBS. Basel III: The Net Stable Funding Ratio. Consultative Document, January 2014, available at www.bis.org/publ/bcbs271.pdf.
116. *See*, BCBS, Basel III Regulatory Consistency Assessment Program: Handbook for jurisdictional assessments, March 2016, available at www.bis.org/bcbs/publ/d361.htm, last accessed, Apr. 27, 2017; *see* also, BCBS (April 2017), Twelfth Progress Report on Adoption of the Basel Regulatory Framework, available at http://www.bis.org/bcbs/publ/d404.pdf, last accessed, Apr. 28, 2017.

Chapter 4: Regulatory Regimes and IFL §4.03[B]

- Capital requirements for bank exposure to central counterparties: came into effect from January 2017.
(b) Basel III leverage ratio: Final adjustments to the definition and calibration of the leverage ratio to be made by 2017, with a view to migrating to a Pillar 1 (minimum capital requirements) treatment on January 1, 2018 based.
(c) Monitoring tools for intraday liquidity management: This standard was developed in consultation with the CPSS. The reporting of the monitoring tools commenced on a monthly basis from January 1, 2015 to coincide with the implementation of the LCR reporting requirements.
(d) Basel III NSFR: The NSFR will become a minimum standard by January 1, 2018.
(e) G-SIB framework: The requirements came into effect on January 1, 2016 and become fully effective on January 1, 2019.
(f) D-SIB framework: Given that the D-SIB framework complements the G-SIB framework, the Committee believes it would be appropriate if banks identified as D-SIBs by their national authorities were required to comply with the principles in line with the phase-in arrangements for the G-SIB framework, i.e., from January 2016.
(g) Pillar 3 disclosure requirements: Took effect from end-2016. Banks are required to publish their first Pillar III report under the revised framework concurrently with their year-end 2016 financial report.
(h) Large exposures framework: will take effect from January 2019.
(i) Interest rate risk in the banking book: The committee issued final standards in April 2016, expected to take full implementation by 2018.

Table 4.1 Basel III Phase-in Arrangements

All dates as of January 1		2013	2014	2015	2016	2017	2018	2019
Capital	Phases							
	Leverage Ratio		Parallel run January 1- January 1, 2017 Disclosure starts January 1, 2015				Migration to Pillar 1	
	Minimum Common Equity Capital ratio	3.5%	4.0%	4.5%				4.5%
	Capital Conservation Buffer				0.625%	1.25%	1.875%	2.5%
	Minimum Common equity plus capital conservation buffer	3.5%	4.0%	4.5%	5.125%	5.75%	6.375%	7.0%
	Phase-in of deduction from CET1*		20%	40%	60%	80%	100%	100%

All dates as of January 1								
Phases	2013	2014	2015	2016	2017	2018	2019
Minimum Tier 1 Capital	4.5%	5.5%	6.0%				6.0%
Minimum Total Capital		8.0%					8.0%
Minimum Total Capital plus conservation buffer		8.0%		8.625%	9.25%	9.875%	10.5%
Capital Instruments that no longer qualify as non-core Tier 1 or Tier 2 Capital	Phased out over 10 years horizon beginning 2013						

All dates as of January 1								
	Phases	2013	2014	2015	2016	2017	2018	2019
Liquidity	Liquidity Coverage Ratio – minimum requirements			60%	70%	80%	90%	100%
	Net Stable funding ratio						Introduce minimum standards	

Source: BIS, Phase-in arrangements. *See,* http://www.bis.org/bcbs/basel3/basel3_phase_in_arrangements.pdf, last accessed July 15, 2015.

* Including amounts exceeding the limit for deferred tax assets (DTAs), mortgage servicing rights (MSRs) and financial – Transition period.

The FSB in its progress report on financial sector regulatory reform to the heads of the G20 leading economies has noted inconsistent implementation of the Basel III standards (*see* above) and in the rules for supervision, recovery and resolution of SIFIs, and shadow banking.[117] Mark Carney, Chairman of the FSB, remarked: *monitoring the shadow banking system is an essential part of our work to strengthen the oversight and regulation of this sector... The FSB will continue to improve its global monitoring exercise to identify the financial stability risks posed by shadow banking as the result of its use of leverage, maturity and liquidity transformation.*[118]

The European supervisory authorities (ESAs) – the EBA, the European Securities and Markets Authority (ESMA) and the European Insurance and Occupational Pensions Authority (EIOPA) – released a report on cross-sector risks and noted, *interest rate volatility, continuing economic weakness and a drawback from cross-border lending within the EU were potential threats, along with the decreased confidence in industry balance sheets and risk disclosures in the light of weaknesses discovered in risk-weighted asset calculations.*[119] The G20's approach beyond the Brisbane Summit will determine *the openness of the global financial system and consequently the strength and sustainability of global growth.*[120] The FSB recommends global standards for resolution of global systemically important institutions; deferring to each other's market regulatory regimes where they achieve equivalent outcomes; peer reviews and impact assessments to ensure consistent implementation (when we get standards right) and refinement of standards (when we get them wrong); and, enhanced cooperation to avoid domestic measures that fragment the global system.[121]

As is obvious from the above, the implementations schedules are inconsistent and provide potential opportunities for regulatory arbitrage across borders. The fear is that such implementation problems tend to induce race to the bottom, making international financial regulatory reforms in vain, and even laying grounds for another financial crisis.[122]

---

117. Shadow banking involves credit intermediation involving entities and activities (fully or partially) outside the regular banking system or in simple words, nonbank credit intermediation, *see for latest monitoring report on shadow banking*, the FSB website at http://www.fsb.org/2017/05/global-shadow-banking-monitoring-report-2016/.
118. *See*, FSB. (Nov. 14, 2013). FSB Publishes Global Shadow Banking Monitoring 2013 Press Release (Vol. No: 87/2013). Available at http://www.fsb.org/wp-content/uploads/r_131114.pdf?page_moved = 1
119. EBA released 'European Supervisory Authorities Highlight Cross-sectoral Risks' in September 2013, available at http://bit.ly/17WB4fb, last accessed, Mar. 6, 2014.
120. Carney, M. (Feb. 24, 2014). Financial Reforms: Progress and Challenges. Letter to the G20 Finance Ministers. Available at https://www.financialstabilityboard.org/publications/r_140222.pdf.
121. *Ibid*.
122. Gu & Liu, *Supra* n. 111.

Table 4.2 Basel Committee on Banking Supervision – Basel III Strengthens micro-prudential regulation and supervision, and adds a macro-prudential overlay that includes capital buffers

Capital				Liquidity
Pillar I		Pillar 2	Pillar 3	Global liquidity standard and supervisory monitoring **Liquidity Coverage Ratio** The LCR will require banks to have sufficient high-quality liquid assets to withstand a 30 day stressed testing scenario that is specified by supervisors. **Net Stable Funding Ratio** The NSFR is a longer-term structural ratio designed to address liquidity mismatches. It covers the entire balance sheet and provides incentives for banks to use stable sources of funding. **Principles for Sound Liquidity Risk Management and Supervision**
Risk Coverage	Containing Leverage	Risk management & supervision	Market discipline	
Capital				

	Capital					Liquidity
Banks	**Quality and level of capital Focus on common equity.** The minimum will be raised to 4.5% of risk-weighted assets, after deduction. **Capital Loss Absorption at the Point of non-viability** Contractual terms of capital instruments will include a clause that allow- at the discretion of the relevant authority- write-off or conversion to common shares if the bank is judged to be non-viable. This principle increases the contribution of the private sector to resolving future banking crises and thereby reducing moral hazard. **Capital Conservation Buffer** Comprising common equity of 2.5% of risk-weighted assets, bringing the total common equity standards to 7%. Constraints on a bank's discretionary distribution will be imposed when bank falls in to the buffer range.	**Securitization** Strengthen the capital treatment for complex securitization. Requiring banks rigorous credit analyses of externally rated securitization exposure. **Trading Book.** Significantly higher capital for trading and derivatives activities, as well as complex securitizations held in the trading book **Counterparty credit risk** Substantial strengthening of the counterparty credit risk framework, which includes: capital incentives	**Leverage ratio** A non-risk-based leverage ratio that includes off-balance sheet exposures will serve as a backstop to the risk-based capital requirements. Also, help contain system-wide buildup of leverages.	**Supplemental pillar 2 requirements.** Address firm-wide governance and risk management; capturing the risk of off-balance sheet exposures and securitization activities; managing risk concentrations; providing incentives for banks to better manage risk and return over the long-term; sound compensation practices; valuation practices; stress testing;	**Revised Pillar 3 disclosure requirements** The requirements introduced relate to securitization exposures and sponsorship of off-balance sheet vehicles. Enhanced disclosures on the detail of the components of regulatory capital and their reconciliation to the reported accounts will be required, including a comprehensive explanation of how a bank	The committee's 2008 guidance principles for sound liquidity Risk Management and Supervision takes account of lessons learned during the crisis and are based on the fundamental review of sound practices for managing liquidity risk in a banking organization. **The Supervisory Monitoring** The liquidity framework includes a set of monitoring metrics to assist supervisors in identifying and analyzing liquidity risk trends at both the bank and system-wide level.

Capital			Liquidity
Countercyclical buffer Imposed within a range of 0%-2.5% comprising common equity. When authorities judge credit growth is resulting in an unacceptable buildup of systematic risk.	for banks to use central counterparties for derivatives; and higher capital for inter-financial sector exposures. **Bank exposures to central counterparties (CCPs)** The committee has proposed that trade exposures to a qualifying CCP will receive a 2% risk weight and default fund exposures to a qualifying CCP will be capitalized according to a risk-based method that consistently and simply estimates risk arising from such default fund.	accounting standards for financial instruments; corporate governance; and supervisory colleges.	calculates its regulatory capital ratios.

Capital	Liquidity
SIFIs: In addition to meeting the Basel III requirements, G-SIFIs must have higher loss absorbency capacity to reflect the greater risk that they pose to the financial system. The Committee has developed a methodology that includes both quantitative indicators and qualitative elements to identify global systemically important banks (SIBs). The additional loss absorbency requirements are to be met with a progressive Common Equity Tier 1 (CET1) capital requirements ranging from 1% to 2.5%, depending on a bank's systemic importance. For banks facing the highest surcharge, an additional loss absorbency of 1% could be applied as a disincentive to increase materially their global systemic importance in the future. A consultative document was published in cooperation with the FSB, which is coordinating the overall set of measures to reduce the moral hazard posed by global SIFIs.	

Source: Basel Committee on Banking Supervision reforms: Basel III, available at http://www.bis.org/bcbs/basel3/b3summarytable.pdf last accessed August 1, 2017.

[C] Basel III: A Critical Assessment

Higher capital requirements provide a buffer against risks and make financial markets resilient however factors like higher compliance costs cannot be ignored. In addition to the higher capital requirements as enlisted in the Pillar I, equally important are the other two pillars of Basel regulation i.e., the supervisory review and market disclosure for keeping financial stability. Until comprehensive market discipline, an effective corporate governance code, and a mechanism to enforce regulatory regime is adopted, *the road to financial stability*[123] would continue to prove increasingly serrated.

Adoption of Basel III faces some important policy and implementation gaps, in particular due to lack of disciplining power and lack of enforcement (these issues are discussed in Chapter 6). For example, the lessons learnt from some of the most damaging cases during the recent economic and banking crisis are mix. The policy makers still have conflicting view on the solutions. Below are a few observations:

- BoE Governor, Mervyn King, suggested splitting up banks and separating riskier activities from more stable businesses (such as taking deposits from utility banking) as the financial sector takes on risk with the support of the taxpayers' money and that reflects not genuine risk-bearing.[124] On the other hand, Nout Wellink, Chairman of the Basel Committee, sounded more confident when he remarked: *[the proposed] combination of much stronger definition of capital, higher minimum capital requirements and the introduction of new capital buffers will ensure that the banks are better able to withstand periods of economic and financial stress, therefore supporting economic growth.*[125]
- The concept of *bail-in measures* (as included in Basel III's agenda) would force creditors to share the cost of propping up large banks before taxpayers shoulder these losses. Lord Turner from the FSA advocated use of new capital and liquidity requirements rather than a structured solution, such as clear institutional separation between classic bank services to the real economy (narrow banking or utility banking) and risky propriety trading activities (investment banking or casino banking).[126]
- The US FDIC Chairwoman, Sheila Bair remarked that the idea of Contingent Convertible Capital instruments (CoCos), a kind of convertible debt would be intriguing but this option may not resolve the underlying crisis of confidence in the institutions. A deeper analysis and comparison reflects that the Dodd-Frank legislation, by contrast, might address the system-wide issues in a better

---

123. *See*, Ashraf, U., Arner, D. W., & Gill, I. M. (2011). A Road to Financial Stability. *Global Journal of Business & Finance Research (GJBR)*, 5(5).
124. King, M. (October 2010). Banking – From Bagehot to Basel, and Back Again: The Second Bagehot Lecture, Buttonwood Gathering. *BIS Review*. Available at http://www.bis.org/review/r101028a.pdf.
125. Wellink, N. (2011). Basel III: A Roadmap to Better Banking Regulation and Supervision. The FSI High-Level Meeting on the New Framework to Strengthen Financial Stability and Regulatory Priorities, June 24. Russia. Available at http://www.bis.org/speeches/sp110524.pdf.
126. King, M. (2010). *Supra* n. 124.

Chapter 4: Regulatory Regimes and IFL §4.04

way than the *bail-in* measures as it would incorporate the idea of *living wills* that would make it easier to wind up such falling institutions in times of crisis.[127]

- The UK made significant effort to correct the balances under the remit of the Independent Commission on Banking (known as the Vickers Commission.[128] The Commission's one of the prime goals was to prevent future bank bailouts at taxpayers' expense). The Vickers Commission recommended, *ring-fencing traditional retail banking and limiting taxpayer guarantees to personal and business depositors,* then government funding of the banking system can be directed to the needs of the businesses that create jobs and growth;[129] however, Basel III doesn't not prescribe anything on those lines.

As a successor to Basel II and Basel I, Basel III's roots lie in the late twentieth century (not in the twenty-first century). The ECB may also play a role by demanding from EU banks to pull their cash and assets out of any such banks that may not have proper risk controls and are not implementing internationally agreed upon reforms measures like Basel III (until such banks meet Prudential Regulatory Authority's enforcement standards). A refusal to access public funds in case of failures of such banks may work as a deterrent to get universal adoption of internationally accepted reform measures.

§4.04 FROM SELF-REGULATION TO REREGULATION: MYTH OR REALITY

If we raise a simple question that what caused this new reregulatory drive, an attempt to answer this brings us following observations (*see* Chapter 2 Section, §2.03 for details):

- That risk assessment and its adequate management are currently the major issues for financial firms and the supervisory bodies. An inaccurate presumption, which prevailed the pre-2008 markets that market-supplied credit and liquidity would continue to be available. This faulty premise led to an overestimation of the market's ability particularly under stressed times. Under capitalization thus turned out to be one prime cause of the crisis.

---

127. FSA. (2009). The Turner Review: A Regulatory Response to the Global Banking Crisis. Available at http://www.fsa.gov.uk/pubs/other/turner_review.pdf.
128. On October 8, the UK authorities announced a comprehensive and system-wide support package that addressed weaknesses in the balance sheets of the banks in the UK. The package aimed at increasing resilience of UK banks by raising the capital requirements in addition to the Special Liquidity Scheme and the provision of guarantees on new debt. Subsequently, other countries adopted system-wide measures with similar underlying principles. *See* Bank of England's publication at, http://www.bankofengland.co.uk/publications/fsr/2008/fsrfull0810.pdf.
129. Wolf, M. (Sep. 15, 2011). Of Course it's Right to Ring-fence Rogue Universals. *Financial Times.* *See,* http://www.ft.com/intl/cms/s/0/f296cc8e-dedc-11e0-9130-00144feabdc0.html#axzz3jYyHDR8Z.

- Secondly, risky innovations in the structured financial products transferred OR to off-balance sheet structures by packaging loans for sale in a Special Purpose Vehicle (SPV) through securitization, and model-based risk assessments rendered it hard to gauge precisely actual risk exposures. Their stress-testing failed to take account of not only unexpected happenings, like total freezing of the inter-bank or commercial paper market-but also of situations like exposures to common shocks.
- Securitization, multi-layered Collateralized Debt Obligations (CDOs),[130] exponential growth in Over-the-Counter (OTC) derivative market, and originate-to-distribute models created perverse incentives for the market. Most of these instruments were created with a view to decentralize *risk* but the nature of the financial markets, the inability of supervisors and misplaced regulatory focus made these risks *invisible* and threw a shadow on the credit quality of counterparties. In fact Basel I encouraged risk-taking off-balance sheet (only was only partly corrected under Basel II) led to a drastic deterioration in mortgage-lending standards and other regulatory risk management practices.
- Weak regulatory standards (e.g., capital requirement under Basel II) coupled with extremely low interest rate policy of short-term (monetary policy) and long-term (government bond) interest rates led to a deluge of less-thoughtful innovative financial products, which resulted in higher securitization trends.[131] At worst, where interest rates did not include a risk premium factor,[132] it encouraged banks in search of avenues to expand their trade into a risky unregulated secondary market through innovative financial instruments such as CDS, credit derivatives and other types of SIVs dominating the shadow banking system.[133]

Basel III regulations are expected to be phased in by 2019 amidst sprawling fears that this focused crackdown on the banking sector would push risk out to the shadow banking sector. It is also feared that this transfer of risk into the shadow sector may serve only to compound any impending crisis. The US subprime mortgage lending was recycled around the globe through this shadow banking mechanism and innovative structures. Frequently, the banking sector and more specifically, the shadow banking

---

130. The term *bespoke tranche opportunity* is being used for the newer forms of CDOs coming into financial markets. Although, bespoke tranche are entirely based on corporate loans – unlike the CDOs which were based on subprime mortgages – and are almost insignificant in volume comparing with the CDOs (USD 20 billion per annum versus a trillion dollar CDO industry), yet Adam McKay's recent movie, The Big Short (2015), mentions these.
131. *See*, Angela Maddaloni., José-Luis Peydró. (October 2010). Bank Risk-Taking,Securitization, Supervision and Low Interest Rates Evidence from the Euro Area and the U.S. Lending Standards. Available at http://www.fundacionbancosantander.com/media/docs/J-L-Peydro_BLS_17092009.pdf.
132. IR = government bond rate + specific risk premium of borrowers.
133. Lopes, J. (July 2010). Re-enactment of the Glass-Steagall Act 1933: Is this a Step in the Right Direction for Global Financial Reform? *Law and Financial Markets Review, 4*, 428-432. Retrieved from http://www.ingentaconnect.com/content/hart/lfmr/2010/00000004/00000004/art00009http://dx.doi.org/10.5235/175214410791942805 p.428, last accessed February 2011.

Chapter 4: Regulatory Regimes and IFL §4.04

sector may require specific shock absorbers for specific activities. The different forms of trading (particularly the proprietary trading) are becoming more and more expensive for the banks due to enhanced capital requirements under the Basel III.

As the US economy began to contract and deleverage, the interest rates plunged to its historical low in the immediate aftermath of the financial crisis.[134] The cheapness of bonds provided companies such as Microsoft, Hewlett-Packard, IBM and e-Bay arbitrage opportunity between the cost of debt and equity.[135] Given that the dividend yield for many companies was higher than the bonds held, this provided those groups the fortuitous option to issue (cheaper) debt and buyback (expensive) equity.[136] However, long-term bonds such as 50-year Goldman bond issues, by contrast, remained pessimistic.[137]

In view of SDCs, Huw van Steenis points at the peripheral nations' debt concerns. The bank funding remained a key risk and a transmission mechanism of sovereign concern, as well as a drag on lending and bank profitability.[138] Such concern can also contribute to a government's contraction in spending, which may occur if the government overspends to propitiate financial default[139] (Greece's notorious swap with Goldman Sachs highlighted the risks on government bonds).[140] Greece used derivatives to disguise its true level of borrowing by arranging a massive swap transactions with Goldman aimed to reduce the cost of financing of country's public debt.[141] The SDC in Greece expanded to the eurozone.[142]

So, from the US, the Irish and Greece's experiences, it is evident that the unfettered markets and self-regulation have not proved the best options.[143] Expensive bailouts and EU's supervisory policies to deal with the crisis sparked the threats that have deepened the crisis beyond financial horizon. Eurozone is facing multiple challenges despite a lapse of almost a decade. The crises are not only financial but monetary, fiscal, and not only threatening political integration of the entity but also are inadvertently impeding reforms.

Before the recent financial crisis, financial innovation was regarded as inextricably linked with economic growth and aggregate welfare. Reviewing virtues and pitfalls

---

134. *See*, Van Duyn, A. & Mackenzie. M. (Nov. 1, 2010). Paper Weight. *Financial Times*, p. 11.
135. *See,* Milne, R. (Oct. 6, 2010). Cheapness of Bonds Helps Fuel Rebound in Share Buy-Backs, *Financial Times*. p. 27; also, International Financial Review, Cash is King for Consumer Issuers, avaiable at http://www.iflr.com/.
136. *See*, Duyn., Mackenzie., *supra* n. 134.
137. Johnson, S., (Nov. 29, 2010)., Long-term Bonds Raise New Bubble Worrries, *Financial Times*, p. 3.
138. Jenkins, P., Sharlene Goff., Patrick Methurin., (Dec. 2, 2010). Bank Ties Across EU Carry Risk Concerns. *Financial Times*, p. 19.
139. *See* Charnovitz, S. (2010)., Addressing Government Failure Through International Financial Law, *Journal of International Economic Law, 13*(3). p. 745.
140. *See* Hope, K. Megan Murphy, Gillian Tett., (Feb. 16, 2010). The Eurozone: Athenian Arrangers, *Financial Times*. Available at https://www.ft.com/content/87c3d0c6-1b30-11df-953f-00144 feab49a last visited, May 4, 2017.
141. *See Id.*
142. *See,* BBC, Eurozone Approves Massive Greece Bail-out (May 2, 2010). The EU and the IMF agreed a EUR 110 billion three-year bailout package to rescue Greece's embattled economy. Available at http://news.bbc.co.uk/2/hi/8656649.stm (last visited Dec. 10, 2010).
143. Coats, *Supra* n. 14, p. 11.

of financial innovation that have marked the history of financial markets in the past three decades, it is important to critically assesses the likely impact of such innovations and corresponding regulations on the future of IFRA.[144] The laissez faire economy believes that financial regulations should largely base on the precept of rational and self-correcting market principles.[145] However, a virtual absence of monitoring of the financial sector's risk analysis by a government can incentivize excessive risk taking for the banks to seek out maximum profits. At times, as we have seen, the problem is not of regulation or reregulation but of having effective, implementable and enforceable regulation.

There are unique angles to look at how regulation works, and also, how regulation or deregulation may not work. Deregulation was a major component of the WC whether applied to financial services, labor markets or elsewhere. Less well known is the IFIs' promotion of deregulation in labor markets. In 2007, the WB bestowed its *Top Reformer of the Year* award for its improved *Doing Business* rating[146] to the Republic of Georgia as the Government did away with most labor regulations. The reform led to Georgia's condemnation by the International Labor Organization for violating fundamental workers' rights.

The international efforts are, more than ever, aimed at devising a system of shock absorbers at various levels of financial governance. The FSB, the IMF, the G20 and the Basel Committee provide forums for regular consultation and cooperation to design acceptable and enforceable universal risk-based management mechanisms. However, the post-crisis regulatory developments have cast a shadow on the role orchestrated by these forums. Even the G20's Declaration *to support an open global economy* by laying the reform foundations in the *Action Plan* could not provide much assurance on the credibility of the new reforms. Agustín Carstens, Chairman of the FSB Standing Committee on Assessment of Vulnerabilities, remarked that *improving bank regulation is not enough* to fully address the weaknesses of the financial system that has been revealed by the crisis. The shadow banking system continues to transform and innovate. The aim is to narrow in on new risks to the financial system,[147] and continue appropriate decision-making encompassing such issues as these arise.

§4.05 CONCLUSION

Banking is central to financial system for efficient functioning of an economy. The consequence of a bank failure, whether due to lender or borrower, impacts nonetheless every aspect of a nation's well-being. Although, unemployment, receding growth rates, diminishing demand and hyperinflation emerged as perpetual issues in the aftermath of the GFC, yet the silver lining is that states, financial institutions and regulatory

---

144. Delimatsis, P. (2013). Transparent Financial Innovation in a Post-Crisis Environment. *Journal of International Economic Law*, 16(1), 159-210.
145. *See*, Fama, E. F. (1970), and, Larsen, P. T (2009). *Supra* n. 29.
146. *See*, Bakvis, P. What Should Replace the Washington Consensus? in, Coats, *supra* n. 14, p. 52.
147. *See*, FSB. (2013). FSB Publishes Global Shadow Banking Monitoring. Ref 87/2013, available at http://www.fsb.org/wp-content/uploads/r_131114.pdf; see also, supra n.117

bodies have become sensitive to closely monitoring regulatory adequacy and financial activities to safeguard failure of financial system. The steady globalization of financial markets contributed to hyperactivity and risk-connectivity of the international financial markets and thus has made bank liquidity and solvency matters of prime international concern. The Basel Accords have provided major milestones in addressing these risk concerns by focusing on the capital adequacy requirements, liquidity, and risk measurement and management approaches. However, history tells otherwise. Pure reliance on Basel III this time too may not provide panacea to all the ills that arise from the next financial crisis.

To sum up all, the above analysis of the existing set of regulations does not reassure our confidence on the regulatory and supervisory instruments available to financial markets currently and therefore, under the circumstances, there is dire need to change, transform, develop and sustain the regulatory architecture. There is need to comprehend fundamental problems in the conceptual philosophy and working of the IFIs, and of IFRs – both in the substantive contents and in their enforcement mechanisms. Sixteen years ago, partly in response to the AFC of 1997, the Basel Committee attempted to overhaul global banking rules through Basel II, which could never achieve full adoption. There is skepticism if Basel III would meet a different fate than its predecessor. There are important variables that can affect the outcomes including politics of global regulation, implementation timelines and sequencing of adoption in determining success of this framework.[148] From banker's perspective, Basel III's rules have increased the amount of capital that banks must hold, and set a core tier 1 capital ratio of 7% that has increased costs of doing business for financial institutions both because of higher capital requirements as well from increased costs of compliance to the new regulatory regime. The technical implementation deadline for Basel III is 2019, but recent developments in the banking market have suggested that even stricter rules may be crafted through another framework, dubbed as Basel IV.[149] The need is for decisions that conform with procedural justice and distributive equity to the ongoing development of relevant laws and standards. A resilient enforcement mechanism with stringent regulatory reforms will make the world a safer place for all the actors including the market players, the regulators and most importantly, taxpayers.

---

148. Lall, R. (2011). From Failure to Failure: The Politics of International Banking Regulation. *Review of International Political Economy, 19*(4), 609-638.
149. Basel IV is likely to include: (1) requiring banks to meet higher minimum leverage ratios (2) emphasizing simpler or standardized models, rather than banks' internal models for calculation of capital requirements and (3) more detailed disclosure of reserves and other financial statistics. *See,* Noonan, L. (Mar. 14, 2016). Basel IV Spectre Looms for Battle-worn Bankers. *Financial Times.* Retrieved from https://www.ft.com/content/a9d6eb94-ce5d-11e5-831d-09f7778e7377.

CHAPTER 5
Enforcement in IFL: The Precarious Case of the EU[*]

Study of the soft-law-based regulatory regimes in the previous chapters has shown that financial market moves much faster than their respective regulators. We found regulators, in peace times trailing behind the market in an attempt to regulate nuances of financial products, while in crises times, responding feebly if at all, and eventually giving in to taxpayer led bailouts. Having seen the abysmal performance of soft law during crises, this chapter is making an attempt reimagine IFL in a treaty-based environment by analyzing the EU's treaty-based regional structure.

A decade ago, to the not too keen eye of an observer, the EU structure would have beautifully illuminated the European canvass presenting a successful and resilient construct under public international law. However, today, the current literature on EU presents a solid case to study a model for a treaty-based international law which had deep fault lines and was faulty from the outset. Let's look at this full circle transformation of the perspective to find lessons, if any, to construct a positive enforcement mechanism in IFL.

§5.01 OLD FISSURES, NEW LESSONS

Lately, we have seen that the SDC which followed the GFC exposed major weaknesses in the economic governance framework of the European Union (EU). We recently have

---

[*] This chapter draws from an initial research conducted for Asian Development Bank's project on Asian Regional Integration, published in the book edited by, Azis, I. J. & Shin,H. S. (2014). Global Shock, Asian Vulnerability and Financial Reform, Edward Elgar Press; and, on an article by, Avgouleas, E., & Arner, D. W. (2013), The Eurozone Debt Crisis and the European Banking Union: A Cautionary Tale of Failure and Reform. *Faculty of Law Research Paper No. 2013/037*, available at http://ssrn.com/abstract = 2347937 Research for this chapter also benefited from two grants awarded under the 'Hong Kong Research Grant Council's project, *Enhancing Hong Kong's Future as a Leading IFC*, to present initial drafts of this research in Europe in 2013.

seen old fissures leading to the dismemberment of at least one of the Member States. We are also watching a transitioning nationalist political backdrop which may be a prelude to many more transformations to come, both local and global. Nonetheless, the EU in the context of (a) its recent crises (SDC, Greece, the Brexit, as well as the rise of far-right political regimes) and, despite all (b) in its continuity to pursue the Union's common framework, provides a *perfect laboratory* to analyze the treaty-based financial market integration structure. What Jean Monnet wrote back in 1970s continues to be the case: *Europe will be forged in crises, and will be the sum of the solutions adopted for those crises.*[1]

The crisis-management mechanism in the EU institutions as it unfolded – first in dealing with the GFC and subsequently with the SDC – gives us an insight to the functioning of hard-law-based supranational institutions of financial governance. The European institutions make a useful belvedere to scale legal complexities involved in the construct and operation of an integrated market. The European Economic and Monetary Union (EMU) is now facing existential threats owing to multiple underlying reasons including huge variation in the financial soundness of its Member States which have become detrimental to its continued existence. The Commission President, Barroso, cognizant of the slipups, said in State of the Union address on September 11, 2013: [T]he EU needs to be big on big things and smaller on small things – something we may occasionally have neglected in the past.[2]

A recent research investigates the impact of the composition of debt in a monetary union, that is, the fraction of *high-debt v. low-debt members, on the occurrence of self-fulfilling debt crises.*[3] Accordingly, a high-debt country may be less vulnerable to crises and have higher welfare when it belongs to a union with an intermediate mix of high-and low-debt members than one where all other members are low-debt. This points to yet another dimension, albeit in sharp contrast to the more populist version, which fancies a union with *only* low-debt members as the most efficient model. These findings invoke us to think deeper on selecting a criterion for an optimal currency area in the presence of rollover crises.

The development of the EU's market institutions followed a piecemeal approach. It started with the establishment of the European Coal and Steel Community (ECSC), through the EEC,[4] it culminated into forming the EU. Aspirations to have a single currency for the union led to the formation of the EMU and the introduction of a single

---

1. *See*, Monnet, J. (1978). *Memoirs*. Garden City, N.Y: Doubleday.
2. Barroso, J. M. (2013). *State of the Union Address by President of the EC, 11 Sep.* Presented at the European Parliament Plenary Session, Strasbourg. *See*, http://europa.eu/rapid/press-release_SPEECH-13-684_en.htm, last accessed, Aug. 25, 2015.
3. Aguiar, M., Amador, M., Farhi, E., & Gopinath, G. (2015). Coordination and Crisis in Monetary Unions. *The Quarterly Journal of Economics*, 130(4), 1727-1779.
4. The EU traces its origins from the ECSC and the EEC, formed by a core of six countries. The ECSC established in 1951, was the first international organization, based on the principle of supranationalism to unify European countries after the World War II. It was formally established under the Treaty of Paris (1951), signed by Belgium, France, West Germany, Italy, the Netherlands and Luxembourg. Its purpose was to abolish trade barriers. The Treaty of Rome established the EEC on broader principles of cooperation. To achieve these, it introduced a number of permanent supranational institutions, such as the EC and the European Court of Justice (ECJ).

currency.⁵ Thus, the Union, during the past couple of decades, has achieved remarkable progress on market integration. However, new threats on the financial horizon (contagions, connectedness, too-big-to-fail issues) as exposed by the 2008 crisis, revealed profound flaws and weaknesses in the cross-border regulatory and supervisory mechanisms. For example, almost all EU jurisdictions lacked comprehensive and effective crisis-resolution mechanisms to withstand impending cross-border cross-sector dimensions of the crisis.⁶

Today, in the midst of exit-movements and the rise of far-right political ideologies the Member States of the Union are struggling to get out of lingering financial woes. These struggles have placed the EU at a critical crossroads. It has to decide whether to continue to further institutional development for Single Supervisory Mechanism (SSM)) is the way to recovery from the Europe-wide financial distress (despite the Brexit; despite the Italian Banks testing the powers that the SSM can dispense *balancing stability v. enforcement of rules*),⁷ or, a return to a nationalist, inward approach (as risk-sharing faces considerable resistance in creditor nations such as Germany or France) would be a safer bet. Jean Monnet wrote in his memoirs 35 years ago: [N]obody can say today what the institutional framework of Europe will be tomorrow because the future changes, which will be fostered by today's changes, are unpredictable.⁸

Given the current status of the post-Brexit political map of the EU, protectionism and the pursuit of narrowly defined national interest seem to dominate the European political canvass but these trends are bound to endanger the single market. Thus, the policy dilemmas being faced by contemporary institution-building within the Eurozone can provide a range of useful lessons to contemplate for any such future initiative, be it regional or global, affecting any aspect of finance, financial regulation or financial markets. So even if the old is dying yet there are new lessons to aspire for.

The chapter is organized as: Section §5.02 begins with an analytical overview of economic and institutional developments leading to the establishment of a treaty-based EU single market for financial services. Section §5.03 discusses crisis in the integration framework triggered by the GFC, which were later intensified by the Eurozone SDC and looks at how these disruptions gradually evolved into serious threats to the most sophisticated regional financial market. The discussion extends to discuss the evolution of institutional infrastructure safeguarding financial stability and effective supervision of financial institutions in the EU from its early stages. Section §5.04 reviews the post-crisis European effort at reinventing the integration mechanism through the formation of the European System of Financial Supervisors (ESFS), the European Single

---

5. The Maastricht Treaty in 1993 also introduced the charter of the European Monetary Union (EMU).
6. *See*, Avgouleas, E. (2012). *Governance of Global Financial Markets: The Law, the Economics, the Politics*. Cambridge University Press, Ch. 6.
7. SSM has to deal with a current EUR 920 billion in non-performing loans out of which EUR 270 billion is from Italian banks. *See*, Claire Jones, Jim Brunsden, (Mar. 22, 2017), *Doubts grow over performance of Eurozone banking watchdog*, Financial Times, available at https://www.ft.com/content/19f809b4-0b1e-11e7-97d1-5e720a26771b last accessed Apr. 5, 2017.
8. Monnet, J. (1978).

Resolution Mechanism (SRM), the EBA, the Integrated Fund, and the DGS on the one hand, and how this new set of EU institutions may strengthen EU's economic and political integration on the other hand. Section §5.05 begins with the discussion on future challenges to a treaty-based mechanism in the EU context and concludes with exploring the possibility of replicating a single market framework for a global setting. This final section §5.06 concludes the thesis that a hard-law-based framework for IFL is not workable at least in the current politico-nationalist environment. Rightfully, the next chapter analyzes short-to-medium-term options to make IFL a more effective tool while living within the soft-law-based framework.

§5.02 FINANCIAL MARKET INTEGRATION

Financial market integration is a complex phenomenon partly due to the risks associated with supranational regulation and supervision of cross-border financial institutions (as discussed in Chapter 4) and related sovereignty issues (as discussed in Chapter 3 and Chapter 6). The complexity of the processes involving power-plays, sovereignty and the supremacy of national interest in a single market is best reflected by the latest political, social and economic developments in the Union. To grasp this complexity that prevails today, it is important to look at the historical account of how this development took place. The following lays down a brief account of the EU financial integration process.

First, let's examine what is this integration in the EU context. Are there different forms of integration, if so, what are those forms. In the EU context, single market includes integration of economic, political, financial and monetary aspects. Let's first define these terms:

- *Economic integration*: refers to integration of national, commercial and economic policies, and elimination of trade barriers and of obstacles to Foreign Direct Investment (FDI) within the single market Member States.[9]
- *Financial sector integration:* implies eliminating restrictions on cross-border capital flows comprising of transactions regarding loans, debt and equity securities. The market for a given set of financial instruments and/or services is believed to be fully integrated if all potential market participants sharing similar characteristics deal with the same set of rules, when they decide to transact in financial instruments and/or provide financial services. Providing such nondiscriminatory access to such financial instruments and/or services to all consumers is vital and it must also extend nondiscriminatory regulatory oversight arrangements.[10]

---

9. The free and reciprocal flow of trade between the various national economies defines economic integration, *see*, Ropke, W. (1950). *The Social Crisis of Our Time*. William Hodge & Co.
10. *See*, Baele, L., et al. (2004). Measuring Financial Integration in the Euro Area. *Occasional Paper Series No. 14: European Central Bank* (April). Retrieved from http://www.ecb.int/pub/pdf/scpops/ecbocp14.pdf p. 7.

- *Political integration:* (linked to economic integration) is equally important. It involves voluntary sharing and pooling of sovereignty, whether in commercial and financial affairs, trade-policy cooperation and coordination, or in relation to justice and national security.[11] On the one hand, lack of political integration can hinder the flow of benefits emanating from monetary and financial integration, while, on the other hand, it can cause many serious frictions among the members. There is a delicate balance which is hard to set in place as we see from the current exit movements.
- *Monetary integration*[12] refers to formal currency alignments and interest rate cooperation among Member States.

[A]   Inception of the European Experiment

The European experience constitutes as an advanced laboratory for a regional economic, monetary and political integration.[13] It is important examining the process as it developed in Europe, in order to discern inherent and artificial obstacles to a well-functioning financial governance regime in an integrated market. The European economic integration and the establishment of Euro as the common currency of 19 EU Member States (as of today) followed an incremental path. This development alternated between periods of strong progress and of slow growth. In general, the single market development has been the product of political expediency and economic efficiency rationale as well as of major setbacks and challenges.[14] For example, the establishment of pan-European banks has been the most potent integrative factor, in an environment marked, at least in its earlier stages, by an absence of regulatory cohesion. At the same time, it was inevitable that the concurrent presence of pan-European banks and of incoherent regulatory structures would lead to financial instability across the

---

11. *See,* for intergovernmental rational bargaining framework, Moravcsik, A. (1993). Preferences and Power in the European Community: A Liberal Inter-governmentalist Approach. *JCMS: Journal of Common Market Studies, 31*(4), 473-524.
12. Monetary arrangements that supplement trade relationships have existed for centuries. In the Roman Empire, for example, the *solidus coin* (a currency with stable metallic content) was circulated widely for centuries. Unsurprisingly when trust in the value of Roman coinage slipped (due to debasing of currency during the reign of Emperor Diocletian to finance the crumbling defenses of the empire), it precipitated fall of the western part of the Roman Empire. In the nineteenth century, there were several well-known arrangements among groups of European countries that set standards for the minting and exchange of specific coins whose value was fixed by their gold or silver content. However, this was not a true monetary union but a common-currency-standard area as each country's monetary policy was separately rooted in a commodity-such as gold or silver. *See,* Meade, E. E. (Mar. 21, 2009). Monetary Integration. *Rethinking Finance Harvard International Review.* http://hir.harvard.edu/rethinking-finance/monetary-integration.
13. Wouters, J., & Ramopoulos, T. (2012). The G20 and Global Economic Governance: Lessons from Multilevel European Governance? *Journal of International Economic Law.* available at http://jiel.oxfordjournals.org/content/early/2012/09/05/jiel.jgs036.short.
14. *See,* Pierson, P. (1996). The Path to European Integration: A Historical Institutionalist Analysis. *Comparative Political Studies, 29,* 123-163; and, Story, J., & Walter, I. (1997). *Political Economy of Financial Integration in Europe: The Battle of the Systems.* Manchester University Press.

single market and the single currency area in the event of any serious market turbulence.[15]

The establishment of a single currency area (the Eurozone) and the pan-European presence of a number of large banks with large cross-border operations lent urgency to the questions about long-term protection of EU-wide financial stability in the absence of appropriate institutional arrangements,[16] the so-called *financial stability trilemma*. This trilemma states that the three objectives of financial stability, financial integration and national financial policies cannot be combined at the same time and that one of these objectives has to be compromised in order to realize the other two.[17] Thus, there is an acute policy trade-off[18] and in spite of assertions to the contrary,[19] establishment of a common currency without accompanied by transnational supervisory structures, would not resolve the trilemma. Through a currency union, EU members could answer the classic monetary trilemma built on the Mundell-Fleming model of an open economy under capital mobility.[20] Therefore, under capital mobility and national monetary policy, fixed exchange rates will invariably break down.[21] However, as the EU remained far from being an optimal currency area under the Mundell model, and there was no fiscal integration or debt mutualization, it was only a matter of time before the first strains on keeping the single market intact would appear.[22]

---

15. *See*, Avgouleas, E., & Arner, D. W. (2013).
16. In 2005 Schoenmaker and Oosterloow conducted a statistical study spanning a four-year period (2000-2003) on the potential emergence of pan-European banking groups. To this effect they gathered a new data set on cross-border penetration (as a proxy for cross-border externalities) of thirty large EU banking groups. They found a home-country bias, but the data indicated that the number of groups having potential to pose significant cross-border externalities within the EU context were not only substantial but also on an increase. Policy makers faced challenge of designing European structures for financial supervision and stability to deal effectively with these emerging European banking groups. *See* for details, Schoenmaker, D., & Oosterloow, S. (2005). Financial Supervision in an Integrating Europe: Measuring Cross-Border Externalities. *International Finance*, 8(1), 1-27.
17. *See*, Schoenmaker, D. (2011). The Financial Trilemma. *Economic Letters*, 111, (February 7), Elsevier, available at http://personal.vu.nl/d.schoenmaker/Financial_Trilemma.pdf, last accessed, Apr. 17, 2017. *See also*, Thygesen, N. (2003). Comments on the Political Economy of Financial Harmonization in Europe. In J. Kremer, D. Schoenmaker & P. Wierts (Eds.), *Financial Supervision in Europe*. Edward Elgar.
18. Lastra and Louis call it *inconsistent quartet* of policy objectives: free trade, full capital mobility, pegged (or fixed) exchange rates and independent national monetary policies. *See*, Lastra, R. M., & Louis, J. (2013). European Economic and Monetary Union: History, Trends, and Prospects. Yearbook of European Law.
19. *See*, Padoa-Schioppa, T. (2000). *The Road to Monetary Union in Europe: The Emperor, the Kings and the Genies*. Oxford University Press.
20. *See*, Mundell, R. A. (1963). Capital Mobility and Stabilization Policy under Fixed and Flexible Exchange Rates. *Canadian Journal of Economics*, 29, 475-485, available at http://jrxy.zjgsu.edu.cn/jrxy/jssc/2904.pdf.
21. Obstfeld, M., Shambaugh, J. C., & Taylor, A. M. (2005). The Trilemma in History: Tradeoffs among Exchange Rates, Monetary Policies, and Capital Mobility. *Review of Economics and Statistics*, 87, 423-438.
22. Mundell, R. A. (1961) A Theory of Optimum Currency Areas. *American Economic Review* 51(4):657-665.

Arguably, an essential prerequisite of financial market integration is importation of a harmonized set of core rules, which border on uniformity[23] and are binding in all jurisdictions comprising the single market. Absence of such uniformity can, in theory, seriously hinder market integration as it can give rise to regulatory arbitrage and hidden protectionism and harm efficient group approaches to capital allocation and risk management within cross-border banks.[24] There is no area where divergence of national rules and regulations is more important than cross-border bank failures.

Thus, protection of financial stability in an integrated financial market characterized by cross-border financial institutions becomes a challenging task, especially when there are incongruent policy measures between national preferences and regional integration requirements. It is the EU that has moved very close to maximum harmonization in the field of financial market regulation however, the overall regulatory edifice in the EU still lacks strong uniformity/consistency in terms of both rule construction and rule enforcement. In addition, there has been a marked absence of institutions that could provide binding guidance in the event of difference of opinion between national regulators, as regards the application and enforcement of financial regulation, or could resolve eventual conflicts of national regulatory actions.

[B]   The Development of the Treaty-Based Mechanism

Financial integration in Europe is a much earlier than late twentieth century phenomenon, at least for the leading European economies. There is convincing evidence which shows that by the mid-eighteenth century European equity markets were well integrated.[25] Professor Neal, who explored operations of international capital market and links between Amsterdam and London in the early eighteenth century, concluded that both markets were well integrated in the pre-World War I period (1870s to 1913). This was, in general, a period characterized by a transition from autarky to integrated world capital markets, and, thus, for many it constituted the very first step toward integration. The term 'financial integration' however, was not used in this sense before the mid-1950s. German neoliberals during the 1950s advocated international integration through removal of trade barriers and the introduction of free convertibility. Machlup associated financial integration with capital mobility.[26] Multilateral trade and free convertibility was only 'a different expression for international integration just as

---

23. Here, *uniformity* refers to the need to have coherent and compatible regulation across jurisdictions.
24. Larosiere, J. d. (2009). *Report of the High Level Group on Financial Supervision in the EU*. Available at http://ec.europa.eu/internal_market/finances/docs/de_larosiere_report_en.pdf.
25. *See*, Neal, L. (1985). Integration of International Capital Markets: Quantitative Evidence from the Eighteenth to Twentieth Centuries. *Journal of Economic History, 45*, 219-226. Retrieved from http://journals.cambridge.org/action/displayAbstract?fromPage=online&aid=4149272 *See also*, Neal, Larry. (1990). *The Rise of Financial Capitalism: International Capital Markets in the Age of Reason*. Cambridge University Press, and, Neal, L. (1992). The Disintegration and Re-integration of International Capital Markets in the 19th Century. *Business and Economic History, 2*, 84-96.
26. *See*, Machlup, F. (1977). *A History of Thought on Economic Integration*. University Press.

bilateralism and capital controls could be another label for disintegration of international economy'.[27] As this argument progresses, the greater the degree of regional integration through multilateralism and convertibility, the larger is the advantage of economic cooperation.[28] Yet evidence of the existence of a direct causal relationship between financial integration and economic growth remains inconclusive.[29] The economic growth as consequence of financial integration depends largely upon a number of preconditions necessary to facilitate the integration process.[30]

[1] Stage I: The Economic Integration

The European economic integration and the establishment of Euro as the common currency of 19 EU Member States (as of today) followed an incremental path. This development alternated between periods of strong progress and of slow growth. In general, the single market development has been the product of political expediency and economic efficiency rationale as well as of major setbacks and challenges.[31] Despite the recent crises in the EU which triggered serious divisions among its Member States – ranging from having a two-speed euro, to an option for parallel domestic currencies for weak currency states to the contagious populist/exit movements – the work on the project integration has not stopped fully.

The six-state EEC was established in 1957 under the Treaty of Rome, formally known as the Treaty establishing the European Economic Community (TEEC), by six states, Belgium, France, Italy, Luxembourg, the Netherlands and West Germany on March 25, 1957. It came into force on January 1, 1958. In the Treaty, political integration was seen as a strong ideal to be achieved in the long-term. This grand ideal was essential in building an EMU and in achieving the progress moving the EU made in economic, monetary and financial sectors by gradually removing national restrictions on the free flow of goods, capital and people. Western European economies always preferred exchange rate stability, following the collapse of the Bretton Woods, when the first set of European exchange rate stability arrangements failed, the world entered into an era of floating exchange rates. The EEC members created the EMS in 1979[32] in order to manage and control currency fluctuations among EMS members.[33]

---

27. Ropke, W. (1950). *The Social Crisis of Our Time*. Hodge. See also, Dorn, J. A., & Xi, W. (Eds.). (1990). *Economic Reform in China: Problems and Prospects*. University of Chicago Press. p. 120.
28. Ropke, W. (1950). As above.
29. Liu, Q., Lejot, P., & Arner, D. A. (2013). *Finance in Asia: Institutions, Regulation and Policy* Taylor & Francis Ltd. Routledge. See, Ch. 12, p. 513.
30. See also, Dorn, J. A., & Xi, W. (Eds.). (1990). *Economic Reform in China: Problems and Prospects*. University of Chicago Press. p. 121.
31. See, Pierson, P. (1996). The Path to European Integration: A Historical Institutionalist Analysis. *Comparative Political Studies*, 29, 123-163. And, Story, J., & Walter, I. (1997). *Political Economy of Financial Integration in Europe: The Battle of the Systems*. Manchester University Press.
32. See, Resolution of the European Council of Dec. 5, 1978 on the establishment of the European Monetary System (EMS) and related matters (1978) Bulletin of the European Communities. Dec., No 12, pp. 9-13. Regulations Nos 380 and 381/78, Dec. 18, 1978, OJEC, No L379, Dec. 30, 1978 (and their modifications); Agreement of Mar. 13, 1979 between the central banks of the Member States of the EEC laid down operating procedures for the European Monetary System. Available at http://ec.europa.eu/economy_finance/emu_history/documentation/compendia/a791231en

EMS was viewed as the *first step* toward permanent exchange rate alignment and it paved the way towards the establishment of the EMU.

It is arguable that the interests of professional intermediaries may have also been a strong force behind the push for further integration. The 1966 Segré report was both very cognizant of the growth potential attached to financial integration and of the potential for this objective to be confounded by commercial interests.[34] Given an excess supply of petrodollars in offshore markets, their scale began to rival national markets in banking and securities.[35] This led to protracted negotiations in the early 1990s between the industry representatives and regulators that brought offshore activity back into the national markets, while subsuming the many disparate local practices. In fact, the early Eurobond market might have played the role of an *imperfect substitute* to financial integration, given that capital mobility was only a secondary EU goal until the 1990s.[36] The path to monetary integration adopted under the Maastricht Treaty (February 7, 1992) by the members of the EC was based on a three-stage process and upon fulfillment of the convergence criteria (albeit weaknesses in the enforcement of the criterion have resulted into real challenges today, including threat to the existence of the Union itself). According to the principles defined at that time, countries meeting the criteria could only gain Eurozone membership.

The Maastricht Treaty's convergence criteria included, *inter alia*, two basic conditions for euro membership: first, a 3% limit on general government annual deficit and a 60% limit on general government gross debt limit. It also included three other metrics, which were: inflation, long-term interest rates and exchange-rate fluctuations. Inflation was to be kept within 1.5% margin over that of any of the three EU countries having the lowest inflation rate. Long-term interest rates were to stay within a 2% margin over that of the three states with the lowest borrowing rates in the EU.[37] As regards, exchange-rate fluctuations, there was a requirement of participation for two years in the European ERM II narrow band of exchange-rate fluctuations. This is to be noted here that the Treaty itself had exceptions to provide political leverage in

---

1771979compendiumcm_a.pdf. *See* for analysis, Giavazzi, F., & Giovannini, A. (1989). *Limiting Exchange Rate Flexibility: The European Monetary System*. Cambridge, Mass: MIT Press. *See also*, Marcello De Cecco, A. G. (Ed.) (1989). *A European Central Bank? Perspectives on Monetary Unification after Ten Years of EMS*. Cambridge University Press.

33. *See* Ch. 2 section §2.02 for details.
34. *See*, Claude Segré et al. *The Development of a European Capital Market: Report of a Group of Experts Appointed by the EEC Commission* (EEC, 1966). Segré argued for harmonization of non-retail national markets in ways later encouraged by the Eurobond market.
35. *See* EC, *The EU Economy: 2003 review* (DG for Economic and Financial Affairs, EC, (2003) No. 6 at 320, http://ec.europa.eu/economy_finance/ publications/publication7694_en.pdf.
36. Genillard, R. (1967). The Eurobond Market. *Financial Analysts Journal 23*(2), 144. The article concludes that the Eurobond market was a fine example of the benefits of international collaboration by bankers in a fully competitive climate. *See also*, Richebacher, K. (1969). The Problems and Prospects of Integrating European Capital Markets. *Journal Money, Credit & Banking*, *1*(3).
37. Article 104c, *The Maastricht Treaty on EU and the Treaties Establishing the European Communities Protocols*. (Feb. 7, 1992) available at http://www.eurotreaties.com/maastrichtprotocols.pdf.

extending membership to certain countries while restricting it for others.[38] Italy, the third largest economy in continental Europe was running general government gross debt in 1998 at 114.9% of GDP (as against 60% required under the Treaty), Belgium's gross government debt (home to the EU capital, Brussels) was at 117.4% of GDP. Given this, formation of a euro block was considered implausible without having both of these countries in the Eurozone. From the get-go, this reflected on the difference in the initial conditions of the European economies at the time of joining the Eurozone. In the longer term, these differences implied a much lesser degree of economic integration would be realizable than had been envisaged in the earlier Werner (1970) and Delors reports (1989) respectively.[39] Consequently, the difference in the macroeconomic *initial conditions* of the founding Member States made it politically difficult to enforce the strict fiscal criteria laid down for EMU membership.[40]

[2]   Stage II: Infancy and the Minimum Harmonization

The first step towards designing legal and regulatory framework for European integration was to develop a harmonized set of minimum regulatory standards based on consensus.[41] The Delors Commission's 1985 White Paper[42] preceded the enactment of the first amendment to the Treaty of Rome in 30 years, the Single European Act.[43] This White Paper outlined the reforms required in the preexisting EEC legal framework in order to build a truly single market in the EEC (as it was) and paved the way to monetary integration.[44] The White Paper also noted that the legislation adopted by the Council and the European Parliament insufficiently adapted to local conditions and

---

38. Art. 104c of the Maastricht Treaty stated that countries could exceed the 3 percent deficit target if "the ratio has declined substantially and continuously and reached a level that comes close to the reference value" or "excess over the reference value is only exceptional and temporary and the ratio remains close to the reference value." Euro area countries could similarly exceed the 60% gross debt target provided that "the ratio is sufficiently diminishing and approaching the reference value at a satisfactory pace." *See, Ibid.*
39. Under the Delors' report, economic union and monetary union form two integral and equally important parts of a single whole and would therefore have to be implemented in parallel (Point 21 of the report) available at http://aei.pitt.edu/1007/1/monetary_delors.pdf. However, the Delors' report adopted a comparatively less centralized approach on economic policy than the Werner report.
40. Countries had differences in terms of *initial conditions* yet, these facts were ignored during the formation of the EEC which neither took into account idiosyncratic characteristics (as alleged by the Greeks) nor embodied inherent mechanisms permitting those *less-than-equal* economies to *catch-up* with the *larger-than-equal* members.
41. Defined as the first EU financial services consensus, see, Avgouleas, E. (2004). The New EC Financial Markets Legislation and the Emerging Regime for Capital Markets. Yearbook of European Law, 321-361.
42. European Commission, *Completing the Internal Market: White Paper from the European Commission to the European Council*, (1985) Com (85) 310 final. (hereinafter 'White Paper' 1985).
43. Single European Act. (1987). *Official Journal of the European Communities* (Vol. O.J. L 169/1), available at http://eur-lex.europa.eu/legal-content/EN/TXT/?uri=OJ:L:1987:169:TOC.
44. The Delors' report provided for the establishment of a new monetary institution to be called a European System of Central Banks to carry out monetary policy and exchange rate policy vis-à-vis third currencies.

experiences, in stark contrast to the original proposals.[45] However, maximum harmonization seemed unattainable at that point, and therefore, the single market and the EC adopted instead the principle of mutual recognition, minimum harmonization and home-country control in the harmonization legislation. The internal market was to be based on minimum harmonization of national regulatory systems and mutual recognition[46] through which Member States would recognize each other's laws, regulations and authorities.[47] Use of minimum regional requirements was intended to limit competitive deregulation by state actors and regulatory arbitrage by commercial parties.[48] It was also a reflection on how political collaboration can encourage adoption of sound market principles and practices.[49]

The EU framework for financial services provided access to the single market unfettered by national borders or restrictions on activity, to be known as single passport facility.[50] Essentially, the purpose of the passport facility was to allow intermediaries to deliver products or services into any part of the internal market and promote cross-border competition.[51] As a consequence, the *passport directives* in financial services delineated the kind of financial intermediary to which they applied, its activities and the market segment, conditions for initial and continuing authorizations, division of regulatory responsibility between the home (domicile) state and the host state, and aspects of regulatory treatment for non-EU Member States.[52] Authorized financial intermediaries that fall within the ambit of one of the passport directive could offer banking and investment services on a cross-border basis without maintaining permanent presence in the target market or through a foreign branch on the basis of a home-country license.[53] The home state would generally be accountable for the licensing and supervision of financial intermediaries, while the host state would account for the conduct both for the clients residing within and outside jurisdictions for clients residing outside.

The Maastricht Treaty, which established the EU as a successor to the EEC, provided an impetus for states to implement prior financial services directives and led to members other than Ireland and the UK adopting legislation foreign to their

---

45. The White Paper, 1985, fn 43.
46. Ibid.
47. *See*, Steil, B. (1996). *The European Equity Markets: The State of the Union and an Agenda for the Millennium*. Brookings Institution Press.
48. Arner, D. W., & Taylor, M. W. (2010). The Global Credit Crisis and the Financial Stability Board: Hardening the Soft Law of International Financial Regulation? *University of New South Wales Law Journal, 32*, 488-513. Retrieved from http://hdl.handle.net/10722/130550.
49. Arner, D. W., Lejot, P., & Wang, W. (2009). Assessing East Asian Financial Cooperation and Integration. *Singapore Yearbook of International Law, 12*, 1-42, 2009.
50. *See*, Cranston, R. (Ed.) (1995). *The Single Market and the Law of Banking* (2 ed.). Lloyds of London Press. *See also*, Ferrarini, G. (1998). *European Securities Markets: The Investment Services Directive and Beyond*. Kluwer Law.
51. Ibid.
52. Ibid.
53. An excellent discussion on the ambit of the provisions for investment firms may be found in Moloney, N. (2011). The European Securities and Markets Authority and Institutional Design for the EU Financial Market: A Tale of Two Competences. *European Business Organization Law Review, 12*(1), 41-86. Retrieved from http://journals.cambridge.org/abstract_S1566752911100026.

traditional market practices. One important influence in the success of the harmonization mechanisms adopted at this stage of EU integration process was the role played by the rulings given by the European Court of Justice (ECJ).[54] Being EU states, it obligated Member States to adopt and implement EU legislation, as national governments could be held liable in damages for failing to comply with EU-level decisions.[55] And, this aspect is of vital importance when it comes to the regulatory sphere. On the one hand, it hardened the otherwise soft-law texture of the *international regulatory law* by safeguarding against any violations or laxity in adoption, and on the other hand, it ensured active participation of each stakeholder (Member States) in framing, negotiation and structuring the supra-state regulatory law applicable across states.

[3]   Stage III: Maturity and the Maximum Harmonization

The passport directives have clearly enhanced financial integration in the EU, although areas of marked divergence, such as retail financial services, remained outside its orbit.[56] Minimum harmonization left the EU with an incomplete regulatory framework, since, in many cases, it merely *augmented* rather than replaced preexisting national laws.[57] Therefore, the drive towards harmonization intensified in the early 2000s following the introduction of Euro and the publication of the EC's FSAP in 1999.[58] Arguably, the most important integrative instrument of that era (which can be viewed as the second EU financial services consensus)[59] was the Directive on Markets in Financial Instruments (MiFID), which established a detailed pan-European regime with respect to conditions of establishment and operation of financial markets and investment intermediaries and the conduct of cross-border financial activities.[60]

---

54. Avgouleas, E., & Arner, D. W. (2013).
55. *Andrea Francovich and Danila Bonifaci and others v. Italian Republic*. References for a preliminary ruling: Pretura di Vicenza and Pretura di Bassano del Grappa, Italy. Failure to implement a directive- Liability of the Member State. Judgment of the Court, Nov. 19, 1991, available at http://eur-lex.europa.eu/legal-content/EN/TXT/HTML/?isOldUri=true&uri=CELEX:61990CJ0006 pp. I-05357.
56. Grossman, E., & Leblond, P. (2011). European Financial Integration: Finally the Great Leap Forward? *JCMS: Journal of Common Market Studies, 49*(2), 413-435. Available at http://onlinelibrary.wiley.com/doi/10.1111/j.1468-5965.2010.02145.x/abstract.
57. *See*, for further discussion of this issue and on the gaps left behind by minimum harmonization, Avgouleas, E. (2000). The Harmonization of Rules of Conduct in EU Financial Markets: Economic Analysis, Subsidiarity and Investor Protection. *European Law Journal*, 6, 72-92.
58. Commission Communication, *Financial Services: Implementing the Framework for Financial Markets: Action Plan*, COM (1999) 232. And, on important changes made to the FSAP implemented in EU Regulation of Financial Services and its impact on the single market *see*, Ferran, E., & Goodhart, C. A. E. (Eds.). (2001). *Regulating Financial Services and Markets in the Twenty-first Century*. Hart publishing. *See also*, Ferran, E., Moloney, N., Hill, J. G., & John C. Coffee, J. (Eds.). (2012). *The Regulatory Aftermath of the Global Financial Crisis*, Cambridge University Press.
59. For a critical discussion of the FSAP legislation, *see*, Avgouleas, E (2005). Evaluation of the New EC Financial Market Regulation: Peaks and Troughs in the Road Ahead. *Transnational Lawyer* 18, 179-228.
60. *See*, EC, Directive 2004/39/EC 2004 of the European Parliament and of the Council of Apr. 21, 2004 on markets in financial instruments amending Council Directives 85/611/EEC and 93/6/EEC, and, Directive 2000/12/EC of the European Parliament and of the Council and

National implementation of MiFID from 2007 onwards represented the *third stage* of single market development.

To answer a number of challenges pertaining mostly to the enactment and consistent implementation of financial services legislation the EU adopted the so-called Lamfalussy process in 2001. It consisted of four levels which started with the adoption of the framework legislation (Level I) and more detailed implementing measures (Level II). To prepare for implementing measures, technical committees made up of representatives of national supervisory bodies (from three sectors, banking, insurance and occupational pensions, and the securities markets), would advise the EU.[61] These committees were: the CEBS,[62] the Committee of European Insurance and Occupational Pensions Supervisors (CEIOPS)[63] and the Committee of European Securities Regulators (CESR).[64] The level III committees would then contribute to consistent implementation of Community directives in the Member States, ensuring effective cooperation between the supervisory authorities and convergence in their practices (Level III), and finally, the EC was to enforce timely and correct transposition of EU legislation into national laws (Level IV).[65] In the aftermath of the GFC, the EU has introduced a number of pan-European bodies with regulatory competences, the most important of which is the development of a common rule book.[66]

---

repealing Council Directive 93/22/EEC, [2007] O.J. L 145/1. For a discussion of the contours of MiFID, *see*, Avgouleas, E (ed.), *The Regulation of Investment Services in Europe under MiFiD: Implementation and Practice*. Tottel. 2008.

61. Avgouleas, E., & Arner, D. W. (2013).
62. The CEBS as an independent advisory group on was established in November 2003 under the 2004/5/E, www.europa.eu/legislation_summaries/internal_market/single_market_services/financial_services_banking/l22025_en.htm. On Jan. 1, 2011, this committee was replaced by the EBA, which took over all existing and ongoing tasks and responsibilities of from the CEBS. The EBA was set by the Regulation (EC) No. 1093/2010 of the European Parliament and of the Council of Nov. 24, 2010 available at, www.esrb.europa.eu/shared/pdf/EBA-en.pdf?79016e64 9558f0a9a741da6c169b806b.
63. The CEIOPS (2003-2010) established under the EC's Decision 2004/6/EC of Nov. 5, 2003, was replaced by the EIOPA under the Decision 2009/79/EC, January 2011, in accordance with the new European financial supervision framework.
64. The CESR was an independent committee of European Securities regulators established by EC on Jun. 6, 2001. On Jan. 1, 2011, CESR was replaced by the ESMA in accordance with the new EFSF. *See* more at http://www.esma.europa.eu/index.php?page=cesrinshort&mac=0&id.
65. *See*, Lamfalussy, A. (2001). *Final Report of the Committee of Wise Men on the Regulation of European Securities Markets*, Feb. 15, 2001, available at http://ec.europa.eu/internal_market/securities/docs/lamfalussy/wisemen/final-report-wise-men_en.pdf For review on the process recommendations, *see also*, Ferran, E. (2010). Understanding the New Institutional Architecture of EU Financial Market Supervision, in, G. Ferrarini, K.J. Hopt & E. Wymeersch (Eds.), *Rethinking Financial Regulation and Supervision in Times of Crisis*: University of Cambridge, Faculty of Law Research Paper No. 29/2011. Ferran examines the recent EU institutional reform of financial market supervision to assess their significance. *See also*, Schaub, A. (2004). The Lamfalussy Process Four Years On. *Journal of Financial Regulation and Compliance*, 13(2), 110-120, available at http://dx.doi.org/10.1108/13581980510621947.
66. *See*, Report of the High Level Group on Financial Supervision in the EU, February 2009 (the de Larosière report), available at http://ec.europa.eu/internal_market/finances/docs/de_larosiere_report_en.pdf.

§5.03 THE SINGLE MARKET AND THE EXISTENTIAL CRISES

[A] External Shocks

It was not until the 2008 crisis, and more solemnly after the outbreak of the Eurozone debt crisis in 2010, that the vexed issue of preservation of *financial stability* in an integrated market came to the forefront of EU policy makers' attention. It should be noted here that the Maastricht Treaty (1992) did not include *financial stability* as a key objective of the ECB, although, Article 127(5) of the Treaty on the Functioning of the European Union (TFEU) underscores *financial stability* as a classic central banking good. Thus, *financial stability* was not designed as one of the four basic tasks to be carried through the European System of Central Banks (ESCB) Article 127(2) of the TFEU and was rather clustered with prudential supervision under the *non-binding tasks* of the ECB.

Until the onset of the GFC in 2008, the *common passport facility* was at the heart of the EU single market. The EU legislative framework based on harmonized standards for financial markets sought equivalence among disparate regulatory and legal systems, so that regional initiatives could recognize national legal and regulatory regimes.[67] A multilevel governance system involves far more complexities mainly arising out of conflicting and at times misunderstood national priorities.[68]

Political considerations also undermined the credibility of rule-based frameworks for coordination of national fiscal policies in the euro area.[69] Arguably, the Maastricht Treaty itself allowed sufficient flexibility in interpreting Stability and Growth Pact (SGP) conditions and its enforcement became a political bargain in the EU at the expense of objective economic criteria.[70] An agreement based on Article 121 and Article 126[1] of the TFEU, among the 28 Member States of the EU, is to maintain the stability of the EMU by fiscal monitoring of members by the EC and the Council of Ministers. The Pact has been strongly criticized on being insufficiently flexible and needing to be applied over the economic cycle rather than in one year. As a result, in the period before the crisis, in a Eurozone that was deeply marked by economic and financial imbalances, debt kept building up. The Union lacked a central fiscal authority which might have afforded it a credible mechanism to enforce budget discipline in the time of crisis.

In addition, trade imbalances and accelerating competitiveness imbalances due to lack of exchange-rate flexibility meant that there were no realistic prospects for fiscal

---

67. *See*, Steil, B. (1996). *The European Equity Markets: The State of the Union and an Agenda for the Millennium*. Brookings Institution Press. p. 113.
68. COM. (2001). *European Governance – A White Paper*. Commission of the European Communities. p. 12.
69. *See*, Bergsten, C. F., & Kirkegaard, J. F. (2012). *The Coming Resolution of the European Crisis [Electronic Resource]* Peterson Institute for International Economics, Washington, D.C. Retrieved from http://www.ciaonet.org/pbei/iie/0024277/f_0024277_19801.pdf.
70. *European Council Presidency Conclusions, Council of the European Union*. (Mar. 22-23, 2005), available at http://www.consilium.europa.eu/uedocs/cms_data/docs/pressdata/en/ec/84335.pdf.

convergence.[71] Accordingly, when the GFC hit in 2008, European economic stability was hampered by a number of preexisting problems whose existence had simply been ignored for far too long. These included: pre-crisis colossal public and private debt, a flawed macroeconomic framework, an incomplete institutional design marked by an imbalanced monetary union which lacked effective fiscal convergence mechanisms, and, institutions tailored for effective crisis management in case of a cross-border banking crisis.

Arguably, during the first decade of its life, the EMU institutional framework was more or less like *a fair weather currency*.[72] It assumed that any macroeconomic or banking system stability shocks could be dealt with at the national level without requiring any transfers from the strongest to the weaker members of the Eurozone, due to the *no bailout* clause in the EMU Treaty.[73] Consequently, the outbreak of the SDC in the Eurozone in 2010 meant that the EU had to enter into the most transformative phase of its history. The enormous taxpayer support (contingent) amounted to a 40% of the total EU GDP (€5.1 trillion during October 2008 to October 2012) undermined the solidity of several Member States' public finances. In the case of some Member States, it contributed to turn a banking crisis into a sovereign crisis. This had the effect of further increasing the fragility of the banking system in the Member States since banks held large volumes of sovereign bonds on their balance sheets.[74]

The EU had to devise both a crisis-fighting capacity and support bailout funding mechanisms in the wake of ensuing Eurozone debt crisis while it was still handling the 2008 crisis. This led to the establishment of an EFSF in 2010 with the objective of preserving financial stability in the Union through providing financial assistance to the Member States facing difficulties. The EFSF was superseded by the European Stability Mechanism (ESM) which was established in 2012 as a permanent firewall for the Eurozone countries in order to provide instant financial access programs with a lending capacity of €500 billion. At the same time, serious steps were taken to build a European banking union based on structures safeguarding centralization of bank supervision and uniform deposit insurance arrangements, as well as centralization of crisis resolution. Thus, the external shocks exposed the internal vulnerabilities (to be discussed in the next section) and faulty integration mechanism that contributed to Eurozone's present state of crisis.

[B] Internal Vulnerabilities

The premise of *home-country control* and the principle of *minimum harmonization* were bound to undermine at some point the stability of the EU banking system. The integration process continued in an increasingly deregulated market following the

---

71. *See*, Grauwe, P. d. (2010). *Economics of Monetary Union* (9 ed.) Oxford University Press.
72. Bergsten, C. F., & Kirkegaard, J. F. (2012).
73. *See* Art. 101 TEU (enshrined in Art. 125 of the Treaty on the Functioning of the European Union, 2008).
74. EC. (April 2013). *European Financial Stability and Integration Report 2012*. Retrieved from EC, Brussels http://ec.europa.eu/internal_market/economic_analysis/docs/efsir/130425_efsir-2012_en.pdf p. 55.

intensification of liberalization efforts in the last quarter of the twentieth century, but the regulatory standards and supervisory principles were not adjusted to suit new realities. The Eurozone crisis brought home with devastating force the potential risks of financial market integration. These risks inevitably led financial institutions operating in the single market to develop very tight links of interconnectedness, which allowed shocks in any part of the market to be transmitted widely and quickly across all other parts. Examples of such rapid transmission of shocks included the failure of Icelandic banks, case of the Fortis bank, the threat of the collapse of Irish and Spanish financial system, and the possibility of a sovereign default (e.g., Greece with potential to a string of more defaults). Each of those crises brought serious tremors to European markets and exposed the structural fragility of the single market and the dearth of policy options available to Eurozone decision-makers. Naturally, the rapid amplification of those crises and their grave consequences has raised serious questions regarding the survival of this treaty-based union.[75]

By contrast, in the US, the response to the crisis came in the form of reregulation of the financial sector. However, in the EU, the diversity of Member States' economies and issues arising out of inherent contradictions between national policy priorities of Member States resulted into a much lower degree of responsiveness to the crisis. The already discussed *financial trilemma* has nowhere manifested itself more clearly than in the Eurozone in recent years. Since the inception of the Euro, European policy makers have been increasingly recognizing the *efficiency gaps* in EU financial supervision against a background of a decentralized institutional architecture for regulation, supervision and financial stability. In the post-2008 scenario, recognition of this gap led to tangible efforts to capture some of the potential efficiency gains through legally binding mechanisms and policy coordination mechanisms like the ESFS.[76]

However, before getting to the stage where the ESFS or the ESM could set to work, the EU as a regionally integrated market with a single currency struggled to preserve both its unified structure as well as its continued existence in the face of challenging internal crises. This was obvious when some of the EMU states experiencing severe crisis than other states gave preference to adopt policies based on their own national needs and interests than considering the single market's larger interest. The following section will look at the peculiar instances where issues of national interest in the Member States trumped regional market stability.

[1] *The Icelandic Banking Crisis*

The collapse of the Icelandic banks – Glitnir, Kaupthing and Landsbanki – presents a classic case of home-country control failure and of the disastrous consequences of lack of centralized supervision and resolution mechanisms in the EU.

---

75. Avgouleas, E., & Arner, D. W. (2013).
76. *See*, Masciandaro, D., & Nieto, M. (2014). Governance of the Single Supervisory Mechanism: Some Reflections. *Baffi Center Research Paper No. 2014-149, available at SSRN: http://ssrn.com/abstract=2384594.*

Back in 2000s, Iceland's banks expanded in a way that exceeded this small country's GDP by a massive 6:1 ratio. The single passport enabled Icelandic banks the ability to enlarge their assets and deposits base through branches and through internet-based operations offering cross-border banking services. In almost no time, the European depositors were attracted to the high interest rates being offered by the Icelandic banks.[77] And by 2008, both the country's economy and its banks were in serious trouble, as we know. While trouble was brewing over several months, the Icelandic bank operations within the EU were being supervised by the home-country authorities, unwilling to take any radical rescue measures. Thus, nothing was done to prevent the ensuing panic. When the Icelandic banks faced difficulties in refinancing their short-term debt, a run on the bank's deposits in the Netherlands and the UK became inevitable. These depositors were not covered by the deposit protection scheme of their home countries.

While both the Netherlands and the UK were, in the beginning unwilling to extend protection to the Icelandic bank depositors, at the same time, Iceland could provide no comfort to foreign depositors, as it was already in the middle of a deep financial crisis. Its government did not want to pay for the mistakes made by private banks with the assistance of politicians and of 'home' supervisory authorities. Harsh responses followed from both the UK and the Netherlands' authorities which annulled the single passport principle. In order to prevent the crisis spreading to the British banking system, the UK Prime Minister, Gordon Brown extended protection to British depositors, which essentially meant that the British taxpayer would cover the loss. Thus, the UK Treasury proceeded with the unprecedented step of issuing a compulsory freezing order of Icelandic bank assets and deposits under the Anti-terrorism, Crime and Security Act 2001, which, of course, antagonized relationships with Iceland. In addition, the UK government announced that it would launch legal action against Iceland over any losses connected to the compensation of an estimated 300,000 UK savers. Icelandic authorities later reached an agreement separately with both the UK and the government of the Netherlands to pay both the UK and the Netherlands a percentage of GDP from 2019-2023 to compensate for the deposit protection made available by these two countries to their own consumers holding investments in Icelandic banks.[78]

The collapse of Icelandic banks led to the economic crisis and mishandling of the crisis brought down the political machinery of the government. In fact, it seems that requisite malpractice involved abuse of insiders' positions (especially in the case of Kaupthing bank, where in a way the bank was buying its own shares) and weak supervisory and institutional oversight. Moreover, the Icelandic banking crisis, and the more recent, Cyprus banking crisis, underscore the perils involved when small countries build an outsized financial services sector. While the Icelandic banking crisis exposed vulnerabilities in the home-country control failure, the Fortis rescue presented

---

77. *See*, for one of the recent publications on the subject, Christodoulakis, G. (Ed.) (2015). *Managing Risks in the European Periphery Debt Crisis: Lessons from the Trade*, Palgrave Macmillan.
78. *See*, Avgouleas, E., & Arner, D. W. (2013).

supremacy of national policy and a failure to preserve single market's sanctity by its Member States.

[2] The Fortis Bank's Case

When the collapse of Lehman Brothers hit global markets, Fortis – a big European bank with strong cross-border presence in France, the Netherlands, Belgium and Luxembourg – came very close to collapse.

In Belgium, Fortis was the country's biggest private sector employer and more than 1.5 million households (about half the country) banked with the group. In 2007, Fortis had acquired parts of ABN Amro through a consortium with the Royal Bank of Scotland (RBS) and Santander bank. In 2008, Fortis had difficulties realizing its plans to strengthen its financial position. Over the summer of 2008, its share price deteriorated and liquidity became a serious concern. Insolvency fear caused its shares to fall to their lowest level in more than a decade gradually losing more than three-quarters of their value.[79]

Fortis was deemed to be systemically important in these three countries. The ECB and ministers from the Netherlands, Belgium and Luxembourg agreed to put EUR 11.2 billion (USD 16.1 billion; EUR 8.9 billion) into Fortis to save the bank. As part of the weekend deal to rescue Fortis, the bank would have to sell its stake in the Dutch bank ABN Amro, which it had partially taken over during the previous year. The Fortis deal would have seen Belgium contributing EUR 4.7 billion, the Netherlands EUR 4 billion and Luxembourg EUR 2.5 billion. However, European Bank's shares fell sharply on worries that other banks could have problems and on concerns from over USD 700 billion bailout plan in the US. One of the biggest casualties was Fortis' rival Dexia, which French and Belgian governments also promised to step in to support. Eventually the joint rescue of Fortis broke down along national lines and each of the three countries (Belgium, the Netherlands and Luxembourg) concentrated only on the part of the group that was most important for their market, in defiance of single market principles and ideals.[80]

[3] The SDC

While the EU was still struggling to recover from the impact of external shocks and internal vulnerabilities exposed by the Icelandic and other banking crises, the sovereign debt crises were simmering in the Eurozone. Therefore, as we study the EU Treaty structure and how it functioned during the crises, we in fact are focusing at four interlocking crises within the EU. These included: a banking crisis, a competitiveness

---

79. *Ibid.*
80. *Ibid.*

Chapter 5: Enforcement in IFL: The Precarious Case of the EU   §5.03[B]

crisis, payment imbalances within the Eurozone indicating structural asymmetries between its Member States, and SDC.[81]

The sharp recession of 2008-2009 and subsequent economic slowdown had a sharply negative impact on the Member States' fiscal position. The operation of automatic fiscal stabilizers and the countercyclical fiscal measures adopted during the crisis seemed to further aggravate the situation. The EU-wide general government deficit increased from 1% of GDP in 2007 to 6.8% of GDP in 2009. At the same time, the Eurozone's aggregate Debt-to-GDP ratio also deteriorated markedly, rising from 61.8% of GDP by 2007 to (projected 82.3% in 2011) 90.0% of GDP by mid-2012, whereas for the EU27, the ratio stood at 84.9% of GDP at the end of the same period. The European Commission's long-term projections indicate that debt-to-GDP ratio could rise to around 110% by 2030 in the absence of appropriate fiscal consolidation plans.

Now, following the escalation of the SDC in the second half of 2011, the EU economy entered a shallow recession by the fourth quarter of the same year. Since then, the outlook for the EU economy slowly improved in the beginning but the situation became extraordinarily fragile. By mid-2012, the risk of a renewed crisis in the EU became more evident. The intensification of the SDC in the first half of the year, raised market concerns about the long-term viability of the euro area itself. The negative fall out from banks' funding pressures and economic activity, together with an unexpected slowdown in non-EU GDP growth and global trade contributed to an overall disappointing global growth performance.

Late in 2013, we saw some sign of recovery in Europe despite a rather low growth momentum with quarter-on-quarter GDP growth rates hovering in a narrow range of between 0.2% and 0.4% in the EU and 0.1% and 0.3% in the euro area. However, six quarters into the economic recovery, GDP remained 0.6% and 2.2%, i.e., below the pre-crisis level of the first quarter of 2008, in the EU and the euro area respectively.[82] The weak short-term growth outlook raises concerns for labor markets where unemployment rates remain much higher, in particular for Italy, Portugal, Greece, Cyprus, Portugal and Spain as these states implement austerity measures. The measures would include reduction in debt through asset sales and reduced spending in social welfare programs. Seasonally adjusted GDP rose by 0.4% in both the Eurozone area (EA19) and the EU (28) during the first quarter of 2015, compared with the previous quarter, according to flash estimates. In the fourth quarter of 2014, GDP grew by 0.3% in the euro area and by 0.4% in the EU28.[83] During the second and third quarter of 2016, the

---

81. Presentation by Avgouleas, E. (July 2012). *Eurozone Crisis and Sovereign Debt restructuring: Intellectual Fallacies and New Lines of Research*, at the Society of International Economic Law (SIEL), 3rd Biennial Global Conference, National University of Singapore.
82. *See*, EC. (2015). *European Economic Forecast*. Retrieved from European Economy 1/2015: http://ec.europa.eu/economy_finance/publications/european_economy/2015/pdf/ee1_en.pdf.
83. Eurostat. (2015). *News-release, Euro indicators*. 84/2015 Eurostat, the Statistical Office of the European Union; 13 May: available at http://ec.europa.eu/eurostat/documents/2995521/6829212/2-13052015-BP-EN.pdf/1444bdf1-65ba-457d-829b-dee843b0c861, last accessed Jul. 11, 2015.

adjusted GDP rose by 0.3% in the euro area (EA19) and by 0.4% in the EU28. A steady and slow growth seems on its way.

After a lapse of almost a decade, the European economic recovery is expected to continue this year and the next albeit the outlook is surrounded by higher-than-usual uncertainty. In its Winter Forecast, the EC expects euro-area GDP growth of 1.6% in 2017 and 1.8% in 2018. GDP growth in the EU as a whole should follow a similar pattern and is forecast at 1.8% this year and next (Autumn Forecast: 2017: 1.6%, 2018: 1.8%).[84]

What we have seen so far? We have seen the Eurozone crisis has triggered a fundamental shift in political dynamics underpinning the EU. We saw that most of the proposed remedies to ease the crisis like austerity, further integration and mutualization of Eurozone members' debts remained enormously contested. We recently saw dismemberment of one Member State from the EU. By the day, we see fragmentation being fed over populist sentiment within the EU seems to be on the rise especially given ever-higher levels of national debt. The fact that many EU banks had invested in EU members' bonds and were also adversely affected by the continuous recession ravaging the periphery of the Eurozone has only made things worse. Admittedly, the more recent issues of free movement of people, heightened security concerns from extremism, and refugees have complicated the financially vulnerable Union. Although the EMU had interest rate setting competence through the ECB, yet until recently it remained without any binding mechanism to enforce even fiscal discipline.

§5.04 THE SINGLE MARKET AND IMPERATIVE REFORM

[A] Preliminary Responses

In November 2008 the EC appointed a High Level Group (chaired by Jacques de Larosiere) to study the Lamfalussy framework in light of the GFC and make recommendations for a new EU regulatory set up.[85] The proposals in the de Larosière report were instrumental to subsequent developments. In order to implement these recommendations, the EU established (through a series of Regulations, normally referred to as the ESAs founding Regulation) an integrated ESFS.

---

84. EC (2017), Winter 2017 Economic Forecast, *see*, https://ec.europa.eu/info/business-economy-euro/economic-performance-and-forecasts/economic-forecasts/winter-2017-economic-forecast_en#all-eu-member-states-economies-set-to-grow-in-2016-2017-and-2018. Last accessed, Apr. 12, 2017.
85. *See*, Larosiere, J. d. (2009). *Report of the High Level Group on Financial Supervision in the EU. See*, http://ec.europa.eu/internal_market/finances/docs/de_larosiere_report_en.pdf, last accessed, February 2014.

[1] Stage I: EFSF and the New Developments

The ESFS came into effect in December 2010.[86] It comprises the ESRB,[87] a decentralized network comprising of existing national supervisors (to carry out day-to-day supervision), and three new ESAs. The ESRB and the three authorities started their operations in January 2011. The authorities include: (a) the EBA,[88] to deal with bank supervision, including the supervision of the recapitalization of banks; (b) the EIOPA dealing with insurance supervision, and (c) the ESMA, which respectively replaced the corresponding Lamfalussy Level III Committees (comprising of CEBS, the CEIOPS and the CESR), deals with the supervision of capital markets and carries out direct supervision with regard to CRAs and trade repositories.

It is to be noted that all of the 28 national supervisors are represented in all of the three supervising authorities. Their role is to contribute to the development of a single rule book for financial regulation in Europe, to solve cross-border problems, and to prevent the buildup of risks and help restore confidence. Furthermore, colleges of supervisors[89] were put in place for all major cross-border institutions. A supervision of strategic decisions at the consolidated level requires a college of supervisors to understand global effects and externalities arising from those decisions.[90] Last but not

---

86. Article 2, ESA founding Regulations, *see*, Regulation establishing a European Securities and Markets Authority, amending Decision No 716/2009/EC and repealing Commission Decision 2009/77/EC: Regulation (EU) No 1095/2010 of the European Parliament and of the Council of Nov. 24, 2010. *See*, Official Journal of the EU, available at http://www.esma.europa.eu/system/files/Reg_716_2010_ESMA.pdf.
87. *See*, EU macro-prudential oversight of the financial system and establishing the ESRB Regulation: EU Regulation No 1092/2010 of the European Parliament and of the Council of Nov. 24, 2010, Published in the Official Journal of the European Union, accessible at http://www.esrb.europa.eu/shared/pdf/ESRB-en.pdf?efba86ec695eea33d6b673acc62578d9. The ESRB established on Dec. 16, 2010 in response to the ongoing financial crisis was tasked with the macro-prudential oversight of the financial system within the Union in order to contribute to the prevention and mitigation of systemic risks to financial stability, under the EU Regulation No 1092/2010 of the European Parliament. *See*, the Official Journal of the European Union, (Vol. L331/1), available at http://www.esrb.europa.eu/shared/pdf/ESRB-en.pdf?49c9d3be4e6566e3eb2c1f0b210d4980.
88. *See*, for EBA, Regulation (EU) No. 1093/2010 of the European Parliament and of the Council of Nov. 24, 2010 Establishing European Banking Authority, amending Decision No. 716/2009/EC and repealing Commission Decision 2009/78/EC. Published in the Official Journal of the EU, available at: http://www.esrb.europa.eu/shared/pdf/EBA-en.pdf?79016e649558f0a9a741da6c169b806b (2010).
89. The colleges are a mechanism for exchange of information between home and host authorities, for planning and performance of key supervisory tasks in a coordinated manner, including all aspects of ongoing supervision, and for preparation and handling of emergencies.
90. This followed similar propositions as to how regulation of cross-border banking in the EU had to be structured. *See*, IRSA. (2009). *Cross-Border Banking in Europe: what regulation and supervision?* Retrieved from Unicredit Group Forum on Financial Cross-border Groups, Discussion Paper No.01, https://www.unicreditgroup.eu/content/dam/unicreditgroup/documents/inc/press-and-media/cross_border_banking_discussion_paper.pdf The Report suggests: the supervision of cross-border banks to be based on three tiers: day-to-day supervision to continue with national supervisors; strategic decisions, affecting the entire group to be supervised by colleges of supervisors, with enhanced, legally binding supervisory powers for each cross-border institution; and, an EBA, whose independence governance follow the proposal of the de Larosiere Group.

least, a Joint Committee was formed by the ESAs to coordinate their actions on cross-sectoral rule-making and supervisory matters. Key competencies envisaged for the ESAs comprised of: (a) legally binding mediation between national supervisors, (b) adoption of binding supervisory standards (c) adoption of binding technical decisions applicable to individual financial institutions (d) oversight and coordination of colleges of supervisors, (e) designation, where needed, of group supervisors, (f) licensing and supervision of specific EU-wide institutions (e.g., CRAs, and post-trading infrastructures), and (g) binding cooperation with the European Systemic Risk Council (ESRC) to ensure adequate macro-prudential supervision.[91]

Since January 2011, three ESAs are dealing with the regulation of financial services across Europe.[92] The ESAs work with the newly established ESRB to ensure financial stability and to strengthen and enhance the EU supervisory framework. Apart from issuing guidance and recommendations to national supervisors,[93] ESAs also seek to formulate a single EU rule book and harmonize technical standards on the basis of powers conferred by the EU commission,[94] which subsequently is to be adopted by the EC and is part of formal and binding EU law.[95]

To ensure consistent application of harmonized legislation, if the ESAs find a national supervisory authority failing to apply EU law, or if the supervisor does not comply with the EC's formal opinion, the ESA may then take decisions binding on firms or market participants to ensure compliance to the EU law. In adverse situations, ESAs assume wide-ranging powers.[96] In a crisis, the ESAs will provide EU-wide coordination.[97] If an emergency is declared, the ESAs may make decisions that are binding on national supervisors and on firms. The ESAs will mediate in certain situations where national supervisory authorities disagree. If necessary, they will be able to resolve disputes by making a decision that is binding on both of the parties to ensure compliance with EU law.[98] They have a role in EU supervisory colleges to ensure that they function efficiently and that consistent approaches and practices are followed.[99] The ESAs will conduct regular peer reviews of national supervisory authorities across the EU.[100] They will be able to collect information from national supervisors to allow them to fulfill their role.[101] This information will be used for analyzing market developments, coordinating EU-wide stress tests and the macro-prudential analysis

---

91. Avgouleas, E., & Arner, D. W. (2013).
92. For comprehensive analysis, Avgouleas, E. (2012), *Supra* n. 6.
93. Article 8 defines tasks and powers of the Authority; *see*, Arts 10-17, ESA founding Regulation, *supra* n. 86.
94. Article 11, exercise of delegation, ESA founding Regulation, *supra* n. 86.
95. Article 10, Regulatory Technical Standards, ESA founding Regulation, *supra* n. 86.
96. Article 18, Action in emergency situations, ESA founding Regulation, *supra* n. 86.
97. Article 31, Coordination function, ESA founding Regulation, *supra* n. 86.
98. Article 19, Settlement of disagreements between competent authorities in cross-border situations, and also, Art. 20, Settlement of disagreements between competent authorities across sectors; Art. 21, Colleges of supervisors, ESA founding regulation, *supra* n. 86.
99. Article 29, Common supervisory culture; Art. 27, European system of resolution and funding arrangements, ESA founding Regulation.
100. Article 30, Peer reviews of competent authorities, ESA founding Regulation, *supra* n. 86.
101. Article 36 on Relationship with the ESRB, ESA founding Regulation, *supra* n. 86.

undertaken by the ESRB.[102] They also have a remit to consider consumer protection issues.[103] The ensuing paragraphs provided a more analytical overview of the competences discharged by the ESRB and the ESAs.

[2]   Stage II: The ESRB

On December 16, 2010, Regulation (EU) No 1092/2010 (to be called the ESRB Regulation) established the ESRB responsible for conducting macro-prudential oversight in the Union in order to prevent or mitigate systemic risks to financial stability. It was created as an independent body with no legal personality and with no legally binding powers – just as many other IFL supervisory bodies. The body was hosted at the ECB, which would direct its work and chair the meetings.

The ESRB aims at detection of excessive risk accumulation, improving surveillance and supervision. Its principal tasks include: conducting operations consisting of prediction, assessment management, and prevention and control of systemic risk, and to collect and analyze all the relevant and necessary information, identify and prioritize systemic risks,[104] issue warnings where such systemic risks are deemed to be significant,[105] and, issue recommendations for remedial action, and where appropriate, making those recommendations public.[106] The ESRB can determine an emergency situation where it may issue a confidential warning addressed to the European Council. This provides the Council with an assessment of the situation[107] in order to enable the Council to adopt a decision addressed to the ESAs determining the existence of an emergency situation.[108] It is for the Council, and not for the ESRB which serves only an advisory function, to make decisions regarding such emergencies. The ESRB works in close cooperation with several other parties to the ESFS,[109] including the European Commission and the EU Economic and Financial Committee (EFC) for surveillance.[110] Jointly with the European Council it performs a collective oversight of systemic stability policies and it cooperates with the IMF, the BIS, and the FSB to identify and assess SIFIs in the EU.[111] Moreover, in collaboration with the ESAs, it maintains a common set of quantitative and qualitative indicators (risk dashboard) to identify and measure systemic risk.[112]

---

102. *Ibid.*, and, Art. 23 on identification and measurement of systemic risk, ESA founding Regulation.
103. Article 9 on Tasks related to consumer protection and financial activities; Art. 26, on European system of national Investor Compensation Schemes, ESA founding Regulations. *Supra*, n. 86.
104. Article 3 ESRB Regulation, *supra* n. 87.
105. Article 3 and Art. 16, ESRB Regulation, *supra* n. 87.
106. *Ibid.*
107. Article 3, ESRB Regulation, *supra* n. 87.
108. Recital 22, ESRB Regulation, *supra* n. 87.
109. Article 16, ESRB Regulation, *supra* n. 87.
110. Dierick, F., Lennartsdotter, P., & Favero, P. D. (2012). The ESRB at Work: Its Role, Organization and Functioning. *Macro-prudential Commentaries, ESRB (1)*, available at http://www.esrb.europa.eu/pub/pdf/commentaries/ESRB_commentary_1202.pdf.
111. Article 3, ESRB Regulation, *supra* n. 87.
112. *Ibid.*

Naturally, there are ambiguities surrounding the ESRB's role. First, as a *soft law body with an informal status*, it is very much dependent for information collection on national supervisory and regulatory authorities. The ESRB's dependence on other bodies to carry out some of its tasks, and more importantly, its mandate implies that it may easily become involved in national and European level political struggles and reputation damaging litigation.

Second, because of the ESRB's closeness with the ECB, which is the effective LoLR in the Eurozone, its credibility and independence may further be compromised by the ECB's policy priorities.[113] It should be noted here that the ECB has a clear role with respect to monetary policy under Article 127(2) TFEU, and Article 18 of the ESCB Statute, but it has only a limited mandate vis-à-vis discharge of the LoLR powers (unlike traditional central banks which are endowed with powers to employ both monetary policy and LoLR instruments during crisis). Also, in the EU's case, until the ESM moves into full action, only fiscal authorities can affect bailouts using taxpayers' money and not the ESRB.

[3] Stage III: The Worsening Crisis

By employing an exploratory approach, this chapter aims at finding how significant the design (a *treaty-based v. soft-law based*) of IFL can be in determining effectiveness of the law as a tool to effectively prevent and manage financial crises. As we will find below, nature of the regulatory architecture itself may not cause a financial crisis, yet the *institutional design* can be very important, in particular, in preventing and later, in resolution of a major financial crisis. Prevention can be achieved by putting in place an effective regulatory framework designed to specifically target and control systemic risk factors. On the other hand, crisis management and resolution requires more elaborate and established supervisory and resolution structures, which in an integrated market, must possess a cross-border remit in order to override or subsume the principle of home-country control.[114]

A historical look at the European Union's institution-building processes reveals an element of experimentation dominated the developmental process than a careful

---

113. Avgouleas, E. (2012). Another perspective argues that the ECB might not necessarily be a tougher supervisor than the national authorities. *See also*, contributions from, Goodhart, C. *Funding Arrangements and Burden Sharing in Banking Resolution*, and, Franklin Allen, Elena Carletti and Andrew Gimber's *The Financial Implications of a Banking Union*. In, Thorsten Beck. (2012). *Banking Union for Europe Risks and Challenges, [electronic resource], Centre for Economic Policy Research (CEPR)* Retrieved from http://voxeu.org/sites/default/files/file/Banking_Union.pdf, last accessed, Apr. 14, 2017. (pp. 105-119).
114. Garicano, L., & Lastra, R. M. (2010). *See also*, The new supervisory framework in the EU, *see* Arroyo, H. T. (2011). The EU's Fiscal Crisis and Policy Response: reforming economic governance in the EU Directorate General for Economic and Financial Affairs, European Commission, available at http://www.oecd.org/gov/budgetingandpublicexpenditures/48871475.pdf.

design.[115] For example, the EU Treaties did not establish clear institutional borders as a prerequisite for efficient functioning of the *multilevel* European governance framework and we saw from the EU's incoherent response to the crises (both after 2008 and SDCs) and a fragile power balance between the EU institutions and its Member States. The Union continues to operate mostly in a reactive mode and continues to face delayed decision-making processes despite the presence of its highly refined constitutional structures with respect to multilevel European governance. *Who does what* in Europe has been occupying policy makers for too many years.[116] A *competence catalogue* was defined under the Lisbon Treaty which has been in force since December 1, 2009 which distinguishes between the EU and the Member State's competences on the basis of the principle of conferral and recognition.

Essentially, for the first time in EU's history it has been explicitly enshrined in the Treaties that competences not conferred upon the Union would remain with the Member States.[117] As a first step, Eurozone Heads of State adopted the intergovernmental Euro Plus Pact. This Pact strengthens the economic pillar of the EMU and aims to improve economic policy coordination with the objective of improving competitiveness leading to a higher degree of convergence. As this remains outside the existing institutional framework, a constitutional amendment to the EMU will be required to enable its implementation.[118] In addition, the European Parliament and the Council adopted a *six-pack* set of new legislative acts, aimed at strengthening Eurozone's economic governance by reducing deficits through tighter control on national finances.[119]

---

115. Schoenmaker, D. (Dec. 19, 2009). The Financial Crisis: Financial Trilemma in Europe *VOX: Research-based policy analysis and commentary from leading economists.* http://www.voxeu.org/article/financial-crisis-and-europe-s-financial-trilemma.
116. COM (2001). *European Governance: A White Paper.* Commission of the European Communities.
117. Wouters, J., & Ramopoulos, T. (2012), *supra* n. 13.
118. Conclusions of the European Council, Mar. 24-25, 2011, EUCO 10/1/10 REV 1, and subsequently revised conclusions, EU. (Jan. 25, 2012). Conclusions of the European Council, Dec. 9, 2011 (Vol. EUCO 139/1/11 REV 1).
119. The legislative six-pack set of European economic governance architecture reforms comprised of five regulations and one directive, proposed by the EC to come into force on Dec. 13, 2011. *See*, Regulation (EU) No 1173/2011 of the European Parliament and of the Council of Nov. 16, 2011 on the effective enforcement of budgetary surveillance in the euro area, OJ 2011, L 306/1; Regulation (EU) No 1174/2011 of the European Parliament and of the Council of Nov. 16, 2011 on enforcement measures to correct excessive macroeconomic imbalances in the euro area, OJ 2011, L 306/8; Regulation (EU) No 1175/ 2011 of the European Parliament and of the Council of Nov. 16, 2011 amending Council Regulation (EC) No 1466/97 on the strengthening of the surveillance of budgetary positions and the surveillance and coordination of economic policies, OJ 2011 L 306/12; Regulation (EU) No 1176/2011 of the European Parliament and of the Council of Nov. 16, 2011 on the prevention and correction of macroeconomic imbalances, OJ 2011 L 306/25; Council Regulation (EU) No 1177/2011 of Nov. 8, 2011 amending Regulation (EC) No 1467/97 on speeding up and clarifying the implementation of the excessive deficit procedure, OJ 2011 L 306/25; Council Directive 2011/85/EU of Nov. 8, 2011 on requirements for budgetary frameworks of the Member States, OJ 2011 L 306/41. Available at http://ec.europa.eu/economy_finance/economic_governance/index_en.htm *See also*, Regulation (EU) No 1175/2011 of the European Parliament and of the Council of Oct. 4, 2011 amending Regulation (EC) No. 1466/97 on strengthening of the surveillance of budgetary positions and the surveillance and coordination of economic policies, OJ 2011 L 306/12, at 15-16.

The EMU has been engaged in adopting radical measures aiming at: stabilizing market conditions, containing impact of the Eurozone debt crisis on the banking system and vice versa, and improving negative feedback loops between banks and the sovereigns debts.[120] Amongst others, critical steps to be taken by Member States for EU's survival include: breaking up the vicious circle of the bank debts piling up on sovereign debt, compliance to the adjustment of internal and external imbalances, and repairing its financial sector to achieve sustainable public finances.[121]

Lately, the financial crisis drew attention to the strain on Member States' public finances where 23 out of the 27 states fall in the so-called *excessive deficit procedure* (EDP). EDP is a mechanism established by the EU Treaties obliging countries to keep their budget deficits below 3% of the GDP, and government debts to be kept below 60% of the GDP. Accordingly, the Member States running any excess deficit must comply with the recommendations and deadlines as decided by the European Council and correct their excessive deficit.[122] We have seen recently the problems being created because of this higher debt levels in certain Member States which raises the cost of borrowing for Eurozone members to unsustainable levels, necessitating continuous bailouts by the wealthier members of the Eurozone in an effort to keep the EMU from breaking up. However, such sovereign bailouts can be not only very expensive but also bear far-reaching impact on keeping the Union intact.

One of the most important of recent integration reforms included the decision to move towards a banking union. The decision was reflected in the legislative proposal for establishing an SSM for the euro area, the entry into force of the ESM and the ECB's decision to undertake Outright Monetary Transactions (OMTs) in secondary markets for the bonds of Eurozone countries. Being conditional on measures implemented at the national level, these policy initiatives aim to support fiscal consolidation and private sector deleveraging.[123] The Liikanen Report[124] proposed to separate deposit-taking banking from the high-risk banking activities. However, preparing a comprehensive EU mandate on structural reform of the EU banking sector may take some time as the EU is currently facing many existential problems.

---

120. *See*, Ferran, E. (2010).
121. EU. (Spring 2012). European Economic Forecast (Vol. European Economy: 1|2012). European Commission: Directorate-General for Economic and Financial Affairs, available at http://ec.europa.eu/economy_finance/publications/european_economy/2012/pdf/ee-2012-1_en.pdf.
122. There is however, mounting criticism of the conditionality of deficit reduction by pursuing austerity measures and tighter control of national expenses, especially on the Member States facing financial stresses. *See* for example, Bellofiore, R. (2013) who perceives a way out of crisis requires not only by means monetary reforms and expansionary coordinated fiscal measures, but also a wholesale change of economic model built upon a new 'engine' of demand and growth that requires a monetary finance of 'good' deficits Bellofiore, R. (2013). Two or Three Things I Know About Her: Europe in the Global Crisis and Heterodox Economics. *Cambridge Journal of Economics*.
123. EU. (Autumn 2012). European Economic Forecast (vol. European Economy: 7|2012). EC: Directorate-General for Economic and Financial Affairs, Retrieved from http://ec.europa.eu/economy_finance/publications/european_economy/2012/pdf/ee-2012-1_en.pdf.
124. *See*, Liikanen, E. (2012). *High-level Expert Group on Reforming the Structure of the EU Banking Sector*. Retrieved, http://ec.europa.eu/internal_market/bank/docs/high-level_expert_group/report_en.pdf.

Finally, irrespective of the progress already achieved on the policy side, the experience of the past two years reflects that reversal of sentiment in financial markets and widening of interest rate spreads can happen very rapidly if the implementation of radical measures does not seem radical enough to meet these requisite challenges. The next few paragraphs will provide an analytical account of the reforms that have been put in place to strengthen EU's financial and monetary stability with particular focus on the SSM and the mooted pan-European resolution and deposit insurance arrangements.

[B] Postliminary Responses

[1] Crisis Management Framework: The EBA

The EBA was established by Regulation (EC) No. 1093/2010 of the European Parliament and of the Council of November 24, 2010[125] and officially started operations as of January 1, 2011. Heads of States and Governments agreed[126] to complete the legislative work underpinning the banking union before the end of 2013. A lot of progress was achieved to meet those milestones by December 2013.[127]

According to the EBA Regulation, oversight, and consumer protection are the main functions. The EBA is required to develop a single European supervisory and recovery and resolution rule book in order to achieve a level playing field for financial institutions. EBA is also committed to enhance consumer protection and promote transparency, simplicity and fairness for consumers of financial products and services across the Single Market.[128] The new rules, which entered into force on January 1, 2015, provide authorities with the means to intervene decisively both ex ante (for instance by ensuring that all banks have recovery and resolution plans in place) and ex post, that is, in the process if they do (for instance the power to appoint a temporary administrator in a bank for a limited period to deal with problems). If, despite these preventive measures, the financial situation of a bank deteriorates beyond repair, the new law ensures through a *bail-in* mechanism that shareholders and creditors of the banks have to pay their share.[129]

---

125. Regulation (EU) No 1093/2010 of the European Parliament and of the Council of Nov. 24, 2010 establishing a European Banking Authority, amending Decision No 716/2009/EC and repealing Commission Decision 2009/78/EC. (Vol. 331/12): Official Journal of the EU, available at http://www.esrb.europa.eu/shared/pdf/EBA-en.pdf?79016e649558f0a9a741da6c169b806b.
126. *See*, A Blueprint for a deep and genuine Economic and Monetary Union (EMU): Frequently Asked Questions, Nov. 28, 2012, (*MEMO/12/909*) available at http://europa.eu/rapid/press-release_MEMO-12-909_en.htm.
127. EU. (January 2014). A comprehensive EU response to the financial crisis: substantial progress towards a strong financial framework for Europe and a banking union for the Eurozone: EC, MEMO/14/57, available at http://europa.eu/rapid/press-release_MEMO-14-57_en.htm.
128. *See*, EBA Work Program 2013. (Sep. 28, 2012), Vol. EBA BS 2012 163 FINAL: The EBA, available at http://www.eba.europa.eu/cebs/media/aboutus/Work%20Programme/EBA-BS-2012-163-FINAL--EBA-work-programme-for-2013-.pdf.
129. EU. (January 2014). A comprehensive EU response to the financial crisis: substantial progress towards a strong financial framework for Europe and a banking union for the Eurozone: EC, MEMO/14/57, available at http://europa.eu/rapid/press-release_MEMO-14-57_en.htm.

The Bank Recovery and Resolution Directive (BRRD) No. 2014/59/EU, on crisis prevention, crisis management and resolution mechanism assigns to the EBA the task to develop a wide range of BTS, Guidelines and reports on these areas of recovery and resolution, with the aim of ensuring effective and consistent procedures across the Union, in particular with respect to cross-border financial institutions. The ultimate objective of this framework is to enhance financial stability, reduce moral hazard, protect depositors and critical financial services, save public money and ensure the smooth functioning of the internal market for financial services.[130] This framework is complemented by the ongoing review of the deposit guarantee directive.

The EC's policy initiative to build EBU (along with the support from the ECB) to help redress risk of a euro breakup has not only imparted strength to the *treaty-based* single financial market but also signaled clear indication of furthering economic and financial integration across the EU. The EU27 is in the midst of challenging circumstances on account of *exit movements*.[131] EBA does acknowledge these risks of an inadvertent *two-speed process* within the concentric circles of the Union and of the potential for fragmentation of the single market in the shadows of more harmonization of supervisory practices within the SSM. The sheer number of various reform proposals and their advanced stages of implementation and adoption reflect policy makers and, in particular, regulators' resolute to do real actions.[132]

[2] The Long-Awaited Panacea: The SSM

To support the ESM, the European Commission took steps for establishing an integrated banking union in the EMU. The SSM places the ECB as the central prudential supervisor of financial institutions in the euro area (including approximately 6,000 banks) and in those non-euro EU countries that choose to join the SSM. The ECB directly supervises the largest banks, while the national supervisors continue to monitor the remaining banks. The SSM has been operational since November 2014, and with a complete set of resolution powers from January 2016. The SSM is the final piece in the banking union jigsaw. Thus, a single EU authority gets the powers and resources to protect taxpayers from banks' failures. The prevalent DGS before establishing the SSM were national in nature. The EC will review the functioning of the DGS

---

130. EBA. (2015). Recovery, resolution and DGS. EBA, available at http://www.eba.europa.eu/regulation-and-policy/recovery-and-resolution/-/activity-list/pPtPvnn3MhOm/more, last accessed Apr. 17, 2017.
131. The recent UK (Brexit) vote to leave the EU has set a major blow to the integration. However, it may take time before deeper implications can be fully explained. The term 'Brexit' connotes the withdrawal of the UK from the EU (a faction of individuals, advocacy groups and political parties were not in favor of the UK to be part of the EEC (the predecessor of the EU, in 1973) however, a continued membership of the EEC was approved in 1975 through a referendum where 67% voted in favor of staying in the EEC. In the June 2016 referendum however, 52% voted to leave, resulting in the complex process of withdrawal which has been initiated on Mar. 29, 2017, putting the UK on course to leave by April 2019. Massive political and economic reshuffles have started in the UK and in EU countries since the June referendum.
132. EC. (April 2013). European Financial Stability and Integration Report 2012. Vol. SWD (2013) 156 final), EC, available at http://ec.europa.eu/internal_market/economic_analysis/docs/efsir/130425_efsir-2012_en.pdf.

Directive by 2019 and see whether, in the context of the banking union, a single pan-European DGS should be set up.

The banking union has, in principle, three pillars: a unified supervision mechanism (the SSM) operated by the ECB, a pan-European DGS and a future single bank resolution mechanism with common backstops. The main task of the ECB and the national supervisors, working closely together within an integrated system is to check that banks comply with the EU banking rules. On November 4, 2013, about one year after the EC proposed to set up a single banking supervision mechanism in the euro area,[133] the SSM Regulation was entered into force.

As mentioned earlier, the whole of the EU's supervisory structure needed fundamental revamp: improving both coordination between national supervisors and enhancing EU-wide supervision to deal with risks and issues with cross-border effects. The rudimentary crisis management and coordination mechanisms that were in place through the Lamfalussy level III committees lacked both, competence and resources to cope with a cross-border banking crisis. Lack of appropriate coordination structures was nowhere more evident than in bank recovery and resolution issues. Similarly, a centralized EU structure dealing with systemic risk monitoring was completely absent. On September 12, 2012, the EC proposed an SSM for Eurozone banks to be run by the ECB and required the Council and the European Parliament to adopt proposed regulations by the end of 2012, together with the three components of an integrated banking union: the single rule book in the form of capital requirements (IP/11/915), harmonized deposit protection schemes (IP/10/918), and a single European recovery and resolution framework (IP/12/570). In the words of the president of the EC, José-Manuel Barroso:

> This new system, with the European Central Bank at the core and involving national supervisors, will restore confidence in the supervision of all banks in the euro area…We should make it a top priority to get the European supervisor in place by the start of next year. This will also pave the way for any decisions to use European backstops to recapitalize banks.[134]

Barroso also explained with authority the main purpose of these arrangements: [W]e want to break the vicious link between sovereigns and their banks. In future, bankers' losses should no longer become people's debt, bringing into doubt the financial stability of whole countries.[135] To this effect, the idea of setting up an asset management company sounds more practical. Although the SSM has reduced regulatory discretion on provisioning,[136] however, traditionally, banks do not have strong incentive to address especially the issues relating to non-performing loans – which has become a huge issue in the EU, in particular, the old hidden losses. This has been

---

133. *See,* Commission proposes new ECB powers for banking supervision as part of a banking union, Sep. 12, 2012 (IP/12/953), available at http://europa.eu/rapid/press-release_IP-12-953_en.htm.
134. Barroso, J. M. (2013), *supra* n. 2.
135. *Ibid.*
136. Thorsten Beck, (April 24, 2017). An asset management company for the Eurozone: Time to revive an old idea, Vox CEPR's Policy Portal, available at http://voxeu.org/article/asset-management-company-eurozone#.WP2mTpi6Kng.linkedin last accessed, April 4, 2017.

suggested in literature by other scholars[137] to subject the institutions selling NPLs to the asset management company to a *structural conditionality*.

[3]   Redefining Roles: The ECB

The desirable ambit of ECB's supervisory powers has been the subject of considerable debate. The institutional foundations of monetary union are the euro and the ECB, which together with the Central Banks of the Member States form the ESCB. This formation however itself produces structural complexities in the system.[138]

The decision to establish the SSM and entrust the ECB with supervisory tasks was a fundamentally political one, taken by the European legislators: the EU Council and the European Parliament in October 2013.[139] Since November 4, 2014 the ECB has assumed responsibility for the supervision of the euro area banking sector. It was nevertheless a major organizational challenge to get the SSM up and running in only one year, while also conducting the comprehensive assessment of the euro area's 130 most important banks. In the EU, given the advanced level of financial market integration as compared to any other part of the world, the current cross-border crisis demanded regional-level reforms to provide for integrated structures and collective solutions and not just single rule book and closer cooperation of national supervisors. Thus, within the unified supervisory system, the ECB has direct responsibility for around 150 banks with assets of more than EUR 30 billion (or those with assets representing more than 20% of a Member State's GDP). National supervisors within the same unified supervisory system will primarily supervise the remaining banks. Finally, while the ECB possess the power to step in to assume direct supervision at any moment, if need be, yet national supervisors are in charge of tasks like consumer protection, money laundering and branches of third country banks.[140] The ECB carried out functions of: (a) licensing/authorizing credit institutions; (b) monitoring compliance with capital, leverage and liquidity requirements; (c) conducting supervision of financial conglomerates; and, (d) early intervention measures (Prompt Corrective Action) when a bank breaches or risks breaching regulatory capital requirements by requiring banks to take remedial action.[141]

The reforms roadmap bequeaths ECB the status of a mother institution for the SSM. The June 2012 statement[142] identified Article 127(6) of the EU's Lisbon Treaty[143] as the legal basis for the SSM, which made the new supervisor a part of the ECB. Under these new arrangements, impartial supervision at Union level under the SSM will make

---

137. Avgouleas, E and C Goodhart (2016), 'An anatomy of bank bail-ins – why the Eurozone needs a fiscal backstop for the banking sector', European Economy 2016(2): 75-90.
138. Lastra, R. M., & Louis, J.-V. (2013).
139. ECB. (March 2015). ECB Annual Report on supervisory activities for 2014: ECB, available at https://www.bankingsupervision.europa.eu/ecb/pub/pdf/ssmar2014.en.pdf, last accessed on Jul. 14, 2015.
140. Avgouleas, E., & Arner, D. W. (2013).
141. *Ibid*.
142. Euro Area Summit, Jun. 29, 2012. *See*, http://www.consilium.europa.eu/uedocs/cms_data/docs/pressdata/en/ec/131359.pdf.
143. Treaty of Lisbon, signed on Dec. 13, 2007, entered into force on Dec. 1, 2009.

bank failures much less likely. And if at all, when they do occur, the European SRM will cover banks overseen by the SSM/ECB. It is made up of a Single Resolution Board (SRB) and a Single Resolution Fund (SRF). Once informed by the ECB that a bank is in trouble, the Board will be responsible for taking most decisions on the best course of action and will prepare for the resolution of the stricken bank. The fund, which will amount to € 55 billion within eight years, will be financed by all the banks in the banking union countries.

In case where the SRF is not sufficiently funded by the banking sector, an effective common backstop will be developed, which will facilitate borrowing by the SRF. The roadmap does not hand over the management of the ESM to the ECB until the new supervisory structures prove their effectiveness. The euro area banking sector will ultimately be liable for repayment by means of levies, including ex post. So a single EU authority will have the powers and resources to protect taxpayers from banks' failures.[144] Empirical evidence suggests that the EC continues to be a powerful player in EU economic governance, but its primary role is changing[145] especially in regard to its role in agenda-setting is on a decline. However, in future as stronger implementation competences would be of significance, its role seems to remain significantly important.

The legislative proposals[146] published by the EC establishing the SSM have still to work out appropriate solutions for some outstanding issues. Beck has argued for having a banking union within a currency union because the close link between monetary and financial stability plays out strongest within a union. In a Union, the link between government and banking fragility is exacerbated because the national governments lack policy tools that are otherwise available to countries with an independent monetary policy.[147] There is possibility of non-Member States to join the framework also depending upon the decision of the euro area Member States have a veto over decisions under Article 127(6).[148] The UK announced the decision not to join the SSM.[149] There is a legitimate concern that adding supervision, which is a politically charged task, to the ECB's responsibilities may compromise its impartiality and independence. There are contrasting views, however, as regards the separation between the two functions, especially during a financial crisis.[150]

---

144. EC. (2015). Banking and Finance, *Understanding Banking Union*. Newsletter, Feb. 27, 2015, available at http://ec.europa.eu/information_society/newsroom/cf/fisma/item-detail.cfm?item_id = 20758&newsletter_id = 166&lang = en last accessed Jul.13, 2015.
145. Bauer, M. W., & Becker, S. (2014). The Unexpected Winner of the Crisis: The European Commission's Strengthened Role in Economic Governance. *Journal of European Integration*, 36(3), 213-229.
146. *See* EC. Sep. 12, 2012. Commission proposes new ECB powers for banking supervision. *Press Release*, A Roadmap towards a Banking Union. Sep. 12, 2012, vol. COM (2012) 510 final. *See*, http://europa.eu/rapid/press-release_IP-12-953_en.htm last accessed October 16, 2017.
147. Beck, T. (2012). *Supra* n. 113.
148. Consolidated version of the Treaty on European Union and the Treaty on the Functioning of the European Union (Mar. 30, 2010). Official Journal of the European Union: C 83/01, Volume 53.
149. Member States who have not adopted the euro are not members of the Governing Council of the ECB.
150. There is an overlap in representation between the Supervisory Board and the Governing Council; therefore, raising Chinese walls between the two highly overlapping bodies would make no sense. *See*, Beck, T., & Gros, D. (March 2013). Monetary Policy and Banking

[4] The DGS[151]

To provide for common mechanisms to resolve banks and guarantee customer deposits, the EC proposed instituting an SRM to govern the resolution of banks and coordinate the application of resolution tool in banks within the EU. The resolution mechanism is aimed at safeguarding the continuity of essential banking operations, to protect depositors, client assets and public funds and to minimize risks to financial stability.[152] This mechanism is considered to be more efficient than a network of national resolution authorities particularly in the case of cross-border failures, given the need for speed and credibility in addressing the issues in the midst of a crisis.[153] The decisions have to be taken in line with the principles of resolution as set out in the single rule book consistent with international best practices and in full compliance with Union state aid rules, in particular that, shareholders and creditors should bear the cost of resolution before any external funding is granted.[154] The main resolution tools, as detailed in the EC's proposal directive for crisis management and resolution, are the following:[155]

- Sale of business tool, whereby the authorities would sell all or a part of the failing bank to another bank, without the consent of shareholders.
- Bridge bank tool, which consists of identifying the good assets or essential functions of the bank and separates them into a new bank (bridge bank). The bridge bank will later be sold to another entity, in order to preserve these essential banking functions or facilitate the continuous access to deposits. The old bank with bad or nonessential functions would then be liquidated under normal insolvency proceedings.
- Asset separation tool, whereby the bad assets of the bank are put into an asset management vehicle. This tool relieves the balance sheet of a bank from bad or *toxic assets*. In order to prevent this tool from being used solely as a state aid measure, the framework prescribes that it may be used only in conjunction with another tool (bridge bank, sale of business or write-down). This ensures that while the bank receives support, it also undergoes restructuring.
- Bail-in tool, whereby the bank would be recapitalized with shareholders wiped out or diluted, and creditors would have their claims reduced or

---

Supervision: Coordination instead of Separation. *European Banking Center Discussion Paper No. 2013-003; published as CEPS Policy Brief.*
151. A Deposit Guarantee Schemes (DGS) simply reimburses a limited amount to compensate depositors whose bank has failed. A fundamental principle underlying DGS is that they are funded entirely by banks, and that no taxpayer funds are used in the process of reimbursement. In the EU's case, depositors' savings are guaranteed up to a sum of EUR 100,000.
152. Avgouleas, E., & Arner, D. W. (2013).
153. *See also*, Beck, T. (2012), *supra* n. 113. Schinasi also distinguishes between immediate crisis resolution and intermediate to long-term measures. *See*, Schinasi, G. (Nov. 5, 2012). European Banking Union: Pros and Cons: A View from Across the Atlantic. *Available at http://www.dsf.nl/assets/cms/File/Events/Garry%20Schinasi_European%20Banking%20Union%20.pdf.*
154. EC. (Sep. 9, 2012). Communication from the EC to the European Parliament and the Council: A Roadmap towards a Banking Union (Vol. COM (2012) 510 final). Brussels.
155. Avgouleas, E., & Arner, D. W. (2013).

Chapter 5: Enforcement in IFL: The Precarious Case of the EU   §5.04[B]

converted to shares. An institution for which a private acquirer could not be found, or an institution which could be complicated to split up, could thus continue to provide essential services without the need for bailout by public funds. This would allow authorities time to reorganize the institution or wind down parts of its business in an orderly manner. To this end, banks would be required to have a minimum percentage of their total liabilities in the shape of instruments eligible for bail-in. If triggered, they would be written down in a predefined order in terms of seniority of claims in order for the institution to regain viability. The choice of tools will depend on the specific circumstances of each case and build on options laid out in the resolution plan prepared for the bank.

A bank would become subject to resolution when (a) it has reached a point of distress such that there are no realistic prospects of recovery over an appropriate time frame, (b) all other intervention measures, as stated above, have been exhausted and (c) winding up the institution under normal insolvency proceedings would risk prolonged uncertainty or financial instability. Thus, entry into resolution will always occur at a point close to insolvency.[156]

These measures aimed at ensuring continuity of policies and uniformity of application throughout the integrated area institute the essential elements necessary for functioning of the entity itself. In consequent, the European Parliament and EU Member States have reached a provisional agreement to complete the single rule book on crisis management for the protection of deposits. It ensures bank deposits in all Member States will continue to be guaranteed up to €100,000 per depositor per bank if a bank fails. The proposal on DGS[157] now agreed will ensure that every Member State has an adequate funding ex ante in their Deposit Guarantee Fund. The text also opens the way to a voluntary mechanism of mutual borrowing between the DGSs from different EU countries. This is the only form of mutualization foreseen at this stage.[158] From a financial stability perspective, this guarantee prevents depositors from making excessive withdrawals from their banks, thereby preventing severe economic consequences within the Union.

---

156. *Ibid.*
157. DGS reimburse a limited amount of deposits to depositors whose bank has failed. From the depositors' point of view, this protects a part of their wealth from bank failures. From a financial stability perspective, this promise prevents depositors from making panic withdrawals from their bank, thereby preventing severe economic consequences.
158. The European Parliament adopted the EC's proposal for a revision of the Directive 94/19/EC on Deposit Guarantee Schemes on Jan.15, 2014. *See*, EU. (January 2014). A comprehensive EU response to the financial crisis: substantial progress towards a strong financial framework for Europe and a banking union for the Eurozone: EC: Brussels, MEMO/14/57, available at http://europa.eu/rapid/press-release_MEMO-14-57_en.htm.

§5.05 CONTINUING CHALLENGES

The weaknesses in the financial and institutional treaty framework of the Union affected the integration process at the EU in two ways: (1) the incomplete harmonization prevented the benefits of full integration, and (2) led to the continuation of fragilities in the structure of financial market.

The recent crisis exposed these fragilities and cracks in the prevalent crisis management frameworks in the EU as well as at the Member State level. These weaknesses have resulted in partial disintegration of the internal market and have caused splits along national lines in at least some of the segments of the single market for capital and financial services.[159] Thus, for the EU, progression to a framework of tighter financial integration as well as putting in place a system of risk controls for the banking system (together with improved governance standards in the monetary and fiscal spheres and centralization of responsibility for financial stability) has become a mandatory one-way road. The ESFS has not remedied the mismatch among the geographic scope of EU bank activities and the regulatory remit of the authorities supervising them. This provides yet another layer of complexity in the EU structures, which has its roots in the dual role performed by the National Central Banks (NCBs). The NCBs are national agencies performing non-ESCB functions and at the same time, NCBs constitute an important part of the ESCB and play this role in conduct of the monetary policy of the Union. This functional complexity has deeper roots that relate to their constitutive laws.[160] Whereas the ECB operates solely under the EC law, the status of the NCBs is governed by both the EC law and through national legislation.

The arrangements advanced under the ESFS for cross-border bank supervision remained compounded and involved too many levels of overlapping competences that could result in significant delays during a crisis.[161] And in the situation, if any European bank or a financial intuition fails, it still has repercussions for states outside the EU, especially when North Asian or North American lenders are involved.[162] These are serious issues worth further thought and part of continued reform process as the aforementioned EU-wide supervisory framework remains far from imposing clear fiscal burden-sharing arrangements between Member States.[163] Therefore, in isolation, no

---

159. ECB. (April 2012). Financial Integration in Europe: European Central Bank. p. 87.
160. Avgouleas, E., & Arner, D. W. (2013).
161. e.g., Jamie Dimon (Jun. 7, 2011) raised a pertinent question with respect to the effectiveness of regulatory reforms: *has anyone bothered to study the cumulative effect of these regulatory and market fixes?* Ben Bernanke, the Fed Chairman issues a statement, as reproduced by Barth, *the central bank doesn't have the quantitative tools to study the net impact of all the regulatory and market changes over the last three years...It's too complicated to study the new regulations' effect.* Reproduced in Barth, J. R., and, Prabha, A. P. (Dec. 3, 2012). *Breaking (Banks)Up is Hard to Do: New Perspectives on Too Big to Fail.* Financial Institutions Centre. Retrieved from http://fic.wharton.upenn.edu/fic/papers/12/12-16.pdf.
162. *See,* Beck, T. (Oct. 25, 2011).
163. This proposal was refined to become an integral part of group level recovery and resolution plans for cross-border banks. *See,* Avgouleas, E, Goodhart, C. & Schoenmaker, D. (2013). Bank Resolution Plans as a Catalyst for Global Financial Reform. *Journal of Financial Stability,* p. 9. Goodhart and Schoenmaker proposed binding burden-sharing arrangement among national governments. If a cross-border bank faces difficulties, the governments would share the costs

Chapter 5: Enforcement in IFL: The Precarious Case of the EU §5.05

institution would be able to perform the complicated and interwoven tasks involving cross-border financial activities in the single financial market.

Moreover, even under the EFSF extensive reliance is placed on the judgment and decisions of the home supervisor.[164] An effective binding mediation mechanism is required to deal with such cross-border supervisory problems. And such binding adjudication, mediation and negotiation mechanisms are quid pro quo (vital constituents) for having any treaty-based framework in place. It has been studied in reference to IFR framework in the previous chapter on Basel implementation issues (*see*, Chapter 4). Without having in place an effective and binding mechanism, some Member States might in future try to limit the branching activities of any firm supervised only by a home supervisor and has been judged to have failed to meet the standards. Such fragmentation would represent a major step backwards for the Single Market.[165]

Current EU reform promise to create a stronger financial and institutional framework in order to strengthen resilience of the single market and mitigate vicious risks from market instability and fragmentation observed during the GFC and the Eurozone debt crisis.[166] Nonetheless, the current integration efforts are high risk as their core only extends to the EMU members[167] and, thus, it might create irreparable fractures for the internal market that remains incomplete at this stage. Moreover, the new arrangements under the SSM need to become *first-best*[168] framework in order to stabilize the euro-area financial instability. Effective supervision, however, will challenge the fiscal sovereignty of the individual states,[169] especially, as the SSM will be able to activate the permanent EU rescue fund in order to directly recapitalize struggling Eurozone banks, such as those in Spain.

Finally, the establishment of the SSM is only a *big first step* on a much longer path towards building crisis management and resolution institutions for the EU banking union. Given the exiting populist sentiment, and ongoing disagreements between the Member States on shouldering the risks, essentially several components such as a European banking charter, a fully-fledged single rule book, a single resolution authority and a more advanced common deposit insurance protection scheme need more refinement.

The EU has experienced an unprecedented economic and financial turbulence since 2007. The European project is still a *work-in-progress* as the interlocking string of

---

according to some predetermined key, for example, according to the distribution of the troubled bank's assets over the respective countries. Under such a burden-sharing approach, a common solution can be found upfront. By pre-committing to burden sharing, governments would give up some of their sovereignty, but in return, the single market in banking serving Europe's businesses and consumers would be saved. Goodhart, C. A. E., & Schoenmaker, D. (2006).

164. *See*, Larosiere, J. d. (February 2009).
165. EU. (Jun. 22, 2012). Country-specific recommendations on economic and fiscal policies: The European Semester, Council of the European Union, available at http://www.consilium.europa.eu/uedocs/cms_Data/docs/pressdata/en/ecofin/131135.pdf.
166. ECB. (April 2012). Financial Integration in Europe: European Central Bank. p. 12.
167. Nineteen Eurozone states and the nine non-euro states are EMU members as of 2015.
168. Schinasi elaborates on *first-best* mechanism in the EU context comprising of single supervisor, uniform deposit insurance, and European resolution mechanism.
169. Schinasi, G. (Nov. 5, 2012). *Supra* n. 153.

crises within the Union has revealed. There are basic flaws in the foundational features of the treaty as well its strict adoption. The crisis does provide prospects to rectify the mistakes committed in the past by addressing those issues and implementing necessary the reform to ensure stability and resilience. The EU needs to strengthen its basic integration framework and that would in turn enhance the Union's international role. This calls for greater sharing of sovereignty by the Member States and with increased legitimacy, accountability and solidarity, in which European institutions are increasingly answerable for the *whole and not only for the sum of its parts*[170] and can keep the integrity of the remaining Eurozone intact. In fact, three mechanisms in the past have shielded the EU's integrity: mostly euro-compatible government formation, avoidance of referendums and delegation to technocratic supranational organizations within the EU. Unfortunately, these three mechanisms are no longer reliably available to the EU. Also, the public opinion has become more Eurosceptic and some of the societal groups have changed their views in certain directions. One of the survey results shows that the negative sentiment towards the EU has increased across all social groups in recent years. However, the results also reveal a paradox of a decline in general support for the EU and an increase in support for the Euro.[171]

This chapter began with analyzing the question of whether and how a treaty-based mechanism has worked in a regional setting with a view to explore if a treaty-based mechanism can function successfully in a global setting under the realm of IFL. This question has been analyzed in the context of the EU that how its enforcement mechanism or the lack of it contributed in many ways to the failures it met in establishing a successfully integrated single market and preventing and managing crises in the Union. The backdrop of the 2008 and 2012 SDC crisis has been used because a crisis can usually provide an opportunity to look for a newer perspective on the outstanding complex issues in an international setting.[172] A return to normalcy without addressing the issues that brought crises can pose a real danger to the survival of such multilateral initiatives. The next section is exploring this expansion of a treaty-based structure for a larger setting.

§5.06 EPILOGUE: CAN THERE BE A GLOBAL TREATY?

The EU as a *polity-in-the-making* provides a real-life laboratory for investigating how far financial integration has advanced in a number of areas within a hard-law-based structure. Simultaneously, the EU's developments highlight real difficulties for IFRA if

---

170. BIS. (2013). Exiting the financial crisis and strengthening European integration: Address by Mr. Carlos da Silva Costa, Governor of the Bank of Portugal, at the Conference of the Portuguese Association of Insurers 'Where is Europe going?', Panel I 'What is the future of the euro?' Lisbon, Oct. 24, 2013. Available at https://www.bis.org/review/r131211d.htm.
171. Clements, B., Nanou, K., & Verney, S. (2014). 'We No Longer Love You, But We Don't Want to Leave You': The Eurozone Crisis and Popular Euro-skepticism in Greece. *Journal of European Integration*, 36(3), 247-265.
172. *See* for example, a detailed discussion of crisis as an obstacle or an opportunity, Tosun, J., Wetzel, A., & Zapryanova, G. (2014). The EU in Crisis: Advancing the Debate. *Journal of European Integration*, 36(3), 195-211.

it were to follow the path of a treaty-based hard-law structure in future. Specifically, it discusses the challenges to the traditional pillars of a treaty-based supra-state structure: identity, legitimacy and solidarity questioning the sustainability of the process of international financial market integration.[173] It also raises questions over representation, governance and control of such multinational/international institutions, the expanding North-South divide, concerns over how pooling and sharing of sovereignty and harmonization of international regulatory standards are going to affect framing of national, international and global financial institutions.

The Eurozone crisis presents a puzzle to the post-functionalist approach to market integration. In spite of unprecedented social hardships, politicization, loss of popular support and political turmoil in the Eurozone, the crisis in the Eurozone has produced major new steps of technocratic supranational integration. Interestingly, another perspective analyzes that integration during the euro crisis can be sufficiently explained by a neo-functionalist account based on path dependency, endogenous preference change and from functional spillover.[174] As the uncertainty of global financial conditions and heightened whammy of a contagion-driven crisis persistently looms over EU financial markets, it cautions others to have adequate and stronger safety nets in place.

The GFC highlighted the necessity of addressing a range of issues at the cross-border level. Before the crisis, financial innovation was regarded as inextricably linked with economic growth and aggregate welfare however, in the wake of the crisis the utility of financial innovation has become more unequivocal. Arner identifies seven aspects of financial regulatory design needed to address systemic risk: (a) robust financial infrastructure, especially payment and settlement systems, (b) well-managed financial institutions with effective corporate governance and risk management systems, (c) disclosure requirements sufficient to support market discipline, (d) regulatory systems designed to reinforce risk management and market discipline as well as setting and monitoring potential risks across all financial institutions, (e) an LoLR to provide liquidity to financial institutions on an appropriate basis, (f) mechanisms for resolving problem institutions, and, (g) mechanisms to protect financial services consumers, such as deposit insurance.[175]

All of these *weaknesses* in the European context are being addressed through reforms that Group of Twenty (G20) is undertaking in coordination with other institutions of international financial governance. Second, in addition to domestic and regional considerations, the crisis implied an enhanced role of the emerging economies within global regulatory and supervisory institutions, such as the IMF and the FSB. The

---

173. *See*, for a debate on pooling of sovereignty in the context of EU, the panel on Sovereignty. (2015). Sovereignty's Revenge: Populism and the Future of European Integration, The Brookings Institution, Washington, D.C. Apr. 23, 2015. *See*, http://www.brookings.edu/~/media/events/2015/04/23-europe-populism/20150423_europe_sovereignty_transcript.pdf last accessed, Jul. 14, 2015.
174. Schimmelfennig, F. (2014). European Integration in the Euro Crisis: The Limits of Post-functionalism. *Journal of European Integration*, 36(3), 321-337.
175. *See*, Arner, D. W. (2011). Adaptation and Resilience in Global Financial Regulation. *North Carolina Law Review*, 89, 101-148. Available at http://hub.hku.hk/bitstream/10722/137052/2/Content.pdf.

IMF, the G20 and the FSB are pursuing structural reforms to allow wider representation with respect to redesigning the global regulatory architecture. While there seems some shift in focus from the western capitalist model towards sustainable and greener financial and regulatory models, this remains a fact that global regulatory regimes are still evolving.

Global financial outlook is susceptible to four significant factors that may grow into bigger threats, these include: over-reliance on the rationality of market forces; faulty LoLR model for bank rescue (using taxpayers' money to foot a banker's bill), and an absence of appropriate reserve-accumulation model; laxity in enforcement and adoption of the agreed models of regulation and supervision; and, weaknesses in institutional mechanisms and legal backstops to carry out financial regulation and supervision. Therefore, to address fallouts emanating from the US and the EU crisis, the reform process must need to bridge these policy and institutional gaps. Begg discusses reform of the EU structure in the aftermath of the GFC from a regulatory and supervisory perspectives, particularly, the home-country control principle, which has been in place since 1980s. He points to the changed scenario after the crisis and highlights EU-wide approaches to design a supranational supervisory system as a way forward. He further speaks of having a quasi-federal system to begin with, which would tone down the political hurdles in the way of European integration.[176]

This is however, not controversial despite the fact that it does challenge the conventional thinking that financial integration may not be advantageous always. For example, in the short term for the Association of South East Asian Nations (ASEAN), the Asian Banking Integration Framework (ABIF) should deliver its promise to facilitate economies of scale, a bigger market, technological transfer and information sharing i.e., *the soft-infrastructure* but in the long term, it should aim for financial stability realized through consolidated integration i.e., *the hard- infrastructure.*[177] This *balanced view* of integration offers further perspectives: first, that the soundness and credibility of domestic policies are not substitutes for global commitments even though, at times when domestic policies are *stuck*, global commitments can help to *tie-hands* and exert external pressure. And, second, rather than imposition of strict benchmarks and milestones to meet the idiosyncrasies of individual economies, the integration framework should facilitate and encourage collective growth while allowing the market to work freely.[178]

While deeper financial integration is often considered conducive to an efficient allocation of resources and risk-sharing, an increasingly important policy concern is whether it also brings along greater vulnerability in times of crisis. To address the latter concern, Xu and Corbett employ a different approach measuring financial integration,

---

176. *See*, Begg, I. (2009). Regulation and Supervision of Financial Intermediaries in the EU: The Aftermath of the Financial Crisis. *JCMS: Journal of Common Market Studies*, 47(5), 1107-1128. Retrieved from http://ssrn.com/paper = 1491805.
177. *See*, Siswanto, J., & Wihardja, M. M. (May 31, 2012). ASEAN banking integration: positioning Indonesia. *East Asia Forum: Economics, Politics and Public Policy in East Asia and the Pacific.* http://www.eastasiaforum.org/2012/05/31/asean-banking-integration-positioning-indonesia/.
178. Avgouleas, E., & Arner, D. W. (2013).

highlighting interconnectedness in a network of financial flows. Applying an adapted version of eigenvector centrality, often used in network analysis, the new measure provides a nuanced picture of financial integration and interconnectedness in the global and regional financial networks.[179] The US and the UK form *the core* in the global banking network with all other countries scattered around *the periphery*.[180] With China rapidly integrating with the rest of the world, the Asian banking network increasingly resembles the structure of a global network. Therefore, this seems to be the beginning of an essential global network to analyze.

§5.07 CONCLUSION

Since the EU in the context of recent integration crisis provides a perfect laboratory to experiment various options, this chapter has looked at the making and the working of EU's crisis-management mechanism in dealing with the GFC and subsequently with the SDCs to get insights for hard-law-based supranational institutions of financial governance. In the course of this analysis, it reviewed the post-crisis European effort at reinventing the integration mechanism through the formation of various crisis-management bodies including the ESFS, the ESRB and the EBA. It scanned how this new set of EU institutions may strengthen EU's economic and political integration and concluded by defining various options to replicate a single-market framework in a global setting. It is important to have standards in GFG however the prevalence of only standards is an insufficient condition for functioning of such a global structure. Quoting from Jean Monnet, who once wrote, *nothing is possible without individuals, but nothing is lasting without institutions.*[181] The rules and institutions form the foundation of any society, and these must be applied effectively and respected by all. Extending this argument to a broader canvass implies that the future of the global village will involve greater share of sovereignty. The discussion on enhanced sharing of sovereignty for responsiveness of IFRA is expanded in the next chapter which explores the nexus between financial market stability and development of a responsible and legitimate IFL.

---

179. Xu, Y., & Corbett, J. (2015). Measuring Financial Integration: The Network Approach (June 14). *CIFR Paper No. WP062/2015*. Available at SSRN: *http://ssrn.com/abstract = 2618283*.
180. *Ibid.*
181. BIS. (2013). Exiting the financial crisis and strengthening European integration: Address by Mr. Carlos da Silva Costa, Governor of the Bank of Portugal, at the Conference of the Portuguese Association of Insurers 'Where is Europe going?', Panel I 'What is the future of the euro?' Lisbon, Oct. 24, 2013. Available at https://www.bis.org/review/r131211d.htm

CHAPTER 6

IFL: Contemporary Issues, Rethinking Alternatives[*]

It is too early to put a caption to this second decade of the twenty-first century and predict where it would lead ultimately but what is certain is that we are in a transition from the late twentieth century's political as well as economic ideas. The future could be anything but continuation of the old financial, monetary, fiscal and in particular, political trends. The regulatory front is not an exception to this transition.[1] The prolonged economic depression and slow growth in the post-GFC period gave birth to amongst others, a massive nationalist-cum-populist political paradigm.

The analysis in this chapter has a focused coverage of issues that directly stem from the nature of the IFL and have arisen from the post-crisis reregulation and include: excessive FML, weaker crisis-management and crisis-prevention systems, legitimacy deficit, weaker governance and representational structures and lack of legal backstop available to regulatory institutions for effective enforcement of regulatory standards. These factors have rendered the existing institutional structures performing poorly in the wake of the GFC. If financial market stability is the uncontested optimal end, IFL then faces multiple inconsistencies on a number of fronts including on the issue of compliance and enforceability of the regulatory standards like international financial risk management framework. Second, whether hard law or the existing soft-law-based model of IFR provides the best fit?

---

[*] An earlier draft of this chapter received valuable comments from Dr. Jasper Finke, Dr. Peter Drahos, and Prof. Dr. Christian Tietje. *See*, Ashraf, U. (Jun. 21-22, 2012). The Reform of the International Financial Regulatory Architecture: Addressing Legitimacy Issues. Paper presented at the 4th Conference on Global Financial Markets, Martin Luther University Halle-Wittenberg.
1. Nationalism has assumed a front seat in the twenty-first century as against regionalism and globalism of the twentieth century. Since the post-Cold War era, conflicting forces operated simultaneously included *globalism v. nationalism, integration v. fragmentation, globalization v. national stratification and democracy v. authoritarianism*. How these conflicting trends are shape the world in the twenty-first century is still largely unknown. *See*, Hettne, B., & Russett, B. (1996), *Globalism and Regionalism*. Presented at the UN University, Global Seminar, September 2-6. Available at, http://archive.unu.edu/unupress/globalism.html.

The discussion raises further questions on the representative nature of the regulatory bodies which are developing regulatory standards (like the IMF) and their decision-making processes, and the legitimacy of these standards (*See*, Chapter 3). In Chapter 5, we have studied a treaty-based hard-law structure functioning (albeit facing challenges) in a regional setting. This chapter reflects on the inconsistencies in the functioning of the IFRA and leads the final debate whether a GFReg (a treaty-based IFL with the power of enforcement, as discussed in Chapter 5) is a panacea to the financial market ills or some focused reforms to the existing soft-law-based IFRA continues to be the best choice available?

Paradoxically, under the new market scenario, regulators are both competitors and essential partners in the international financial system, with varying and, at times, shifting incentives with respect to whether and how, and how much to cooperate and to coordinate on the market reformatory initiatives. Thus, it is an apt moment to analyze the dynamics of the current financial and regulatory architecture and explore basic issues of *whether to co-operate and co-ordinate*, and if so, how to, and how much coordination is required on what areas between the regulated and the regulators in this new and essentially interconnected world.

This chapter is organized as follows: Section §6.02 looks at the variables underpinnings of the relationship between institutions and development of financial markets by employing a three-pronged strategy. It looks at the role of these institutions in development, the relationship with law, and how this nexus between the two has shaped over time. Part of this section while defining the undefined term, *financial stability* expands the debate on to *instability factor* and pins down its inherent challenges – (including those from FML). The last part of this section combines theoretical conceptualizations of the previous section with the character of the post-2008 IFL and identifies significant paradoxes.

The theme in this section draws on the current reforms taking place at the global level in response to the GFC to highlight fundamental *inconsistencies* in the reform processes that may form breeding ground for future crisis. Gaps, in compliance with and in enforcement of financial standards engender the debate whether to strengthen only the financial institutions of global governance or the framework of IFL itself needs to be strengthened in tandem with institutional reform. The *universal-adaptability-appeal-through-inherent-flexibility* model transcends mostly in partial compliance with these soft standards because these standards though have global applicability yet can mobilize only a group of influential actors. Frequently, a number of jurisdictions embracing these standards have lesser, or at times, no significant contribution in the drafting processes – thus creating *democratic deficit* in IFL and its regulatory regimes. Analysis of these institutions reveals legitimacy deficit in the standard-formulation processes, representation imbalances in their membership, and skewed decision-making models. This is the third theme discussed here. If financial market stability is the uncontested optimal end, then IFL faces many inconsistencies on a number of fronts. Questioning these conceptual foundations of legitimacy and ingenuity of law forms the fourth theme.

§6.01 WHAT'S WRONG WITH THE WORLD OF FINANCE?

A common axiom is that markets foresee everything except crises. Another adage is that a risk is the most significant common denominator extant in all crises. Globalization has brought many advantages to the world especially to the world of finance, but among many not-so-good implications, systemic risk stands out as the most challenging as it continues to remain challenging: hard to foresee, difficult to contain and manage.

The *endless finance*, that is, finance based on perpetual postponement of payments is one of the primary obstacles to perpetual peace which could be secured through international cooperation, argued Kant. He further remarked that *it would be commerce to avoid war* through the formulation of a system of *perpetual alliances* to avoid war or to establish peace. The natural state is *a state of war and not a state of peace* and the persistence of *global financial imbalances* structurally vitiate the possibility of materializing a global political and economic peace. Interestingly, Kant's concern about peace is not divorced from finance. Peace can never be an automatic product of a scientific calculation or in any way a *natural state*. It is something that must be established, not through technical means or partial adjustments but has to be expressly established, so as to be adequate to what it must ensure. These certainly are the *lex latae* (and not *lex strictae*) conventions of warfare. The only difference the twenty-first century may have made in this *war and peace* implications from Kant's eighteenth century is that military terror of his time has now been eclipsed by economic seductions[2] rendering perpetual peace an eternally unrealizable dream.

In the post-Napoleonic era, nationalism and internationalism were considered as *soul-mates*. Mazower claimed[3] that this philosophy underpinned the creation of the EU which started in the 1950s with the Schuman Declaration proposing establishment of the ECSC.[4] However, by the mid-1980s after the establishment of the Bretton Woods system, faith in the precept that international cooperation and national sovereignty complement each other began to dwindle. Here again, the trigger was the liberalization of capital controls. The free flow of capital reversed the economic gains arising from international cooperation.[5]

More recently, when the financial oscillation of 1929 questioned market efficiency phenomenon and challenged its ability to exercise discipline, stringent policy measures (like the Glass-Steagull Act (GSA) was adopted in the US in 1933) were implemented. The GSA by narrowly defining the finance restrained financial activities into respective spheres in order to protect against risk spillovers. Roosevelt's financial package, also known as *regulatory capitalism,* while restraining finance aimed at separation of all three financial sectors i.e., banking, insurance and securities. The whole system of legislation was readopted from free market ideology to Keynesian

---

2. Kant, E. (1995). *Perpetual Peace: A Philosophical Sketch*. Hackett Publishing Company.
3. *See,* for an account of European political developments, Mazower, M. (2013). Governing the World: The History of an Idea, 1815 to the Present: Penguin Books.
4. The ECSC, the forerunner to the EU, was established by the Treaty of Paris in 1951 to unify European countries after World War II.
5. *See,* Ch. 2 for details.

model of command and control economy propagating a tough and closed system of regulation.

Amato and Fantacci[6] make a bold supposition about the aggrandized role of market and money in today's financial system believe that financial oscillations are not built into the system, hence, crises can be avoidable. For them, the only befitting way to enter into debtor/creditor relationship should be by assuming the risks it involves in the constitution of the financial institutions and financial transactions.[7] This coincides with the Islamic finance principle where the primacy of risk brackets and distribution forms an integral requirement (further discussed in subsequent text). For broader systemic stability, IFR needs to be redesigned in a fashion so to address the risk allocation factors to circumvent systemic risk repercussions.

Yet another dimension of internationalization (a direct result of globalization) is the fact that a number of international banks and financial institutions operate across the globe, including in developing countries, where their services provide key channels to local persons and businesses to access international finance. The 30 largest institutions around the world are deeply international, with 53% of their assets abroad, and have on an average 1,000 subsidiaries, of which 68% operate abroad and 12% in offshore financial centers.[8] However, an absence of international standards and codes on the regulation of bank size and cross-border resolution mechanism carries particular salience for regulators in both the developing and industrialized countries, as has become evident in the aftermath of the recent crisis.

The focus of the post-crisis reform is converging on maintaining systemic financial stability. Kant's *Peace* concern marked the eighteenth century as *nationalism* marked the 19th and the first half of the twentieth century. The last part of the twentieth century was marked by internationalization, globalization and deregulation (the *'tion'* regimes). The twenty-first century so far replete with crisis seems to be focusing on the theme of attaining stability. The questions are: *why and, how this transformation took place?* This section, while defining financial stability, links the debate to describe financial system as it exists now, and underpins the interrelationship of systemic risk and FML in the context of financial stability as the ultimate goal.

§6.02 FINANCIAL STABILITY: WHAT IS THIS UNDEFINED TERM?

Surprisingly, like the word terrorism, *international financial stability* has no clear definition. More commonly, it is defined by what it is not than by what it constitutes.

---

6. *See*, Amato, M., & Fantacci, L. (2012). The End of Finance. Polity Press.
7. Risk-sharing and risk-distribution as necessary pre-requisites to maintain international financial market stability. *See* details in Ch. 7.
8. ICMB. (2010). *A Safer World Financial System: Improving the Resolution of Systemic Institutions* (12). Retrieved from International Center for Monetary and Banking Studies & Centre for Economic Policy Research; Geneva Reports on the World Economy: available at http://personal.vu.nl/d.schoenmaker/Geneva12.pdf. *See also*, Claessens, S., Herring, R. J., & Schoenmaker, D. (2010). A Safer World Financial System: Improving the Resolution of Systemic Institutions. CEPR's Policy Portal, July 8. Retrieved from http://www.voxeu.org/article/safer-world-financial-system.

In simple and more frequently employed terms it has been defined as *an absence of major financial crises.*[9] Michael Foot suggests that there is no easy definition of financial stability except for a homely definition by Walter Bagehot in 1870s. To him, it would constitute financial stability when there is (a) monetary stability in a country, (b) employment level close to the economy's natural rate, which combines with (c) the confidence in independent operation of key financial institutions and of markets, and, (d) where there are no relative price movements of either real or financial assets within the economy that undermines (a) or (b).[10]

The Group of Ten (G10) defines financial stability as *a state when financial system environment [is] resilient to events that trigger a loss of economic value, confidence, or uncertainty to the extent that they will not have significant adverse effects on the real economy.*[11] Recently, under the new financial order, the definition of financial stability[12] has been expanded (due to a tremendous escalation of risk both in intensity and frequency of the crises) which now includes *normal operation* of financial intermediaries and markets, and, economic growth and development of the country as a whole.

The role of financial stability in maintaining a steady economy and therefore development, it has lately been classified in the category of *a public good.*[13] In the more recent literature financial stability has grown from a *homely* exercise to a much complex international concept. The concept may now be described as in which the financial system[14] (comprising of financial intermediaries, markets and market infrastructures) is capable of preventing disruptions and withstanding shocks in the financial intermediation processes which significantly impairs allocation of savings to profitable investment opportunities. Hence, a stable financial system: (a) allows an efficient and smooth transfer of resources from savers to investors, (b) provides a reasonable and an accurate risk pricing and its assessment, and, (c) has capacity to absorb financial and economically disruptive surprises.

---

9. Das, U. S., Quintyn, M., & Chenard, K. (May 2004). Does Regulatory Governance Matter for Financial System Stability? An Empirical Analysis. IMF Working Paper No. WP/04/89. Retrieved from http://www.imf.org/external/pubs/ft/wp/2004/wp0489.pdf.
10. Foot, M. (Apr. 3, 2003). What Is Financial Stability and How Do We Get It? The Roy Bridge Memorial Lecture. Available at http://www.fsa.gov.uk/library/communication/speeches/2003/sp122.shtml.
11. G10 Report, Consolidation in the Financial Sector, (2001). No. 126. Available at: http://www.imf.org/external/np/g10/2001/01/eng/index.htm.
12. Schinasi, G. J. (October 2004). Defining Financial Stability. IMF WP/04/187, International Capital Markets Department. Available at http://cdi.mecon.gov.ar/biblio/docelec/fmi/wp/wp04187.pdf.
13. Quintyn, M., & Taylor, M. (March 2002). *See also,* Shirakawa, M. (Oct. 14, 2012). [International financial stability as a public good. Keynote address by Governor of the Bank of Japan, at a high-level seminar, co-hosted by the Bank of Japan and the International Monetary Fund, Tokyo, available at http://www.bis.org/review/r121015c.pdf?frames=0].
14. The three parts of the financial system: Financial intermediaries, such as banks, insurance companies and other institutional investors that direct funds from those willing to invest/lend to those who want to borrow. Financial markets, where lenders and borrowers meet. Examples are money markets and stock exchanges, and through financial market infrastructures money and financial assets flow between buyers and sellers. Examples are payment systems and security settlement systems.

Understood this way, safeguarding of financial stability requires identifying the main sources of risk and vulnerability such as inefficiencies in the allocation of financial resources from savers to investors and the mispricing or mismanagement of financial risks.[15] Gari Schinasi defines financial stability as an ability to facilitate and enhance economic processes, manage risks and absorb shocks. He considers financial stability along *a continuum* which is changeable over time and is consistent with multiple combinations of the constituent elements of finance. In other words, *a financial system is in a range of stability whenever it is capable of facilitating (rather than impeding) the performance of an economy, and of dissipating financial imbalances that arise endogenously or as a result of significant adverse and unanticipated events.*[16]

Since the crisis in 2008, IFIs with newer mandates are promoting cooperation on global issues including on the transient nature of financial stability and related risks in the market. In doing so, the working has also brought to the fore many conflicting interests. Quintyn and Taylor have brought to prominence the important link between financial stability and regulatory and supervisory independence.[17] An uncertain or turbulent market condition (national or international) can pose significant obstacles to growth, development and even political and social stability of a country. Financial stability is a global public good as against financial instability which has been characterized as a *global public bad* because it spreads across countries through negative externalities and that collective action problems have led so far to an under provision of the international public good of financial stability. Given the large number, frequency, severity and higher societal as well as financial costs of recent crises, much emphasis in contemporary writing has been on combating the global public bad of financial instability.[18] Let's look at what ingredients are required to have functioning liberal financial markets and what actions normally a state undertakes in order to protect this freedom both in peace time as well in crises.

---

15. ECB. (December 2012). Financial Stability Review: European Central Bank, available at http://www.ecb.europa.eu/pub/pdf/other/financialstabilityreview201212en.pdf?fd9bfe9f040ef32a1195c0767d6427f3.
16. Schinasi, G. J. (October 2004). Defining Financial Stability. IMF WP, International Capital Markets Department, available at http://cdi.mecon.gov.ar/biblio/docelec/fmi/wp/wp04187.pdf, WP/04/187, p. 9. *See also*, Schinasi, G. J., & (June 2003). Responsibility of Central Banks for Stability in Financial Markets IMF Working Paper No 03/121, available at SSRN: http://ssrn.com/abstract=879197, 1-19.
17. Quintyn, M., & Taylor, M. (2002). Regulatory and Supervisory Independence and Financial stability. IMF WP/02/46. p. 8 Available at https://www.imf.org/external/pubs/ft/wp/2002/wp0246.pdf.
18. Financial stability is an especially crucial global public good. In 1975-1998, there were 244 significant international financial crises: 158 currency crises, 54 banking crises and 32 crises involving both currency and banking. Recent examples include the East Asian financial meltdown of 1997-1998, Russia's 1998 debt crisis and Turkey's 2001 currency crisis. The Argentine debt crisis shrank its national economy by 5%-10% in 2002, and hiked unemployment to over 20%. The cost of banking crises alone is at about USD 8 trillion since the late 1970s and this excludes the magnitude of losses from the Asian financial crisis and the 2008 crisis. *See*, briefing n. 3, UNDP report, available at http://web.undp.org/globalpublicgoods/globalization/pdfs/b-note3.pdf, *See* for details, Kaul, I., Conceição, P., Goulven, K. L., & Mendoza, R. U. (Eds.). (2003). *Providing Global Public Goods: Managing Globalization*. Oxford University Press.

In crude terms, financial liberalization constitutes a stronghold of finance capital over state and aims at liberating finance from the control of the state however, in praxis it is the state that acquiesce control on finance. Thus, state institutions (regulators, supervisors) remain skeptical of the growing reach of laisses-fair market.

A few indicators can reveal the extent of free market in a society and include variables such as:[19] (a) elimination of interest rate controls, an end to government-imposed differential interest rate schemes and, autonomy of the Central Bank from State's influence. Lowering of bank reserve requirements and independence of banks in their lending decisions, and abandonment of all priority sector lending targets make part and parcel of ensuring markets exercise their freedom. And, (b) privatized banks, with the removal of restrictions on the ownership of banks and an absence of nationally owned banks as well as ensuring freedom to foreign banks to compete in the market. That is, complete freedom of finance to move into and out of the economy, which implies full convertibility of currency,

In other words, financial liberalization implies greater access to international capital facilitated in part through an expanded role for foreign banks and nonbank financial institutions. Given this perspective, modern financial markets can be characterized by the following variables:

- markets marked with high capital mobility are *global* in nature only at the wholesale level but are at best, international at the retail level;
- fiercely *competitive* among financial services providers;
- *monetary system* based on floating rates between major currencies, and many other currencies have pegged their currencies to the major currencies through various mechanisms;
- Historical separation between financial services providers and actors kept at low;
- largely unrestricted and widely dispersed *capital flows*;
- frequent financial *crises* marked with strong contagions;
- risk as a major factor in monitoring and supervising regulatory activities affecting an increase in the costs for investors, regulators and financial institutions;
- innovative financial services and instruments marked by rising volume of derivative trade especially in Over-the-Counter (OTC) market, securitization, subprime mortgages and lending, along with a parallel revolution in technological advancements in computing, information technology and communications;
- regulated markets coexist with a large and liquid unregulated institutional market;
- extensive and rising international cooperation through financial and trade connectivity, development and cooperation;

---

19. Beim, D., & Calomiris, C. (2001). Emerging Financial Markets New York. McGraw-Hill.

- primarily driven by the EU, the WTO, the FSF/FSB, the European Bank for Reconstruction and Development (EBRD), the BIS and through its technical committees on banking, securities and related standards;
- liberalization and deregulation as the dominant philosophies under the WC (until the 2008 crisis), currently the emphasis on raising capital bars, sound risk management, liquidity provisions and reform of regulatory and legal institutions;
- In a struggle to create order through internationalization, integration and adoption of common policies despite the sheer fragmentation in interests following the prolonged recent recession. Markets are striving to standardize in particular the capital requirements and risk measurement strategies given more than 200 jurisdictions on the world map with distinct laws, supervisory practices, domestic regulatory standards and risk controls, legal systems, corporate and governance laws, and currencies and customs.

After the Great Depression, the financial sector, particularly (but not only) in the US was reregulated most notably by the GSA in 1933 which controlled the markets for the next 40 years. However, since the 1970s there has been far-reaching deregulation both at national and international levels. Capital mobility grew out of the collapse of the Bretton Woods institutions which eliminated cross-border capital controls. Since the 1980s, there have also been frequent and deep financial crises, both in the developing and the developed worlds. These crises have been extremely costly in terms of growth and development. Barry Eichengreen[20] and Reinhart and Kaminski have provided the staggering estimate that over the last quarter of a century, currency and banking crises have reduced incomes of developing countries by 25%. They established the correlation that problems in the banking sector typically *precede* a currency crisis which in turn not only deepens but also activates a vicious cycle of banking crisis, and FML often precedes banking crises. Anatomy of these episodes suggests that crises occur as an economy enters into recession following a prolonged boom in economic activity fuelled out of easy credit, capital inflows and an overvalued currency[21] elsewhere, Kaminsky and Schumukler studied *short-run but more painful consequences* of FML.[22]

---

20. Eichengreen, B. J. (2004). *Financial Development in Asia: The Way Forward*. Institute of Southeast Asian Studies.
21. See, for a deeper correlation between financial liberalization, capital inflows and problems in banking sector leading to economic crises; Kaminsky, G. L., & Reinhart, C. M. (June 1999). The Twin Crises: The Causes of Banking and Balance-of-Payments Problems. *The American Economic Review*, 89(3).
22. Literature before the GFC and onwards remains generally inconclusive in categorizing financial liberalization as a positive good, however, post-GFC regulatory reforms indicate the necessity to put into practice appropriate regulatory tools to channel financial liberalization. See, for positive correlations; Kaminsky, G., & Schumukler, S. (2003). Short-Run Pain, Long-Run Gain: The Effects of Financial Liberalization. NBER Working Paper No. 9787, available at http://www.nber.org/papers/w9787.pdf, See also, Bekaert, G., Harvey, C. R., & Lundblad, C. (July 2005). Does Financial Liberalization Spur Growth? *Journal of Financial Economics, Elsevier*, 77(1), 3-55, available at http://ideas.repec.org/p/nbb/reswpp/200405-200409.html.

Since, the crises in the 1990s mostly remained limited to the emerging markets invariably the causes were rooted mostly in institutional weaknesses of these markets. Not surprisingly, reforms in that era combined placing systemic risk controls along with the institution-building efforts in those economies.

In contrast, the crisis in 2008 remained exclusive to the developed economies with sophisticated financial and support institutions and necessary systemic risk controls in place. The reforms warranted for the first time a redirection. *We must not let financial regulation slip off the policy agenda. We simply cannot carry on with the financial sector that gave us the GFC crisis,* remarked the Managing Director of the IMF.[23] For the 2008 crisis, once again, this time is different[24] and as much for the causes of the crisis which calls for strenuous remedies and reforms. The crisis consists precisely in the fact that the old is dying and the new cannot be born; in this interregnum a great variety of morbid.[25]

§6.03 CONTEMPORARY CRITICAL ISSUES IN IEL

[A] IFL and the Conflict of Laws

It is imperative to see how IFL (governing financial markets among nations) positions under the umbrella of IEL (governing economic relations among nations). This is an inclusive field and encompasses a vast array of interests[26] ranging from public international law of trade to private international law of trade to certain aspects of international commercial law and the law of international finance and investment. IEL is conceptualized primarily from a cosmopolitan citizen's perspective as a system of norms and legal practices to promote not only economic efficiency and sustainable development but also to comply with human rights obligations of the UN Member

---

23. Lagarde, C. (Jan. 23, 2012). Global Challenges in 2012. Speech by the MD IMF. Berlin. Available at http://www.imf.org/external/np/speeches/2012/012312.htm.
24. Reinhart, C. M., & Rogoff, K. S. (2009). This Time Is Different: Eight Centuries of Financial Folly. Princeton University Press.
25. Gramsci, A. (1971). Selections from the Prison Notebooks. (editors: Quentin Hoare and Geoffrey Nowell Smith). Elec Book. Available at http://courses.justice.eku.edu/pls330_louis/docs/gramsci-prison-notebooks-vol1.pdf.
26. An attempt at defining IEL would broadly conceive it as a field of international law that encompasses the conduct of sovereign states in international economic relations, as well as the conduct of private parties involved in cross-border economic and business transactions. This also includes, among other things, international trade law, law of international financial institutions or IFL, and traditional private international law fields. IEL Law Interests Group of the American Society of International Law (ASIL) includes the following non-exhaustive fields under IEL: (1) International Trade Law, (2) International Economic Integration Law, (3) Private International Law, (4) International Business Regulation – which includes antitrust or competition law, environmental regulation and product safety regulation, (5) IFL – inclusive of private transactional law, regulatory law, the law of foreign direct investment and international monetary law, that is, the law of the International Monetary Fund and the World Bank, (6) Law and Development, (7) International Tax Law and (8) International Intellectual Property Law.

States and a democratic self-government.[27] Petersmann criticizes traditional power-oriented Westphalian conceptions of international law among sovereign states which fails to protect citizens against widespread abuses of foreign policy clouts and undersupply of international public goods.[28] To replace Westphalian law, Petersmann urges for a paradigm shift[29] and builds case for a new *cosmopolitan theory* of the IEL[30] in which IEL is *defined and legitimized* in conformity with the human rights obligations of the UN Member States.[31] Petersmann also calls for *constitutionalizing the IEL*.[32] For him, a major task of a cosmopolitan theory of IEL is to go beyond regulating national self-interest and relations among state agents by extending constitutional safeguards to citizens for their transnational economic cooperation.[33] He presses the case for IEL to be conceived as a *layered, multilevel legal order* based on *respect for legitimate constitutional pluralism*.[34] In another recent research, Cervone explores prospects for harmonization and development of global standards given the context of current regime fragmentation and individual rule-making. Accordingly, to her, harmonization in international law could be achieved easier in an era of deregulation by reaching agreement on a low common denominator.[35] While keeping an in-depth focus on global standards for CRAs, her scholarship however, goes beyond the specificities of jurisdiction, technical capacity and differing levels of financial development to the extraterritorial effects of various financial rules (by analyzing the EU regulation and its extraterritorial effects) and conflict-of-laws-literature.

While talking of conflict of laws, we cannot ignore the IFI's case of privileged exceptionalism. The IFIs have a dual character in discharging their public purposes and transactions commercial in nature. These intergovernmental organizations are created by their Member States collectively for a public purpose. The IFIs draw their authority and mandate from an international agreement to which their member institutions and states are a party. As the subjects of international law, the rights and obligations arise from applicable public international law principles and at the same time these organizations engage in financial transactions which despite their public purposes by nature are akin to market-based financial transactions. Unfortunately, an absence of appropriate principles of international public law to address such legal situations dealing with the dual character of the IFIs gives rise to many ambiguities.[36] On the one hand, IFIs as international organizations clearly fall under the domain of international

---

27. Steve, C. (2014). International Economic Law in the 21st Century. Constitutional Pluralism and Multilevel Governance of Interdependent Public Goods. By Ernst-Ulrich Petersmann. *Journal of International Economic Law*. p. 14.
28. *Ibid.* p. 11.
29. *Ibid.* p. 2.
30. *Ibid.* p. 24.
31. *Ibid.* p. 302.
32. *Ibid.* p. 437.
33. *Ibid.* p. 24.
34. *Ibid.* p. 497.
35. Cervone, E. (2015). Credit Rating Agencies: The Development of Global Standards. In, C. L. Lim., & B. Mercurio. (Eds.). *International Economic Law after the Global Crisis: A Tale of Fragmented Disciplines*, Cambridge University Press. p. 46.
36. Bradlow, D. D., & Hunter, D. (Eds.). (2010). *International Law and the Operations of the International Financial Institutions*. Kluwer Press. Ch. 1, p. 1.

law and hence are accountable for compliance to applicable international legal regime, while at the same time, IFIs insist that not all the customary law principles are applicable to them hence they are not obligated to comply with the treaties they are not signatories to. This *privileged exceptionalism* is gets compounded when IFIs claim extensive immunity under domestic legal regimes.[37]

In short, IFIs produce set of rules, standards and practices under the realm of IFL which governs international financial markets and transactions.[38] Again the prime objective of the law here is to ensure smooth supply of an important international public good, that is, market stability. This international public good endeavors the test of local and national jurisdictions, where each state follows its own governance standards best suited to pursue its national interests, challenged by the conflict of international commitments and of domestic priorities. This is furthered by challenges from increasing globalization, technological development and financial innovation (which is neither linear nor same across states) and this multiplicity and variance in conditions render conceiving universal standards a formidable task and its enforcement and compliance even more menacing. Another challenge arises from the fact that the financial institutions are international in life but become national in death.[39] As we saw the chaos in the collapse of the Northern Rock, and later the Lehman Brothers, the cost of rescue got to be borne ultimately by home-country national authorities.[40] For resolution of crises which affect global markets, a coherent approach needs to be adopted like the EU did in the case of European Common Market by establishing the Colleges of Supervisors[41] for coordinated crisis management.

As far as the purpose of IEL is concerned, it is to help governments and individuals overcome market failure, government failure and particularly to facilitate undersupply of public goods to both. One of the most essential public good includes the availability of international institutions for the collective supply of interdependent international public goods. International financial stability is a public good (as discussed above) and financial instability falls under the category public bad, IEL therefore, aims to ensure supply of international financial stability through its network of international institutions. These institutions act as a fourth branch of government which – like the other three branches, i.e., legislative, administrative and judicial –

---

37. *Ibid.* p. 388.
38. *See*, Wood, P. R. (2008). *Law and Practice of International Finance*. Sweet and Maxwell. *See also*, Bamford, C. (2011). *Principles of International Financial Law* (1 ed.). Oxford University Press. *See also*, Scott, H. S. (Dec. 15, 2005). An Overview of International Finance: Law and Regulation, available at http://papers.ssrn.com/sol3/papers.cfm?abstract_id=800627. *See*, Scott, H. S., & Wellons, P. A. (2010). International Finance: Transactions, Policy, and Regulation (17 ed.). Foundation Press.
39. Mervyn King famously remarked in 2009, *Global banks are global in life but national in death*.
40. FSF. (April 2008). *Report of the FSF on Enhancing Market and Institutional Resilience*. Retrieved from http://www.financialstabilityboard.org/wp-content/uploads/r_0804.pdf?page_moved=1 last accessed Aug. 21, 2015.
41. Under the EU law, colleges of supervisors have to be established for EEA banks with subsidiaries or significant branches in other EEA countries. They may include supervisors in non-EEA countries, where relevant. The initiative has been taken in the EU but must be replicated at global level.

require constitutional constraints and democratic legitimation.[42] Essentially, international treaties and agreements need to be translated into domestic legislation to ensure enforcement of such agreements.

For economists, international finance traditionally implies *a study of exchange rates*, however, to policy makers and lawyers it has always meant much more.[43] Generally, it involves a study of international financial transactions (transactions that have some cross-border element with respect to payment, credit or investment) or involve a financial contract.[44] Zooming in on IFL reveals that IFL is an area of modern law which can be treated as a separate discipline. It represents an area of law subject to a set of rules which, taken together, are not merely the sum total of national legal rules (nor simply the sum total, for example, of the recognized rules of Public International Law).[45] Notwithstanding the countless counts of fragmented streams within IFL's gambit of international standards, this specific area of law is one that possesses an underlying unifying theme, method and approach which is identifiable and distinctive to it, though not necessarily exclusive.

[B] Consolidating the Discipline: Is it a Good Idea?

The question is how deeply this specific area of law with a unifying underlying theme is fragmented from within? We find a real case of fragmentation in IFL especially in matters of (state) authority,[46] and in matters ascertaining a concerted line of action (especially in times of crisis for regulatory content) due to an uneven normative and institutional development in inter-state relations. The voluntary compliance operational model common to IFL institutional norms remained generally weak except in situations where it triggered the formation of a consensus on application of minimum standards – for example, at the Basel Committee, the G20 and at the FSB in developing global common standards on the supervision of financial markets. The process of harmonizing minimum standards needs to be organic and should continuously evolve to respond, adapt and expand to encompass newer financial market developments. For example, the first step towards a consolidated DGS in the EU could involve devising the scheme (which was a hot issue in the late 1990s in response to the Asian crisis) as one of the structural conditionality providing a way out from a banking crisis facing the union members.[47] The positive inferences from extraterritoriality of EU regulation on credit rating standards have been documented in a recent research which found that:

---

42. Steve, *Supra* n. 27.
43. Scott, Dec. 15, 2005. *Supra* n. 38, p. 1.
44. *Ibid.*
45. *See,* for IFL as an academic and professional discipline, Sebastianutti, P. (2009). What Is This Thing Called International Financial Law? *Law and Financial Markets Review, 3*(1), 64-71. Retrieved from http://search.informit.com.au/documentSummary;dn=710655244810779;res=IELHSS.
46. A good read on authority fragmentation, *See,* C. L. Lim., & Mercurio, B. (Eds). 2015. *International Economic Law after the Global Crisis: A Tale of Fragmented Disciplines*, Cambridge University Press.
47. Fischer, S. (2001). *The International Financial System: Crises and Reform*. The Robbin Lectures at the LSE, London, Oct. 29-31, 2001.

[t]he equivalence regime introduced by the EU Regulation on CRAs enhanced the benefits of equivalence as a form of mutual recognition of regulatory standards among countries and, generally, recognition of compliance with global standards. The extraterritorial effects of the EU Regulation (accompanied by robust additional requirements for certification of third-country credit ratings to be used in the EU) may then lead to stronger global standards in the industry.[48]

[1] Consolidation and Arbitrage

An appreciable degree of legal uncertainty has been described by liberal political scholars like Max Weber (who considered it one key condition for the success of a capitalist economy) however, the existing regulatory regimes are not very helpful in this regard. The current regulatory standards, rules and legislation (if any) produce regulation which is mostly vague at its best. In addition to being vague, inconsistent implementation and adoption leads to inconsistent expectations, outcomes and risk profiles. This raises serious questions on the complexity of existing legal and policy tradition. The increasing complexity of financial markets and intricate financial products cause equally complex regulatory regimes (resulting into even more uncertainty and thereby arbitrage opportunities) however, it is important to note a few subtle distinctions.

First, markets act much faster than their counterpart regulators and supervisors, thus setting regulators in a *frisbee-catching* exercise (which is hard to master, see Chapter 4). Therefore, it is not uncommon to find complex regulation becoming obsolete in almost no time.[49] Second, that financial institutions and often financial products have become not only international but also global, whereas regulators almost invariably remain essentially local or domestic in their method, approach and jurisdictions. Another mostly overlooked peculiarity of the regulatory standards is that not all of them are shaped by, or are necessarily in response to market initiatives. A correlated fact to be discounted is that not many regulations are designed for universal applicability, thereby creating natural arbitrage opportunities. Also, not all the jurisdictions follow same rules for similar range of financial instruments and hence, such business activities fall naturally outside the scope of IFR even if these have been consented to by the respective jurisdiction. Another important challenge lies in fragmented approaches to regulate nuances in financial products. Banking crises are serious issues. The run on banks ensued by financial crisis requires immediate and effective control measures because of their inherent contagious nature. The extent of deposit insurance or LoLR responsibility assumed by central banks needs to be spelled out clearly along with response time.[50]

---

48. Cervone, *supra* n. 35 p. 71.
49. Capital reserve requirements under the Basel III were found to be insufficient for G-SIFIs so FSB suggested a higher shock absorbing cushions for G-SIFIs in addition to having in place recovery and resolution plans (the living wills).
50. For the Northern Rock in September 2007, and the Lehman Brothers a delayed response affected the course and the outcome of the crisis deeply. *See*, Arner, D. W. (2009). The Global Credit Crisis of 2008: Causes and Consequences. The International Lawyer, 43, 91-136.

For cross-border wholesale and investment banks, the Financial Services Authority (FSA) and most of the other regulators were following an approach that assumed primary responsibility for ensuring prudential soundness with the home-country supervisors. One of the underlying causes of the GFC was the divergence between domestic regulatory structures and that of the global finance.[51] Failure in international coordination can lead to duplication of processes and efforts apart from setting the stage for regulatory arbitrage. The resolution framework for handling failed financial institutions needs to take into account the multinational structure of these institutions. Clearing houses and exchanges for derivatives need to handle internationally traded derivatives which may be subject to different requirements in different countries.[52] Securitized debt markets are global and thus standards for origination and disclosure as well as regulation of CRAs require global coordination. Not to mention that convergence is imminent between the US Generally Accepted Accounting Standards (GAAP) and IFRS to address the accounting treatment gaps in various financial markets for similar financial instruments. The time is ripe to ensure greater global coordination.[53] States must work together to avoid cross-border harms that are not fully taken into account in national decision-making to avoid detrimental regulatory arbitrage In order for each state to reduce risk through regulatory reform.

[2]   The US Case

Fragmented regulators in the US are not a product of careful design but something that has evolved in layers of accretion since the Civil War.[54] After the 1929 financial crisis, Roosevelt's regulatory capitalism[55] separated financial sectors i.e., banking, insurance and securities by separating control and regulation of these industries (perforated controls by the regulators were considered part of the problem in the GFC of 2008). Subsequently, the Dodd-Frank Act and Volcker's Package were brought in order to further redress the regulatory gaps; however, these legislations were primarily domestic in jurisdiction and influence. For finance, which became an international subject after the 1970s, the US continued to preserve its unique domestic market system and regulatory preferences irrespective of the various initiatives taken by Basel Committees.

The report by the Committee on Capital Market Regulation[56] claims that it has survived largely unchanged, despite repeated unsuccessful efforts at reform, not because it has been functional or effective but because it has served the interests of

---

51. FSF. *Supra* n. 40 p. 11.
52. *See*, Botched rescue of Fortis, Icelandic Banks, Ch. 5.
53. Hubbard, R. G., Thornton, J. L., & Scott, H. S. (May 2009). The Global Financial Crisis: A Plan for Regulatory Reform: A Report by the Committee on Capital Markets Regulation. P. vi.
54. CCMR. (May 2009). *The Global Financial Crisis: A Plan for Regulatory Reform*. Retrieved from http://capmktsreg.org/app/uploads/2014/07/TGFC-CCMR_Report_5-26-09.pdf last accessed, Aug. 19, 2015.
55. Wood, *Supra* n. 38.
56. CCMR *supra* n. 54, P.v.

industry, regulators and politicians,[57] while failing the national economic interest of the American public. The Committee's statement of January 14, 2009 entitled, Recommendations for Reorganizing the US Regulatory Structure, proposed a new *consolidated* structure comprising the Fed, US Financial Services Authority, the Treasury Department and possibly a consumer and investor protection agency while believing that risk from future financial crises would be substantially slashed. Since *global crises demand a global solution*,[58] coordination with other national regulators and cooperation with regional and international authorities will be required for any effective crisis resolution mechanism to work. Whether there is a genuine need to harmonize legal nods for cross-jurisdiction financial products and transaction remains a valid question for the experts. The practice of pigeonholing the financial sector institutions needs to be revised because the cross–sector risk transfer mechanisms are on an increase more than ever due to the growth of risks in the derivatives and hedge markets.[59] The authorities responsible to maintain financial stability need to attend to the dynamics of the overall system.

[3]   Consolidation Through Increased Regulation?

The post-GFC analytics reveal that the most precarious sectors of our financial system were already subject to a great deal of regulation, albeit woefully *ineffective* implementation. Hence, an enhanced regulatory ambit or increased government's control of the markets would not redress the wrongs. According to the more popular stance, market outcomes should not be overridden unless there is a specific justification for government regulation, such justifications may include: (a) externalities (the most important being systemic risk), (b) correction of information asymmetries, (c) principal-agent problems, (d) preservation of competition and (e) limitation of moral hazard arising from government support of the financial system.[60] In practice however, the demarcations where such interventions are justifiable are often more fluid.

Yet another factor to consider is incremental cost of regulation. On the policy making front, any increase in the cost of a financial service (or a product) to a consumer in any jurisdiction needs to be taken into account while drafting universally applicable standards. Any new regulation needs to be promulgated only when its benefits outweigh its costs (and at the least possible cost).[61] Ms Lagarde pointed out that the banks are spending millions to kill some of the new regulations they consider

---

57. *Ibid.* p. 17.
58. *Ibid.* p. 19.
59. Paul Tucker, Deputy Governor Bank of England.
60. This recommendation is broadly similar to reforms proposed in: *Special report on Regulatory Reform: Modernizing the American Financial Regulatory System, Recommendations for Improving Over-sight, Protecting Consumers, and Ensuring Stability.* (2009). Retrieved from Congressional Oversight Panel, January 2009: https://www.sec.gov/comments/4-579/4579-24.pdf last accessed Aug. 19, 2015.
61. *See, Ibid. See also,* CRMPG. (August 2008). Containing Systemic Risk: The Road to Reform. Retrieved from http://www.crmpolicygroup.org/docs/CRMPG-III.pdf last accessed, Aug. 21, 2015.

burdensome[62] (both to comply with and to their customers) in order to stay competitive in the markets where cost of the same product varies. Some critics, however, believe that the increased regulatory costs to the market are nothing compared to the costs that the world had to pay putting together those seven years of crisis since 2008.[63]

In matters of enforcement, domestic political institutions have an advantage over the IFIs. It is hard for unelected central bankers and regulators to wield power on politically elected office bearers. Although Keynes tenaciously expected that ideas would retain preeminence over power politics but the issues of power are hard to circumvent when it comes to economic paradigms and market interests.[64] Mainstream economics stubbornly denies a bigger role to power dialectics. The policy paradigm and institutions within which the current global crisis is being addressed reflect power structures of the past which are now under mounting pressure to transform. Many have argued, for example, that the current crisis ensued as consequence of neoliberal ideology[65] which had also conditioned the mainstream analysis of the crisis as well as the policy responses in a complex way.[66] To many, the mainstream analysis has not only significantly failed (in predicting and analyzing the crisis) but also provides scanty theoretical justification of the interventions made in the early stages of the crisis.[67] And bankers are not the only ones who failed us advocating for less regulation in pursuit of their selfish interests but also the economists who monopolized the dogmatic theorization of financial capitalism and have failed both in providing logical explanation of the crisis as well as in admittance of their inability to do so. Amato and Fantacci raise an interesting point, that those who have been instrumental in creating the problem are being asked to find solutions.[68] This definitely demands rethinking of the issues.

---

62. Hodgson, J., & Sibonney, C. (2012, October 25). IMF's Lagarde Urges Action on Unfinished Financial Reforms. *Reuters*. Business News. Retrieved from http://www.reuters.com/article/2012/10/26/us-imf-lagarde-idUSBRE89P00420121026, last accessed Jul. 14, 2017.
63. Up to 2012 – which makes it 6th year of the crisis that began in 2008 – more than 200 million people lost their job; the US and the EU GDP remained 10%-15% lower compared to the figures if there were no crisis; international trade has declined by more than 30%. These figures have been taken from various statistical websites including: Trade liberalization statistics, available at http://www.gatt.org/trastat_e.html (accessed Aug. 21, 2015); *See*, Losing Jobs: The real impact of the Economic Crisis (2009), available at http://www.waronwant.org/media/losing-jobs-real-impact-economic-crisis (last accessed Aug. 15, 2015); and, *Rethinking Poverty*. (2009). Retrieved from Department of Economic and Social Affairs, UN: http://www.un.org/esa/socdev/rwss/docs/2010/fullreport.pdf (last accessed, Aug. 22, 2015).
64. Keynes, J. M. (1936). *The General Theory of Employment, Interest and Money*. Macmillan; reprint 1973, Collected Writings, vol. VII.
65. *See*, for example, Palma, J. G. (2009). The Revenge of the Market on the Renters. Why Neo-liberal Reports of the End of History Turned Out to Be Premature. *Cambridge Journal of Economics, 33*(4), 829-869.
66. *See*, Callinicos, A. (2012). Contradictions of Austerity. *Cambridge Journal of Economics, 36*(1), 65-77.
67. *See*, Dow, A., & Dow, S. (2013). Economic History and Economic Theory: The Staples Approach to Economic Development. *Cambridge Journal of Economics. 38*(6), 1339-1353. *See also*, on lack of theoretical scholarship on institutions, Allen, F., & Carletti, E. (2013). New Theories to Underpin Financial Reform. *Journal of Financial Stability, 9*. Available at http://finance.wharton.upenn.edu/~allenf/download/Vita/new%20theories%20to%20underpin%20published.pdf.
68. Amato & Fantacci *Supra* n. 6.

The universally applicable principle of Basel risk-weighting capital requirements seems prudent yet it incentivizes institutions to structure the asset side of their balance sheets in such a way as to minimize the use of capital resulting in hiding risks under the complexity of various financial structures. Such a cycle of increasing complexity raises both compliance costs and enforcement costs.[69] Alternatively, higher capital requirements based on the leverage ratio, as opposed to overly complex risk-weighting schemes, might lower both compliance and enforcement costs while achieving similar or better outcomes in terms of the safety and soundness of individual institutions as well as overall financial stability. Thus question comes down to smarter regulation and not necessarily more regulation.

The idea of smarter regulation however raises another question: whether uniformity of standards and consolidated regulation is more valuable and cost effective? In the EU as a remedial action it is now expected from the Colleges of Supervisors to resolve conflicting responsibilities between home and host-country supervisors. Generally, conflicts between home and host supervisors are legion and may impose heavy compliance costs on internationally active banks and can add to competitive distortions, thereby jeopardizing financial stability.[70] Increased complexity in itself hinders consistent and uniform enforcement of regulatory standards and rules. Gaps in regulatory effectiveness provide arbitrage opportunity as well as add uncertainty to the regulator's behavior, hence undermining both the effectiveness of the financial system and credibility of the regulatory regimes. Here, we explore essential links between financial stability and financial system's architectural design and find inconsistency in regulatory enforcement as the most challenging menace.

§6.04 SELECT STRUCTURAL INCONSISTENCIES IN IFL: RETHINKING ALTERNATIVES

[A] The Soft-Law of International Finance

[1] Understanding the Soft Law

Joseph Gold comments that the most essential ingredient of soft law is an expectation that states accepting these instruments will take their content seriously. A few important postulates of soft law may include: (a) a common intent implicit in soft law as it is formulated and this common intent, when elucidated, is to be respected, (b) a soft law when promulgated, its legitimacy is not challenged, (c) a soft law not deprived

---

69. Plosser, C. I. (Apr. 8, 2014). Simplicity, transparency, and market discipline in regulatory reform. Presented by the President of the FRB, Philadelphia, at the conference *Enhancing Prudential Standards in Financial Regulations*, at Wharton Financial Institutions Centre and the Journal of Financial Services Research. Available at http://www.bis.org/review/r140409b.htm p.2.
70. Herring, R. J. (2007). Conflicts Between Home & Host Country Prudential Supervisors. In D. D. Evanoff, G. G. Kaufman & J. R. LaBrosse (Eds.), *International Financial Instability: Global Banking and National Regulation*. World Scientific Publishing Co. Available at http://fic.wharton.upenn.edu/fic/papers/07/0733.pdf last accessed, Aug. 17, 2015.

of its quality as law due to a failure to observe it and (d) a conduct that respects soft law cannot be deemed invalid.[71]

Based on the above postulations, existence of collective intent is a *must* condition among the parties constituting to observe and implement (soft-law-based) principles. Second, presence of a desire within the parties to transform these principles into hard law is a must. The basic ingredient is the legitimacy that is derived from the collective intent of the parties adopting such standard. It would therefore be illegitimate, for a state to be expected to comply with a standard if its consent was not obtained during the drafting process. Unfortunately, it is the legitimacy, i.e., the collective intent of all stakeholders to do or to undo a change and which constitutes the basic ingredient is mostly missing from the soft-law-based IFRA and therefore, raises many doubts on the adequacy of this framework. Main elements of a hard-law-based legal system on the other hand includes: (a) precision of rules, (b) degree of obligation and (c) delegation of authority for adjudicating compliance, and sanctions and enforcement.[72]

Referring to Seidl-Hohenveldern's lectures, Gold remarked that the distinctive characteristic of soft law in relation to economic matters appears to be an intended vagueness of the obligations that it imposes. This kind of law can be obtained in treaties or in other instruments whether or not adopted under the authority of a treaty that shows the softness of their contents by such titles as guidelines or declaration of principles. Soft law comprises of:[73] (a) expectation, that the states shall take the contents seriously, (b) a common intent, both implicit and respected. Here, it is important to distinguish that for a state to be expected to comply with a standard – if its consent was not obtained beforehand – will be considered illegitimate (next section brings forth the question of legitimacy where non-Member States are not represented in the decision-making or standard-setting stage, but later are expected or forced through market discipline, competition and reputational risk elements to observe such standards), (c) legitimacy, of the law itself is not challenged, (d) quality of law, a failure to observe it is not in itself a breach of obligation and (e) a conduct respecting soft law, cannot be deemed invalid.

In a similar fashion, Zaring outlines a six-point framework that makes IFR function despite the absence of an enforcement and court system in the existing IFL. Accordingly, a national treatment principle (i.e., a principle of nondiscrimination between national and foreign financial institutions); a most-favored nation (MFN) principle (not explicitly stated though yet these networks have made an explicit commitment to MFN) – these two are the substantive pillars of GFR; a preference for rule-making (the third operational pillar of GFR) over adjudication; a subsidiary

---

71. Gold, J. (July 1983). Strengthening the Soft International Law of Exchange Arrangements. *American Journal of International Law, 77*, 443-489. Retrieved from https://litigation-essentials.lexisnexis.com/webcd/app?action = DocumentDisplay&crawlid = 1&doctype = cite&docid = 77 + A.J.I.L. + 443&srctype = smi&srcid = 3B15&key = 19414869f627648522a95539eaabe4c2.
72. Wellens, K., & Borchardt, G. (1989). Soft Law in European Community Law. *European Law Review, 14*(5). Abbott, K. W., Keohane, R. O., Moravcsik, A., Slaughter, A.-M., & Snidal, D. (2000). The Concept of Legalization. *International Organization, 54*(3), 401-419. For elements of a legal system, *see*, Alexander, K., Dhumale, R., & Eatwell, J. (2006). *Global Governance of Financial Systems: The International Regulation of Systemic Risk*. Oxford University Press.
73. Gold, *supra* n. 71. p. 443.

principle of enforcement (closer to the EU model); a peer-reviewed model of enforcement (subsidiary and paired with peer review for oversight over domestic application of the soft law); and finally a network model of institutionalization are the factors that make IFL work on the pattern of a legal system despite the fact that the intent behind the soft law as well as the initiators do not act with the force of law.[74]

While talking of the last principle of the network model, international rules (standards, guidelines, best practices) for IFL are primarily fashioned by administrative agencies and not by the heads of state (as is the case of the WTO, where technically the experts design rules and or treaties, while the heads of states negotiate for enactment) which is in stark contrast to the practice with IFL. Domestic regulatory authorities are responsible for enacting the laws, standards and procedures of enforcement in their home jurisdictions and for oversight (partly due to the technical expertise needed and to fulfill domestic legislative mandate). The WTO has become a mature legal regime and largely avoids those structural deficiencies which IFL more commonly cannot avoid. IFL from the outset lacked supportive institutional base. After the end of the Gold Standard era, the decade of 1930s welcomed liberalization initiatives, and financial markets witnessed tremendous developments albeit unaccompanied by a parallel development of supportive regulatory and supervisory frameworks.

[2]   The Dialectics of Hard Law

IFRs have always been conceptualized as soft law[75] based on the laissez-faire principle. The formal process starts off from an informal negotiation among the Central Bank governors and finance authorities of various countries to build a mutually agreed framework for a particular segment of financial product. It involves consultations with the stakeholders (the shareholders of banks and financial institutions, legal and technical experts). Historically, the evolutionary process of developing a regulatory framework continued taking various forms in various jurisdictions however, each time shaped by a major politico-financial affair. For example, in the UK, it was a customary convention-based system, run by the *raised eye-brow*[76] of the BoE. Later, it was the supervisory approach backed by force of *moral suasion*[77] and *supervisory best practices*[78] from time to time. Strong respect and adherence to the convention system provided necessary sanction to the success of the *force of example* principle in the UK. On the other hand, at the global level, internationally agreed *high standards* based on

---

74. Zaring, D. (2012). Finding Legal Principles in Global Financial Regulation. *Virginia Journal of International Law.* 52. pp. 683-722.
75. Soft law is based on the precept of implementing and adopting nonbinding standards of IFRA. See for discussion on how it works, Arner, D. W. (2007). *Financial Stability, Economic Growth and the Role of Law.* Cambridge University Press.
76. In old days, Bank of England's raised eyebrow used to serve the purpose of regulating financial institutions. However, this force of *convention* got eroded gradually by the slush of foreign financial institutions in the UK who were not accustomed to abide by the strong convention-based system as was prevalent in the UK.
77. Unwritten rules of the city of London based on consultation, persuasion and informal dialogue.
78. The original principle came forth from the *Cassis de Dijon* case Judgment of the European Court of Justice, February 1979, EC reports 1979.

voluntary adoption prevailed in the regulatory and supervisory spheres.[79] More recently, the pressure created by the credit ratings of sovereigns and other financial institutions have created another kind of sanction by the rating agencies. The 2008 crisis however, shattered the credibility attached to the rating agencies).[80]

Unlike the realm of other subfields of international law, for example, human rights law or more specifically within related fields under trade or monetary law, the structure of IFL lacks basic instruments of formality like treaties, or contractual obligations. The only mechanism engendering *compliance pull emanates from reputational costs* as the rational-choice theorists of PIL have distinguished it from soft-power theorists (under which soft law is essentially a coordinating and cooperation tool), and from the characterization of the use of the soft law as *a risk mitigation device* (contractarian analysis).[81] Most of the soft law sources being of informal quality facilitate negotiating agreements between regulators and thereby, to an extent control the costs of (and also of benefits) such legal standards.[82] The costs of experimenting with hard-law instruments can be harsh and astronomical due to the complexities involved in enforcement as well as of winding back such treaties as we can see in the case of the EU, the costs of the Brexit may outweigh the costs of staying in for the British.

The defining characteristic of IFL is the absence of a legal instrument to seek observance. The absence of consequences and legal repercussions in instances of noncompliance to such soft law affords regulators to cherry-pick aspects of best practices, international commitments, and important obligations for a responsible behavior. The ultimate effect of this voluntary adoption and cherry-picking creates opportunities for arbitrage and a near absence of coordination in regulations for cross-border institutions.

Theoretically, employing a soft law mechanism is a unique tool of mobilizing low-cost international coordination on important issues of global finance and its regulation. A strong argument in favor of soft law approach to IFL has always prevailed[83] based on the low compliance cost advantages that it offers. However, looking at the magnitude of what financial crises have cost to the world, the implementation cost of hard law seems negligible if translated in its dollar value. Kenneth Abbot and Duncan Snidal underscore that legalization is a tool that enhances

---

79. Kaufman, H. (Apr. 28, 2009). How Libertarian Dogma Led the Fed Astray. *Financial Times*. Retrieved from http://economistsview.typepad.com/economistsview/2009/04/libertarian-dogma-and-the-fed.html.
80. Taleb, N. N. (2007). *The Black Swan-The Impact of the High Improbable*. Random House. As Taleb explains, Black Swan is a highly improbable event with three principal characteristics being: unpredictable, carries a massive impact, and, after the fact, we concoct an explanation that makes it appear less random, and more predictable, than it was. For example, the astonishing success of Google was a black swan.
81. *See*, Brummer, C. (2012). *Soft Law and the Global Financial System: Rule-Making in the 21st Century*. Cambridge University Press. p. 124.
82. Brummer, C. (2011). How International Financial Law Works (and How it doesn't). *Georgetown Law Journal*, 99, 257-261.
83. *See*, for example, Raban, O. (Jun. 14, 2009). The Fallacy of Legal Certainty: Why Vague Legal Standards May Be Better for Capitalism and Liberalism. *Boston University Public Interest Law Journal*, 19(175). available at http://papers.ssrn.com/sol3/papers.cfm?abstract_id = 1419683.

credibility by increasing the costs of reneging.[84] Earlier on, hard commitments encoded at the Bretton Woods Conference were thought to be necessary as the soft arrangements during the War years proved inadequate. Simmons made a forceful point that *legalization strengthens commitment*.[85] As mentioned earlier, regulators are both *competitors and partners* with the international financial system therefore, such an absence of enforcement authority creates disparate costs and benefits to the otherwise equal members of the system. Also, regulators *self-enforce* only what incentivizes their domestic financial markets as against anything which could be otherwise detrimental to the international financial market stability.

Irrespective of any advantages and disadvantages of hard law, the most important contribution that hard law can make in regulatory sphere is in its inherent ability to contribute to institution building. The financial system so far, favors the rich banks in the developed countries at the expense of the poor in the poor countries. It is the unique role of law that protects the unprivileged. The IFL, although it is called law has no binding force, no formal compliance and accountability mechanism to solicit respect and compliance from all Member States equally. Its toothless nature served hardly any protection to the poor in poor countries where uncontrolled capital flows exploited their less-advantageous positions and assisted in taking loans injurious to their economic stability in the long run.[86]

The GFC highlighted the need to redesign both the global and domestic financial regulatory systems not only to suitably address systemic risk but also to support its proper functioning. Lastra, in rethinking the role of the IFIs brings out comprehensive economic, historical and legal perspectives for national, European and international framework of monetary laws and financial regulation.[87] Others suggest maintaining the existing system. To many political theorists, especially realists who differentiate little between international law and international politics, it is always power (and not law) which promotes promulgation of international standards. While emphasizing importance of the force of sanction in IFL, Brummer suggested introducing a *few more teeth* to the existing soft law structure transforming it effectively into a rather *hard-soft-law*.[88] Brummer believes in the soft nature of financial law when bolstered by reputational and market discipline along with institutional sanctions (framed by domestic regulatory and administrative agencies). To him, IFL does not operate in a purely soft law manner, rather in many ways hard law and soft law both operate along a spectrum and

---

84. *See*, Abbott, et al. *supra* n. 72. *See also*, Abbott, K. W., & Snidal, D. (2000). Hard and Soft Law in International Governance. *International Organization, 54*, 421. Retrieved from http://ssrn.com/abstract = 1402966.
85. Simmons, B. A., (2000). The Legalization of International Monetary Affairs. *International Organization, 54*(3), 573-602.
86. Buckley, R. P. (2005). Why Are Developing Nations So Slow to Play the Default Card in Renegotiating Their Sovereign Indebtedness? *Chicago Journal of International Law*, 347-362. 155.
87. Garicano, L., & Lastra, R. M. (2010). Towards a New Architecture for Financial Stability: Seven Principles. *Journal of International Economic Law, 13*(3), 597-621.
88. *See*, for an authoritative account, Brummer, C. (2010a). Why Soft Law Dominates International Finance and not Trade. *Journal of International Economic Law, 13*(3) Oxford University Press, p. 20.

both are not dichotomous or qualitatively different forms of regulatory controls.[89] Guzman and Mayer endorse the view that urges usage of and present four theories describing why and under what situations states prefer employing soft law. And, this state behavior (of preferring to opt for soft law) itself provides explanation to the operational effectiveness of soft law as the analytical category in itself.[90] The initiative taken under the *Santiago Principles* also endorsed soft nature and nonbinding rule-based framework.[91] At another place, Golden argued for creation of an International Court of Finance (IFC), thereby, providing another perspective to the IFL from arbitration regimes.[92]

In order to understand soft law's value as a coordinating mechanism, institutional assessment of the way the law is enforced is indispensable. Brummer recommends improving *procedural level* of the regulators which can be done through, amongst other means, by outlining procedures for joint enforcement mechanism.[93] For this, cooperation among the supervisory authorities through enhanced information sharing is a prerequisite. There is another innovative approach where soft law instruments are made implementable through the hard-law tongs. In the case of the Basel rules and standards for example, these are not enforceable under the international law but the IMF conditionality incorporates compliance to Basel standards under Article IV surveillance program and this incorporation makes these soft law standards enforceable, having a force of sanction against the noncomplying Member States. Similarly several of such standards have been incorporated as benchmarks for various IMF and WB lending programs. There is however, an interesting alternative perspective:

> The IMF conditionality and sanction is invoked against the borrowing state, and thus it becomes inevitable for such states to comply with the standards and rules attached to such conditionality. However, there is no conditionality to the lender. By extension of the same argument, if *compliance* conditionality is extended to the lender states as well, it would have addressed to the gap in compliance for Basel II earlier, and for Basel III in future where the same compliance pattern is again expected especially from the developed and more influential states like the US.

[3] What Soft Law Offers?

There is an abundance of instances where the flexile nature of soft law has been instrumental in galvanizing consensus on complex financial issues. The law relating to

---

89. Brummer, *supra* n. 82 See also, Abbott & Snidal *supra* n. 84.
90. Guzman, A. T., & Meyer, T. (August, 2010). International Soft Law. *The Journal of Legal Analysis, UC Berkeley*. Public Law Research Paper #1353444, 2(1), retrieved from http://ssrn.com/paper=1353444.
91. *See*, for detailed discussion on *Santiago Principles* and the making of IFL, Norton, J. J. (2010). The 'Santiago Principles' for Sovereign Wealth Funds: A Case Study on International Financial Standard-Setting Processes. *Journal of International Economic Law, 13*(3), 645-662. *See also*, IWG. (September 2008). *Preliminary Agreement on Generally Accepted Principles and Practices – 'Santiago Principles'*. Retrieved from http://www.iwg-swf.org/pr/swfpr0804.htm.
92. Golden, J., & Burn, L. (2010). Editors' Note. *Capital Markets Law Journal, 6*(1), 1-2.
93. *See*, Brummer, *supra* n. 89.

exchange arrangements offers the best example of such usefulness of soft law. For instance, where a retreat from hard law becomes indispensable, only soft law can offer alternative to an otherwise anarchistic outcome. However, this may be noted that the inverse can be true as well. For example, collapse of the Bretton Woods' par system reflected this process of gradually evolving into a body of hard law can actually lead to dissolution of international legal obligations if states so decide. Capital requirements under the Basel regulation offer another peculiar instance where a skewed adoption by some jurisdictions has negatively influenced across-the-board implementation of standards.

It remains an effective instrument when it comes to adoption and implementation of standards involving multiple jurisdictions as it offers a flexible way to regulators to adjust quickly to the new needs as these arise and vary from one jurisdiction to another jurisdiction. There are however, conceptual hitches in the soft law discourse, not to mention definitional difficulties in elaborating the concept itself. The dialectics of law necessarily emanating from the state and being judicially enforceable are unending. The English Common law, a customary law to this day, is more comfortable with more diffused sources of law and is less fixated on the state. Second, recent experiences over the past decade with the international financial standard (as both diagnostic and prophylactic tools) have decidedly been mixed, in fact, largely unsatisfactory. Third, the soft law discourse in international finance appears strangely remote from the daily grind of international commercial practice, where the discourse is largely unknown: international commercial practitioners do not much think about state authority or judicial enforcement in going about their business. Their studies are *granular*; a reference to IFL would evoke bewilderment, as being devoid of meaning.[94]

Usually, enforcement issues in IFL sit at the bottom of the list. IFL law keeps intact the tradition of soft-law based standards even after the 2008 financial crisis. This status quo has been derived from concerns over sovereignty and regulatory uncertainty. Although soft law has merits in pragmatic rule-making and flexible rule implementation, soft law is not always an efficient design for IFR. The soft law tradition has led to difficulties in implementing G20-led IFRA's reform against the 2008 financial crisis.[95] Not only can a stronger financial stability institution facilitate the implementation of reforms but also can help devise credible dispute resolution mechanism (which constitutes an indispensable part of the enforcement concept). The 2012 Global Financial Stability Report find that the progress, if any, on post-crisis reform has only been *limited* so far, in part because of poor implementation. It is implementation that determines success of a safer financial system.[96]

---

94. Jordan, C. (Oct. 3, 2013). How International Finance Really Works. *7 Law and Financial Markets Review*. 2, available at SSRN: http://ssrn.com/abstract=2349215 See also, Jordan, C. (Jul. 24, 2012). International Financial Standards and the Explanatory Force of Lex Mercatoria. Georgetown Public Law: Center for Transnational Legal Studies Paper No. 12-120. Available at http://ssrn.com/abstract=2107943.
95. Gu, B., & Liu, T. (2014). Enforcing International Financial Regulatory Reforms. *Journal of International Economic Law*, 17 (1).
96. *See, Changing Global Financial Structures: Can They Improve Economic Outcomes*, in, IMF's Global Financial Stability Report: Restoring Confidence and Progressing on Reforms (October 2012). Available at https://www.imf.org/external/pubs/ft/gfsr/2012/02/pdf/text.pdf.

§6.05 PROCESSES AND LEGITIMACY CRITIQUE IN IFL

[A] What Is Legitimacy: Defining the Gaps

The democratic theory poses a strong challenge when it comes to critique of international financial regulatory structures and its processes. International legal theorists from Immanuel Kant to Thomas Franck have all argued that states should only and only conform to legislation and rules that have been produced through a legitimate process. The previous section stated that enforcement of IFL is directly dependent on state's incorporation of international customs and agreements into national laws through adjudication and legislation. Empirical evidence suggests that states facilitate standards to be incorporated and translated into local laws and enjoy force of sanction only when they are themselves involved in the standard-formulation processes.

In today's financial world, structural inequities and lack of representativeness in global rule-making bodies pose legal and normative challenges. Lately, criticism has been mounting on the gap in democratic representation in regulatory organizations and IFIs. The GFC has intensified this debate making it indispensable to follow inclusive and democratic processes. This section is going to dissect legitimacy gap, its relevance, impact and the reasons the gap continues to persist.

Let's define first what we mean by legitimacy. It is *popular* acceptance of authority, usually a governing law or a regime. A related term, *rational-legal legitimacy* is derived from a system of institutional procedures, wherein government institutions establish and enforce law and order in public interest.[97] It is, therefore, through public trust that the government will abide the law that confers rational-legal legitimacy, and here legitimacy gap in IFL's processes draws strong criticism. Unless Member States get involved in the rule-making processes to adopt such regulation in greater public interest, compliant to such regulation or a law contravenes the underlying philosophy. As Franck posits, a community which is organized around rules, compliance is secured at least in part by *perception of a rule as legitimate* by those to whom it is addressed. Their perception of legitimacy will vary in degree from rule to rule and time to time. It becomes a crucial factor however, in the capacity of any rule to secure compliance when, as in the international system, there are no other compliance-inducing mechanisms.[98] Legitimacy is a political and often a very standardized concept and can be

---

[97]. Only this is relevant here, there are, however, other forms including: (a) traditional legitimacy, which derives from societal custom and habit that emphasize the history of the authority of tradition; and (b) charismatic legitimacy which originates from the ideas and personal charisma of the leader. A charismatic government usually features weak political and administrative institution. *See* references at, n. 99 below.

[98]. Franck, T. M. (1988). Legitimacy in the International System. *American Journal of International Law, 82*, 705-759. *See also*, Franck, T. M. (2006). The Power of Legitimacy and the Legitimacy of Power: International Law in an Age of Power Disequilibrium. *The American Journal of International Law, 100*(1), 88-106; *See*, for a detailed discussion on the concepts of legitimacy, fairness and distributive justice as it transpires to the international or global institutions under the realm of international financial law, Franck, T. M. (1995). Fairness in International Law and Institutions: Oxford and Clarendon Press. *See also*, for a contrasting view, Keohane, R. O., Macedo, S., & Moravcsik, A. (2009). Democracy-Enhancing Multilateralism. *International*

categorized into[99] (a) input legitimacy, which involves a more explicit conception of consent by the governed. It relates to the functioning and machinery of an institution; how members are selected, the procedures by which decisions are made and power is exercised, and so on; and, (b) output legitimacy, which connotes an implied consent based on the optimality of the rule that the governors produce. It refers to the public assessment of the relevance and quality of the institution's performance.

Legitimacy in its both forms expresses public assessment of the worth of an institution but input legitimacy is a matter of the *design of the institution* while output legitimacy must be *earned by* the institution's performance and its accomplishments.[100] The institutions and their regulation should meet the standards of transparency, legitimacy and accountability to secure compliance from Member States which is realizable only when domestic public trusts these policies – deprived otherwise of input legitimacy. However, in the case of IFL, compliance, also pointed by Franck, cannot be assumed as the only or the principal indicator in gauging if a country's national practice reflects its adherence to and respect for international rules and standards. The question of legitimacy when it comes to IFIs confines around the role these bodies play in preserving global financial stability (which is a global public good). Let's look briefly at the parameters of accountability and transparency.

Accountability glues with the concept of legitimacy of financial regulatory processes. It gauges the extent to which regulators are responsive to stakeholders and to their public when wielding their powers. Its key objectives include that the individuals subject to regulation be protected from arbitrary governmental intrusions and that the government officials act with due care. It also aims at ensuring that the governmental authorities internalize the costs of their decision-making so that these are rewarded when effective and punished when their decisions undermine general public welfare.

The concept of *transparency* despite being more qualitative (i.e., involving a question of degree and not whether the actors are accountable to their principals in an absolute sense), it is glued with legitimacy and accountability. It functions as a condition precedent to determine the output legitimacy of an actor.[101] Another pertinent aspect is the provision for stakeholders to assess, evaluate and to take a critical review of sub-optimal decisions. Masciandaro analyzed the trends and determinants of financial supervisory governance by calculating levels of supervisory

---

Organization, 63(01), 1-31. The authors challenge the notion that multilateral institutions can enhance quality of national democratic processes even in well-functioning democracies in a number of important ways.

99. *See, supra* n. 98 for understanding the concept of legitimacy, and *See also,* Harlow, C. (2010). The Concepts and Methods of Reasoning of the New Public Law: Legitimacy *LSE Law, Society and Economy* WP 19/2010, LSE, available at http://eprints.lse.ac.uk/32891/1/WPS2010-19_Harlow.pdf.
100. Sharman, C. (2008). Political Legitimacy for an Appointed Senate. IRPP Choices, (Institute for Research on Public Policy), 14 (11), available at http://www.irpp.org/assets/research/strengthening-canadian-democracy/political-legitimacy-for-an-appointed-senate/vol14no11.pdf.
101. Brummer, C. (2012).

independence and accountability in 55 countries. The econometric analysis of determinants indicates that the quality of public sector governance plays a decisive role in establishing accountability arrangements. It also shows that decisions regarding levels of independence and accountability are not mutually connected. The results also reflect that the likelihood of establishing adequate governance arrangements is higher when supervisor is located outside the Central Bank.[102]

The IFIs provide the best barometers to gauge IFL and its processes' legitimacy, accountability and transparency. Unfortunately, the Bretton Wood institutions both as to input and output legitimacy remain under heavy shadow. As is the general rule, any organization, whether business or political is more likely to comply with regulations when it has participated in the design of such regulatory framework. However, this relationship only holds true when the firm sees authorities attentive to its inputs it makes. On the other hand, a firm's participation may actually be when authorities are seen to be less sensitive, poorly democratic or following not very participatory processes. Studies in psychology and organizational behavior also indicate that individuals are more likely to follow rules they have had the opportunity to influence. A similar dynamic between participation and compliance applies among businesses as well. Strengthening governance practices of international institutions means strengthening rules and making them effective to preserve the fundamental values of the members, in a context of collective decisions. Quoting Jean Monnet again, *nothing is possible without individuals, but nothing is lasting without institutions.*[103]

Although the reform debate predates 2008 yet substantial achievements remain a distant dream. The crisis in 2008 has provided an opportunity to IFL, to IFIs and to the financial markets (including the EU which hosts a number of bodies like the BIS and the FSB) to adopt new reforms. The old messianic deal of European integration needs a *de novo look* within the frame of democratic legitimacy and accountability with essential preservation of a social state.[104] The section below is looking closely at the issues involving governance reforms at the IMF and the WB to look at how these half-baked reform proposals would strengthen the institutional framework of IFL that remains weak largely on account of inherently weaker soft-law-based enforcement mechanisms.

§6.06 FINANCIAL INSTITUTIONS AND THE SOFT REFORM AGENDA

The first globally influential IFIs were the Bretton Woods institutions comprising of the WB and the IMF in 1944. The role and the function of these IFIs evolved with time and

---

102. Masciandaro, D., Quintyn, M., & Taylor, M. (June 2008). Financial Supervisory Independence and Accountability: Exploring the Determinants. *IMF WP/08/147*, available at http://www.imf.org/external/pubs/ft/wp/2008/wp08147.pdf.
103. BIS. (2013). Exiting the financial crisis and strengthening European integration: Address by Carlos da Silva Costa, at the Conference of the Portuguese Association of Insurers, *Where is Europe going? What is the Future of the Euro?* Lisbon, Oct. 24, 2013, available at https://www.bis.org/review/r131211d.htm.
104. Gerapetritis, G. (2013). Europe's New Deal: A New Version of an Expiring Deal. *European Journal of Law and Economics*, 1-25.

have greatly been influenced and shaped by the situational context. Let's see how these IFIs evolved under the soft umbrella of IFL and how these new developments interacted in shaping the discipline.

[A] The IMF

[1] Facts, Beyond Facts, and to Challenges

Originally the function of the IMF was to employ its financial resources to create and support a rule-based IMS based on stable exchange rates and to facilitate a relatively free payments system for current transactions.[105]

As of now, the role has been transformed. The IMF works to foster global growth and economic stability. It provides policy advice and financing to members in economic difficulties and also works with developing nations to help them achieve macroeconomic stability and reduce poverty.[106] It also promotes international monetary cooperation and balanced growth of international trade. However, in the wake of the GFC, its focus even more narrowly shifted to help ensure stability of the international system.[107] The IMF relies on a three-pronged strategy: keeping track of the global economy and the economies of member countries; lending to countries with balance-of-payments difficulties; and giving practical help to members.[108] Going back, this transformation of role and character is distinguishable into four epochs: (a) cooperation and reconstruction (1944-1971), (b) the end of the Bretton Woods system (1972-1981), (c) debt and painful reforms (1982-1988), societal change for Eastern Europe and Asian upheaval (1989-2004) and (d) globalization and crisis (2005-present).

How the IMF makes decisions? The Board of Governors is the highest decision-making body of the IMF. It has delegated most of its powers to the IMF's Executive Board. It consists of one governor and one alternate governor from each member country. It meets once a year together with the World Bank Group during the IMF-WB Spring and Annual Meetings to discuss the work of their respective institutions. Its members are usually the Finance Minister or the head of Central Bank of the member country. The Board of Governors appoints or elects executive directors. It has the right to approve quota increases, SDRs allocation, membership extension to new countries, withdrawal of old members and amendment to the Articles of Agreement and By-laws. It is the ultimate arbiter on issues related to the interpretation of the IMF's Articles of Agreement. The annual meetings are chaired by a Governor of the WB or the IMF.

---

105. Articles of Agreement of the IMF, (1945). *See* the Website http://www.imf.org/External/Pubs/FT/AA/ and, Art. 1 is available at http://www.imf.org/External/Pubs/FT/AA/#art1.
106. *See also, Rethinking Poverty.* (2009). Retrieved from Department of Economic and Social Affairs, United Nations http://www.un.org/esa/socdev/rwss/docs/2010/fullreport.pdf.
107. *See,* IMF's activities, what we do? Available at http://www.imf.org/external/about/whatwedo.htm.
108. *See,* Our Work: Surveillance, Lending, Technical Assistance, at the IMF's Website available at http://www.imf.org/external/about/ourwork.htm.

The IMF has two ministerial committees: the International Monetary and Financial Committee (IMFC), and the Development Committee. The Development Committee has the dual task of advising the Board of Governors of both the IMF and the WB on economic-development-related issues in emerging and developing economies. The committee has 24 members representing the full membership of the IMF and the WB and serves as a critical forum for government level discussion processes on critical issues. The IMFC has 24 members drawn from 187 governors. It is based on 24 constituencies and thereby represents all of its member countries. Its structure reflects on the Executive Board's structure. Specifically the committee discusses matters of common concern affecting global economy and advises the IMF. At the end of the meetings, which are held twice a year at the time of the IMF's Annual Meetings, a joint communiqué is issued. This sets guidance for the IMF's work till the time it meets again for its second biannual meeting. The decision-making process is consensus based hence no voting is carried out.

Who represents what? The Executive Board comprises of 24 members representing all 187 countries. The bigger economies like the US and China has their own seat, however, most of the countries are represented by grouped constituencies which are formed usually of four countries or more. Such largest constituency comprises of 24 countries. The Executive Board is responsible to carry out discussions and decisions on almost everything relating to the daily business ranging from matters relating to the IMF staff salaries or pension benefits to the issues of global economy. Most of the time the consensus-based decision-making model is applied, however, at times, the Board may seek formal voting on certain issues. At the end of the formal meetings, summing up is issued which reflects Board's views.

Global politico-economic variables have been shaping the mandate and governance structure of the IMF. Unfortunately, despite massive global economic shifts, the governance and power structure at the IMF kept stagnant. It didn't evolve with the new geopolitical and economic landscape dominated by emerging economies. Past couple of decades of tremendous developments in East has dramatically changed our world traditionally dominated by western ideologies and influence. Despite repeated pledges to undertake overarching reforms following the 1980s and 1990s Asian Crisis, meaningful progress in substantive reforms remained trivial. The post-GFC has shaken up the low momentum though.

Some of the factors hindering progress on governance reforms include: (a) reluctance of the European members to give up their disproportionate higher representation, (b) an uneven pressure for change from the US that affects negatively on reducing influence of the traditional western powers in the governance of these institutions, and (c) a lack of *policy coherence* between the new emergent players in particular reluctance to share sovereignty.

An unstable and non-linear development of IFL and regulatory reforms (discussed in Chapters 2-5) provide compelling reasons for structural reforms of the IFRA. Increasing developing country participation in GFG require: (a) incorporating developing country participation in the FSB where at present they do not participate substantially in the rule-making process, even though they are invited on the working groups, (b) enhanced representation and participation of developing and transition countries on the IMF's Board (appointment of the Managing Director needs to be opened to EMEs)[109] and, (c) increasing participation of developing countries in the BIS (there is insufficient representation and participation of the EMEs) and in BCBS (where there is no formal participation, though consultation has been increased).

After addressing the quota[110] reform and adjustment to the representational issues at the Fund's Board, further expectations to change could include: (a) all BRIC (Brazil, Russia, India and China) countries to be the top 10 IMF shareholders, while the European economies to hold two lesser seats. By doing this, a total of 110 countries will gain or maintain quota share, of which 102 would be either EMEs or developing countries, (b) more than 6% shift in quota share to be given to dynamic Emerging Market and Developing Countries (EMDCs). The bulk of this (about 80%) would come from reduction in the shares of advanced economies and major oil producers, and (c) once reforms in place, rebalancing to be mirrored in IMF's Executive Board, and all Executive Directors to be elected through an agreed and equitable process.[111]

[2] The Reform Process at the Fund

The process has been underway since 2006 without a substantial outcome. However, we see the emerging economies have taken their own separate initiatives[112] and are no longer awaiting legitimate representation the US/EU dominated IFIs. The required changes in the institutional structure of the Fund needs to correspond to the respective roles and responsibilities of the Board of Governors, the IMFC, the Executive Board and the Fund's management. In 2008, a committee, headed by Trevor Manuel, Minister of Finance of South Africa, was appointed to assess and report on the efficacy of the current structure and to point out areas where reforms are imminent. The committee presented its report in March 2009 but the work on the reforms remains underway. The 14 General Reviews conducted by the IMFC (IMFC advises IMF on policy changes) called for a fresh review of the realignment of quota shares and the size of the quota increase in April 2009. In April 2010, the IMFC requested completion of the review process before January 2011 (this was two years ahead of the original schedule that was due for early 2013). In 2009, G20 leaders called for a shift in quota shares to EMDCs from overrepresented to underrepresented countries in addition to preserving voting

---

109. *See*, Griffith-Jones, S. (No date). New Financial Architecture as a Global Public Good. Available at http://www.ids.ac.uk/files/griffithj4.pdf last accessed Jul. 29, 2017.
110. The current quota formula is a weighted average of GDP (weight of 50%), openness (30%), economic variability (15%), and international reserves (5%). For this purpose, GDP is measured through a blend of GDP based on market exchange rates (weight of 60%), and on PPP exchange rates (40%). The formula also includes a *compression factor* that reduces the dispersion in calculated quota shares across members. *See*, IMF Quotas, available at http://www.imf.org/external/np/exr/facts/quotas.htm.
111. IMF Governance Reform, (Nov. 5, 2010). IMF Board Approves Far-Reaching Governance Reforms, IMF Survey online, available at http://www.imf.org/external/pubs/ft/survey/so/2010/NEW110510B.htm.
112. The One Belt, One Road (OBOR), the New Development Bank (NDB or the BRICS Bank), and the AIIB (Asian Infrastructure Investment Bank) are a few such instances.

share of the poorest members, using the current quota formula as the basis to work from.¹¹³ This call was also endorsed by the IMFC.

At the meeting in Cannes in 2011, it was agreed that the G20 would make a diagnosis to verify that the resources available to the Fund are enough. It was also agreed to continue working on the implementation of the 2010 Contributions and Government Reform of the IMF, including the review process of the formula that determines the contributions to the Fund, so that they reflect adequately the relative weight of the economies within the global system.[114] As of May 16, 2013, 150 members having 78.4% of quotas as of November 5, 2010 had consented to their proposed quota increases under the 14th General Review of Quotas. As of the same date, 137 members having 72.2% of the total voting power had accepted the proposed Board Reform Amendment. Overall, the membership achieved the quota threshold for effectiveness of the quota increases under the 14th General Review of Quotas and the required number of members for entry into force of the Board Reform Amendment. However, the membership is about four-fifths of the way towards meeting the second threshold, namely the voting power threshold, for entry into force of the Board Reform Amendment, which is also necessary for effectiveness of the quota increase. It remains critically important to reach the required voting power threshold as soon as possible.[115] The representatives of the G20 Finance Ministries and Central Banks, and experts from the IMF, WB, OECD, BIS and the Group of Twenty-Four (G24) reaffirmed the need to continue the work towards increasing legitimacy of the IMF's governance structure and complete the process by January 2014 (as originally planned) in accordance with the agreed commitments.[116]

However, the 2008 Voice and Participation Amendment could only be entered into force on the scheduled date of March 3, 2011. The Executive Board deeply regretted the delay in implementing the Fourteenth Review quota increases and the Board Reform Amendment. As a result, it has not been able to complete its work in connection with the Fifteenth Review in accordance with the timetable set forth in the Board of Governors Resolution No. 66-2. Given the delay, the Executive Board concluded that additional time will be needed to complete its work on the Fifteenth Review. The *IMF needs to adapt-* was the call by the Managing Director in her recent

---

113. *See,* for example, Rustomjee, C. (2005). Improving Southern Voice on IMF Board: Quo Vadis Shareholders? In B. Carin & A. Wood (Eds.), *Enhancing Accountability in the International Monetary Fund*: Aldershot: Ashgate. *See also,* Woods, N., & Lombardi, D. (2006). Uneven Patterns of Governance: How Developing Countries Are Represented in the IMF? *Review of International Political Economy, 13*(3), 1-35. Retrieved from http://www.uquebec.ca/observgo/fichiers/66828_patterns.pdf.
114. Kuribrena, J. A. M. (Feb. 26, 2012). *Remarks by the Secretary.* Paper presented at the G20 Mexico City meeting. Available at http://www.g20mexico.org/en/news-room/speeches/236-palabras-iniciales-del-secretario-jose-antonio-meade-kuribrena-durante-la-conferencia-de-prensa-sobre-reunion-de-ministros-de-finanzas-y-gobernadores-de-bancos-centrales-del-g20, last accessed Feb. 29, 2012.
115. IMF (May 16, 2013). Proposed Amendment on the Reform of the IMF Executive Board and the Fourteenth General Review of Quotas: Status of Acceptances and Consents. Available at http://www.imf.org/external/np/pp/eng/2013/051613.pdf.
116. The IFA WG meeting, Feb. 13, 2013, Moscow. http://www.g20.org/news/20130213/781184424.html.

article.[117] The reforms at the IMF await approval by the US Congress. Every US president since World War II has supported strong US engagement with the Fund, especially, Ronald Reagan, George H.W. Bush and Bill Clinton backed legislation to increase the Fund's resources. Making it reflective of its global membership through quota and voting power reforms would broaden the IMF's funding base as well which is more than ever imminent under the existing crisis circumstances. The Board Reform Amendment of 2010 though faced endless delay and refusal in particular by the US congress for almost 7 years. Recently, the much awaited Board Reform Amendment of 2010 to increase quota got approved (after an endlessly cumbersome process) on April 24, 2017 by 184 members having 99.757% of total quota.[118]

To iterate the obvious that a lackadaisical governance reform process that commenced from early 2000s at the Fund has led to disappointment and frustration for the emerging economies who are exploring local alternatives to these traditional IFIs breed. As much as we can appreciate indigenous institutions capable to reflect emerging economies' true weight, interests and priorities, nonetheless it will be a critical setback to efforts at harmonizing standards for international markets. IFL needs to respond to these new realities in a *harder* way in order to continue to be called *international*.

[B]   The World Bank and the Emergent Challenges

The World Bank despite having its portfolio dominated by developing countries' interests, its governance structure remains in want of reform as much as the IMF. The IBRD was created to help finance reconstruction of Europe and economic development of its erstwhile colonies with a few independent states in Asia, Africa and Latin America having prime focus on physical infrastructure-development-related projects.[119] However, the world has changed dramatically and so the functions of the IBRD also evolved. Its membership has expanded to more than 180 states with a steady rise in the scope of its functions.

There has been a steady rise in Regional Development Banks (RDBs) as well as IFIs both in terms of the outreach and scope of the activities they used to engage in. Amongst the RDBs, the African development Bank (AfDB), the Asian Development Bank (ADB), the EBRD, the Inter-American Development Bank (IDB), and some other Multilateral Development Banks (MDBs) like Islamic Development Bank (IDB), the International Fund for Agriculture Development (IFAD) and European Investment Bank (EIB), have been operating under a prescribed mandate and delivering specified functions. The legal structure and governance functions of the most of these regional institutions are built upon the WBG structure.

---

117. Lagarde, C. (Mar. 24, 2014). Congress Can Help the US by Reforming The International Monetary Fund. *The Wall Street Journal*, Asia. p. 11, available at http://search.proquest.com/eproxy2.lib.hku.hk/docview/1509802603/fulltext/865EA218CF0C43E8PQ/1?accountid=14548# accessed 1 May 2014.
118. *See*, the IMF website, https://www.imf.org/external/np/sec/misc/consents.htm.
119. *See*, IBRD, Articles of Agreement. Available at http://siteresources.worldbank.org/EXTABOUTUS/Resources/IBRDArticlesOfAgreement_links.pdf.

The original role of the WB (to help finance reconstruction of Europe and economic development of its erstwhile colonies) has transformed significantly. The World Bank Group consists of the IBRD which lends to governments of middle-income and creditworthy low-income countries; the IDA that provides interest-free loans called *credits* and grants to governments of the poorest countries; the IFC which is the largest global development institution focused exclusively on the private sector; the MIGA, created in 1988 to promote FDI into developing countries to support economic growth, reduce poverty and improve people's lives. MIGA fulfills this mandate by offering political risk insurance (guarantees) to investors and lenders; and, the ICSID which provides international facilities for conciliation and arbitration of investment disputes.[120] The WB's Agenda 2030 aims to end extreme poverty by decreasing the percentage of people living on less than USD 1.25 a day to no more than 3% and promote shared prosperity by fostering the income growth of the bottom 40% for every country.[121] Let's now focus on the not-so-good side. In the WB's view, a law's value for economic development lies in its ability to provide a stable investment environment necessary for markets to operate. In a way, reducing law's value to be a facilitator in utility maximizing exchange and optimal market allocation, a view that informs many of the Bank's specific law reform projects. The Bank's turn to law actually undergirds many continued neoliberal assumptions and masks a continuation of neoliberalism's core tenets.[122] The question arises on the need to revisit *Political Prohibitions* in the Charters of IFIs.[123]

Following the sporadic crisis episodes of the 1990s and post-crisis regulatory reforms, Kern Alexander argued in 2001 for greater linkages between various international economic governance institutions for regulatory harmony and supervisory uniformity. Today, the dynamics of GFG have changed dramatically owing to the 2008 financial crisis. Now, strengthened linkages are required both in terms of supervision and regulation at global as well as regional level. Given a burgeoning growth of regulatory bodies and consequent not-so-well-coordinated development of standards and their uneven application, adoption and partial compliance by the member countries has resulted into a vast but loosely coordinated – and at times uncoordinated mechanisms to respond to crisis situations. This *patchwork* of regulatory initiatives is in want of harmonization and lacks universal applicability appeal in order to be efficient and effective as voices for globalization mandate.

---

120. *See,* the WB's website, Organizations and their corresponding functions, http://web.worldbank.org/wbsite/external/extaboutus/0,,contentMDK:23063010 ~ menuPK:8336848 ~ page PK:50004410 ~ piPK:36602 ~ theSitePK:29708,00.html.
121. *See,* for details, WB's website, *What We Do* at http://www.worldbank.org/en/about/what-we-do. *See also,* Shinohara, N. (Jun. 3, 2013). The Financial Crisis, Capital Flows, and Global Liquidity, Keynote Speech, the Deputy MD, IMF, Bank of Korea International Conference, Seoul, accessible at http://www.imf.org/external/np/speeches/2013/060313.htm.
122. *See,* Krever, T. (2011). The Legal Turn in Late Development Theory: The Rule of Law and the World Bank's Development Model. *Harvard International Law Journal, 52*(1),available at http://www.harvardilj.org/wp-content/uploads/2011/02/HILJ_52-1_Krever.pdf last accessed October 16, 2017.
123. *See,* WB. (2012). International Financial Institutions and Global Legal Governance. In, H. Cissé, D. D. Bradlow & B. Kingsbury (Eds.), *The World Bank Legal Review: WB Law, Justice, and Development Series 3.*

The IMF's *rescue* of the EU economies following the GFC and the SDC invoked a heavy critique.[124] As part of the regional integration and SSMs, the European Commission wants ECB to oversee all Eurozone banks from 2014.[125] There are also suggestions to establish an *International First Responder*[126] with significant resources. The proposal gets backing from dire liquidity needs, the contagion risk, too-big-to-fail (TBTF) problem and the risky momentum and amounts of financial flows that the recent crisis have brought to the fore. One important difference to bear is: this and similar proposals could provide *ex-post remedies* for financial disruptions at best leaving the need to address the fundamental issues unresolved.

At the time of establishing the Bretton Woods institutions, the principle delineating authority, and influence was the relative weight and strengths of the founding members. Decline in the power and authority of these old founding members coincide with a steady rise in the influence, economic weight and rise of the BRICS (Brazil, Russia, India, China and South Africa) and in particular, of China demanding fair representation and voice in the decision-making processes. The IFIs established to reform and direct international financial landscape however failed to reform and directs their own processes. The new politico-economic reality demanded reforms to enhance voice and representation of the EMDCs including the poor and the low-and-middle-income countries to better reflect changes in relative weights of Member States in the global economy.[127] The recent agreement among the BRICS countries to establish the NDB is an apt response from the disillusioned emergent economies that have *less-than-just* role in the decision-making processes of the IFIs. South African President Jacob Zuma remarked that for the NDB, we have agreed that the initial capital contribution should be substantial and sufficient for the bank to be effective in financing infrastructure.[128]

There are serious flaws with the current formula. Several steps are therefore required to address the existing deficiencies. Although, over the past couple of decades, relative economic weights of countries have changed substantially but the IFI's governance, quota and representation pattern fail to reflect adequately new realities of the economic horizon despite a huge demand for reforms. IFRA, thus, remains archaic,

---

124. The IMF's decision to fund one-third of all financing for Europe's rescue packages was harshly criticized by the emerging-market IMF members as a special deal for the West, *See*, Robert Kahn (Feb. 25, 2016). IMF's Next Five Years: No Rest for the Weary. Available at https://www.foreignaffairs.com/articles/2016-02-25/imf-s-next-five-years last accessed Apr. 2, 2016.
125. ICFR (Aug. 31, 2012). EC Wants ECB to Oversee all Eurozone Banks from 2014. Available at http://archive-org.com/page/288006/2012-09-08/http://www.icffr.org/Resources/News/European-Commission-Wants-ECB-to-OverSee-all-Euroz.aspx accessed, May 1, 2014. *See* Ch. 5 for European post-crisis SSM.
126. Reference, the traditional LoLR function by Bagehot was in the domestic context. Here, the suggestion for establishing an International LoLR came in response to the GFC where contagion affect and the TBTF banks triggered thoughts on establishing an ILoLR. *See*, Lagarde, *supra* n. 23.
127. *See*, Rustomjee, C. (2004). Why Developing Countries Need a Stronger Voice in Finance and Development. Available at http://www.imf.org/external/pubs/ft/fandd/2004/09/pdf/rustomje.pdf.
128. *See*, Zuma, J. (Mar. 23, 2013). *Statement by BRICS Leaders on the Establishment of the BRICS-LED Development Bank*. Fifth Summit, S. Africa.

obsolete and devoid of legitimacy (both input and output). Given a disappointingly slower pace of reforms, lately, some alternative proposals have surfaced to establish new institutions, both global[129] and regional to fill this void.[130] Another relatively new challenge to the traditional MDBs is arising from the NDB, the AIIB and other China-led infrastructure related development projects in Africa, Asia, and even parts of Middle East. The WB Group has a key role to address this want of legitimacy and proportional representation.

§6.07 THINKING ALTERNATIVES

There has always been an increasing mismatch between globally integrated financial markets and the corresponding supervisory and regulatory structures. These disproportions continue to be a causal factor to crises. Institutional design and allocation of authority to a financial regulator (with domestic jurisdiction and authority) to manage global market risk (under the IFL with no authority to seek compliance) has become a major reform challenge that the twenty-first century financial institutions are facing. This challenge is compounded by the soft nature of IFL. The section above looked at the painfully slow reform that the WB and the IMF were able to incorporate despite having a comparatively stringent authority to do so. This is not to deny that the international community has taken important and valuable steps in mobilizing globally coordinated regulation such as establishing the FSB, extending the scope and work of the Basel Committees and by establishing international colleges of supervisors.

In terms of new institutional arrangements to seek uniformity in compliance to the international regulatory processes as devised by the FSB and Basel Committees (like the Basel III), it is essential to keep domain of the market consistent with the domain of the regulator to avoid many a regulatory slippages leading to gaps in compliance. There are basically two options: (a) a hard-law-based regime, and (b) the soft law based. The current IFL and IFRA lies somewhere between the two albeit tilting more towards the softer-side of the fulcrum, hence, attracting criticism on its ineffectiveness to seek compliance. We have critically looked at both of the approaches (Chapter 5 for Hard law & Chapter 6 above for soft law) and everything in between the two (Chapter 3, section on the existing IFRA). The section below analyzes whether a Global Regulator can be the panacea to the regulatory ills followed by an alternative scenario based on scholarly opinions where *only tweaking the existing soft-law* can deliver the most illuminating outcomes. Let's explore both.

[A] Scenario I: Whether a Global Regulator

Different prescriptions and alternatives to the soft-law-based existing system have been forwarded as viable policy options. Amongst many ideas, the proposal for establishing

---

129. *See*, last section of this Chapter for proposals on alternative IFR institutions.
130. For example, the IMF specifically acted more like a *fire brigade* since 1980s. *See* for reference, Sandström, S. (1998). The East Asia Crisis and the Role of the World Bank: Speech, MD of the Bank at the Bretton Woods Committee; February 13.

a GFReg seems quite desirable to help provide the necessary regulatory coordination and market stability needed for today's truly global markets. Both academics[131] and some market actors[132] have since long called for creating such an institution.

Hypothetically, a GFReg would design standards to be applied by all countries and jurisdictions, and adopt appropriate surveillance mechanisms guaranteeing adoption. The institutional set up would leave room to adapt regulations to different national conditions, and in this sense as well as in the area of supervision, operate essentially as a network of national regulators with strong international coordination. For example, countercyclical regulation criteria could be agreed internationally, but then be implemented nationally depending on the state of the cycle in each country. Such national regulation would best be applied by host regulators on local banks and systemic subsidiaries.

States have for long resisted a call establishing GFReg because of their unwillingness to give up national sovereignty, a precondition to establish an institution of GFG. In one view, global financial markets, to the extent that these are unregulated, are profoundly unaccountable. To the extent that financial markets are global, one option to make IFL effective and its regulatory architecture meaningful could materialize by pooling sovereignty among governments through global arrangements. Therefore, in one view, by sharing sovereignty with other states, Member States will gain sovereignty through their enhanced influence and control over financial markets other than their own in the pursuit of public policy goals such as of providing global financial stability to everyone. This could be construed as a superior option in a way in terms of exercise of sovereignty and joint supervision comparing to a scenario where individual governments remain unable to regulate international aspects of domestic financial products and their market.

However, one of the major criticism on this is from the developing countries who increasingly are unwilling to support the creation of such a GFReg, and rightly so due to the fear of being shadowed by states with deeper and larger financial markets who would assume leadership of such an organization and overriding influence in the design of regulatory priorities and larger policy space. On the other hand, for the industrialized countries, sharing their sovereignty with smaller states and having their preferences incorporated into global laws especially those not having a larger footprint on the financial map of the world is challenging in another way.

And, so are the challenges of establishing a GFReg even if the issues of enforcement and compliance and its direct implications on a state's sovereignty are pushed aside temporarily. The Canvas of IFL is as rampant with suggestions as are the inconsistencies in its formulation and ineffectiveness in its operations. Nonetheless, its soft nature and its lack of legal sanction have been instrumental in addressing crises situations. The world today is in the midst of major political transformation. We have seen the recent G20 meeting in July 2017 with an entirely transformed agenda from what the G20 had back in November 2008. International relations are directly affecting

---

131. *See*, Eatwell, J. & Taylor, L. (2001). Global Finance at Risk: The Case for International Regulation. Polity Press.
132. *See* Kaufman, H. (2008). The Principles of Sound Regulation. *Financial Times*, p. 11.

the interaction relation of states, the IFIs and the IFL. There is though hope in applying the GAL to the problem of democratic deficit in the IFIs and international regulatory bodies.

Alexander's argument stems from the global nature of the financial markets, therefore, for him, *the domain of the regulator should be the domain of the regulated* and since existing markets are international hence regulator should also have its authority and domain necessarily international. Eatwell's World Financial Authority (WFA) is mandated to perform those functions in the international market what domestic regulators do in the domestic markets. He draws attention to the performance of functions required from such an authority and not the authority itself. A considerable component of the function of WFA would therefore entail provisions for surveillance, enforcement and policy development.[133] Another view underlines the need for formal legal institutions for micro and macroeconomic stability. While combining law and economics with regulatory regimes, this view builds up a case for a global supervisor to function as a global watchdog on the one hand, and also strongly believes on the parity of the regulator and the regulated on the other.[134]

An important issue is to ensure necessary steps are taken to enhance representation in international regulatory bodies, both of the countries and of nonfinancial stakeholders, along the lines outlined above. There are no significant barriers to submitting an entry in the save-the-world-financial system game. Eichengreen commented once, most of the plans floating around are politically unrealistic, technically infeasible, or unlikely to yield significant improvements in the way crises are prevented, anticipated or managed and it holds almost alike today.[135] The dilemma in realizing a truly representative forum where keeping national sovereignty intact without compromising international financial market stability and steady growth remains one of the outstanding challenges.[136] It requires more importantly political will to bring about fundamental changes in the traditional power play.

A key question is whether a new customized institution should be created to fulfill this function judiciously. Given the difficulty of achieving consensus for creating new IFIs, adapting, transforming an existing one would perhaps be an only option (unless another major crisis paves the way for it), and the only option is nonetheless a complex alternative. We have seen G20's tremendous role right after the GFC which more recently has significantly transformed and dwindled at least from the financial regulatory sphere. One way could be to have the BIS or the FSB, given its set of expertise in dealing with systemic risk in financial markets, high quality of its analysis and its close links with other central banks and regulatory bodies. However, a precondition for the BIS to provide raw basis for a global financial authority rests on the premises that it expands its membership considerably, with the aim of creating a universal body, with developing countries adequately represented on its Board,

---

133. Dhumale & Eatwell, *supra* n. 72.
134. Ferran, E. & Goodhart, C., (Eds.). (2001). Regulating Financial Services and Markets in the Twenty First Century. Hart publishing.
135. Eichengreen, *Infra* n. 149.
136. *See,* Chs 3 and 5 for a debate on challenges posed by sovereignty issue.

management and staff. Some steps have been taken in this direction, but these are clearly insufficient (*see* Chapter 3). This does not eliminate the possibility of segmenting national markets by introducing capital controls that should remain the right of national authorities. The desire to introduce capital controls will increase if regulation is seen as insufficient to curb volatility of capital flows.

This brings us to the second scenario: to rethink if by tweaking the existing system we can reap more benefits than reconstructing yet another global institution. Many IFL scholars indeed believe that *reforms* can go a long way in bringing legitimacy, fairness and effectiveness to the existing IFRA.

[B] Scenario II: If Less Is More

International prudential regulation developed in a relatively fragmented and weak institutional context. IFL provides, at best, an authority that springs from persuasion and is embedded in consensus. Perspectives on reform thus rest upon subtle modifications to substantive reform to the existing IFRA but nowhere close to a complete revamp. Below, we sketch some of these policy choices. Although many of these ideas are not new, but in the aftermath of the recent crisis, these have been expressed and articulated more cogently.

More specifically at the global level, a number of propositions attract much attention including for example, by Jeffrey Sachs who advocated formation of an international bankruptcy court.[137] George Soros called for establishing an *international deposit insurance corporation*. Henry Kaufman recommends creating a *Single Global Super Regulator* for financial markets and institutions, and an International Credit-Rating Agency, endowed both with broad supervisory and regulatory powers to enforce common standards.[138] Jeffrey Garten[139] proposed a World Central Bank with responsibility for overseeing a new global currency.[140] Fischer made the case that, with a range of improvements in the system, a multilateral lender could effectively perform the main functions of an LoLR even without being able to issue currency. Golden argued creation of an *IFC*, to strengthen legal framework of IFL by the addition of an arbitration dimension.[141]

---

137. Sachs, J. (April 1995). Do We Need an International Lender of Last Resort? Frank D. Graham Lecture at Princeton University. Available at http://www.ksg.harvard.edu/cid/ciddirector/publicat.htmlWorking & Sachs, J. D., & Warner, A. (1995). Economic Reform and the Process of Global Integration. Available at https://www.brookings.edu/wp-content/uploads/1995/01/1995a_bpea_sachs_warner_aslund_fischer.pdf.
138. Kaufman, H. (Jan. 28, 1998). Preventing the Next Global Financial Crisis. *Washington Post*.
139. *See*, Garten, J. (Sep. 25, 1998). In This Economist Chaos, A global Central Bank Can Help. *International Herald Tribune*.
140. *See*, Rogoff, K. (1999). International Institutions for Reducing Global Financial Instability. *Journal of Economic Perspectives*, 13(4). At http://www.jstor.org/stable/2647011?seq=1#page_scan_tab_contents.
141. Golden, & Burn, *supra* n. 92.

Many writers, for example, Mishkin,[142] Meltzer,[143] Garten,[144] Calomiris,[145] Giannini[146] and Fisher[147] have proposed a typology of international institution to perform different functions including for an international LoLR. On capital controls, Paul Krugman[148] suggested that economists need to rethink their traditional antipathy towards controls on capital outflows, while Barry Eichengreen[149] is among many who advocated Chilean-style controls on capital inflows. The Clinton proposal offered at the October 1998 G7 meeting fell in line with the same argument.[150] When it comes to questions of having an LoLR, most often it is implied having the IMF offering a new emergency line of credit,[151] for which countries would have to prequalify by meeting certain macroeconomic and regulatory standards. The existence of such line of credit would stave off speculative attacks so that very few countries would actually ever have to draw on the facility. Undoubtedly, the obstacles to having international deep pockets[152] style LoLR are formidable.

---

142. Mishkin, F. S. (1994). Preventing Financial Crises: An International Perspective. *NBER Working Paper No. 4636 available at http://www.nber.org/papers/w4636.*
143. Meltzer, A. (Feb. 24, 1998). Asian Problems and the IMF. Testimony Prepared for the Joint Economic Committee of the US Congress.
144. Garten, *supra* n. 139.
145. *See*, the classical work of Calomiris, C. (Oct. 7, 1998). Blueprints for a New Global Financial Architecture. *Mimeo, Columbia Business School.* Retrieved from http://www.jec.senate.g.ov/public/_cache/files/edcf86a0-93eb-45de-830c-bae1f65ca100/charles-w.-calomiris-blueprints-for-a-new-global-financial-architecture.pdf.
146. Giannini, C. (1999). Enemy of None but Friend of All? An International Perspective on the Lender of Last resort Function. *IMF WP No 99/10.* http://www.imf.org/external/pubs/ft/wp/1999/wp9910.pdf.
147. Fischer, S. (1999). On the Need for an International Lender of Last Resort. Presented at the American Economic Association and the American Finance Association, New York, available at https://www.imf.org/external/np/speeches/1999/010399.htm.
148. *See*, Krugman, P. (Sep. 7, 1998). Saving Asia: It's Time to Get Radical. Fortune. *See also,* Krugman, P. (Sep. 28, 1998). Heresy Time. Available at http://web.mit.edu/krugman/www/heresy.html.
149. Eichengreen, B. J. (1999). *Toward a New International Financial Architecture: A Practical Post-Asia Agenda.* Institute for International Economics. DC. Also, he has been strongly suggestive of Chilean-style capital controls. *See*, Eichengreen, B., & Hausmann, R. (1999). Exchange Rates and Financial Fragility. *NBER Working Paper No. 7418.* Retrieved from http://www.nber.org/papers/w7418.
150. The proposal was to establish a new *mechanism* for dispensing IMF aid to provide countries with large lines of credit they can tap at will. The new mechanism would have some advantages over the previous IMF rescues that flopped, notably Russia's – but also some drawbacks. *See*, Blustein, P. (Oct. 30, 1998). G7 Backing of US Plan Predicted. *Washington Post.* Retrieved from http://www.washingtonpost.com/archive/business/1998/10/30/g-7-backing-of-us-plan-predicted/32475611-7740-4783-9a48-b0b14b23134c/ last accessed, Aug. 17, 2015.
151. For the IMF, Total quotas as of Mar. 13, 2015 were: USD 362 billion; additional pledged or committed resources of: USD 885 billion. It has committed amounts under current lending arrangements for USD 163 billion, of which USD 137 billion have not been drawn. *See*, fast Facts on the IMF, available at http://www.imf.org/external/np/exr/facts/glance.htm The IMF's lendable resources USD 655 billion (SDR 477 billion) after the 14th General Review. *See*, IMF. (2010). IMF Executive Board Approves Major Overhaul of Quotas and Governance. Press Release, available at http://www.imf.org/external/np/sec/pr/2010/pr10418.htm IMF Quota and Governance Publications (2006-2013) accessible at http://www.imf.org/external/np/fin/quotas/pubs/index.htm.
152. Rogoff, *supra* n. 140.

For many political theorists (especially realists who differentiate little between international law and international politics), it is power and not the law that promotes the promulgation of international standards. Right in the aftermath of the GFC, Buckley and Arner reiterated a set of most imminent reforms and underlined the urgency to reshape both the global as well as domestic financial regulatory landscape in order to address intensifying systemic risk.[153] Lastra, while rethinking role of the IFIs, called for taking into account economic, historical and legal perspectives while conceiving national, regional and international framework of monetary laws and financial regulation.[154] One of the premises indicates to replicate European integration at the pattern of the Champion's League for pan-European financial institutions, essentially a hybrid of national and European rules for advantages of synergy and coordination (*see*, Chapter 5).

The importance of the force of sanction in IFL has been underscored by scholars including Brummer who propose instituting *a few more teeth to the existent* soft-law structure would sufficiently work as a mechanism transforming the existing *soft-law into a hard-soft law*.[155] Brummer, who presents one of the most objective and realist option, believes in the soft nature of the IFL which is bolstered by reputational and market discipline on the one hand, while, institutional sanctions framed by the domestic regulatory and administrative agencies on the other.

IFL does not operate in a purely soft-law manner, rather in many ways hard law and soft law both operate along a spectrum and are not dichotomous or qualitatively different forms of regulatory controls. Guzman and Mayer make a discussion on the nature and usage of soft law and present four theories describing why and under what situations states prefer employing soft law. Accordingly, the state behavior itself provides justification for the *coherence of soft law* as an analytical category itself.[156] The initiative taken under the Santiago principles endorses soft nature of the law and its nonbinding rule-based framework.[157]

International law is a rational-choice theory that states employ to further their national interest and is far beyond a whet for appetite for power or security. IFI's lack of compliance (under both the customary international law and the general principles of law) has been discussed widely. The IFIs have a critical role to play in shaping IFL but the architecture requires to be redesigned to address lack of representation and imprecise mandate. The issues of state sovereignty, interdependent global economy, and constitutionalism, the interaction and linkages between domestic rules and international standards need to be considered in order to strengthen IFRA.

---

153. Buckley, R. P., & Arner, D. W. (2011). *From Crisis to Crisis: The Global Financial System and Regulatory Failure.* Kluwer Law International. Available at http://ssrn.com/paper = 1980010.
154. *See*, Garicano & Lastra, *supra* n. 87.
155. Brummer, *supra* n. 89 p. 20.
156. Guzman & Meyer, *supra* n. 90.
157. *See*, Norton, *supra* n. 91.

§6.08 CONCLUSION

We reviewed inconsistencies in the development processes of IFL and regulatory regimes. We also reviewed a range of issues from FML to weaker crisis-management and crisis-prevention system to the legitimacy deficit and weaker governance structures of the IFIs to find lack of legal backstops and enforcement mechanism in IFL in this chapter. We analyzed a spectrum of issues with both the soft-law-based reforms as well as hard-law-based solutions to pin down inherent challenges that IFL is bearing. We find both, the soft-law-based and the hard-law-based new conceptions of IFL and IFRA present tremendous challenges, be it adoption, standardization, implementation or compliance. We spotted numerous *inconsistencies* within markets, IFIs, within the reform process affecting the discipline of IFL. In the last section, we found, continuing with the soft-law-based framework is not an option either if a strong and resilient financial system remains the end goal. We thus have called for an analytical rethink of the ongoing reform process. The next and final chapter recommends therefore alternatives outside of the realm of traditional IFL structures.

CHAPTER 7
Conclusions, Challenges and Recommendations

§7.01 OVERVIEW

Crises and responses are constantly defining contours of international finance, which is in a perpetual state of flux. The existing soft-law-based financial regulatory architecture failed repeatedly in preventing and managing crises. These failures have recently threatened global financial stability. International Financial Law's (IFL) mechanisms also failed in addressing multifaceted issues arising from the interconnected nature of financial institutions and complex cross-border transactions. An absence of financial accountability in irresponsible lending/borrowing behaviors in one jurisdiction emulated similar behavior in other regions threatening global financial stability and far deeper challenges to the discipline of IFL itself.[1] This book claims that financial risk must be prevented and managed by enforcing an accountable behavior possibly through a hard IFL (based on the enforcement of financial standards and regulations) to achieve relatively stable global financial markets.

To achieve global financial stability, this research recommends both the need to refine and improve the existing tool kit of IFL and proposes alternative perspective to the existing financial regulatory framework. The post-2008 IFL keeps intact its soft-law-based nonbinding tradition for regulatory regimes (as seen from Basel III and the

---

1. Primary objective of IFL is *to create international financial stability*. This stability has to be created in an environment of national jurisdictions, each pursuing their own national interest and governance standards, and is constantly threatened by the consequences of increasing globalization, technological development and financial innovation. See, International Financial Law. *Peace Palace Library*. Retrieved from http://www.peacepalacelibrary.nl/research-guides/economic-and-financial-law/international-financial-law/, date accessed, Aug. 20, 2015. *See also*, reference work by, Wood, P.R., Law and Practice of International Finance, Sweet and Maxwell, 2008, also, Bamford, C. (2011). Principles of International Financial Law (1 ed.): Oxford University Press.

Financial Stability Board (FSB)'s mandate, *see* Chapters 4 and 6 respectively). Although, in certain ways, a few states (and regions like the European Union (EU)) put in place stringent domestic financial regimes (like the Dodd-Frank in the US), however, processes of IFL essentially remains unaltered:

> This study argues for fundamental changes to the design of IFL and its crisis and risk management processes to ensure global financial stability, which is an essential international public good. A responsible IFL derived from legitimate legal order, rooted in accountable institutions and based on enforceable standards is essential to ensure stability in the financial world.

The discipline of IFL is shaped by both the national and the international policy dimensions.

In the real world national interest almost always takes precedence over the more abstract compliance to a global order. In international law's realm, states generally comply with the commitments they have voluntarily entered into; however, in a crisis, narrowly defined national interest almost always trumps foreign and other considerations. In practice, however, pursuit of pure national interest in situations with foreign spillovers is hardly ever an easy choice. States are members of an international system and despite being sovereign are not entirely independent in following isolated actions on international issues without invoking the threat of similar responses from other members of that international system. International law thus does not ensure an *externality-free context* where sovereign states are truly sovereign in all domestic matters. Hertogen finds that in reality, *states' domestic affairs are exposed to the external adverse effects of other states' actions* due to a lack of limits on states' exercise of their sovereignty.[2] To address such gaps only a mechanism, which brings accountability to violators can command respect and ensure compliance to regulatory standards in an international setting. This is particularly relevant when the goal of maintaining systemic stability collides with preservation of national financial institutions.[3]

This book begins with Chapter 1, which raises a number of questions. We looked for answers through the succeeding chapters. Chapter 2 sketched the development of IFL during the twentieth century and observed recurring financial crises shaping its contours. Chapter 3 focused on the development of International Financial Institutions (IFIs), their role in maintaining financial stability and the design of the regulatory architecture as it evolved through time. Chapter 4 analyzed Basel processes (Basel I, II and III) to see if the existent regulatory framework (Basel II) served effectively as crisis prevention/management tool. It evaluates Basel III's resilience vis-à-vis a future crisis.

---

2. Hertogen, E. (2015). Roadblocks and Pathways Towards Inter-state Cooperation in Increasing Interdependence. In C. L. Lim & B. Mercurio (Eds.), International Economic Law after the Global Crisis: A Tale of Fragmented Disciplines. Cambridge University Press.
3. We have seen during the Icelandic banking crisis the issues between the Icelandic government and the authorities in the Netherlands and the UK which were resolved only afterwards. *See* for details, Chapter 5 section 4. Morgenthau associated lack of enforcement to imply that law doesn't cover those areas of international affairs where states do not comply, *see*, Morgenthau, H. (1948). Politics Among Nations. Knopf.

Chapter 7: Conclusions, Challenges and Recommendations §7.01

Chapter 5 analyzed a treaty-based structure by exploring the EU's integration framework to find, if any, parallels that can be drawn for the working of international financial markets. Chapter 6 summarized the various legal and policy aspects as discussed from Chapters 2-5 and evaluated the post-Global Financial Crisis (GFC) reform effort for its adequacy in establishing a stable and resilient archetypal IFL. This final chapter enlists further challenges that IFL continues to weather despite the post-GFC reform and provides *conclusions and recommendations* for fundamental reform of the existing international financial system.

Chapter 2 looked at the chronological development of IFL under the controlled regimes of the twentieth century and at the transformation of the financial regime under the liberalization and de-regulatory periods. It examined the various crises episodes and how these shaped the development of IFL, and the drastic transformation of *finance* from a *domestic concept* to an *international phenomenon* under the de-regulatory philosophy of market fundamentalism. It examined the current state of IFL by studying the GFC and how IFL and its regulatory institutions responded to the crisis and took up the post-crisis reform agenda.

Chapter 3 addressed two distinct streams: the first stream focused on ideological and political ethos underpinning the development of financial markets and how these contoured the formation of the regulatory institutions. Stream II rigorously studied structural manifestations of IFL through its regulatory network and considered its institutional heritage (which was influenced from the post-War and the post-Bretton Woods time) to evaluate the role of law in the development of international financial markets. In the process, it surveyed the ethos of the Washington Consensus and the New International Financial Architecture (NIFA), and analyzed the structure, role and functions of the most important pillars of the International Financial Regulatory Architecture (IFRA) to identify obstacles to reform. It questioned the resilience of the prevalent regulatory architecture in the wake of the next crisis.

The next three Chapters 4-6 appraise whether an enforcement mechanism in the realm of IFL is crucial in the post-crisis reconstruction of the regulatory architecture. In this context, Chapter 4 focused exclusively on risk/crisis prevention and management regulations. It raised the question whether the newly evolving soft-law-based regulatory framework is resilient enough against future crises, and contrasted its regulatory substance (i.e., the standards) against the regulatory objectives on the one hand, and the requisite legal backstops and availability of appropriate mechanisms for implementation of the regulatory substance, on the other hand. This focused *substance* and *processes* analysis reviewed institutional objectives and regulatory goals against the prevalent national and international financial practices. The post-2008 phase focuses on Basel III critique in terms of its contents, in comparison to Basel II, adoption timeline and implementation hiccups. Clearly, the Basel II capital buffers in the pre-2008 scenario were inadequate and scanty, while the Basel III framework is to be judged against future financial flare-ups.

Chapter 5 explored the treaty-based regional single market structure of the EU in order to evaluate relevance of a hard-law-based integration mechanism for international financial market. Since the EU in the context of the recent integration crisis provides a perfect laboratory to experiment various options, this chapter looked at the working of EU's crisis-management mechanism in dealing with the GFC and subsequently with sovereign debt crisis (SDC) to get insight for hard-law-based supranational institutions of financial governance. In the course of this analysis, it reviewed the post-crisis European effort at reinventing the integration mechanism through the formation of various crisis-management bodies including the European Financial Stability Facility (ESFS), the European Systemic Risk Board (ESRB) and the European Banking Authority (EBA). It scanned how this new set of EU institutions may strengthen EU's economic and political integration and concluded by defining various options to replicate a single market framework in a global setting.

Chapter 6 reviewed the inconsistencies in the development of IFL, regulatory regimes and in the current regulatory reforms. These included a range of issues from excessive financial market liberalization to weaker crisis-management and crisis-prevention systems to legitimacy deficit and weaker governance and representational structures to the lack of legal backstops available to regulatory institutions for effective enforcement of regulatory standards. This chapter expanded the debate on the financial *instability* factor and pinned down its inherent challenges calling for fundamental *reform of the reforms underway*. It pointed out the *gaps and inconsistencies*, in compliance to the enforcement of financial standards and engenders the debate whether to strengthen only the financial institutions of global governance or the discipline of IFL only or both.

This final chapter concludes the research by providing recommendations for further development of IFL as a discipline and subsequent development of the IFRA in order to have stable, reliable and robust international financial markets. Based on the previous analysis, it provides conclusive recommendations to build an IFRA embodying crisis-prevention mechanism and yet for unseen, unknown unknowns, crisis-management mechanism fully primed to address such situations. It recommends for a strong IFL and a stronger IFRA empowered to comprehend unseen financial shocks.

§7.02 CHALLENGES AND LIMITATIONS

[A] Where Do We Stand Today?

There were higher expectations for 2015 to be a *turning point* in terms of implementing most of the post-crisis reregulatory agenda, however persistence of commotions on the financial front make us doubt having implemented successfully the reform agenda. The continuity of crisis – from GFC to the SDC – and perpetual market influx has shifted away our focus from implementing more thorough and long-awaited structural reforms. Instead, the focus invariably has been to put in place short-term crisis-management responses for the more pressing issues. In fact, the mayhem in the

Chinese financial market in 2016 sent off distress alarms to the US/European markets. It seemed as if the world could be on the brink of another financial crisis.[4]

[1] The Anti-regulatory Debate and Misaligned Incentives

The anti-regulatory argument by the pro-market factions is much easier to peddle politically, largely because of low apparent cost of softer or no-regulations comparing to putting in place costlier regulations in order to achieve longer-term unseen benefits of lowering the risk potential from future crises. As these benefits accrue only to the next generations (who are not physically or virtually there to vote in favor), it is challenging to implement such reforms whose beneficiaries are not there to defend effectively.[5] Arguably, it is also true that the cost of compliance to various regulatory regimes (involving cross-national financial transactions) has increased significantly due to extraterritoriality of the regulatory initiatives. Regulatory incentives need to be aligned for not only addressing arbitrage opportunities but also to streamline increasing fragmentation within the discipline of IFL and thereby reducing the cost of regulatory compliance.

[2] The Reform Fatigue

Long-term reforms are prone to lose momentum as time passes and recovery process can slowdown implementation of a heavy reform agenda (which seems to be the case currently). This is particularly the case with the GFC. The GFC became a protracted series of complex crises events. We saw the SDC following the GFC and both crises spanned over a significant number of years involving many countries in Europe, the US and even in Asia. The G20 took on an ambitious pledge in 2008 however the support for regulatory reforms dwindled as G20's agenda progressed to include many other emergent issues requiring immediate policy attention. It is therefore, imperative to press on with the reform agenda and not to succumb to reform fatigue.

---

4. Larry Summers remarked, *we could be on the brink of another 2008 financial crisis.* (2015). Retrieved from http://myinforms.com/en/a/15725590-larry-summers-says-we-could-be-on-the-brink-of-another-2008-financial-crisis/ see his twitter posts, *as in August 1997, 1998, 2007 and 2008 we could be in the early stage of a very serious situation,* Retrieved from https://twitter.com/LHSummers/status/635814574374170624.
5. *See,* Carney, M. (2014). *The Future of Financial Reform.* Retrieved from speech given by the Governor of the Bank of England, Chair of the Financial Stability Board, at the Monetary Authority of Singapore, Lecture on 17 November 2014, available at, http://www.financialstabilityboard.org/wp-content/uploads/The-future-of-financial-reform.pdf, *see also,* Carney, M. (Feb. 24, 20 14). *Financial Reforms: Progress and Challenges. Letter to the G20 Finance Ministers and Central Bank Governors,* FSB. Retrieved from https://www.financialstabilityboard.org/publications/r_1 40222.pdf.

[3] Markets Have Failed Us

The BCBS Chairman in a speech referred to the incapacity of the pre-crisis regulatory framework to outsmart the increasing complexity of the existing financial system.[6] While talking about the incapacity of self-regulating markets (which, in the pre-crisis period, assumed to have 'graduated'), Fischer said:

> [w]e need to remind ourselves that the principle underlying Basel II was that the private sector would manage risk efficiently and effectively, since the last thing a bank would want would be to fail. That did not work out as predicted.[7]

It is important to note that the gist of this research is not to advocate for bringing in more regulation. This research has expanded on the distinct weaknesses of the IFL, its regulatory architecture and its enforcement mechanism. It is about strengthening the discipline of IFL through an enforcement mechanism to make the financial system more responsive to the crisis in an effective way. Over-regulation and/or centralized state controls can stifle growth prospects besides being too costly both for consumers and for regulators. The Chair of the FSB while underlining the importance of *trust* in the financial system argued that the succession of financial scandals alludes to the *real problem*, which is not of simply *a few bad apples*,[8] but, according to him, *the problem lies with the barrels in which those apples are stored* i.e., the existing financial system itself has deeper problems.[9]

---

6. He further stated that, during the last 20 years, *the average risk weight has declined* from 70% to below 40% but this reduction did not represent a genuine reduction in risk in the banking system. See, Ingves, M. S. (November 2014). Implementing the regulatory reform agenda – the pitfall of myopia: FSB, speech by the Chairman, Basel Committee on Banking Supervision and Governor, at the Federal Reserve Bank of Chicago, available at http://www.financialstabilityboard.org/wp-content/uploads/Stefan-Ingves-Implementing-the-regulatory-reform-agenda-the-pitfall-of-myopia.pdf.
7. Fischer, S. (Jun. 1, 2015). [What Have We Learned From the Crises of the Last 20 Years? Remarks by the Vice Chairman, Board of Governors of the Federal Reserve System, at the International Monetary Fund Conference, Toronto, Ontario, available at http://www.federalreserve.gov/newsevents/speech/fischer20150601a.pdf].
8. This view contrasts to the market who view not infrequently that post-crises reforms and increased regulation have made the system complex and skewed to favor excessive regulation. See, Carney, M. (2014). '*The future of financial reform*', speech given by the Governor of the Bank of England, Chair of the Financial Stability Board, at the Monetary Authority of Singapore, Lecture on 17 November 2014, available at http://www.financialstabilityboard.org/wp-content/uploads/The-future-of-financial-reform.pdf/.
9. In good old days, the financial system including the present day banking originated on the basis of trust. It also resembles the tenets underlying the sharia' based Islamic finance whose principles emanate from *trust* which essentially is rooted in the concept of risk-sharing finance. Risk-sharing finance is trust intensive, and trade financing during the Middle Ages was based on risk sharing, which, in turn, was based on mutual trust. However, with the passage of time, due to wars, misery and other devastations, scarcity led to the breakdown of trust and the financial horizon developed to address the changed realities. See, for an elaborate account of Middle Ages, Evans, H. C. (Ed.) (1964). *Age of Transition: Byzantine Culture in the Islamic World*. The Metropolitan Museum of Art. The Islamic finance, despite being only a few decades old discipline, draws its roots from the basic sharia tenets of *trust* which is rooted in the concept of risk-sharing. A financial system based on risk-sharing (where all stakeholders share any losses arising) makes the entire stakeholders act responsibly.

[B] Is Financial Stability Still an International Public Good

Financial stability is an *international public good*[10] and national governments as well as global governance institutions both owe this right to their publics. However, this critically important right has not been incorporated in the Universal Declaration of Human Rights (UDHR).[11] Since financial stability is an international public good, domestic regulation may be needed when firms or financial institutions do not bear all the risks following from their policies and actions. In such situations, Trachtman suggests adopting the subsidiarity concept at a higher level of institution. Accordingly, international regulation is needed when states do not bear all the risks of their regulatory actions, where states acting individually would otherwise underinvest in a global public good, or where states may regulate more efficiently by working together.[12]

Some scholars equate *constitutional legitimacy* of International Economic Law (IEL) in its consistency with respect to *human rights* and *democracy*.[13] IFL has been lately under scrutiny for being devoid of legitimacy and for not adopting itself to the changed realities, which demanded adequate representation of various groups of economies on its institutional and decision-making platforms (*see* Chapters 3 and 6). This extends to both the input legitimacy of IFL (which relates to the functioning and machinery of an institution for example, decision-making processes at the FSB), and

---

10. *See*, Kaul, I., Conceição, P., Goulven, K. L., & Mendoza, R. U. (Eds.). (2003). Providing Global Public Goods: Managing Globalization. Oxford University Press. Charnovitz, S. (2014). International Economic Law in the 21st Century: Constitutional Pluralism and Multilevel Governance of Interdependent Public Goods. By Ernst-Ulrich Petersmann. *Journal of International Economic Law, 17*(1), 178-183. Shirakawa, M. (14 October, 2012). [International financial stability as a public good. Keynote address by Governor of the Bank of Japan, at a high-level seminar, co-hosted by the Bank of Japan and the International Monetary Fund, Tokyo, available at http://www.bis.org/review/r121015c.pdf?frames = 0]. Griffith-Jones, S. (No date). New Financial Architecture as a Global Public Good. *Available at http://www.ids.ac.uk/files/griffithj4.pdf.* Kindleberger, C. P. (1986). International Public Goods without International Government. *The American Economic Review, 76*(1), 1-13. Retrieved from http://www.jstor.org/stable/1804123 Kindleberger, C. P. (1981). Dominance and Leadership in the International Economy: Exploitation, Public Goods, and Free Rides. *International Studies Quarterly, 25*(2), 242-254. Retrieved from http://www.jstor.org/stable/2600355 Petersmann, E.-U. (2014). Need for a New Philosophy of International Economic Law and Adjudication. *Journal of International Economic Law, 17*(3), 639-669.
11. *See*, for example, Petersmann, E.-U. (2014). Need for a New Philosophy of International Economic Law and Adjudication. *Journal of International Economic Law, 17*(3), 639-669; He also spotlights the 'human right to have *international rights*' which is also not spelled out in the UNHR declaration, *see*, Petersmann, EU. (2012). JIEL Debate: Methodological Pluralism and its Critics in International Economic Law Research. *Journal of International Economic Law, 15*(4), 921-970.
12. Trachtman, J. P. (Aug 2011). *Fragmentation and Coherence in International Law*. Retrieved from SSRN: http://ssrn.com/abstract = 1908862, http://dx.doi.org/10.2139/ssrn.1908862 Last accessed, Aug. 24, 2016.
13. Petersmann (2012), *see also*, Franck, T. M. (2006). The Power of Legitimacy and the Legitimacy of Power: International Law in an Age of Power Disequilibrium. *The American Journal of International Law, 100*(1), 88-106. *See also*, Franck, T. M. (1988). Legitimacy in the International System. *American Journal of International Law, 82*, 705-759. Retrieved from http://nw18.american.edu/~dfagel/Philosophers/TOPICS/HumanitarianIntervention/Legitimacy%20In%20The%20International%20SystemSmaller.pdf.

the output legitimacy (the public assessment of the relevance and quality of the institution's performance, for example as expressed by market outcomes).

§7.03 CONCLUSIONS AND RECOMMENDATION

Recalling Bagehot's words:[14]

> I fear that I must not expect a very favorable reception for this work. It speaks mainly of four sets of persons... and I am much afraid that [none] will altogether like what is said of them... (Walter Bagehot, Lombard Street).

In the following section, some bold recommendations are enunciated to address financial crises posing unremitting threats to financial market stability. Regulators or the markets may not give a favorable reception to the recommendations. To address incessant crises and instability, there are two basic recommendations that this research strongly advocates: strengthening responsiveness and coherence within the discipline of IFL; and, correcting structural inadequacies extant in the existing financial system by adopting risk prevention/management models.

[A] Approach I: Strengthening Responsiveness Within

An impartial and detached look at the relative gains from the post-2008 regulatory reform indicates a few gains that we made: first, improved policy coordination, for example by establishing the FSB. Second, the post-2008 reform resulted in broadening of perspective, mobilizing consensus on enhanced capital and liquidity standards, and, in an inclusive debate on the role of institutions, regulators and markets. Third, we made progress towards a more inclusive financial system, for example, the Emerging Market Economies (EMEs)'s increased membership in the institutions of financial governance like the Basel Committee on Banking Supervision (BCBS). Finally, the crisis increased the involvement of significant global financial and political leadership in the reform of IFL and its regulatory structures, for example, through the participation of the G20 in the reform agenda.

Notwithstanding the *gains,* it is to be noted that in many subtle ways soft-law-based IFL is experiencing a gradual hardening process.[15] In reference to the adoption and implementation of Basel standards – which most of the countries have already *committed* to adopt into their domestic legislation and implement – some consider having *committed* to the soft-standards of IFL is more profound than having an IFL embedded in a *binding* structure. This has been, however, contested through existing

---

14. Calomiris, C. (1998). Blueprints for a New Global Financial Architecture. Mimeo, Columbia Business School, October 7. Retrieved from http://www.jec.senate.gov/public/_cache/files/edcf86a0-93eb-45de-830c-bae1f65ca100/charles-w.-calomiris-blueprints-for-a-new-global-financial-architecture.pdf. Walter Bagehot's Lombard Street is available online at http://www.econlib.org/library/Bagehot/bagLom2.html last accessed, Aug. 25, 2015.
15. *See,* Abbott, K. W., Keohane, R. O., Moravcsik, A., Slaughter, A.-M., & Snidal, D. (2000). The Concept of Legalization. *International Organization, 54*(3), 401-419.

Chapter 7: Conclusions, Challenges and Recommendations §7.03[A]

evidence as well as by historical facts.[16] The underestimation of risks in good times incentivizes excessive risk taking without contemplating fallouts of a distress during a crunch (which can trigger devastating consequences, as happened in the UK in 2007 in the case of the Northern Rock).

Also, in the post-recovery periods the complacency of peaceful times reassures faith in the stability of markets, which while feeding on itself, boosts market's confidence in its ability to shoulder higher debts and undertake much higher risks, potentially leading to, what Minsky calls, *the third stage of debt, the Ponzi finance* (could end in *Minsky moment*).[17] Global financial markets experienced that *Minsky moment* recently in 2008. The economist Hyman Minsky integrated human tendency to be over-confident into his famous financial instability hypothesis,[18] according to which, *seeds of a crisis are sown in times of stability.*[19] Therefore, the crisis moment may provide an enabling environment to commit to bold and hard choices. The GFC has been a defining moment of the twenty-first century and post-GFC reform had the potential to become a defining moment in the development of the discipline of IFL.[20] It, however, didn't materialize. In the discipline of IFL, finance is a means to an end. The end is economic development and providing global financial market stability. The ends are achievable by developing accountable, responsive and effective institutions with strong legal framework. The G20's emergence in the post-2008 era as *high table of*

---

16. For example, the Basel capital rules though came with *stringent requirements*, yet due to an absence of an enforcement mechanism; the USA, Russia and Argentina are in the process of adoption of Basel I and II where the rest of the world has almost started the adoption or implementation of Basel III.
17. A Minsky moment is a sudden major collapse of asset values, which is part of the credit cycle or business cycle. Such moments occur because long periods of prosperity and increasing value of investments lead to increasing speculation using borrowed money. *See*, Did Hyman Minsky Find the Secret Behind Financial Crashes? (Mar. 24, 2014). *BBC Magazine*. Retrieved from http://www.bbc.com/news/magazine-26680993 last accessed Aug 26, 2015; *see also*, The Fed Discovers Hyman Minsky. (Jan. 7, 2010). *The Economist*. http://www.economist.com/blogs/freeexchange/2010/01/the_fed_discovers_hyman_minsky.
18. For example, Minsky, H. (1992). The Financial Instability Hypothesis. Levy Economics Institute of Bard College, Working Paper No. 74. Retrieved from http://www.levyinstitute.org/pubs/wp74.pdf, last accessed Aug. 26, 2015. *See also*, Minsky, H. (1986). Stabilizing an Unstable Economy: Yale University Press, A pdf is available at http://digamo.free.fr/minsky86.pdf. and, Did Hyman Minsky Find the Secret Behind Financial Crashes? (Mar. 24. 2014). BBC Magazine. Retrieved from http://www.bbc.com/news/magazine-26680993, last accessed Aug. 26, 2015.
19. The G-SIFI assets increased from $2.6 trillion to $30 trillion during 1993 to 2003 (a 12 times increase), as against the capital funding to provide for these assets, which rose from $125 billion to $890 billion (a seven times increase) despite having in place Basel I and Basel II capital adequacy frameworks in place. *See* the speech, Carney, M. (2014). 'The future of financial reform', speech given by the Governor of the Bank of England, Chair of the Financial Stability Board, at the Monetary Authority of Singapore, Lecture on 17 November 2014, available at http://www.financialstabilityboard.org/wp-content/uploads/The-future-of-financial-reform.pdf.
20. *See*, The post-crisis 'moment' forms the context and backdrop to the theme of fragmentation while the editors trace the evolution of international economic system from its original Bretton Woods design to the present day. *See*, Lim, C. L., & Mercurio, B. (Eds.). (2015). p. 6.

economic governance[21] has done little structural or substantive change in the methods of international economic regulation meant to provide global financial stability.[22]

While talking of instituting a treaty-based IFL, the dilemma of asymmetrical sovereignties is considered as the biggest obstacle to cross for formulating such system. Not too long ago, in the post-GFC scenario, the G20 and the FSB while exercising leadership in setting up post-crisis reform agenda faced irreconcilable issues of keeping intact the autonomy of Member States and their own independence of action.[23] The structural predicaments in the current global regulatory institutions are not least the result of an asymmetric sovereignty as Member States can assert only a marginal impact on international financial markets. However, the Member States are liable in times of crisis due to G-SIFIs and financial institutions being constantly engaged in cross-border financial transactions which erode national boundaries. It is thus, indispensable in this situation to set aside issues of national sovereignties and rationalize financial policies affecting multiple jurisdictions.[24]

For global financial market issues, we require global solutions. A comprehensive legal framework for enforcement of financial regulations could be the key to the success of the initiatives that the FSB and the G20 are unrolling. Here, it may be pertinent to look at the World Trade Organization (WTO) and the FSB's implementation surveillance[25] platform and possibly at the Dispute Settlement Mechanism

---

21. *See*, Buckley, R. P. (2015). From Regional Fragmentation to Coherence: A way Forward for East Asia. In C. L. Lim & B. Mercurio (Eds.), International Economic Law after the Global Crisis: A Tale of Fragmented Disciplines. Cambridge University Press. p. 114.
22. In the same volume as above, An Hertogen comments that despite the lofty pronouncements at the G20 about the need for cooperation, states have so far agreed on few effective limits. *See*, Hertogen, E. (2015) in C. L. Lim & B. Mercurio (Eds.).
23. The Global Financial Crisis: Lessons from History, Brookings event: Eichengreen, Lipton, Chris, and Wessel, Jan 14, 2015 Available at http://www.brookings.edu/events/2015/01/14-global-financial-crisis-lessons-from-history?utm_campaign=Hutchins+Center&utm_source=hs_email&utm_medium=email&utm_content=15564612&_hsenc=p2ANqtz--4sykOGKR94Q50E_eRaUoIY5_EznMYx6Sw8D0FrklUfS5m0o2PB3Ru62VQeAYl5wFsS7B2k0yv4uyUfwBrZ4ImGWNGrg&_hsmi=15564612.
24. Dieter, H., & Krummenacher, M. (2013). The G-20 and the Dilemma of Asymmetric Sovereignty: Why Multilateralism Is Failing in Crisis Prevention. Retrieved from SWP comments 2013/C 30 Sep, Stiftung Wissenschaft und Politik, German Institute for International and Security Affairs, available at http://www.swp-berlin.org/fileadmin/contents/products/comments/2013C30_dtr.pdf.
25. *See*, Gu, B., & Liu, T. (2014). Enforcing International Financial Regulatory Reforms. *Journal of International Economic Law*. Chapter 1.

Chapter 7: Conclusions, Challenges and Recommendations §7.03[B]

(DSM)[26] of the WTO[27] (in particular at the provision for retaliation).[28] The DSM can facilitate mutual compliance[29] as the DSM lends the necessary legitimacy for bilateral retaliation, vis-à-vis self-initiated *tit-for-tat* process. In order to maintain a responsive and resilient international financial system, consistent and prompt adoption of its legal rules remains essential. The post-GFC experience leaves little doubt on the prospect for a hard-law-based structure to be adopted any time soon; however, what has become certain is that the soft-law-based post-crisis regulatory institutions and regulations have added to the existing incoherence and fragmentation of IFL regime.

[B] Approach II: Looking Ahead, Beyond Within

[1] Financial Market Risk Prevention and Management Mechanism

If the objective of financial regulation is global market stability, it is important to take reform decisions that conform to procedural justice and distributive equity. Such decisions must not only constructively contribute to the development of IFL but also manifest through its regulatory architecture (stated in Chapter 1, Research Objectives). For a safer financial market system, it is recommended revisiting the foundations of the existing financial system, which operates on debt-based model (and has forgone substantive roots in real assets) and is devoid of sufficient risk-prevention and management mechanism.[30] Originally and historically, financial systems were not

---

26. The WTO mechanism in simple words works as follows: the DSM of the WTO recommends a defaulting member, following the DSM finding, to comply with the member's commitments under the WTO agreement. The DSM suggests ways to implement its recommendations, pending the defaulting member's choice of means to implement. Typically, the defaulting member should state its intention to implement the recommendation within 30 days after the recommendation being adopted. If immediate implementation is not feasible, then there comes a determination of a *reasonable period* of time for implementation, either made by private agreement or arbitration but not exceeding 15 months. The power of this DSM lies where the prevailing member may request the DSM to authorize retaliation by suspending the prevailing member's concessions owed to the defaulting member, if the latter fails to implement the DSM's recommendations properly.
27. Trachtman, J. P. (2010). The International Law of Financial Crisis: Spillovers, Subsidiary, Fragmentation, and Cooperation. *Journal of International Economic Law, 13*(3). Retrieved from Available at SSRN: http://ssrn.com/abstract = 1630523 or http://dx.doi.org/10.2139/ssrn.1630 523.
28. The retaliation system is rational and persuasive, partially because it takes account of the concerns of the non-implementing member who may rebuke the level of authorized retaliation by arbitration. Retaliation is LoLR in the WTO system.
29. Scholarship has since long talked about addressing the absence of conflict resolution mechanism in IFL. This gap has specially been highlighted since the tested effectiveness of the DSM as exists in international trade law (under WTO), under the various investment regimes and other related areas of IEL. *See* for example, Trachtman, J. P. (2010). The International Law of Financial Crisis: Spillovers, Subsidiary, Fragmentation, and Cooperation. *Journal of International Economic Law, 13*(3). Retrieved from Available at SSRN: http://ssrn.com/abstract = 1630523 or http://dx.doi.org/10.2139/ssrn.1630523.
30. A debt-based financial system with fractional reserve banking is inherently fragile and prone to periodic instability. According to some scholarship (influenced by Minsky, low returns on loans render banks unable to raise interest rates on their loans, and these low rates coax banks to adapt to a liability-management mode by increasing interest rates on their deposits, and this vicious

based on debt but had footings in real assets and therefore were less prone to various kinds of risks.[31] One recent example of a stable financial system (the late nineteenth century) was based on *gold standard*[32] *of exchange* (the system lasted until the World Wars) and was inherently stronger, and resilient to various financial market risks primarily due to its design.[33] A financial system based on tangible assets (i.e., backed by real assets and not on fiat currency) can function to stop the currency wars, major exchange fluctuations and restraining issues of capital flows.[34] However, for such a system (unlike the gold standard which was easy to wiggle out), it is important to have well-defined legally-backed financial standards to provide the required capacity to

---

circle continues to pick up momentum. Gradually, the liability management transforms into Ponzi financing and eventually leading to bank-runs.

31. Brouwer has traced the evolution of the modern-day corporation in the European context and has described how the equity-based *commenda* organizations supported trade in medieval Europe. The Commenda organization, which slowly and gradually evolved over centuries to become present-day limited liability companies were functioning across Italy (Pisa and Venice) at that time. These organizations at that time were based on *equity financing*, as opposed to debt financing. *See*, Brouwer, M. (2005). Managing Uncertainty through Profit Sharing Contracts from Medieval Italy to Silicon Valley. *Journal of Management & Governance*, 9(3), 237-255. Scholarship has found strong the linkages between the Commenda organizations and its origins in Islamic finance. *See*, Askari, H., Iqbal, Z., & Mirakhor, A. (2009). Islamic Finance, Conventional Finance, and Globalization *and Islamic Finance* (pp. 59-77): John Wiley & Sons (Asia) Pte. Ltd. *See also*, Askari, H., Iqbal, Z., & Mirakhor, A. (2010). Globalization and Islamic Finance: Convergence, Prospects and Challenges. John Wiley & Sons. And also, Askari, H., & Krichene, N. (2014). Islamic Finance: An Alternative Financial System for Stability, Equity, and Growth. PSL Quarterly Review, 67(268), 9-54. available at http://ojs.uniroma1.it/index.php/PSLQuarterlyReview/article/view/11984/11824.
32. G20's inaugural meetings following the crisis in 2008 were dubbed as a version of twenty-first century version of Bretton Woods. Some others call it or bringing back the Bretton Woods II.
33. As stated above (fn 30), fractional reserve banking is inherently prone to risks whereas a risk-sharing finance model by design is trust intensive. Going back in history, trade financing during the Middle Ages was based on risk sharing, which, in turn, was based on mutual trust, however, the catastrophic wars (Crusades, Mongol invasions) led to the deterioration of trade routes and customs; famines and traumatic experiences of the Middle Ages ultimately led to the gradual breakdown of trust in the society, which spread rapidly throughout the then-known world across its various systems including the financial system. For the history of Byzantine culture, *see*, vans, H. C. (Ed.) (1964). Age of Transition: Byzantine Culture in the Islamic World. The Metropolitan Museum of Art. For a more recent read on how trust develops and deteriorates, *see*, Alesina and La Ferrrara who document the phenomenon of 'how individual experiences and community characteristics influence how much people trust each', *see*, Alesina, A., & La Ferrara, E. (2002). Who Trusts Others? *Journal of Public Economics*, 85(2), 207-234. Going back to the financial system as it evolved in the Middle Ages from a 'trust and trade' basis to the debt-based modern day financial system, economic historians document that in old days, these trade flows were supported by a financial system sustained by an expanding risk-sharing credit structure based on *commenda* and *maona (where Commenda, has strong parallels in* mudarabah, and maona seem to originate from either musharakah or mudarabah – the Islamic finance's permissible forms of partnerships. *See* for details on this subject, the groundbreaking work from Postan, which illustrates the origin of Commenda rooted deep in Islamic finance's tradition of risk sharing. *See*, Postan, M. (1928). Credit in Medieval Trade 1. *The Economic History Review*, a1(2), 234-261.
34. The existing financial system is based on fiat currency and requires a need for constant growth with unlimited access to resources (i.e., capital, which is raised through issuance of debt) for its continued functioning. As stated above(fn 30), this debt-issuance model comes to a halt as the existing economic levels face diminishing returns from debt and to continue increasing returns, more debt needs to be issued and the cycle perpetuates resulting into expansion of debt-based economy without the real assets to back the growth.

absorb financial shocks[35] (through the risk-sharing mechanism where all shareholders and stockholders share gains and shoulder losses) and manage crisis. This could base for example on the underlying principles of *Islamic Finance*[36] in which risk-management strategy is based on *equity stake rather than debt*. A financial transaction based on debt-financing and profit-sharing only is inherently risk-prone in comparison with an equity which accounts for probable risks and ensures stability. Islamic finance is based on asset-backed securities and thus risk is shared between all the stakeholders unlike conventional finance, which is debt-based and interest profits.[37] Since asset-based finance provides best risk-hedging strategy,[38] its principles of risk management, if are adopted into conventional finance would draw a parallel to the gold standard's central principle of having *real* assets backing the economy.[39]

The purpose of a financial system, whether it is conventional or Islamic, *should aim at mobilizing* financial resources, minimizing risk and providing an enabling environment to its participants to enhance their welfare. The following Islamic finance principles have potential to contribute to the conventional financial system:

- First, prohibition of uncertainty (principle of *gharaar,* as is called in Islamic finance) which restricts any exchange in which there is an imprecise, ambiguous, or uncertain element, and may include speculation, gambling, derivatives (but not forward purchase in certain situations). Recently, regulation of Global-Systemically Important Financial Institutions (G-SIFIs) and Global-Systemically Important Banks (G-SIBs) has emerged as the biggest challenge in the post-2008 financial markets and an application of the principle of 'gharaar' certainly will outlaw *immeasurable risks* from the speculative nature of financial system by itself.

---

35. Although *euro* provided that stringent system yet questions on its capacity to absorb shocks are yet to resolve.
36. Islamic financial institutions manage about an estimated USD 1 trillion in assets globally, and as a whole, the Islamic finance industry's annual growth rate has averaged 23% since 1994. *See,*for an alternative treatment of risk under Islamic finance, Askari, H., Iqbal, Z., Krichne, N., & Mirakhor, A. (2012). Risk Sharing in Finance: The Islamic Finance Alternative. John Wiley & Sons.
37. The phenomenon of *interest* in the practice of *Shari'ah*-compliant business activities was triggered a few decades ago by the expansion of conventional *interest-based* commercial banking in the Arab and Muslim world. In the late nineteenth century, a formal critique and opposition to the element of *interest* started in Egypt when Barclays Bank was established in Cairo to raise funds for the construction of the Suez Canal.
38. Islamic institutions appear to have largely avoided the fallout of the crisis due to lack of exposure to the subprime mortgage market and the absence of complex structured products, *see*, John Aglionby, Islamic Banks Urged to Show the West the Sharia Way Forward, *Financial Times*, London, Mar. 3, 2009, p. 3.
39. The Islamic Financial Services Board (IFSB) was established with the support of the IMF in 2002 by central banks and the Islamic Development Bank, to frame prudential standards and guidelines for international application by banking supervisors in the supervision of Islamic finance products. See, Archer, S. & Karim, R. A. A. eds., Islamic Finance: The Regulatory Challenge. John Wiley & Sons, 2007. *See also*, in the same volume, Archer, S. & Karim, R. A. A. Measuring Risk for Capital Adequacy: The Issue of Profit-Sharing Investment Accounts, 223-235.

- Second, the principle of *asset-backed financing* or tangibility of underlying assets (which is similar to the gold standard ethos)[40] intrinsically makes the finance and the financial system stable.[41] The ABS requirement will restrict or curb subprime loans and mortgages, securitization, derivative, and debt-based industry. The system based on sharing of risk, finance, skills and other contributions in the form of various joint ventures does not stifle innovative business financing.
- Third, the principle of partnership in gains and risks i.e., profit-or-loss-sharing is another taking that the existing conventional finance can emulate. Essentially based on sharing of loss and profit (both) in a pre-defined ratio and providing for *equity-sharing* rather than raising capital (by issuing debt-based instruments)[42] distributes risk on all stakeholders and saves taxpayers from shouldering costly crises.

Despite the myriad post-crisis reforms, laudable commitments to implement them, and initiatives to establish newer institutions, legislation, regulation and reversal of many policy changes, the fact remains that the financial system continues to be fragile. The argument to integrate principles from gold standards (or of Islamic finance)[43] has been discussed undoubtedly at many forums but could not get much attraction. The misconceptions and political considerations trumpeted – whether deliberately or not – many opportunities to incorporate elements from the asset-backed finance model (i.e., gold standards and/Islamic finance). According to the analysis drawn in this research, the gold standard could provide a solution for addressing international financial instability[44] if only it is anchored in 100% reserve banking (an essential pillar of Islamic finance as well).

---

40. See a recent work on the subject, Askari, H., & Krichene, N. (2014). *Gold Standards Anchored in Islamic Finance* Palgrave Macmillan US.
41. See, Askari, H., & Krichene, N. (2014). Islamic Finance: An Alternative Financial System for Stability, Equity, and Growth. *PSL Quarterly Review, 67*(268), 9-54.
42. In the absence of frictions, a firm's financial structure would be indifferent between debt and equity, showed Franco Modigliani and Merton Miller in 1958. However, in the real world, the two important frictions (of taxation and of information) make debt financing and debt-based contracts as the better option. The tax treatment of equity returns and interests is heavily biased against equities and so are the informational issues (information asymmetry and the subsidies and policies that encourage moral hazard and adverse selection). See, Modigliani, F., & Miller, M. H. (1958). The Cost of Capital, Corporation Finance and the Theory of Investment. *The American Economic Review, 48*(3), 261-297.
43. This research is NOT primarily talking about incorporating principles of Islamic finance. In all its advocacy, the recommendation is to look into some of these principles, which exist in Islamic finance but also formed the foundations of the gold standards as well as the remaining hallmarks of all the financial systems (including in the Middle Ages), which were based on 100% reserve banking or ABS. The exception is the post-gold standard debt-based system or the fractional reserve banking system. See for a thorough discussion of the topic why crises are becoming more and more frequent, severe, and how the reforms initiatives are littered with gaps between the theory and the practice, See, Alrifai, T. (June 2015), Islamic Finance and the New Financial System: An Ethical Approach to Preventing Future Financial Crises. John Wiley & Sons.
44. The caveat is anchoring the financial system in reserve banking. The shift from fractional reserve to reserve banking could be gradual and perhaps may not reach full 100%, however, a gradual transition towards reserve banking (asset-backed) could bring back the lost *trust* in the existing financial system. To find the best balance between the existing fractional reserve and 100%

Thus to conclude, a reconstruction of the discipline of IFL and its regulatory architecture is indispensable for the long-term financial market stability and economic growth. It requires increased risk management by putting in place crisis-prevention and crisis-management tool kits, and by empowering IFL to seek compliance to the regulatory frameworks which Member States commit to adopt and implement:

> We become just by performing just actions, temperate by performing temperate actions, and brave by performing brave actions. (Aristotle).

[2] Further Research

In the context of developing financial system with an inbuilt risk-prevention mechanism and post-crises risk-management strategies, a comprehensive independent research must be conducted to find the best balance between the existing debt-based (fractional reserve) and an asset-based (100% reserve banking) financial system. This can take into account the underlying principles of gold standard and of the concept of ABS in order to devise such a framework. This would involve designing up structural specifics for putting in place such a financial system.

---

reserve requires further research, which is beyond the scope of this study. *See*, Askari, H., & Krichene, N. (2014). Gold Standards Anchored in Islamic Finance Palgrave Macmillan US.

Index

A

ABIF. *See* Asian Banking Integration Framework (ABIF)
Accountability, 2, 5, 15, 33, 67, 78, 86, 107, 109, 120, 122, 190, 215, 219–220, 235–236
Argentinian crisis, 41–42
Arner, 4, 39, 191, 233
Asian Banking Integration Framework (ABIF), 192
Asian Financial crisis, 5
Asian Monetary Fund (AMF), 41
Association of South East Asian Nations (ASEAN), 192
Avgouleas, 54

B

Bank for International Settlements, 3, 20, 27, 37, 52, 71–75, 85, 88, 89, 93–96, 101–102, 105–107, 126, 177, 202, 220, 223, 224, 230
Basel Capital Accords
　Basel 2.5, 137
　Basel I, 71, 118
　Basel II, 71, 74
　Basel III, 71, 74
　Basel IV, 153
　BCBS (*see* Basel Committee on Banking Supervision (BCBS))
　capital ratios, 119, 135, 146
　CARs, 75, 81, 120, 122, 126, 153
　First Concordat, 118
　Revised Concordat, 118
Basel Committee on Banking Supervision (BCBS), 51, 52, 59, 71, 74, 80, 84, 85, 88, 89, 95, 98, 107, 133, 136, 138, 223, 240, 242
Brazil, 36, 37, 39, 42, 78, 102, 223, 227
Brummer, 215, 216, 233
Buckley, 4, 39, 233

C

Chiang Mai Initiative (CMI), 41
Committee on Payment and Settlement Systems (CPSS), 52, 74, 88, 89, 95, 139
Committee on the Global Financial System (CGFS), 52, 74, 88, 89, 95
Compliance
　cost, 116, 119, 148, 211, 214
　regulatory compliance, 2, 13, 119, 123, 239
Credit Rating Agencies (CRA)
　credit rating, 87, 206, 207, 214, 231
Crisis management
　prevention, 2, 13, 14, 70, 105, 178, 182, 195, 234, 236–238, 249

D

Debt crisis, 13, 36–37, 68, 69, 74, 168, 169, 180, 189, 238
Delors Report
　Colleges of Supervisors, 175, 176, 205, 211, 228

Index

Deposit Guarantee Scheme (DGS), 13, 158, 182, 183, 206
Development Theory
    Law and Development, 61–64
Dispute Settlement Mechanism (DSM), 244, 245
Dodd-Frank Act (DFA), 55, 82, 208

E

Eichengreen, 18, 19, 21, 27, 48, 202, 230, 232
Emerging Market Economies (EMEs), 67, 70, 114, 223, 242
Enforcement
    regulatory enforcement, 211
European Banking Authority (EBA), 13, 91, 135, 143, 158, 175, 181, 182, 193, 238
European Central Bank (ECB), 32, 34, 73, 88, 91, 103, 149, 168, 172, 174, 177, 178, 182–185, 188, 227
European Coal and Steel Community (ECSC), 156, 197
European Commission (EC), 34, 35, 82, 91, 93, 100, 101, 123, 131, 163, 165, 167, 168, 173, 174, 176, 177, 181–183, 185, 188, 227
European Community (EC), 34
European Economic and Monetary Union (EMU), 34, 41, 73, 156, 162, 163, 168–170, 174, 179–182, 189
    European single market, 13, 34, 109, 157–160, 162, 164, 165, 167–190, 193, 237, 238
    European Union (EU), 89, 109, 155, 168, 178, 236
European Economic Community (EEC), 34, 73, 156, 162, 164, 165
European Exchange Rate Mechanism (ERM), 34, 38, 163

European Financial Stability Facility (ESFS), 13, 157, 170, 174, 175, 177, 188, 193, 238
European Payments Union (EPU), 27, 73
European Securities and Markets Authority (ESMA), 91, 143, 175
European Single Market Institutions, 179
European Single Resolution Mechanism (SRM), 158, 185, 186
European Systemic Risk Board (ESRB), 13, 93, 175, 177, 178, 238
European System of Financial Supervisors (ESFS), 13, 157, 170, 174, 175, 177, 188, 193, 238
Euro Plus Pact, 179
Exchange Rate Mechanism (ERM), 34, 38, 163

F

Financial Action Task Force (FATF), 84
Financial Innovation
    liberal financial markets, 200
    liberalization, 66, 75, 201
    market integration, 156, 158–167, 170, 184, 191
    market liberalization, 13, 238
Financial Market Stability (FMS), 11, 12, 14, 16, 18, 32, 45, 60, 70, 105, 193, 195, 196, 215, 230, 242, 243, 249
Financial Services Authority (FSA), 53, 112, 126, 148, 208, 209
Financial Stability Board (FSB), 2, 95, 236
Financial Stability Forum (FSF), 2, 15, 51, 70, 74, 79, 87–90, 93, 95, 102, 107, 202
Financial Stability Trilemma, 160
The Fortis Bank, 170, 172
Fractional Reserve Banking, 249
Fragmentation, 2, 4, 87, 174, 182, 189, 202, 204, 206, 239, 245
FSB Secretariat, 93

Index

G

General Agreement on Tariffs and Trade (GATT), 27, 28, 32, 58, 89
General Agreement to Borrow (GAB), 30, 101
Glass-Steagall Act (GSA), 23, 49, 75, 113, 197, 202
Global Financial Crisis (GFC) 2, 237
   financial crisis, 10, 12, 16, 36, 39, 41, 50, 104, 115–117, 143, 151, 153, 171, 178, 180, 185, 207, 208, 217, 237, 239
Globalization 63, 67, 68, 74, 104, 153, 197, 198, 205, 221, 226
   Global Financial Regulator (GFReg), 67, 196, 229
Global Systemically Important Banks (G-SIBs) 99, 135, 138, 139, 147, 247
   Global Systemically Important Financial Institutions (G-SIFIs), 100, 115, 133, 147, 244, 247
Gold Standard
   classical, 18–23
   reconstructed, 18
Gramm-Leach-Bliley Act (GLBA), 49–51, 113
Group of Ten (G10), 30, 70, 73, 74, 78, 88, 95, 101, 126, 137, 199
Group of Thirty (G30), 102, 112, 113
Group of Twenty (G20), 5, 15, 25, 51–53, 68–71, 82–84, 89–108, 132, 133, 143, 152, 191, 192, 206, 217, 223, 224, 229, 239, 242–244

H

Hard law
   informal law making (IN-LAW), 7–9, 109
   soft law, 6, 7, 10, 11, 158, 195, 196, 211–217, 228, 233, 234, 237, 245
Harmonization
   home-host recognition, 125
   maximum, 161, 165–167
   minimum, 164–166, 169, 206
Historical recognition, 124–126

I

Icelandic Banking Crisis, 170–172
Integration
   economic, 74, 158, 159, 162–164
   monetary, 159, 163, 164
   political, 13, 151, 158, 159, 162, 193, 238
International Accounting Standards Board (IASB), 52, 71, 84, 85, 88, 89, 102
International Association of Insurance Supervisors (IAIS), 52, 71, 79–85, 88, 89, 91, 95, 102, 106
International Economic Law (IEL), 60, 203–205, 241
International Financial Institutions (IFI), 11, 14–16, 52, 63, 67, 68, 71, 80, 88, 89, 102, 112, 119, 152, 153, 200, 204, 205, 210, 215, 218–221, 223, 225–227, 230, 233, 234, 236
International Financial Law (IFL), 1, 235
International Financial Regulation (IFR), 118, 153, 189, 195, 198, 207, 212, 213, 217
International Financial regulatory Architecture (IFRA)
   IFR (*see* International financial regulation (IFR))
   regulatory architecture, 9, 11, 12, 55, 57–108, 110, 133, 153, 178, 192, 196, 229, 235–237, 240, 245, 249
International Financial Reporting Standards (IFRS)
   Generally Accepted Accounting Principles (GAAP), 84, 208
International financial stability
   FMS (*see* Financial Market Stability (FMS))

global financial stability, 10, 37, 217, 219, 229, 235, 236, 244
International Monetary Fund (IMF)
conditionality, 37, 41, 69, 71, 216
Governance Reforms, 100, 107, 220, 222
IMF Governance Reform, 100, 107, 220, 222, 225
Special Drawing Rights (SDRs), 30, 37, 221
International Monetary System (IMS), 18, 20, 24, 28, 58, 73, 221
International Organization of Securities Commissions (IOSCO)
IOSCO By-laws, 77
regulatory structures, 4, 43, 94, 105, 111–113, 159, 208, 218, 228, 242
securities regulation, 71, 75–79
supervision, 52, 56, 68, 71, 74, 77, 81–83, 87, 91, 102, 105, 111–113, 115, 116, 118–120
International Regulatory Bodies, 230
International trade
GAB (*see* General Agreement to Borrow (GAB))
GATT (*see* General Agreement on Tariffs and Trade (GATT))
General Agreement to Borrow (GAB), 30, 101
ITO (*see* International trade organization (ITO))
WTO (*see* World trade organization (WTO))
International trade organization (ITO), 27, 58
Islamic finance
asset backed system (ABS), 14, 247–249
debt-based financial system, 20, 21, 36, 59, 132, 245–249
equity-based financial system, 6, 114, 132, 245, 247, 248
gharaar (uncertainty), 247

J

Joint Forum, 52, 82–84

L

Lamfalussy process, 167, 174, 175, 183
Legal risk, 123
Legislations
DFA, 55, 82, 208
Directive on Markets in Financial Instruments (MiFID), 166, 167
Dodd-Frank legislation, 54, 55, 148
EBA Regulation, 181
ESAs Founding Regulation, 174
Legitimacy
input legitimacy, 219, 241
output legitimacy, 219, 220, 242
Lehman Brothers, 44, 45, 47, 50, 172, 205
Lender of Last Resort (LoLR), 19, 20, 22, 35, 43, 67, 75, 178, 191, 192, 207, 231, 232

M

Maastricht Treaty, 34, 73, 163, 165, 168
Market risk, 119, 120, 122, 131, 138, 228, 245–249
Maynard Keynes
Bretton Woods Institutions, 1, 26, 29, 34, 42, 58, 71, 202, 220, 227
1944 Conference, 25
Keynes' Plan, 24–26, 67
Mexico crisis, 36–37
Minsky Moment, 243
Monetary Policy
IMS (*see* International Monetary System (IMS))
Monetary System, 10, 18–21, 26, 201
Multilateral Development Banks (MDBs), 225, 228

N

New Institutional Economics (NIE)
  New International Financial Architecture (NIFA), 4, 11, 12, 17, 23, 38, 42, 57, 70, 87, 108–110, 237
Northern Rock (NR), 44, 45, 133, 205, 243

P

Public good
  International public goods, 200, 204, 205, 236, 241–242

Q

Quantitative Impact Studies (C-QIS), 134, 135

R

Reinsurance
  Insurance Core Principles (ICPs), 81, 84
Risk
  advanced measurement approaches (AMAs), 120, 124, 125, 127–131
  Bankhaus Herstatt, 74, 116, 118
  basic indicator approach (BIA), 120, 124, 125, 127–130
  Herstatt risk, 74, 76
  Internal Ratings-based Approach (IRA), 119
  operational risk, 13, 110, 119–132
  operational risk pillars, 110, 126
  standardized approach (TSA), 119, 124, 125, 129, 130
Risk Management
  prevention, 12, 13, 105, 110, 242, 245, 249
Risk-sharing
  equity-sharing finance, 248

Risk-weighted assets, 136, 145
Russian crisis, 37–38

S

Santiago Principles, 216, 233
Schuman Declaration, 197
Securitization
  collateralized debt obligations (CDOs), 48, 121, 150
  sub-prime loans, 45, 47, 117
Single Resolution Fund (SRF), 185
Single Supervisory Mechanism (SSM), 157, 180–185, 189
Smithsonian Conference, 31, 32
  Smithsonian Agreement, 32, 101
  Smithsonian Mechanism, 33
Snake Mechanism, 33, 73
Sovereign Debt Crisis (SDC), 13, 42, 109, 151, 155–157, 169, 172, 173, 190, 227, 238, 239
Stability and Growth Pact (SGP), 168
Systemically Important Financial Institutions (SIFIs), 51, 115, 143, 147, 177, 244
Systemic risk, 35–43, 51, 55, 76, 77, 79, 87, 94, 96, 99, 101, 116, 118, 176–178, 183, 191, 197, 198, 203, 209, 215, 230, 233, 238
  credit risk, 47, 49, 74, 82, 83, 117, 119, 120, 123, 124, 126, 131, 135, 138, 145

T

Too-Big-To-Fail (TBTF), 227
Transparency, 43, 44, 67, 70, 78, 85, 96, 100, 120, 133, 181, 219, 220
Triffin's dilemma, 31
Twin Peak Structure, 113–114

V

Volcker's Rule
  Volcker's Package, 55, 208

Index

W

Washington Consensus (WC)
  the Consensus, 68–69, 85, 110, 222
Werner Report, 33, 34
World Bank (WB)
  International Bank for Reconstruction and Development (IBRD), 58, 225, 226
World Financial Authority (WFA), 230
World Trade Organization (WTO), 7, 27, 32, 67, 69, 103, 202, 213, 244, 245

INTERNATIONAL BANKING AND FINANCE LAW SERIES

1. Jan Job de Vries Robbe, *Innovations in Securitisation. Yearbook 2006*, 2006 (ISBN 90-11-2533-7).
2. Jim Bartos, *United States Securities Law: A Practical Guide*, Third edition, 2006 (ISBN 90-411-2362-8).
3. Hui Huang, *International Securities Markets: Insider Trading Law in China*, 2006 (ISBN 90-411-2557-4).
4. Barth et al., *Financial Restructuring and Reform in Post-WTO China*, 2007 (ISBN 90-411-2573-6).
5. Zhongfei Zhou, *Banking Laws in China*, 2007 (ISBN 978-90-411-2519-4).
6. Jan Job de Vries Robbe & Paul Ali, *Expansion and Diversification in Securitization Yearbook 2007*, 2007 (ISBN 978-90-411-2661-0).
7. Ross Buckley, *International Financial System. Policy and Regulation*, 2008 (ISBN 978-90-411-2746-4).
8. Jan Job de Vries Robbe, *Securitization Law and Practice: In the Face of the Credit Crunch*, 2008 (ISBN 978-90-411-2715-0).
9. Phoebus Athanassiou, *Hedge Fund Regulation in the European Union: Current Trends and Future Prospects*, 2009 (ISBN 978-90-411-2856-0).
10. Jan Job de Vries Robbe, *Structured Finance: On from the Credit Crunch: The Road to Recovery*, 2009 (ISBN 978-90-411-2787-7).
11. Gaetane Schaeken Willemaers, *The EU Issuer-Disclosure Regime: Objectives and Proposals for Reform*, 2011 (ISBN 978-90-411-3394-6).
12. Panagiotis Delimatsis & Nils Herger (eds), *Financial Regulation at the Crossroads: Implications for Supervision, Institutional Design and Trade*, 2011 (ISBN 978-90-411-3355-7).
13. Raffaele Scalcione, *The Derivatives Revolution: A Trapped Innovation and a Blueprint for Regulatory Reform*, 2011 (ISBN 978-90-411-3430-1).
14. Douglas Arner & Ross Buckley, *From Crisis to Crisis: The Global Financial System and Regulatory Failure*, 2011 (ISBN 978-90-411-3354-0).
15. Anton P. Trichardt, *Letters of Comfort: A Trans-Systemic Analysis*, 2012 (ISBN 978-90-411-3600-8).
16. Eddy Wymeersch, *Alternative Investment Fund Regulation*, 2012 (ISBN 978-90-411-3690-9).
17. Asif H. Qureshi & Xuan Gao (eds), *International Economic Organizations and Law: The Perspective and Role of the Legal Counsel*, 2012 (ISBN 97890-411-3427-1).
18. Rhys Bollen, *The Law and Regulation of Payment Services: A Comparative Study*, 2012 (ISBN 978-90-411-3818-7).
19. Ramandeep Kaur Chhina, *Standby Letters of Credit in International Trade*, 2012 (ISBN 978-90-411-4560-4).

20. Dirk A. Zetzsche (ed.), *The Alternative Investment Fund Managers Directive: European Regulation of Alternative Investment Funds*, 2012 (ISBN 978-90-411-4044-9).
21. Lorenzo Sasso, *Capital Structure and Corporate Governance: The Role of Hybrid Financial Instruments*, 2013 (ISBN 978-90-411-4843-8).
22. Pablo Iglesias-Rodríguez, *The Accountability of Financial Regulators: A European and International Perspective*, 2013 (ISBN 978-90-411-3874-3).
23. Seraina Neva Grünewald, *The Resolution of Cross-Border Banking Crises in the European Union: A Legal Study from the Perspective of Burden Sharing*, 2014 (ISBN 978-90-411-4909-1).
24. Megan Bowman, *Banking on Climate Change: How Finance Actors and Transnational Regulatory Regimes are Responding*, 2015 (ISBN 978-90-411-5223-7).
25. Jin Sheng, *China's Listed Companies: Conflicts, Governance and Regulation*, 2015 (ISBN 978-90-411-5925-0).
26. Sven Schelo, *Bank Recovery and Resolution*, 2015 (ISBN 978-90-411-4959-6).
27. Luis M. Hinojosa–Martínez & José María Beneyto (eds), *European Banking Union: The New Regime*, 2015 (ISBN 978-90-411-5263-3).
28. Gill North, *Effective Company Disclosure in the Digital Age*, 2015 (ISBN 978-90-411-3815-6).
29. Hanneke Wegman, *Investor Protection: Towards Additional EU Regulation of Investment Funds?*, 2016 (ISBN 978-90-411-5252-7).
30. Ruth Plato-Shinar, *Banking Regulation in Israel: Prudential Regulation versus Consumer Protection*, 2016 (ISBN 978-90-411-6791-0).
31. Bader Alkhaldi, *Saudi Capital Market: Developments and Challenges*, 2017 (ISBN 978-90-411-8351-4).
32. Yves Mauchle, *Bail-In and Total Loss-Absorbing Capacity (TLAC): Legal and Economic Perspectives on Bank Resolution with Functional Comparisons of Swiss and EU Law*, 2017 (ISBN 978-90-411-8998-1).
33. Uzma Ashraf Barton, *Rethinking Regulation of International Finance: Law, Policy and Institutions*, 2018 (ISBN 978-90-411-8838-0).